INSIDERS' GUIDE® TO

ALBUQUERQUE

HELP US KEEP THIS GUIDE UP TO DATE

We would love to hear from you concerning your experiences with this guide and how you feel it could be improved and kept up to date. Please send your comments and suggestions to:

editorial@GlobePequot.com

Thanks for your input, and happy travels!

INSIDERS' GUIDE® SERIES

INSIDERS' GUIDE® TO

ALBUQUERQUE

TANIA CASSELLE

INSIDERS' GUIDE

GUILFORD, CONNECTICUT

AN IMPRINT OF GLOBE PEQUOT PRESS

All the information in this guidebook is subject to change. We recommend that you call ahead to obtain current information before traveling.

INSIDERS' GUIDE®

Editor, Travel: Amy Lyons
Project Editor: Ellen Urban
Layout Artist: Maggie Peterson
Text Design: Sheryl Kober
Maps by Daniel Lloyd © Morris Book Publishing, LLC

ISBN: 978-0-7627-5341-3

Printed in the United States of America
10 9 8 7 6 5 4 3 2 1

CONTENTS

Directory of Maps

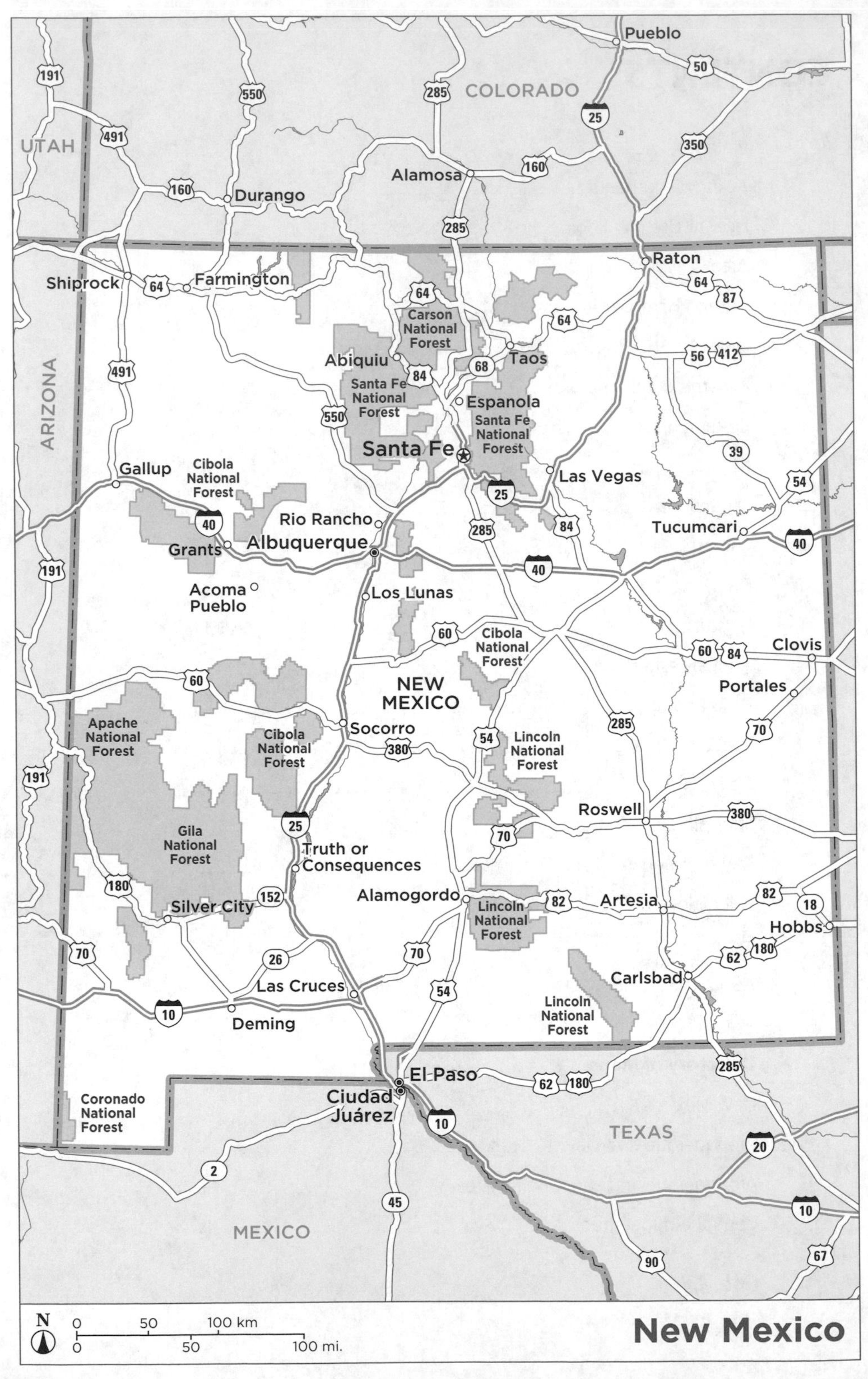
Pueblo
COLORADO
UTAH
Alamosa
Durango
Raton
Shiprock
Farmington
Carson National Forest
Abiquiu
Taos
Santa Fe National Forest
Espanola
Santa Fe National Forest
Santa Fe
ARIZONA
Gallup
Cibola National Forest
Las Vegas
Rio Rancho
Tucumcari
Grants
Albuquerque
Acoma Pueblo
Los Lunas
Cibola National Forest
Clovis
NEW MEXICO
Portales
Apache National Forest
Cibola National Forest
Socorro
Lincoln National Forest
Roswell
Gila National Forest
Truth or Consequences
Alamogordo
Silver City
Lincoln National Forest
Artesia
Hobbs
Carlsbad
Las Cruces
Deming
Lincoln National Forest
El Paso
Ciudad Juárez
Coronado National Forest
TEXAS
MEXICO
N
0 50 100 km
0 50 100 mi.
New Mexico

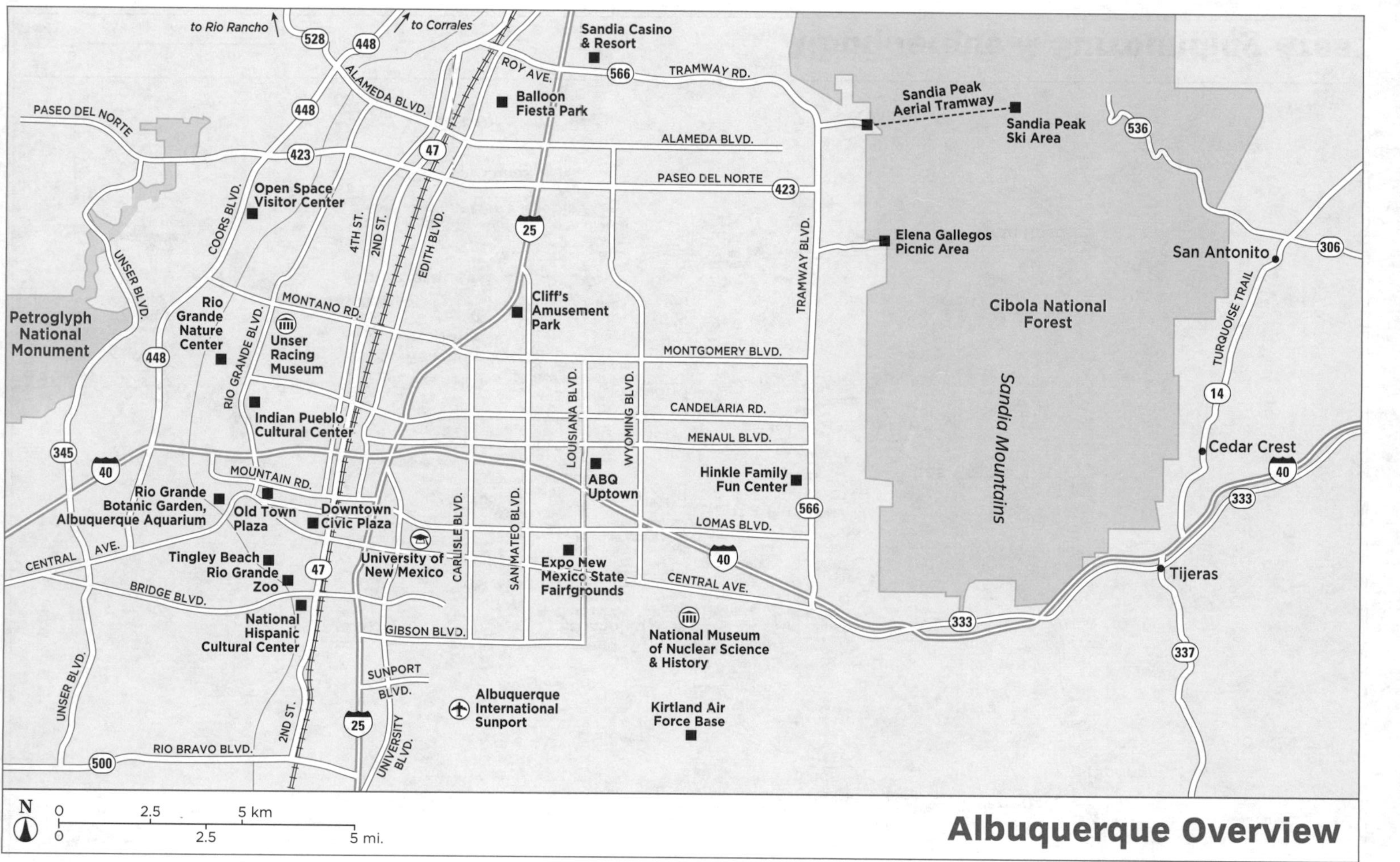

Albuquerque Overview
to Rio Rancho
to Corrales
528
448
Sandia Casino & Resort
Roy Ave.
566
Tramway Rd.
Alameda Blvd.
Balloon Fiesta Park
Paseo del Norte
423
47
Sandia Peak Aerial Tramway
Sandia Peak Ski Area
536
Open Space Visitor Center
Coors Blvd.
4th St.
2nd St.
Edith Blvd.
25
Tramway Blvd.
Elena Gallegos Picnic Area
San Antonito
306
Unser Blvd.
Rio Grande Nature Center
Montano Rd.
Rio Grande Blvd.
Unser Racing Museum
Cliff's Amusement Park
Cibola National Forest
Turquoise Trail
Petroglyph National Monument
Montgomery Blvd.
Sandia Mountains
14
Indian Pueblo Cultural Center
Louisiana Blvd.
Wyoming Blvd.
Candelaria Rd.
Menaul Blvd.
345
40
Mountain Rd.
ABQ Uptown
Hinkle Family Fun Center
Cedar Crest
333
Rio Grande Botanic Garden, Albuquerque Aquarium
Old Town Plaza
Downtown Civic Plaza
Carlisle Blvd.
San Mateo Blvd.
Lomas Blvd.
Central Ave.
Tingley Beach
Rio Grande Zoo
University of New Mexico
Expo New Mexico State Fairgrounds
Tijeras
Bridge Blvd.
National Hispanic Cultural Center
Gibson Blvd.
National Museum of Nuclear Science & History
337
Sunport Blvd.
Albuquerque International Sunport
Kirtland Air Force Base
2nd St.
University Blvd.
Rio Bravo Blvd.
500
N
0 2.5 5 km
0 2.5 5 mi.

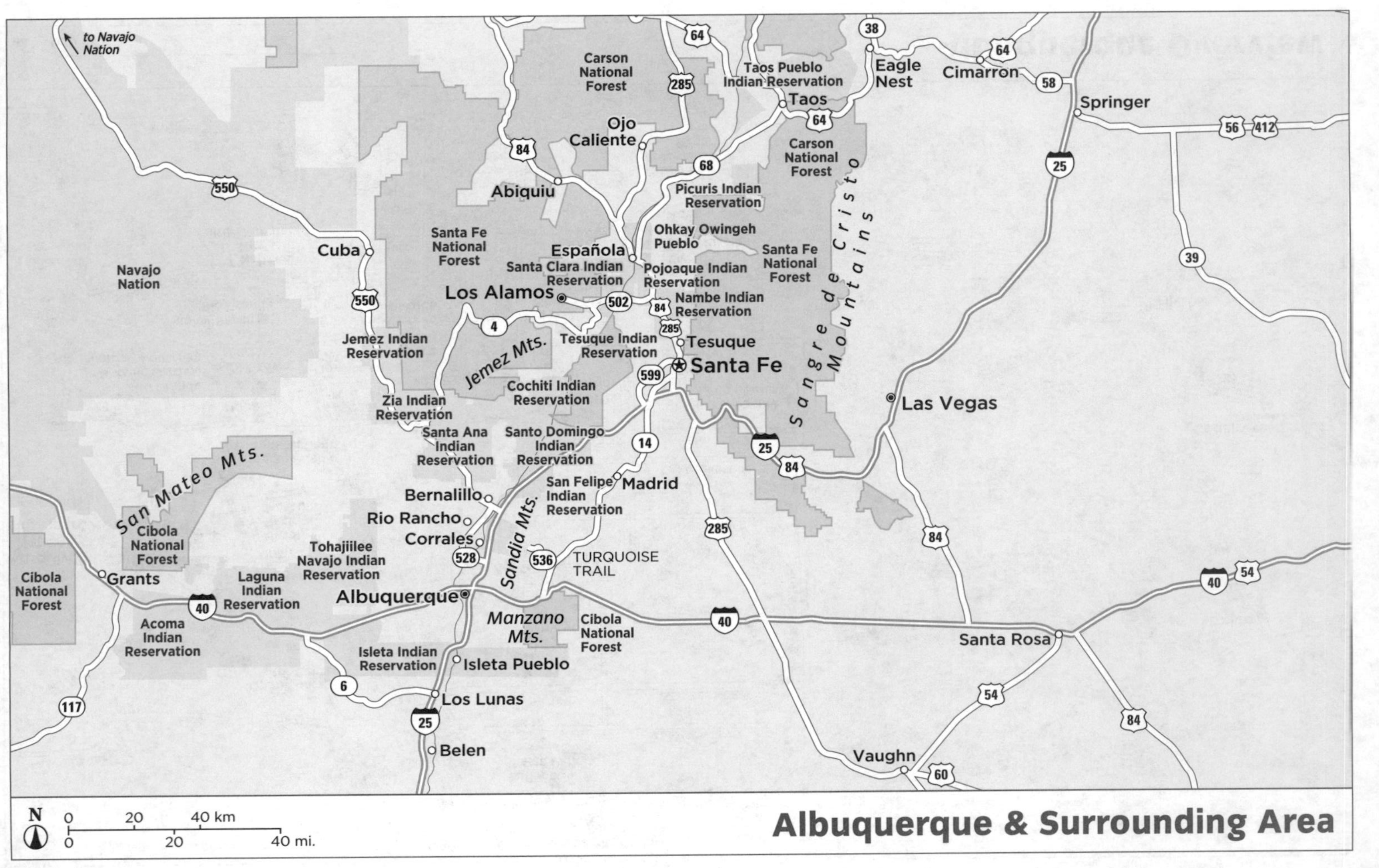
Albuquerque & Surrounding Area
to Navajo Nation
Navajo Nation
Cuba
Carson National Forest
Ojo Caliente
Abiquiu
Santa Fe National Forest
Española
Santa Clara Indian Reservation
Los Alamos
Taos Pueblo Indian Reservation
Taos
Eagle Nest
Cimarron
Springer
Carson National Forest
Picuris Indian Reservation
Ohkay Owingeh Pueblo
Pojoaque Indian Reservation
Nambe Indian Reservation
Santa Fe National Forest
Sangre de Cristo Mountains
Tesuque
Santa Fe
Tesuque Indian Reservation
Jemez Indian Reservation
Jemez Mts.
Cochiti Indian Reservation
Zia Indian Reservation
Santa Ana Indian Reservation
Santo Domingo Indian Reservation
Las Vegas
San Mateo Mts.
Bernalillo
Rio Rancho
Corrales
San Felipe Indian Reservation
Madrid
Sandia Mts.
Cibola National Forest
Tohajiilee Navajo Indian Reservation
TURQUOISE TRAIL
Grants
Laguna Indian Reservation
Albuquerque
Manzano Mts.
Cibola National Forest
Santa Rosa
Acoma Indian Reservation
Isleta Indian Reservation
Isleta Pueblo
Los Lunas
Belen
Vaughn
N
0 20 40 km
0 20 40 mi.

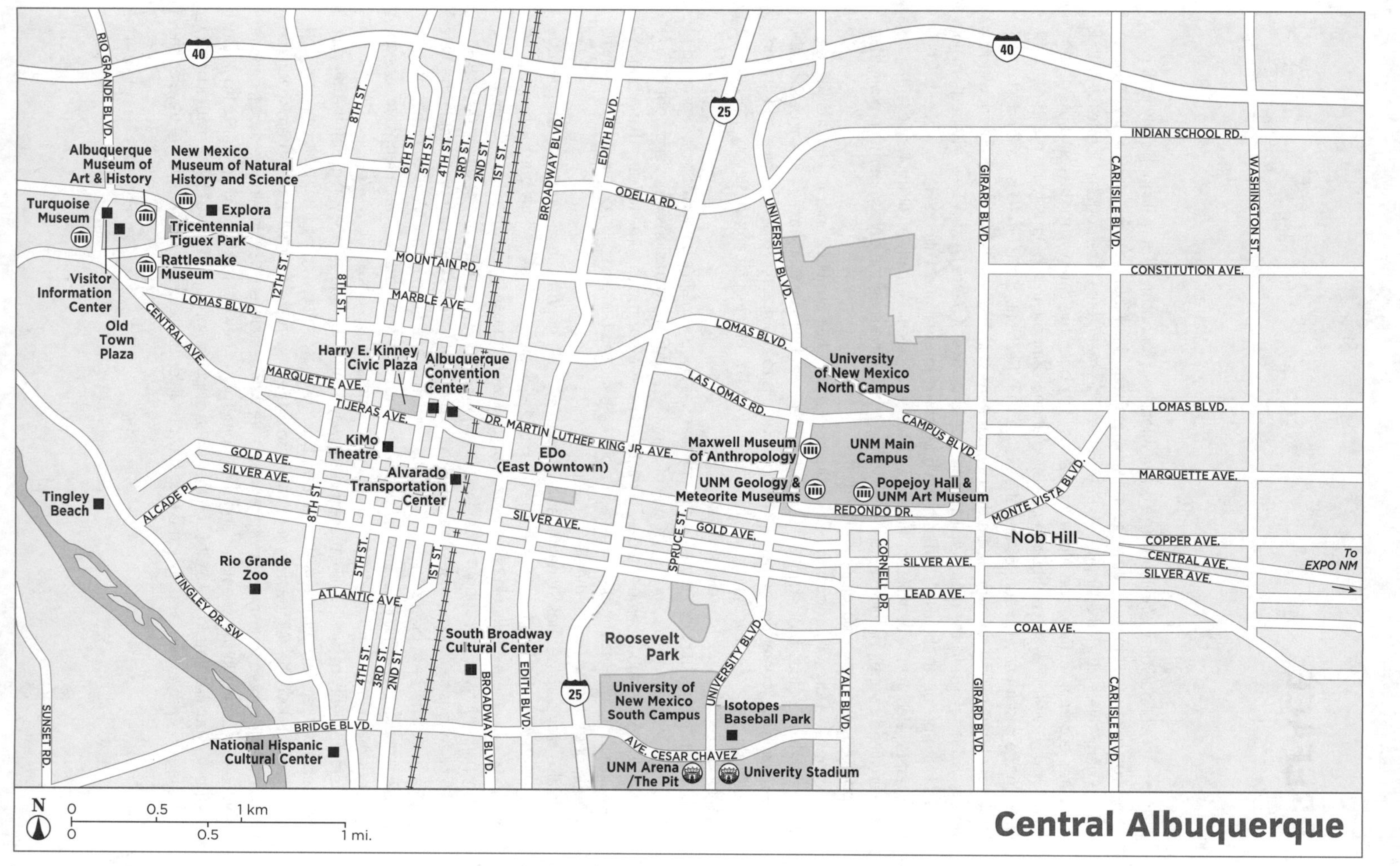
Central Albuquerque
Albuquerque Museum of Art & History
New Mexico Museum of Natural History and Science
Explora
Turquoise Museum
Tricentennial Tiguex Park
Rattlesnake Museum
Visitor Information Center
Old Town Plaza
Harry E. Kinney Civic Plaza
Albuquerque Convention Center
KiMo Theatre
Alvarado Transportation Center
EDo (East Downtown)
Tingley Beach
Rio Grande Zoo
South Broadway Cultural Center
National Hispanic Cultural Center
Roosevelt Park
University of New Mexico South Campus
Isotopes Baseball Park
UNM Arena /The Pit
Univerity Stadium
Maxwell Museum of Anthropology
UNM Geology & Meteorite Museums
UNM Main Campus
Popejoy Hall & UNM Art Museum
University of New Mexico North Campus
Nob Hill
To EXPO NM
RIO GRANDE BLVD.
8TH ST.
6TH ST.
5TH ST.
4TH ST.
3RD ST.
2ND ST.
1ST ST.
BROADWAY BLVD.
EDITH BLVD.
ODELIA RD.
UNIVERSITY BLVD.
GIRARD BLVD.
CARLISILE BLVD.
WASHINGTON ST.
INDIAN SCHOOL RD.
CONSTITUTION AVE.
MOUNTAIN RD.
MARBLE AVE.
12TH ST.
LOMAS BLVD.
CENTRAL AVE.
MARQUETTE AVE.
TIJERAS AVE.
DR. MARTIN LUTHER KING JR. AVE.
LAS LOMAS RD.
CAMPUS BLVD.
MONTE VISTA BLVD.
REDONDO DR.
GOLD AVE.
SILVER AVE.
ALCADE PL.
SPRUCE ST.
CORNELL DR.
LEAD AVE.
COAL AVE.
COPPER AVE.
ATLANTIC AVE.
TINGLEY DR. SW
YALE BLVD.
BRIDGE BLVD.
AVE. CESAR CHAVEZ
SUNSET RD.
40
25
N
0
0.5
1 km
1 mi.

PREFACE

Welcome to Albuquerque! Whether you're on vacation, here for business, or making the city your new home, you have a treat in store. It may sound strange to say that Albuquerque is one of New Mexico's hidden gems. After all, it's the largest city in the state. The metro area is responsible for nearly half of the state's economic activity, and Albuquerque has long been the gateway to the "Land of Enchantment." Today's visitors arrive via Albuquerque International Sunport and the crossroads of I-25 and I-40, while in the past it was via Route 66 and the old Camino Real. Still, Duke City—as it's fondly known, in honor of the Spanish duke for whom the city was named in 1706—has often been overlooked by visitors rushing north to the more familiar tourist destinations of Santa Fe and Taos. Although major events bring people to the city (such as the Albuquerque International Balloon Fiesta, where 800,000 balloonatics celebrate the high life in a nine-day October spectacular), many of Albuquerque's treasures have remained a secret for those "in the know," while others have seen the city as not much more than a stepping-stone to someplace else.

Meanwhile, Duke City citizens have quietly gone about their business, enjoying an arts scene to rival much bigger cities; basking in 310 sunny days a year in a climate that's rarely too hot or too cold, with amazing outdoor leisure, from Sandia Mountain trails to championship golf courses; and savoring a tricultural history of Native American, Hispanic, and Anglo cultures that enriches every aspect of life from food to architecture to entertainment.

But increasingly, the word is out on the city that has been in plain sight all along . . . speaking of which, the TV series *In Plain Sight* is just one of many TV and film productions produced right here at the state-of-the-art Albuquerque Studios. It might come as a surprise to some to learn that Albuquerque is a major movie-making city (if you're one of those, see this book's section on film, which explains Albuquerque's starring role on the silver screen).

It also may surprise those who linger a while to see just how much green space Albuquerque enjoys. Visitors are delighted to discover the thick, oasis-like green belt of luscious bosque forest along the Rio Grande, the majestic old cottonwoods and blossoming gardens of the North Valley, and the 286 city parks sprinkled throughout even the most urban areas. The terrific range of dining options also converts new fans to Albuquerque's relaxed and affordable lifestyle, as they pull up a seat in the leafy courtyards of family-run places serving generous portions of traditional New Mexican dishes or sleek upscale restaurants offering innovative cuisine paired with New Mexico wines. (Burqueños are passionate about their food . . . and visitors get to reap the rewards of that passion.)

There are plenty of surprises like these tucked away in Albuquerque—once you get off the freeway. The media has recently turned its spotlight on Duke City, repeatedly citing it in "best city" lists, and while residents love the acknowledgment, they also express a wry sense of "what took them so long to find out?" Unlike more touristy cities where visitors are a dime a dozen, here in Albuquerque locals are genuinely interested in the people visiting their hometown. They like to know where you're from and whether it's your first time in Duke City, and they often display a contagious pride for the natural beauty of the region, keen to help you have the best stay possible. In researching this guide I've traveled the city from west mesa to east mountains, revisiting favorite places, discovering new ones, and at every stop I found myself chatting with people who've lived here all their lives and newer arrivals fiercely loyal to their adopted home. In nearly every case Burqueños are quick to strike up conversation and share their strong opinions on the best places to go and things to do. And when I ran into visitors and asked about their Albuquerque experiences, the responses were universal: "Spectacular" . . . "Friendly" . . . "I want to live here" . . . "Wow!"

Whether you're in Albuquerque for a few days, for a few weeks, or as a new resident, you'll find information in these pages to help you discover the many facets of this "hidden gem" and get the best out of your time here in the Land of Enchantment.

ACKNOWLEDGMENTS

In researching this book I spent many hours talking with Albuquerque old-timers, newcomers, and travelers passing through and had a lot of fun doing so! Thank you for sharing your opinions, experiences, and tips on city life. My affection for Albuquerque has grown over the last dozen years, and it was great to have an excuse to dig even deeper. I especially appreciated the many guys and gals on the front line—the waitstaff; park workers; ticket takers; and employees at museums, shops, attractions, golf courses, cultural and nature centers, and a host of other public places—who really didn't have anything to gain by answering the nosy questions of this woman with a strange accent but who did so with courtesy and good humor even before they knew my reasons for cornering them. Once I did divulge my purpose, they were delighted to hear that a new Insiders' Guide would focus on their city, and they couldn't resist adding their own two cents on what makes it special, including suggestions of their own favorite places. As the public face of Albuquerque, you do a grand job in making this city so friendly and welcoming.

Thanks also to the business owners, arts and nonprofit organizations, and city officials, who patiently answered my many fact-checking questions.

In the course of research I relied on numerous resources for background information.

Thank you to the Albuquerque Convention and Visitors Bureau and to Megan Mayo in particular. Albuquerque Economic Development provided much useful data on the city.

Deep appreciation to the Albuquerque Historical Society archives and especially to historian Mary Mortensen Diecker, who generously read over the History chapter draft and did not stint in sharing her considerable knowledge to help me untangle the threads of Burque's long and complex history. Gratitude to Laura Lynch for her great assistance with research and fact-checking on portions of this manuscript, and special thanks to Deanna McMain, who went above and beyond in providing insights, research, and fact-checking in her enthusiasm for this project and her very apparent love for her home city.

Fiona Thompson was stalwart in her wise and witty support; Jane Graham added reflections from a visitor's point of view; and John Chapman hit a hole in one with his golfing expertise. My husband, Sean Murphy, was not too distressed at tagging along on a few of my adventures exploring new places, but as a fellow writer he also provided helpful ideas and comment on pages and generally kept the home fires burning in between the fun bits. I am eternally in debt to Prefab Sprout's hot dogs and jumping frogs for putting Albuquerque on my radar a decade before I set foot in the city.

The *Albuquerque Journal,* weekly *Alibi* newspaper, and biweekly *Local IQ* and their respective archives provided valuable background on current and past events. Duke City is fortunate to have so many dedicated journalists and writers today and in the past, including the authors of the books mentioned in the history chapter and not forgetting the works of Rudolfo Anaya and Tony Hillerman.

Finally, much appreciation for the guidance of my stellar editor Amy Lyons, who had the smart idea that Albuquerque was due its own Insiders' Guide in the first place.

HOW TO USE THIS BOOK

Maybe you're coming to Albuquerque on vacation or a business trip, looking for a great meal, the must-see attractions, inspiration as to fun things to do and fascinating places to explore, and practical information on how to make the most of your time in the city. Or perhaps you've just joined Albuquerque's growing population or are thinking about it—as a student at the University of New Mexico, as a family relocating for work or for quality of life, or as a retiree looking forward to a wonderful 310 days of sunshine a year and great leisure and entertainment opportunities.

Whatever your reasons for tipping your hat in Duke City's direction, this book will guide you through the many options Albuquerque has to offer and help you discover exactly what makes it such a unique place to visit and live.

Throughout the book the insiders' tips, indicated by **i**, share nuggets of useful information or interesting background of the kind you'd hear if a local were showing you around. Close-ups give the scoop on the things that make Albuquerque so distinctive, including historic Route 66, the KiMo Theatre and its resident ghost, the UNM Lobo sports teams and the infamous "Pit" (Go, Lobos!), and an introduction to Old Town.

The book kicks off with an Area Overview to acquaint you with the character of Albuquerque, key facts, and an outline of the various geographical districts referred to throughout. Subsequent chapters focus on specific subjects of interest to a traveler or newcomer so you can quickly and easily find the information you are looking for.

For example, the Getting Here, Getting Around chapter orients you to what to expect when you arrive by plane or car, plus city transportation, and how to find your way around once you get here. If you want to treasure hunt for antiques or slip into true southwestern style by picking up a pair of cowboy boots, head to the Shopping pages. The Parks and Recreation chapter points you to gorgeous outdoor spaces where you can picnic, hike, fish, spot wildlife, and see 700-year-old petroglyphs. Of course, this chapter also gives you the full lowdown on how to fly high, enjoying one of Albuquerque's most famous pleasures: a balloon ride. If you're eager to hit the links, you'll find plenty of choices in the Golf chapter.

The youngest members of the family get a Kidstuff chapter all to themselves, with suggestions from amusement parks to where to pet an alpaca. The Attractions chapter tells you about the things to see and do, including museums, historic sites, and how to ride to the top of 10,378 foot Sandia Peak in 15 minutes for panoramic views and a spot of lunch at the top. If you're fond of critters, the same chapter points out where to see the city's earliest animal inhabitants (dinosaurs, at the Museum of Natural History and Science), its crawliest creatures (at the Rattlesnake Museum), and a whole Noah's Ark of beasts at the Rio Grande Zoo.

These chapters and others, such as The Arts and Spectator Sports, are subdivided by topic, as Albuquerque is relatively small and fast to drive around, and location is less likely to be a deciding factor than, for example, whether you want to see theater or dance or take in a baseball game or watch football. The themed subdivisions make it easy to put your finger on the information you need.

The chapters on Restaurants and Accommodations are organized by geographic area, however, to help you quickly find a nearby place to eat or reserve a bed in an area convenient for your stay. Within chapters and subsections, places are listed alphabetically.

The Annual Festivals and Events chapter is organized chronologically throughout the year, to show you the festivals, shows, and celebrations that coincide with your visit or perhaps even inspire you to time your visit for those events. This chapter also indicates when Albuquerque might be especially busy. During Albuquerque International Balloon Fiesta, the Gathering of Nations, and the New Mexico State Fair, the city swells with visitors, so you know you should book your hotel room and reserve restaurant tables early! The range of events in this chapter—from wine to world music, from the spicy foods show to Cinco de Mayo celebrations—also gives a taste of the city's lively and diverse character.

The History chapter offers a capsule overview of the colorful history of the region, from Clovis Man to the current day. Spending time with this chapter will enhance your experience of the Albuquerque area, as so much of today's culture and areas of interest are born from the rich, and often conflicted, past.

Price guides, indicating what you can expect to pay, are provided in the chapters on Restaurants, Accommodations, Attractions, and Kidstuff. For destinations a little farther afield, you'll find a guide on approximate driving time or mileage. Mileages given are from the Downtown Albuquerque Civic Plaza unless otherwise noted.

Albuquerque city limits cover an area of 187 square miles, but the formal boundary lines are not that evident to a visitor traveling around the city. In many instances the places described in this book fall outside strict city limits, into neighborhoods that are continuous with the city and may even be very close to Downtown Albuquerque but are in fact part of the greater metropolitan area. In order to avoid tedious repetition, and as it's largely irrelevant to visitors just looking for a good time on their trip, the references to Albuquerque within these pages don't always spell out whether we're talking city or metro. If a place feels like it's part of the Albuquerque experience, even if it's technically outside city limits—it's included!

Still, it's impossible to include everything to see and do in one guidebook. The Insiders' Guide approach is to select and suggest some of the brightest and best to suit every budget and taste. On your journeys you'll no doubt discover much more to enjoy—and this is as it should be in a destination with as much to discover as Albuquerque, and it's also part of the joy of travel.

Although every effort is made to ensure accuracy, in a city as dynamic and fast-growing as Albuquerque, changes are bound to occur as businesses close; new ones spring up in their place; and contact information, prices, and hours change. New Mexico in general tends to experience fast turnover and a "go with the flow" approach to opening hours. If you're making a special trip to a destination, it's worth calling ahead to make sure you are not disappointed.

Finally, if you find any errors in this book or want to share your experiences at the places featured here or recommend places that are not included but should be in a future edition—it would be great to hear from you! Insiders' Guides are regularly updated, and reader feedback, recommendations, and your own insider tips are noted and appreciated.

AREA OVERVIEW

New Mexico is a land of extremes, and Albuquerque is no exception. As the main gateway to the state, Albuquerque, founded in 1706, has a rich tricultural history, and although the city is now known for technology industries, it still carries the spirit of the Old West. That spirit is seen in everything from the architecture—old adobe buildings and the kitschy nostalgia of Route 66's neon signs—to the personality of the people. Albuquerque folk are feisty and individualistic, pioneers at heart, whether their family has been here for generations, they are descended from the original Spanish settlers, or they're recent Anglo transplants to this high-desert environment. The Native American peoples, who were here long before anyone else, endured their own hardships to dwell in this glorious land. Although indigenous peoples inhabited the Albuquerque area for thousands of years, by the 1300s larger populations had migrated from the drier Four Corners area to sustain their families along the banks of the Rio Grande, the life-giving vein of the region.

Burqueños are also mighty friendly. When you live in a city packed with great arts, leisure, and employment, in some of the most beautiful landscapes on earth, what's to be grumpy about? People arrive in New Mexico seeking adventure on the frontier, and in Albuquerque they find it. The Albuquerque Convention and Visitors Bureau slogan, "It's a trip," says something of the quirky Burque character and lifestyle—this is not a homogeneous cookie-cutter city. Often vacationers decide to stay; witness the many tales of travelers passing through the state whose vehicles break down; or they're otherwise delayed; or they simply fall in love with the land, the light, the laid-back atmosphere; and the next thing they know they've picked up sticks and moved here. New Mexico is known as the Land of Enchantment, but locals fondly call it the Land of Entrapment—once you step foot here, you might never leave.

Visitors, and even those who've lived here for years, are magnetized by the natural beauty of the Sandia Mountains. Sandia means watermelon in Spanish, and under our famous New Mexico sunsets, the Sandias do indeed glow the luscious pink of ripe watermelon. The Rio Grande provides irrigation to the green belt of the bosque, with its whispering cottonwoods, while the high-desert sunlight has drawn artists and photographers from around the world. Duke City, as it's called, after the Duke of Alburquerque, for whom it was named (that first "r" was later dropped), is colorful in every sense. Its residents are into enjoying life and living outside the box, with lots of room for creative types and for innovative minds of every stripe. Bill Gates's Microsoft started in Albuquerque, and the city has long been a center of science and inventive technology. Today nanotechnology, biotechnology, energy technologies, and green technologies, including solar energy, are part of the dynamic business mix. Albuquerque—or Tamalewood, as some have dubbed it—is also flourishing as a movie city, with a film industry that contributed $130 million to city coffers in 2008. *Terminator Salvation* is one of many productions shot at the new and top-notch Albuquerque Studios complex, and the Emmy Award–winning TV series *Breaking Bad* is also set in the city.

People come to Albuquerque to enjoy life at the highest level—literally! At 5,326 feet above sea level, Albuquerque lies more than a mile high and enjoys mile-high rankings, too, in "best cities" lists for quality of life, leisure, health, and fitness and as a relocation destination.

i The City of Albuquerque's official elevation of 5,326 feet makes it the highest metropolitan city in America. (Stretching just a notch above mile-high Denver at 5,280 feet.) However, elevations range from 4,500 feet in the Rio Grande Valley to 6,500 feet in the foothills of the Sandia Mountains and 10,378 feet at Sandia Peak if you take the Sandia Peak Tramway to its dizzy heights. Sandia Crest tops off at 10,678 feet.

The Albuquerque metropolitan area has grown from a population of just shy of 600,000 in the 1990 U.S. Census, to an estimated 859,000 in 2009, and urban sprawl is a community concern and a challenge to city planners. However, there are many green oases and open spaces throughout the city—including 28,000 acres of dedicated open-space lands, 286 parks, and 113 miles of developed trails—all offering wonderful recreation opportunities. You can ski in the morning, play a round of golf in the afternoon, and be back Downtown in time for a gourmet New Mexican dinner.

The city lies at the feet of the Sandia Mountains to the east, a base for skiing, hiking, and biking. Or you can zip to the top of Sandia Peak on the longest aerial tramway in the world, for stunning views over 11,000 square miles, including the dormant volcano area stretching to the west, a prehistoric landscape where you'll find the Petroglyph National Monument. Maybe you'll spot balloons bobbing past; Albuquerque is the ballooning capital of the world, and the city celebrates the high life in October at the Balloon Fiesta, which brings around 800,000 visitors to Albuquerque to watch over 700 balloons soar into the turquoise skies.

The lively arts scene includes over 100 art galleries and studios and performing arts from classical music at the University of New Mexico's stately Popejoy Hall, to innovative theater at the Filling Station, a converted 1930s gas station on old Route 66. The historic KiMo Theatre, a flamboyant former vaudeville house built in Pueblo Deco style, hosts everything from poetry slams to ballet, but even if you don't catch a show, it's worth a look—or even a tour—as you cruise along Central Avenue.

The University of New Mexico (UNM), founded in 1889, played a vital role in establishing Albuquerque as a center for artists, scholars,

Historical Sites

Visitors may take a tour of the Puye Cliff dwellings, home from the late 1100s to 1580 to the ancestors of the current Santa Clara Pueblo people (today's pueblo lies 10 miles east of Puye). Several tours of varying durations are offered daily, and no reservations are needed. The Puye Welcome Center is approximately one and three quarter hours north of Albuquerque via Santa Fe and near Española (888-320-5008; www.puyecliffs.com). Trips to Petroglyph National Monument or Coronado State Monument also give fascinating insights into New Mexico's earliest residents (see Attractions chapter), as do the cliff dwellings at Bandelier National Monument. Bandelier was inhabited starting over 10,000 years ago and abandoned by 1550 when the residents moved to today's pueblos of Cochiti, San Felipe, San Ildefonso, Santa Clara, and Santo Domingo. Bandelier National Monument is approximately two hours north of Albuquerque via Santa Fe, near Los Alamos (505-672-0343; www.nps.gov/band).

i **While we certainly enjoy the unique character of our Land of Enchantment, New Mexicans are surprised to discover that some people think we're a foreign country. People so often muddle the U.S. state of New Mexico with the country of Mexico that the state publication *New Mexico Magazine* has fun with the blunders in its column "One of Our 50 is Missing." Readers write in with their experience of officials, businesses, and people they've dealt with who insist New Mexico is an overseas territory, and there's never a shortage of stories. We do share a border with Mexico, but let's put the record straight: The last time we looked we were tucked between Texas, Arizona, Colorado, and a sliver of Oklahoma, and the last time we did our tax returns, we paid money to the feds!**

and thinkers, broadening its horizons from being just another frontier town. The 25,000 students attending UNM's 600-acre campus in the heart of town keep the city buzzing with youthful energy and contribute to the artsy, intellectual atmosphere in the University and Nob Hill areas.

Over a third of New Mexico's population is bilingual, with the great majority of those speaking Spanish and English. You'll hear Spanish spoken in Albuquerque and a hearty peppering of Spanglish, too, and many roads and districts have Spanish names. If you don't know Spanish, you'll have no problem communicating, as English is used for everyday business. Get out into New Mexico's rural villages, though, and you might still run across a few people who only communicate in Spanish.

Albuquerque is the largest city in New Mexico, although the state capital is Santa Fe. In 2012 New Mexico will celebrate its 100-year anniversary of becoming part of the United States. It joined the Union as the 47th state on January 6, 1912, so if Americans still sometimes mistake New Mexico as a foreign country—and they do—we can't be too surprised. Rest assured, no passport is required.

THE CITY OF ALBUQUERQUE AND THE METROPOLITAN AREA

The City of Albuquerque is located in Bernalillo County in central New Mexico and covers 187 square miles. Population in the 2000 census was 448,607, and city government estimates it at 535,000 for 2010. The city lies between the Sandia and Manzano Mountains on the east and Petroglyph National Monument on the west and is bordered north and south by Sandia and Isleta Pueblos.

The greater Albuquerque Metropolitan Area covers four counties: Bernalillo, Sandoval, Valencia, and Torrance. Population for the entire metropolitan area is estimated at around 859,000 in 2009. This is up from 729,649 in the 2000 census. (For apples-to-apples comparison this 2000 figure is adjusted to include Torrance County, which wasn't included in the Metropolitan Statistical Area in the 2000 census but was added in 2003.) Nearly half of all economic activity in New Mexico is generated in the Albuquerque metro area, which includes the mushrooming Rio Rancho, the second largest city in the metro area after Albuquerque. The University of New Mexico Bureau of Business and Economic Research predicts that the metropolitan-area population will reach over 1.5 million by 2035.

i **In recent years a single letter has been the cause of some controversy, as the letter "Q" has been presented as a new nickname and logo for modern Albuquerque. Although it makes for snappy graphics, some citizens are staunch in their defense against being "branded" as The Q, arguing in favor of the traditional Duke City and Burque nicknames.**

Older Burqueños remember when the villages and towns around the city of Albuquerque had clear boundaries, with space in between. With the population growth and new construction over recent decades, communities that were once distinct have merged together. Travelers

Duke City Kudos

Albuquerque has been praised in many surveys of American cities. Here are some of the rankings, ratings, and media reports that demonstrate yet more reasons to visit Duke City.

* No. 6 of Best Cities in America 2009 list—*Outside* magazine, August 2009
* In the 10 Best Cities for Local Food—*The Huffington Post,* July 2009
* In the 10 Best Cities to Live in 2009—*U.S. News & World Report*
* In the Top 10 Best Cities to Live in 2009—*Relocate-America*
* 2nd in 10 Best Cities of 2009—*Kiplinger's Personal Finance,* 2009
* 5th Best Big City Art Destination—*American Style Magazine,* April 2009
* 5th Fittest City in the U.S.—*Men's Fitness magazine,* January 2009
* 5th best city to live as an independent moviemaker—*MovieMaker Magazine,* February 2009
* Included in "Hollywood's Favorite Cities"—Forbes.com, December 2008
* 3rd best city with 500,000-plus populations that have the safest air—*Health* magazine, October 2008
* 18th for 2008 U.S. Sustainability Rankings and 1st place amongst Desert Cities—*SustainLane,* 2008
* Top 10 Cities for Hispanics—*Hispanic Magazine,* August 2008
* 21st in America's Most Walkable Neighborhoods in the Top 40 U.S. Cities—Walkscore.com, 2008
* Paseo del Bosque Trail Ranked No. 1 for Top 10 City Bike Rides—*Sunset* magazine, July 2008
* Among the Top 66 Places Where Owning Real Estate Makes Sense—RealEstateMSN.com, 2008
* 5th best place to build personal wealth—Salary.com, 2008
* 2nd most affordable destination in North America—*AAA Annual Vacation Costs Survey,* 2008
* Ranked in the Top Towns for Empty Nesters—Forbes.com, April 2008
* The Albuquerque BioPark appeared in *Sunset* magazine's Top 10 City Parks, April 2008
* No. 16 of America's 50 Greenest Cities—*Popular Science* on their popsci.com Web site, February 2008
* Top 10 Movie Cities of 2008—*MovieMaker* magazine, January 2008
* Among Top 10 Cities for Jobs—*Forbes,* October 2007
* Top 50 Best Places to Live and Play—*National Geographic Adventure,* September 2007

from Santa Fe can leave I-25 at an exit north of Albuquerque, drive south through Bernalillo, on into Rio Rancho and then the Village of Corrales, swoop down into the North Valley, passing through the Village of Los Ranchos, and arrive in Downtown Duke City, and although each area has its own atmosphere and style, it's effectively one contiguous string of neighborhoods.

For a casual visitor, it's hard to tell when you're passing in and out of Albuquerque city limits and when you're entering independently incorporated villages such as Los Ranchos or crossing the borders of Indian reservation lands. What technically falls into the City of Albuquerque (with a capital "C") or the greater metropolitan area is irrelevant to most visitors, who'll simply experience this wonderful patchwork of communities as all part of the Albuquerque adventure.

City and Metro Areas

Old Town

Albuquerque was founded in Old Town in 1706, and a walk around the plaza is a walk into history, surrounded by beautiful old adobe dwellings, many now home to shops, galleries, and restaurants. The San Felipe de Neri Church, built in 1793, dominates the north side of the plaza with its white towers and is still an active Catholic church. The plaza, with its central gazebo, remains the heart of the community for fiestas and holiday celebrations, and here and in the side streets all around, you'll hear live music, from mariachi to flamenco and salsa. You can wander through courtyards spilling with flowers and even join a nighttime ghost walk if you've courage enough. Along "museum row," on Mountain Road to the east of the plaza, you'll find the Albuquerque Museum of Art and History, the New Mexico Museum of Natural History and Science and Planetarium, and the Explora children's museum and discovery center. The Turquoise Museum and the Rattlesnake Museum are also within Old Town, as is Tricentennial Tiguex Park. Although the historic Old Town district is centered around the plaza, the broader area is defined as reaching north to I-40, east to 15th Street and is bordered by the sweeping curve of the Rio Grande. Within that area lie the Albuquerque Aquarium and Rio Grande Botanic Garden and Tingley Beach.

Downtown

Downtown is an oasis of high modern buildings in the otherwise mainly low-rise cityscape and is booming as a result of a 10-year $350 million revitalization program.

New businesses, restaurants, and nightlife abound, as well as trendy apartment and loft developments. The Alvarado Transportation Center is the Downtown transport hub, and in this district you'll find the Albuquerque Convention Center, City Hall, and the city and county courthouses. The many arts and entertainment destinations include the KiMo Theatre with its Pueblo Deco architecture; the 14-screen Century 14 Theatres complex; plus live music venues, nightspots, and art galleries, especially around Central Avenue (the old Route 66) and Gold Avenue a block south of Central. The Harry E. Kinney Civic Plaza, with its fountain, sculptures, a large performance stage, and capacity for over 20,000 people, is the gathering place for city events, including free summer music, entertainment, and movies. The neighorhood nicknamed EDo (East Downtown), is receiving a facelift of its own and is home to some excellent restaurants along Central Avenue between the railroad tracks and I-25.

i **Harry E. Kinney Civic Plaza is named for Albuquerque's first elected mayor. The much-admired mayor Harry Kinney, known as "Harmonious Harry," was elected in 1974. He served two terms and later took up cab driving, apparently because of his great affection for the city of Albuquerque and his pleasure in meeting the people. He reportedly liked driving around pointing out things that were a result of his years in office. The former Civic Plaza was renamed in his honor after he died in 2006, and a statue of the late Mayor Kinney by sculptor Reynaldo "Sonny" Rivera was unveiled in the plaza in June 2009. As the renaming is so recent, many locals are still in the habit of referring simply to the Civic Plaza or Downtown Plaza.**

University/Midtown

This area reaches from the University of New Mexico's 600-acre campus, up and around the Big I interchange where I-40 meets I-25. UNM's presence along the stretch of Central Avenue between Downtown and Nob Hill ensures a college-town vibe, with trendy restaurants and shops geared for a student's pocketbook. Popejoy Hall, the city's premier performance-arts venue and home to the New Mexico Symphony Orchestra, is on the UNM campus, as is the UNM Art Museum, which contains the state's largest fine art collection and the Jonson Gallery. Also

Albuquerque Vital Statistics

Albuquerque city area: 187 square miles

Population: City of Albuquerque 535,000 (2010 estimate). **Greater metropolitan area** 859,000 (2009 estimate). State of New Mexico 1,829,146 (2000 U.S. Census).

Time zone: Mountain Time

Elevation: 5,326 feet

Average temperature:
July—high 92, low 64
January—high 47, low 23

Average number of sunny days a year: 310

Average rainfall: Approximately 9 inches

Nicknames: Duke City, Burque, ABQ, The Q

Albuquerque founded: April 23, 1706

City incorporated: 1891

New Mexico statehood: January 6, 1912

Language: English and Spanish are both official languages in the State of New Mexico.

Major college: University of New Mexico

Newspapers: Daily—*Albuquerque Journal;* **Weekly**—*Alibi*

Major employers (Metro area): Kirtland Air Force Base, University of New Mexico, Albuquerque Public Schools, Sandia National Laboratories, Presbyterian (hospital and medical services), City of Albuquerque, State of New Mexico, UNM Hospital, Lovelace (hospital and medical services), Intel Corporation

Military base: Kirtland Air Force Base

Major airport: Albuquerque International Sunport

Major interstates: I-25 North-South, I-40 East-West

Public transportation: ABQ Ride city bus service, New Mexico Rail Runner Express

Alcohol laws: You must be 21 to drink, buy, or serve alcohol in New Mexico. Bars may stay open till 2 a.m. or midnight on Sunday. There are no alcohol sales before noon on Sunday. Establishments holding only a beer-and-wine license may only serve these beverages accompanied by food. In New Mexico it is illegal to drive with a blood alcohol content of 0.08 or more.

Driving laws: Seat belts and child restraints are mandatory. Children under 1 year must sit in the back seat of the car in a rear-facing restraint seat. Children 1 to 5 and under 40 pounds must be in a child-restraint seat. In Rio Rancho children under 12 must sit in the back seat. Drivers are prohibited from driving while talking on a cell phone unless using a hands-free device. See "Alcohol laws" above for DWI information.

Sales tax: New Mexico charges a gross-receipts tax on goods and services. The amount varies by location and is added to your check or purchase price. In Albuquerque the tax is 6.875 percent.

Room tax: A 6 percent lodgers' tax is charged on accommodations, in addition to the gross-receipts tax, bringing the total tax on accommodations to 12.875 percent.

Area code: 505

Mayor: Richard J. Berry

NM governor: Bill Richardson

Capital of New Mexico: Santa Fe

Other major NM cities: Santa Fe, Las Cruces, Los Alamos, Taos, Roswell

Resources and visitor centers:

Emergency Services: 911

Albuquerque Convention & Visitors Bureau
Suite 601, 20 First Plaza NW
(800) 284-2282
www.itsatrip.org

African American Chamber of Commerce of New Mexico
Suite C, 100 Arno Street NE (by appointment only)
(505) 243-3949, (866) 585-5992
www.aaccnm.com

Airport Visitor Information Center: On Level One by Baggage Claim Four

Albuquerque Economic Development (AED)
Suite 203, 851 University Boulevard SE
(505) 246-6200, (800) 451-2933
www.abq.org

Albuquerque Hispano Chamber of Commerce
1309 Fourth Street SW
(505) 842-9003, (888) 451-7824
www.ahcnm.org

City of Albuquerque Citizen Contact Center: Dial 311 within city limits or (505) 768-2000 from other areas.

Greater Albuquerque Chamber of Commerce
Suite 201, 115 Gold Avenue SW
(505) 764-3700
www.abqchamber.com

New Mexico Tourism Department: (800) 733-6396, www.newmexico.org

Old Town Visitor Information Center: Plaza Don Luis on Romero NW, across the road from San Felipe de Neri church

Rio Rancho Convention & Visitors Bureau
3001 Civic Center Circle, Rio Rancho
(505) 891-7258, (888) 746-7262
www.rioranchonm.org

Town of Bernalillo Information
(505) 867-3311
www.townofbernalillo.org

Village of Corrales Information: www.visitcorrales.com

Village of Los Ranchos Information: www.villr.com

you'll find the Maxwell Museum of Anthropology, UNM Meteorite Museum and Geology Museum, and the Tamarind Institute. This is an area of architectural note, as many UNM buildings were designed by famed architect John Gaw Meem. Midtown around the Big I interchange is rather less aesthetically charming, but here and along Menaul Boulevard there are good-value accommodations that provide a convenient base from which to get anywhere around town with ease.

Nob Hill

Fashionable Nob Hill plays up its Route 66 heritage, extending along a mile of Central Avenue just east of the university. The historic district's neon lights, retro signage, and many original buildings give a good sense of how the city would have appeared to the new automobile tourists arriving during the Route 66 heyday. This isn't a center for accommodations, but don't miss a visit to this artsy and avant-garde neighborhood for its chic boutiques, specialty stores, and galleries and the thriving nightlife in restaurants and bars. It's also home to the 1966 art house Guild Cinema. The 1940s Nob Hill Shopping Center (3500 Central Avenue SE) was designed by Louis Hesselden, featuring Territorial Revival and Moderne design elements. Nob Hill offers a satisfying blend of retro Americana and up-to-the-minute design savvy, and many eateries have sidewalk patios where diners watch the passing parade. Historic Nob Hill is generally a good bet to find places that stay open later, although shops here may start the day's business later, too.

i **Call 311 to reach the City of Albuquerque's 24-hour hotline with inquiries about city services, including attractions, leisure facilities, and transportation. Outside the city limits, call (505) 768-2000. The helpful Citizen Contact Center operators find speedy answers for visitors and locals alike. They also answer questions on Twitter, using the Twitter tag @cabq. (This number is for nonemergency requests only—call 911 for emergencies.)**

Uptown

Uptown is a modern business and retail district, with bright and shiny new developments, such as the ABQ Uptown outdoor shopping mall. This major commercial area also includes the Coronado Center mall, the Uptown Transit Center, and many hotels and restaurants. EXPO New Mexico at Uptown's southern edge is a venerable 236-acre site that hosts the New Mexico State Fair, the weekend flea market, and many annual festivals and events. Tingley Coliseum and the Downs at Albuquerque Racetrack & Casino are also located on the EXPO New Mexico grounds.

i **Albuquerque has nine sister cities around the world: Alburquerque, Spain; Ashgabat, Turkmenistan; Chihuahua, Mexico; Guadalajara, Mexico; Helmstedt, Germany; Hualien, Taiwan; Lanzhou, China; Sasebo, Japan; Rehovot, Israel**

Eastside

The Eastside runs from Wyoming Boulevard to the foothills of the Sandias, and the most famous visitor attraction here is the Sandia Peak Tramway. It's the world's longest aerial passenger tramway, offering a 15-minute ride to spectacular views from 10,378 foot Sandia Peak. There are restaurants at both the bottom and the top of the tramway and excellent views from the base station, too. The tramway accesses the Sandia Peak ski area, and other sporty and outdoor options on the Eastside include the Elena Gallegos Picnic Area and Albert G. Simms Park with lots of hiking, biking, and other leisure activities; the Los Altos Golf Course, municipal park, and 35,000-square-foot skate park; the Jerry Cline Tennis Complex; and Outpost Ice Arenas. Kids will enjoy the Hinkle Family Fun Center, and the National Museum of Nuclear Science & History moved to the Eastside, from Old Town in 2009.

Balloon Fiesta Park/North I-25

On the north border of Albuquerque along the I-25 corridor, this area surrounds Balloon Fiesta

Park, the stomping ground for around 800,000 spectators at the nine-day Albuquerque International Balloon Fiesta every October. The park is also home to the Anderson-Abruzzo Albuquerque International Balloon Museum, the Golf Training Center driving range, and the Albuquerque Wine Festival on Memorial Day weekend. Also within this area you'll find the Journal Center—a campuslike business park housing the Albuquerque Publishing Company's daily *Albuquerque Journal* newspaper, plus health-care, banking, and high-tech industries. Cross streets around the Journal Center on Jefferson sport newspaper-inspired names such as Masthead and Headline. Hotels are strung along the I-25 corridor, and there is plenty of play potential at the Arroyo del Oso municipal golf course and the summer-only Cliffs Amusement Park.

Airport

Unlike many cities where you just want to get away from the airport as soon as possible, the area around Albuquerque International Sunport is a good-value place to stay for close proximity to the University area and Nob Hill, with a quick zip up Yale Boulevard. And it's just beside I-25, with easy access to other parts of the city. Sporty destinations near the airport include the University of New Mexico Championship Golf Course and the Puerto del Sol Golf Course. Isotopes Park, home to the Isotopes Minor League baseball team, is here, as well as the University of New Mexico Stadium and Arena for football and basketball, respectively. UNM's arena (the Pit) hosts other events, including the annual Native American Gathering of Nations Powwow. Kirtland Air Force Base, Sandia National Laboratories, and the New Mexico Veterans' Memorial are also in this area. The 12,000-capacity Journal Pavilion outdoor concert venue presents major international bands and lies south of the airport.

i **Albuquerque's phone area code is 505. In 2007 the state split into two area codes: Albuquerque, Santa Fe, Los Alamos, Farmington, and Gallup retained the 505 code, along with other towns in an area designated as the northwest region. The remainder of the state changed to 575, including Taos, Las Cruces, Socorro, and Roswell.**

Barelas and the South Valley

This is one of the oldest communities in Albuquerque, and the early Spanish roots in Barelas and the rural South Valley are still very much in evidence. Adobe homes as old as 300 to 400 years can be found here, dating back to original settlers who farmed the fertile river lands by the old Camino Real trading route from Mexico City. This area nudges up against the southern edge of Downtown and crosses west of the Rio Grande. The National Hispanic Cultural Center is in the Barelas neighborhood, as are the Rio Grande Zoo, the South Broadway Cultural Center, and the Mother Road Theatre Company and Filling Station Arts & Performance Space. The Barelas Rail Yards, dating back to the 1880s, are in a process of redevelopment.

Westside

West of the Rio Grande, the prehistoric landscape is shaped by five volcanoes—all dormant, although they sent up smoke as recently as 1881. Any snowfall melts faster around the ground of the cooling volcanoes. On the far horizon stands 11,301-foot Mount Taylor, about 60 miles from Albuquerque and a sacred site to many Native American tribes. Closer to home, Petroglyph National Monument is located on the Westside, along with the Open Space Visitors Center and the large Cottonwood Mall shopping complex with a multiscreened movie theater. Double Eagle II Airport serves charter, private, and corporate flights. Recreation includes the Ladera Golf Course, the Sierra Vista West Tennis Complex, the West Mesa Aquatic Center, and the Mariposa Basin city park. If you take a balloon ride, you're likely to launch from the Westside. As the population of Albuquerque has grown, vacant land on the Westside has been developed into suburban residential areas. Coors Boulevard is a major

Native American Pueblos

New Mexico is home to nineteen pueblos, two Apache tribes (Mescalero Apache reservation in South Central New Mexico and Jicarilla Apache Nation in the north of the state), and a part of the Navajo Nation.

The best way to get an overview of Native American history and the cultures of the state's nineteen pueblos is to visit Albuquerque's Indian Pueblo Cultural Center, which includes a museum with narrative displays that take you through the history of the region's Native peoples and exhibits showing the unique arts and crafts of each pueblo. Indian dances take place here on the weekend and some weekdays in summer. See the Attractions chapter for details (2401 12th Street NW, 505-843-7270, 866-855-7902, www.indianpueblo.org).

The nineteen New Mexico pueblos are Acoma, Cochiti, Isleta, Jemez, Laguna, Nambe, Ohkay Owingeh, Picuris, Pojoaque, Sandia, San Felipe, San Ildefonso, Santa Ana, Santa Clara, Santo Domingo, Taos, Tesuque, Zia, and Zuni. These pueblos are living communities, not tourist attractions, and each is its own self-governing sovereign nation. Some pueblos are conservative in retaining traditional customs despite great pressure from the outside world, and they are either closed to visitors or do not encourage them. Others are open to visitors or have leisure- and tourism-related businesses.

The ancient villages of the mesa-top Acoma Pueblo (an hour west of Albuquerque) and Taos Pueblo (two and a half hours north), with its multistory apartment-style dwellings, are both well geared to receive visitors and are recommended for their outstanding architecture and locations. Tours are available at both pueblos, and a visit will provide great insight into the culture and history of these communities. Details on both are in the Day Trips and Weekend Getaways chapter.

In the immediate area around Albuquerque, tourists are catered to with leisure amenities that include casinos, resorts, and golf courses on the pueblo lands of Sandia, Isleta, Santa Ana, and San Felipe. These businesses are located separately from the actual tribal communities, and policies on visiting the pueblo communities vary. For example, aside from tribal gaming at San Felipe's Casino Hollywood (30 miles north of Albuquerque at exit 252 of I-25) and occasional public festival days, San Felipe pueblo generally prefers to keep its privacy. In the village of Isleta Pueblo (about 3.5 miles southwest of the casino and resort), visitors are free to see the beautiful St. Augustine mission church rebuilt in 1716, after the Pueblo Revolt, on the foundation of the original 1612 mission church. Photography on the pueblo is restricted to the church only.

The Pueblo of Jemez, about 50 miles northwest of Albuquerque, is closed to visitors except on feast days, but the pueblo's Walatowa Visitor Center and Museum of History and Culture is open daily with exhibits, nature walks, guided hikes of Jemez red-rock canyons, and pottery and other arts and crafts for sale (7413 Highway 4, Jemez Pueblo, 575-834-7235, www.jemezpueblo.com).

Most pueblos hold feast days (named for each pueblo's patron saint) that are open to the public at various times of year, as well as other days of dance, song, and ritual celebration, notably around Christmas and the New Year. Consult the Indian Pueblo Cultural Center for details about feast days (a feast-day calendar and directions to pueblos are also available on their Web site: www.indianpueblo.org) and other celebration days open to visitors at the pueblos, or check with the tribal offices of individual pueblos.

PUEBLO ETIQUETTE

When visiting a pueblo, please remember that these are living communities just like any other and respect individuals' privacy. Dances and other traditional events that are open to non-Pueblo people are not entertainment or staged performances, but religious ceremonies.

It is a privilege to be invited to witness them, and many visitors come away with a sense of awe, honored that they have been allowed to be present at these sacred rituals. If you act as you would in a house of worship, maintaining silence and paying respectful attention to proceedings, you'll be unlikely to offend. Pueblos have their own cultures and their own codes of etiquette. By observing courteous behavior, you will avoid offending your hosts and ensure that future guests are welcome.

- Each pueblo has its own government and its own rules for visitors. Please familiarize yourself with these in advance or on arrival, and observe the regulations while on pueblo lands.
- Call ahead to confirm access to tribal lands and event dates. Access is sometimes restricted due to private ceremonies or other reasons, and schedules may change. Please keep visits to daylight hours unless there is a specific evening ceremony open to the public (such as Christmas Eve dances).
- Pueblos may charge an entry fee, and each pueblo has individual policies regarding permits for photography, sketching, painting, and video and audio recording. Some prohibit all photography. Check with the pueblo, and do obey regulations; otherwise cameras, film, or other equipment may be confiscated. Never take photos of tribal members without their prior permission.
- Don't enter private homes uninvited or wander outside the public areas. (It's common sense—act as you would like people to act if they came visiting in your neighborhood.)
- Respect any signs that show off-limit areas; don't enter kivas or cemeteries or climb on walls or other structures. Also don't drop litter—nature is sacred, and littering is prohibited. Refrain from wading in rivers or creeks—they may be a source of water for the pueblo.
- Don't take alcohol, drugs, or weapons onto Native lands. No pets, either.
- Leave your cell phone behind—pueblo officials may confiscate them if they could be used for photography or recording, and ringing phones are intrusive to pueblo life.
- Don't talk during dances and ceremonies or ask questions about the meanings and other details of ceremonies if the information isn't offered (pueblo people are very private about their religious traditions). Don't wave and point or intrude on or walk across the ceremonial space or do anything to distract the dancers. Leave them their space as they enter or leave the dance area or are resting, and don't approach dancers to talk or ask questions.
- Applause at any point is inappropriate.
- On feast days (or any other day) only enter a pueblo home by invitation. On a feast day, even if you don't know anyone at the pueblo, someone may invite you in to eat. If so, it's polite to accept, but don't linger at the table as your host will want to serve other visitors. Thank your host, but it is not appropriate to offer payment or a tip.
- Do not pick up or remove artifacts, pottery shards, or other objects.
- Be aware that ceremonies are not conducted by the clock but by natural events or in a ceremonial sequence that may happen out of the public eye and not be evident to you. Relax and be patient. It's worth the wait!
- Please dress modestly, and avoid revealing clothing such as shorts and skin-revealing or skimpy tops.
- Keep your youngsters close so they don't go scaling that incredibly tempting ancient wall!
- Obey all speed limits and other traffic and parking directions. Pueblo police are diligent in enforcing these, and lower speed limits protect children who may be playing by the roads, as well as other community members. Also watch out for livestock on pueblo lands that may wander on or near roads.

thoroughfare running north/south through the Westside, parallel to the Rio Grande.

New Mexico's official nickname is the Land of Enchantment. Author Lilian Whiting first coined the phrase in her 1906 book *The Land of Enchantment: From Pike's Peak to the Pacific,* although she was writing about several southwestern states. In 1935 New Mexico used the term in a tourism brochure, and starting in 1941, the name appeared on New Mexico license plates and became common usage. In 1999 Land of Enchantment was officially adopted as the state nickname.

North Valley and Los Ranchos

The North Valley is a verdant strip bordering the Rio Grande, starting from I-40 and reaching north to Corrales. Many visitors are surprised to see this pastoral oasis in the desert and the lush bosque cottonwood forest that is home to much wildlife. Because of the North Valley's fertility, it was a natural choice for early settlers to farm, and it retains its agricultural atmosphere today, especially in the area close to the river. The Village of Los Ranchos de Albuquerque lies at the heart of the North Valley and was incorporated as its own municipality in 1958. Just 7 miles north of Downtown Albuquerque, Los Ranchos has a population of around 5,000 and holds tight to its rural roots. Its main streets are Rio Grande Boulevard and 4th Street. The north stretch of Rio Grande Boulevard is bordered by grand old trees, horse pastures, and agricultural fields. The line of antiques shops known as Antique Mile is found on North 4th Street—part of the original Camino Real. The North Valley and Los Ranchos are home to the Indian Pueblo Cultural Center, the Rio Grande Nature Center, the Rio Grande Valley State Park, access points to the 16-mile Paseo del Bosque trail, the Unser Racing Museum, wineries, picturesque bed-and-breakfast inns, and authentic New Mexican restaurants.

Corrales

Tucked between busy Rio Rancho and the Rio Grande, the Village of Corrales is a sweet retreat from the pace of the city. Corrales has a long agricultural history and retains a peaceful pastoral atmosphere, with a single winding Main Street lined with orchards, mature cottonwoods, and old adobe buildings housing restaurants, cafés, and art galleries. Corrales is also home to wineries and a grower's market, and several bed-and-breakfasts. The arts influence is strong—the Corrales Society of Artists has about 120 members. The partially reconstructed Casa San Ysidro hacienda—part of the Albuquerque Museum of Art and History—is open at certain times for public tours, and music concerts are held at the Old San Ysidro Church. The Village of Corrales was formally incorporated in 1971, although the southern part still lay within Bernalillo County. Since 2005, all of the incorporated area is located in Sandoval County. Corrales is about 19 miles north of the airport.

Rio Rancho

On the northwest border of Albuquerque, Rio Rancho is a young city, incorporated in 1981. The self-styled City of Vision is New Mexico's fastest growing metropolitan area, with an estimated population of over 80,000 in 2009. A business center and high-tech mecca, Rio Rancho's largest employer is the Intel Corporation. Attractions here include the J&R Vintage Auto Museum and the Santa Ana Star Center, a venue for concerts, car shows, sporting events, ice shows, and trade shows. Rio Rancho covers over 100 square miles north of Albuquerque's Westside area and is about a 30-minute drive from Albuquerque Inter-

In Spanish words, "ll" is pronounced as if it were a "y"; e.g., Bernalillo = Ber-na-LEE-yo. "J" is pronounced as if it were an "h"; e.g., frijoles = fri-HO-lez; or Jemez = Hemez. A tilde on an ñ gives it a "ny" sound; e.g., mañana = man-YA-na; or Piñon = Pin-yon. Sandia has an emphasis on the "i" = San-DEE-a.

Around the Houses

Acequia: Irrigation ditch, in a network of ditches fed by the acequia madre, or mother ditch. It's traditionally a community project each spring to clear debris and silt from the acequias, to keep the water flowing to everyone's land.

Adobe: Thick New Mexican mud mixed with straw, formed into bricks and dried in the sun. The bricks are mortared into walls with more mud, and the walls are plastered with another layer of adobe. As the surface adobe layer cracks in the elements, annual remudding is traditionally needed to maintain a building's exterior, which can become a whole-community project for adobe churches! The word *adobe* is also used to describe the warm earth color. Modern buildings attempt an adobe look with adobe-toned stucco, but you can tell authentic from faux adobe, because real adobe homes and churches usually have softly rounded contours. It's hard to shape true adobe into perfectly straight planes and right angles. So if a building has sharp corners, it's a look-alike.

Banco: A built-in bench, traditionally adobe and jutting out from an adobe wall, often around a fireplace.

Casita: A small house (casa) or cottage. Casitas are often on the land of a main house and are used as a guest house.

Corbel: Carved wooden bracket supports.

Coyote fence: Rustic fence of branches or saplings wired together to keep the coyotes away from the livestock—or just used as a decorative fence.

Horno: Adobe outdoor oven, shaped like a beehive and used to bake bread, typical of Indian pueblos.

Kiva fireplace: An arch-shaped adobe fireplace, usually built into a corner.

Latilla: Saplings laid close together across vigas (roof beams) to form a ceiling, sometimes in straight rows, sometimes diagonally in herringbone patterns.

Linea: A long narrow parcel of land. When families bequeathed their land grants to their offspring, the land was divided into strips, often running from higher ground into valleys. In this way, everyone had an equal share of the irrigated and fertile land in the valley bed and of the higher, less-productive land. As the lineas were divided further over generations, some became very narrow.

Nicho: A small arched recess in an adobe wall, used to display religious icons or other objects.

Portal: Covered porch along the front or back of a building, also used as a walkway. The prime example in Albuquerque is in Old Town Plaza.

Viga: Peeled logs used as ceiling beams and left exposed. The large timbers extend outside the walls of the building.

national Sunport. The shops, hotels, restaurants, and pubs in this new urban center cater to the local Rio Rancho community and business travelers. If you are visiting Rio Rancho on business, a short drive into the neighboring Village of Corrales, between Rio Rancho and the Rio Grande, brings a rural change of scene. Driving north on the modern strip through Rio Rancho on NM SR 528 leads you to Bernalillo.

Bernalillo

Historic Bernalillo is about 17 miles north of Downtown Albuquerque and with a population of 8,500 keeps a small town feel on its main street, Camino del Pueblo, part of the old El Camino Real and Route 66. The Town of Bernalillo, confusingly enough, does not lie within Bernalillo County but is the county seat of Sandoval County. The town was founded by Don Diego de Vargas in 1695. Bernalillo's winemaking lineage goes back to 1883, and it hosts the New Mexico Wine Festival every Labor Day weekend, the oldest wine fair in the state. Other town events include Las Fiestas de San Lorenzo in August, a rodeo, and classic and custom car shows. Access Bernalillo from I-25 exit 240 or from exit 242, which takes you to the busy main drag of US 550, where you'll find the Coronado State Monument with Kuaua Pueblo ruins. Also off US 550 are the Santa Ana Pueblo facilities: Santa Ana Star Casino, Santa Ana Golf Club, and Hyatt Regency Tamaya Resort and Spa and Twin Warriors Golf Club. Bernalillo also has a New Mexico Rail Runner Express station.

Sandia, Isleta, and Santa Ana Pueblos

The pueblos are sovereign nations, with independent authority to govern within their territories. The Pueblo of Sandia lies on the northern border of Albuquerque and has been on this site since at least the year 1300. You're actually on reservation land when driving across the east-west section of Tramway Boulevard at the north end of Albuquerque. The pueblo reports fewer than 500 tribal members now. The 22,877-acre reservation includes the Sandia Resort & Casino, an impressive hotel, spa, and casino development with an open-air amphitheater that hosts music concerts and other events, and the Sandia Golf Club, with an 18-hole championship golf course designed by Scott Miller. Sandia Resort & Casino also has a 50,000-square-foot convention and events center, home to the annual Fiery Foods and Barbecue Show. Sandia Lakes Recreation Area offers year-round fishing, plus trails, wildlife watching, and picnic and softball facilities. You can buy Native American jewelry, arts, and crafts at Sandia Pueblo's kiva-shaped Bien Mur Indian Market Center.

Isleta Pueblo borders Albuquerque to the south and was established around the 1300s. There are 4,441 enrolled tribal members, and businesses operated by Isleta Pueblo includes a casino resort, scheduled to be rebranded as the Hard Rock Hotel & Casino Albuquerque in spring 2010, with a 30,000-square-foot convention center, the Isleta Eagle 27-hole golf course, and a lake fishing and recreation area.

The Pueblo of Santa Ana, north of the town of Bernalillo, dates back to the 1500s. On Santa Ana lands you'll find the Hyatt Regency Tamaya Resort and Spa, a beautifully designed property that fits sensitively into the natural environment. There are two golf courses: the championship Twin Warriors, designed by Gary Panks, at the Hyatt resort and the 27-hole Santa Ana Golf Club. The tribe also operates the Santa Ana Star Casino, with a bowling center, 30,000-square-foot conference facility, and live entertainment at the Bosque Event Center.

i **Air is thinner at Albuquerque's high elevations, and it can take a few days for a body to adjust, so take it easy. Day one of your trip is not the day to tackle climbing Sandia Peak. To avoid dehydration, drink plenty of water. Because of Albuquerque's high-desert climate, you dehydrate faster here than at sea level. Even if you don't feel sticky and sweaty, because of the low humidity, you'll be losing water, and you must replenish it. Be aware that alcohol is also dehydrating. Clue: If you notice you're urinating less frequently than usual or if you get headachy, tired, or irritable or have a hangover feeling, you are probably dehydrated. Topping up on H_2O also helps defend against altitude sickness. Symptoms include headaches, dizziness, fatigue, weakness, shortness of breath, loss of appetite, nausea, disturbed sleep, irritability and a general feeling of malaise. If you feel you're coming down with altitude sickness, drink some water and consult a medical professional immediately. The sun's UV rays are stronger at this high altitude, so wear high-SPF sunscreen at all times and year-round—even on the occasional cloudy day. Also shield your eyes by wearing sunglasses with UV-protection lenses.**

New Mexico State Symbols

State Question: "Red or green?" In other words, what kind of chile would you like with your meal? If in doubt, answer Christmas—you'll get a bit of both.
State Aircraft: Hot-air balloon
State Bird: Greater Roadrunner, also called the chaparral bird and el paisano
State Cookie: Biscochito. The anise-flavored cookie traditional to Spain made New Mexico the first state to enjoy an official state cookie.
State Fish: Rio Grande cutthroat trout
State Fossil: Coelophysis, from the dinosaur *Coelophysis bauri,* which lived about 228 million years ago
State Flower: Yucca flower
State Gem: Turquoise
State Grass: Blue grama
State Mammal: American black bear. New Mexico's most famous bear was Smokey Bear, a cub found injured after a forest fire in Lincoln National Forest, near Capitan. Starting in 1950, Smokey Bear starred in U.S. Forest Service ads for fire prevention. He died in 1975 and is buried in Smokey Bear State Park, Capitan.
State Neckwear: Bolo tie
State Reptile: New Mexico whiptail lizard
State Slogan: "Everybody is somebody in New Mexico."
State Tree: Piñon pine, also called the two-needle piñon
State Vegetables: Chile pepper (*Capsicum annum L.*) and frijoles, otherwise known as pinto beans. The state legislature couldn't decide between these two treats that pair so beautifully in New Mexican dishes, so they plumped for both.

The full and illustrated list of state symbols and the stories behind them can be found at the Secretary of State's Web site: www.sos.state.nm.us/KidsCorner/StateSymbols.html

i Keep a lookout for bison roaming the fields alongside Tramway Boulevard in the area of Sandia Pueblo, south of the Bien Mur Indian Market Center. The herd is cared for by Sandia Pueblo's preservation program.

East Mountains

The Sandia Peak Ski Area lies on the east "green side of the mountains," where the heavily wooded alpine landscape is a great contrast to the more rugged western face. There are trails here into the Cibola National Forest. A series of funky old mountain villages and mining towns is strung along the scenically beautiful Turquoise Trail National Scenic Byway. The Turquoise Trail threads behind the Sandias from Albuquerque to Santa Fe, and villages en route include Cedar Crest; Sandia Park; Golden; Madrid, with its galleries and cafés; and Cerrillos. Other places of interest are the quirky folk art Tinkertown Museum and the superb Paa-Ko Ridge golf course designed by Ken Dye.

WEATHER

Albuquerque enjoys an average 310 days of sunshine a year, and the low humidity keeps even the summer highs comfortable. Average annual rainfall is around 9 inches, and about half the year's total precipitation falls from June through September. Average relative humidity is 44 percent. Winters are comparatively mild, and although snow occasionally falls—working out to 4.2 days of snow a year—it remains moderate in the valley and usually melts off fast, while the mountain peaks hold on to their sparkling white crowns! The Sandia Mountains have their own microclimate, with an average annual snowfall of approximately 111 inches and 40 inches of rain. In the valley the four distinct seasons are most visibly evident in the changing flora, fauna, and foliage.

Average Temperature, High/Low

	°F	°C
January	47/23	(8/–5)
February	53/27	(12/–3)
March	61/33	(16/1)
April	70/41	(21/5)
May	79/50	(26/10)
June	89/59	(32/15)
July	92/64	(33/18)
August	89/63	(32/17)
September	82/56	(28/13)
October	71/44	(22/7)
November	57/31	(14/–1)
December	48/24	(9/–4)

i **Even on the warmest days, temperatures drop once you go up to higher elevations, and the high desert can cool quickly after sundown. It's always a good idea to wear layers, to adjust to shifts in temperature.**

SURFING IN DUKE CITY—FREE WIFI HOTSPOTS

The City of Albuquerque offers free wireless Internet access at various locations for residents and visitors. Here are some of the most convenient, organized by geographical quadrant so you can hotfoot it to the nearest hotspot. The Rapid Ride Red Line bus route 766 also has WiFi along the length of its route, which passes through all four quarters of the city. Other locations may be added, so check the latest list at the City's Web site, www.cabq.gov/wifi. Many hotels, restaurants, cafés, and other businesses also offer WiFi to their customers.

Southeast

Albuquerque International Sunport, 2200 Sunport Boulevard SE

Crosswinds Weekly Rapid Ride Station, Central Avenue SE & Carlisle Boulevard SE

Ernie Pyle Library, 900 Girard Boulevard SE

KOB-FM Pop Rapid Ride Station, Central Avenue SE & Carlisle Boulevard SE

San Pedro Library, 5600 Trumbull SE

UNM Rapid Ride Station, Central Avenue SE & Yale Boulevard SE

Southwest

Alamosa/Robert L. Murphy Public Library, 6900 Gonzales SW

South Valley Library, 3904 Isleta Boulevard SW

Westgate Library, 1300 Delgado SW

Northeast

Cherry Hills Public Library, 6901 Barstow Street NE

Erna Fergusson Library, 3700 San Mateo NE

Juan Tabo Library, 3407 Juan Tabo NE

Lomas Tramway Library, 908 Eastridge NE

Special Collections Library, 423 Central Avenue NE

Uptown Transit Center, Uptown Boulevard NE & Indiana Street NE

Wyoming Library, 8205 Apache Avenue NE

Northwest

Albuquerque Aquarium and Botanic Garden, 2601 Central Avenue NW

Albuquerque Civic Plaza, One Civic Plaza NW

Albuquerque Convention Center, 401 2nd Street NW

4th Street Mall, Copper Avenue NW & 4th Street NW

Main Public Library, 501 Copper Avenue NW

North Valley Library, 7704 2nd Street NW

Old Town Plaza, 303 Romero Street NW

SW Mesa Park and Ride, Central Avenue NW & Unser Boulevar. NW

Taylor Ranch Public Library, 5700 Bogart NW

GETTING HERE, GETTING AROUND

Although Albuquerque has sprawled over recent decades, and the city can seem daunting to first-time visitors, it's actually pretty easy to find your way around, with wide, clearly signed roads and the best compass of all in Mother Nature. To orient yourself in the city, remember that the mountains are to the east.

Albuquerque addresses are divided into four quadrants: northwest, northeast, southwest, and southeast, with the letters NW, NE, SW, and SE appearing in the address to tip you off on the general area. Central Avenue marks the north/south divide. The railroad tracks (just east of First Street, or west of I-25) split east/west.

Historically, transportation has played a major part in shaping Albuquerque—quite literally from the ground up! Consider the famous roadways of the Camino Real, the major trading route in the city's early days, and Route 66, which helped put Albuquerque on the map as a tourism destination. The railways also performed a vital role in the city's development and its current geography. Finally, we take to the skies, with Albuquerque's important ballooning and aviation history, not forgetting the Sandia Peak Tramway, the longest aerial passenger tramway in the world. You quickly start to see transportation's influence on Albuquerque's economy, character, and culture. You can read more about that in the History chapter, but first let's focus on the information you'll need when you arrive.

ARRIVING BY AIR

ALBUQUERQUE INTERNATIONAL SUNPORT

2200 Sunport Boulevard SE
(505) 244-7700
www.cabq.gov/airport

You couldn't hope for a better welcome to New Mexico than to land at the charming, friendly, and easily navigable Albuquerque International Sunport. The airport is close to the center of Albuquerque, about 4 miles south of the major business district. As you fly in you'll enjoy terrific mountain and city views, including if you arrive at night when Downtown is lit up and the radio masts twinkle red on Sandia Peak.

Although Albuquerque International Sunport is small in scale compared to many city airports, it has plenty of muscle, handling nearly 6.5 million passengers in 2008, in an average of 494 flight departures or landings each day. Passenger numbers have grown by an average of 2 percent a year over the last 15 years. The airport code is ABQ—an acronym that has become a popular shorthand for Albuquerque itself.

You immediately know you're in the Land of Enchantment when you arrive in the attractive adobe and turquoise Sunport terminal. It's a true southwestern reception, with huge carved beams painted with native symbols stretching the width of the arrival hall. Art and sculpture by New Mexican artists is dotted throughout the terminal from the airport's permanent collection of over 100 pieces. You'll also spot a dramatically positioned original 1914 Curtiss Pusher Design Biplane in the Great Hall. You might even be welcomed by live music in the Sunport Serenades series of concerts featuring local classical, mariachi, jazz, or even polka bands.

Albuquerque International Sunport (AIS) is the state's largest commercial airport and therefore the main gateway to New Mexico, served by nine major commercial airlines: AeroMexico, American, Continental, Delta, Frontier, Northwest, Southwest, United, and US Airways. Southwest

Close-up

Route 66

Route 66, also known as the Mother Road, was commissioned in 1926, joining many existing sections of local roads into one continuous highway. Although its purpose was practical, in a few decades Route 66 came to symbolize the freedom of the American spirit and the independence of ordinary families who now had access to motor vehicles and were determined to explore their country from sea to shining sea. Well, not quite from sea to sea; more like windy lake to shining sea. Route 66 stretched 2,448 miles from Lake Michigan in Chicago to Santa Monica's Pacific Ocean, and the United States Highway Association promoted Route 66 as the Main Street of America. It passed through eight states, including New Mexico, and brought many Americans to the Land of Enchantment for the first time. Once experienced, it was never forgotten, and a flourishing tourist industry sprung up in Albuquerque. Restaurants and retailers as well as many new motor hotels—or motels—with their iconic neon signs established themselves along Route 66 to serve the adventurous travelers.

Originally, between 1926 and 1937, Route 66 ran north-south through Albuquerque along Fourth Street, as part of a huge S-curve connecting Santa Rosa, Santa Fe, Albuquerque, Los Lunas, and a number of Indian reservations. This somewhat tortuous route of 506 miles of mainly unpaved road through New Mexico was shifted after federal money was granted in 1931. The realignment to a straight east-west direction was more in keeping with the rest of Route 66 and positioned the route along Albuquerque's Central Avenue. By 1937 the complete length of Route 66 was paved, and the New Mexico section was a much improved and straighter 399 miles.

It's worth noting that Central Avenue had already been an important thoroughfare since 1880, when it was called Railroad Avenue following the arrival of the Atchison, Topeka and Santa Fe Railway. However, before the motorcar was king, traffic on Railroad/Central was made up of horse-drawn carriages, and then electric streetcars, moving between the "New Albuquerque" district around the railroad depot and Old Town a mile and half to the west.

Early travelers on Route 66 weren't always there for the thrill of it. During the Great Depression, they included desperate Americans heading to California to seek their fortunes and equally despairing families migrating from the Great Plains to escape the Dust Bowl. John Steinbeck's Pulitzer Prize–winning novel *The Grapes of Wrath* immortalized Route 66 as "The mother road, the road of flight."

After World War II Route 66 truly enjoyed its heyday. It became less a road of salvation than a road of exploration, as thousands of former GIs took to the wheel to discover the farthest reaches of their country and all the possibilities it could offer them. In 1946 one of those young men, an ex-marine from Pennsylvania named Bobby Troup, set off on the drive from Chicago to California to pick up his career as a composer. When he pulled into Los Angeles 10 days later, he not only had a journey under his belt, he'd written a song that captures the essence of Route 66 in all its glory. Nat King Cole had a hit with Troup's song, and the rest is history. We've been getting our kicks on Route 66 ever since.

By the 1950s Route 66 was in its prime, even as federal plans were made to create a new system of interstate highways that would ultimately replace Route 66 as a major national artery. To accommodate Route 66's tourist traffic, the road through Albuquerque was widened at both its east and west ends and the commercial strip pressed out in both directions, too.

Visitors from the east entered through Tijeras Canyon, one of the few passing places through the mountains, and caught their first glimpse of Albuquerque and the gorgeous Rio Grande valley. Tijeras Canyon was home to Paleo-Indians at least 900 years ago, and today you'll pass through the Canyon to drive the Turquoise Trail (see the Day Trips and Weekend Getaways chapter). Route 66 exited Albuquerque via Nine Mile Hill to the west.

During the 1950s the motels grew bigger, and their neon signs grew bigger and brighter, too. Albuquerque's city population grew to match, doubling to 201,000 over the decade. Many of the old postcards celebrating Route 66 date to this period, showing the motels, bars, and nightclubs that offered glamour and escape in this exotic landscape to visitors from across the country. Gas stations, diners, and drive-ins featured dramatic designs to catch the eye of passing motorists. Some of those vintage buildings and signs still exist. Newer businesses have reproduced their unique style, too, evoking the nostalgia of Route 66 and the ever-tempting allure of the open road, with all the glittering delights to be discovered on the highway that's the best.

Many of today's visitors will no doubt recall their first introduction to the Mother Road from the early 1960s CBS television series *Route 66,* where characters Tod (Martin Milner) and Buz (George Maharis) freewheeled across the country in a stylin' Corvette convertible. Route 66 was decommissioned in 1985, bypassed by the zoom of traffic on I-40. It remains on the National Scenic and Historic Byway system, and it most certainly remains a vibrant part of Albuquerque's life today. The revitalized Central Avenue buzzes with trendy restaurants, boutiques, and nightlife around Nob Hill, the University of New Mexico, and along into Downtown. Central also leads you past the southern edge of Old Town; the Pueblo Deco KiMo Theatre; the Alvarado Transportation Center; the Rio Grande Botanic Garden; Albuquerque Aquarium; and EXPO New Mexico, home to the state fair, the Downs Racetrack & Casino, and many of Albuquerque's major annual festivals.

The east end of Central, beyond the revitalized Nob Hill area, has a number of original motels that are closed and in disrepair or derelict. It's still worth a trip by these "ghost motels," as they give a good sense of the old architecture and just how fabulous and extensive Route 66 was at its peak.

The ABQ Ride bus route 66 takes you the length of Central and, at $1 for a one-way adult fare or $2 for a day pass so you can jump on and off, is a great way to explore the old Route 66. Kids under 10 ride free when accompanied by an adult. For an abbreviated version of the same experience, the Rapid Ride Red Line 766 bus for the same fare has fewer stops and covers the key middle section of Central.

Each of the Nob Hill, UNM, Downtown, and Old Town sections of Route 66 are easy to walk, so you can pick a section to explore on foot.

Or hop in your car and crank up the volume on a track of "Route 66" on your CD player. In addition to the original Nat King Cole version, musicians including Bing Crosby, Jerry Lee Lewis, Chuck Berry, Bob Dylan, the Rolling Stones, Depeche Mode, Tom Petty, and John Meyer have covered it, so there's plenty to choose from. Then cruise the length of Central Avenue. Even if you aren't driving a convertible, imagine your hair blowing in the breeze, sing along to the song, and drink in the excitement and history of America's, and Albuquerque's, spiritual Main Street.

i **Albuquerque International Sunport was named as a result of a contest held by the city in the 1960s. The Sunport suggestion beat around 2,000 other entries. Other finalists were the rather unimaginative Albuquerque Airport, and the more whimsical Albuquerque Enchantoport.**

is the largest carrier into the city, handling just shy of 60 percent of Albuquerque's passengers in 2008. There are also regular in-state commuter services with Great Lakes Airlines and New Mexico Airlines.

The airport provides nonstop service to 30 cities, including major hubs. Currently, these are Atlanta, Baltimore, Chicago, Chihuahua, Dallas, Denver, El Paso, Houston, Kansas City, Las Vegas, Los Angeles, Lubbock, Midland/Odessa, Minneapolis/St. Paul, Oakland, Orlando, Phoenix, Portland, Salt Lake City, San Diego, San Francisco, Seattle/Tacoma, St. Louis, Tampa (on a seasonal basis), Tucson, and Washington, D.C. In-state commuter flights serve Alamogordo, Carlsbad, Clovis, Hobbs, and Silver City.

AIS has a single 574,000-square-foot terminal, which was expanded in the 1980s and again in 1996. It now has 23 gates in two concourses for major commercial airlines, plus a separate commuter airline gate area. Set over three levels, the terminal has a good range of restaurants, gift shops, and kiosks plus several ATMS, both before and after the security checkpoint. Smart Carts for luggage cost $3 by cash or credit card. Free wireless Internet access is available throughout the terminal. The Albuquerque Visitor Center booth, staffed by volunteers, is located by Baggage Claim Four on Level One, with information on accommodations, attractions, and transportation. There are also courtesy phones to about 15 hotels. An Interfaith Meditation Room is on Level One, just past Baggage Claim Eight. Look for the glass tiles set into the wall. This small but serene space also provides information on Albuquerque places of worship, and chaplains are on call. Wheelchair users will find accessible restrooms, elevators, and drinking fountains. There is also Braille signage and telecommunications devices for the hearing impaired (TDD).

i **Find real-time information on Albuquerque International Sunport flight arrivals and departures at www.cabq.gov/airport.**

The airport also shares its runways with Kirtland Air Force Base, and you often see military planes zooming dramatically over the mountains. Kirtland Air Force Base provides aircraft rescue and firefighting services for the airport.

Albuquerque International Sunport is a U.S. Port of Entry with its own customs facility. Exporters can ship freight directly and pay duties locally.

Private Planes

Most private planes and charter services arrive into Albuquerque International Sunport, where there are two fixed-base operators: Cutter Aviation (505-842-4184, 800-678-5382, www.cutteraviation.com) and Atlantic Aviation (505-842-4990, www.atlanticaviation.com). An alternative for charter, private, and corporate flights is Double Eagle II Airport on the Westside of Albuquerque, near the Petroglyph National Monument. The fixed-base operator here is Bode Aero Services (505-352-0292, 877-384-9813, www.flybode.com).

Commercial Airlines Contact Information:

AeroMexico:
(800) 237-6639, www.aeromexico.com
American Airlines:
(800) 433-7300, www.aa.com
Continental:
(800) 525-0280, www.continental.com
Delta: (800) 221-1212, www.delta.com
Frontier: (800) 432-1359, www.frontierairlines.com
Northwest: (800) 225-2525, www.nwa.com
Southwest: (800) 435-9792, www.southwest.com
United: (800) 241-6522, www.united.com
US Airways: (800) 235-9292, www.usairways.com

Commuter Airlines Contact Information:

Great Lakes Airlines (Clovis and Silver City): (800) 554-5111, www.greatlakesav.com

New Mexico Airlines (Alamogordo, Carlsbad, El Paso and Hobbs): (888) 564-6119, www.flynma.com

If you arrive without accommodation, pick up one of the coupon booklets at the visitor service area by baggage claim. The coupons provide great discounts for walk-in guests, although you can't use them to reserve in advance. In the same area there's also a free phone to selected hotels, to check availability and arrange shuttles if provided.

On the Ground at AIS

One of the joys of arriving at Albuquerque International Sunport is that you can make a speedy exit so you don't waste a minute of your trip to the city! The airport is rarely congested, and international visitors have already passed through customs and passport control at their airport of entry. As there is only one terminal, it's a quick walk from your gate to the baggage claim area, and luggage is processed quickly and efficiently. So unless you're tempted to stop for a welcoming margarita at one of the airport bars, you're usually on your way within 20 minutes of disembarking from your flight. As you leave the terminal, there are outdoor sculptures from the permanent collection of the Sunport Arts Program along Sunport Boulevard and by the Rental Car Center.

Meeters and Greeters

After 9/11, when meeters and greeters could no longer amble directly to the gate to welcome arrivals, people used to stand around waiting by the security checkpoint, which created a collegial atmosphere as we peered over everyone's heads to spot our loved ones, but was rather cramped and uncomfortable. However, following renovations to the security area, there is now a dedicated Greeters' Lobby, with windows facing the Sandia Mountains and also overlooking some of the gates. Additionally, the airport has created a Cell Phone Waiting Area outside the terminal. Greeters can wait here in their vehicles until their passengers call to say they are ready for pickup; then it's just a minute's drive round to the front of the terminal. Follow the signs on the arrival level to this free lot just east of the main parking structure on Girard. You must remain with your vehicle while in this lot. Two free Aircraft Observation Areas also serve as cell phone waiting lots. One is on Girard east of the terminal and near the main Cell Phone Waiting Area. The other is on Spirit Drive, south of the terminal and just east of University.

Parking

A four-level parking structure at the AIS terminal provides short-term parking for 3,400 vehicles. Rates payable by cash or credit card start at $1 for 30 minutes to $7 for 24 hours and $10 a day after 3 days. A long-term parking lot has 500 spaces, charging $6 for the first 24 hours and $8 a day after 3 days. Sunport handicapped parking is free for the first 24 hours. The parking information hotline is (505) 842-7030. If you have trouble getting your car to start, 24-hour assistance is available from the parking office (505-244-7884) or the main AIS phone number (505-244-7700). There are also several off-site parking companies serving the airport, with frequent shuttles circulating to the terminal.

Car Rental

The Sunport Car Rental Center is at 3400 University SE, about half a mile from the terminal. Free car rental shuttles run every five minutes outside Level One of the terminal. There is also a car rental courtesy phone on Level One. The Sunport Car Rental Center opened in 2001 and features striking art and sculpture by New Mexico artists.

Advantage Rent A Car: (505) 247-1066, (800) 777-5500, www.advantage.com

Alamo Rent A Car: (505) 724-4500, (800) 462-5266, www.alamo.com

Avis Rent A Car: (505) 842-4080, (800) 331-1212, www.avis.com

Budget Rent A Car: (800) 527-0700, www.budget.com
Enterprise Rent A Car: (505) 765-9100, (800) 736-8222, www.enterprise.com
Hertz Car Rental: (505) 842 4235, (800) 654-3131, www.hertz.com
National Car Rental: (800) 227-7368, www.nationalcar.com
Thrifty Car Rental: (505) 842 8733, (800) 847-4389, www.thrifty.com

Taxis

Metered taxis wait outside the terminal from Albuquerque Cab Company (505-883-4888) and Yellow Cab Company (505-247-8888). A taxicab fare for one person from the airport to the Downtown Civic Plaza costs around $16 to $18.

i Many Albuquerque hotels provide free shuttle services to guests, even those that aren't right by the airport, so check when booking.

Shuttle

SUNPORT SHUTTLE
(505) 883-4966, (866) 505-4966
www.sunportshuttle.com

The Sunport Shuttle is part of the Albuquerque Cab Company and offers shared-ride shuttles between the airport and any city destination. A detailed list of their rates to most Albuquerque hotels can be found at the Web site. The fare as we go to press to the Downtown Civic Plaza is $11 for the first person including tax and $5 for each additional passenger in your party. You save money by booking a round trip; this Downtown Civic Plaza example would be $20 round trip. Advance reservations are accepted by phone or via the Sunport Shuttle Web site. The shuttle counter at the airport also takes walk-up passengers without reservations. It's open between 9 a.m. and 10 p.m., on Level One of the terminal, opposite Baggage Claim Three.

Buses

Albuquerque International Sunport is not very well served by public buses, but as a budget option there are two ABQ Ride buses between the airport and the Alvarado Transportation Center in the Downtown area. Here you can find further transportation options or connect with the New Mexico Rail Runner Express. Route 350 is a nonstop express that takes 15 minutes, and six buses a day run on weekdays only. Route 50 runs via Yale and the University of New Mexico, with stops along the way, so it takes about 20 minutes. It operates on weekdays about every 30 minutes and on Saturday at approximately 70-minute intervals.

A third airport bus, Route 222, connects Albuquerque International Sunport with the Rio Bravo station for the New Mexico Rail Runner Express. Approximately 8 buses a day run weekdays only, and the journey takes about 19 minutes. The 222 also goes east to Kirtland Air Force Base.

The adult fare for all routes is $1. Exact change is required.

All three services are quite limited in their hours and schedules are subject to change, so check the timetables posted on the City of Albuquerque's ABQ Ride Web site, www.cabq.gov/transit, or call (505) 243-7433.

ARRIVING BY BUS AND RAIL

Amtrak serves Albuquerque on the Southwest Chief train route that runs from Chicago to Los Angeles (800-USA-RAIL, www.Amtrak.com). Greyhound buses (800-231-2222, www.greyhound.com) also run through the city. Both the Amtrak and Greyhound stations are located in the Downtown Alvarado Transportation Center, 100 First Street SW, on the corner of First and Central.

ARRIVING BY CAR

Albuquerque sits squarely on the junction of two interstate highways. I-40, the Coronado Interstate and the third longest interstate in the nation, runs east to west, from Wilmington, North Carolina, to Barstow, California. It's bisected in Albuquerque by I-25, the Pan American Freeway, which stretches north to south, from Buffalo, Wyoming, to Las Cruces, New Mexico.

As interstate access to Albuquerque is so good, and as it's preferable to have a car when touring the city, many visitors arrive by road. You frequently see license plates from neighboring and nearby southwestern states: Texas, California, Arizona, Utah, Nevada, Oklahoma, and Colorado. But it's not uncommon to see license plates from much farther afield. The idea of a freedom-finding road trip to New Mexico's Wild West, with Albuquerque's links to the iconic Route 66, attracts young and old alike. If you play a game of spot-the-state-license-plate, it won't be too long before you've filled your card—for the lower 48 states, at least!

i Outside Albuquerque city, you'll often drive through Indian pueblos and reservations. Speed limits can drop suddenly on these highways, so keep a close eye on signs to avoid a speeding ticket from vigilant reservation police.

Approximate Driving Distances

Journey length obviously depends on your start and end point between these large cities and the route you take, but as a rough guide here are some approximate driving distances in miles.

Atlanta, Georgia—1,392
Chicago, Illinois—1,345
Cleveland, Ohio—1,616
Dallas, Texas—646
Denver, Colorado—449
El Paso, Texas—270
Houston, Texas—907
Las Vegas, Nevada—586
Los Angeles, California—802
Minneapolis, Minnesota—1,256
New Orleans, Louisiana—1,169
New York, New York—2,029
Oklahoma City, Oklahoma—540
Phoenix, Arizona—458
Salt Lake City, Utah—617
Seattle, Washington—1,460
St. Louis, Missouri—1,042

DRIVING IN ALBUQUERQUE

Once you arrive here, the two interstate highways remain important for getting around. I-40 and I-25 form "The Big I" intersection in the center of the city, and the cross they make divides ABQ into four easily accessible areas. You can reach most city locations quickly from one or the other arm of the interstate "cross."

The Big I is an amazing spaghetti-junction superstructure and the result of a $291 million reconstruction completed in 2002. This was the largest public works project in the history of New Mexico and was one of the 10 biggest highway projects in the country. The original Big I, designed in 1966, was planned to handle 40,000 vehicles daily. By 2002, as the busiest intersection in the state, it handled 10 times that traffic, 400,000 vehicles a day. It was the tenth most congested interchange in the nation before the rebuilding project to improve safety and efficiency started in June 2000. When work finished in May 2002, a month ahead of schedule, the project established a world record at the time for the fastest completion of a major interchange still supporting traffic. The entire intersection has fifty-five bridges, and the design, with its curving loops, has a certain grace. It even has a traditional New Mexico color scheme of adobe and turquoise.

Other major arteries to look out for are Central Avenue, the old Route 66 that runs east/west through Old Town, Downtown, and the University and Nob Hill areas (see the Close-up on Route 66 for some background on this historic road). Lomas and Menaul are two other big east/west routes. If you're on the north end of town, Paseo del Norte is an efficient way to cross the valley from Tramway Boulevard under the Sandias to the east, right across the Rio Grande to Coors Boulevard on the west. Coors is a fast road running just west of and parallel to the

i Drivers talking on a cell phone must use a hands-free device. The fine for using a hand-held cell phone while driving is $100.

Rio Grande, leading up to Rio Rancho and Corrales. It's mirrored on the east side of the river by Rio Grande Boulevard, which runs fairly quickly from Old Town up to around Montano, but at its northern stretch progress becomes more stately, with speed bumps and low speed limits. It's worth taking a spin up the length of Rio Grande Boulevard, however, as the slower section leads you through the beautiful village of Los Ranchos de Albuquerque along the bosque, with its fertile lands from the river, horse pastures, and impressive houses. Another good route to head north from Downtown, still west of 1-25, is 2nd Street. In Midtown, the busy San Mateo Boulevard is a key arterial north/south road. If you're trying to get north/south on the east side, try Tramway Boulevard, a straight and fast-moving road, often quite free of traffic, with the benefit of up-close mountain views.

i Adults must wear seatbelts in moving vehicles. Children under 1 year must be seated in a rear-facing restraint seat in the back seat of the car. Children 1 to 5 and under 40 pounds must be in a child-restraint seat. If you drive into Rio Rancho, children under 12 must be in the back seat.

The majority of Albuquerque's roads are laid out on a grid, so they're easy to navigate. Most are two-way roads, although in the Downtown area some roads are one way only. Around Old Town, of course, some roads are narrower and a bit of a maze, which is part of this historic district's charm. To go into Old Town itself, you're better off parking on the edge and taking to foot; otherwise you might circle the plaza for some time trying to find a parking space. In any case, walking is by far the best way to experience this delightful area.

City roads are wide and well sign-posted. Traffic rarely becomes so congested as to cause a delay, although it's worth avoiding I-25 and I-40 in morning and evening rush hours if you can and also the busy bridges crossing the Rio Grande. In general the average drive in the inner city is 20 minutes or less. Although most drivers in Albuquerque are courteous and relaxed, driving habits can occasionally be more cowboy than careful and attitudes toward using turn signals notoriously casual. The meaning of a red light can be taken somewhat liberally, too (red-light cameras are installed at major intersections). There's also an ongoing problem with drinking and driving throughout the state, leading to alcohol-related accidents. So it's worth being extra alert on the roads. Drive defensively, and always check both ways even when traffic lights are in your favor.

If a man's home is his castle, it could be said that a Burqueño's castle is his car. You'll spot lots of customized cars, vintage and retro models, some lowriders, hot rods, trucks jacked up on big wheels, and motors tricked out with all kinds of decoration, or at the very least a Virgin of Guadalupe on the dashboard. Pickup trucks often have a pooch or two riding in the open back, their ears flapping in the breeze. If you want to rent a more unusual car for your stay, perhaps a Mini Cooper S Turbo or a Jeep Wrangler, try RC Exotic Cars (505-688-4431, www.rcexoticcars.com). For a more traditional car rental, Albuquerque has most of the national chains. See the agencies listed in the airport car-rental section above.

i Albuquerque had the eighth highest vehicle theft rates for metro areas in 2008, according to the National Insurance Crime Bureau, and car break-ins can be a problem throughout New Mexico, whether you're in a city or a peaceful village. Take the same precautions that you'd take anywhere else: Always lock car doors and park in populated, well-lit areas at night. Never leave valuables in the car or anything that even looks enticing, such as a bag or camera case, even if it's empty. If you have to leave any gear, lock it in the trunk, although official advice is to remove all property.

PUBLIC TRANSPORT AROUND ALBUQUERQUE

Albuquerque folk are very attached to their cars, and it's true that driving is the most convenient way to get around if you want to explore beyond popular and easily accessible areas like Old Town, Downtown, and Nob Hill. However, the City has expanded its public transportation in recent years, including alternative-fuel and hybrid vehicles. Fares are reasonable or even free in the case of the D-Ride.

ABQ RIDE BUSES
(505) 243-RIDE, (505) 243-7433
Phone enquiries Mon–Sun, 8 a.m. to 5 p.m.
www.cabq.gov/transit or www.myabqride .com

The ABQ Ride network of buses extends across the city, and you can find a route map and schedules at the Web site. If you're not too handy with a bus map, the Web site also features a trip planner, where you enter your start point, final destination, and date and time of travel, and it provides the buses and routes you can take. There is also an ABQ Ride Customer Service Center open Monday to Friday, 8 a.m. to 5 p.m., at the Alvarado Transportation Center. You can pick up maps here, get advice on trip planning, or buy bus passes. Outside business hours there's a self-serve kiosk to buy one-day bus passes.

You must have the exact fare to pay on the bus, either coins or $1 bills. Fare boxes do not give change. One-way fares as we go to press are $1 for an adult and free for children under 10 accompanied by an adult. Students age 10 through high school age pay 35 cents but need valid school or ABQ Ride ID. "Honored Citizen" fares are 35 cents, including passengers 62 or older, or with disabilities, or holding a Medicare card. See the Web site for details on required Student and Honored Citizen ID. If you plan to hop on and off several buses, it's cheaper to buy a pass. A one-day adult pass for unlimited rides on any bus is $2. A pass for two or three consecutive days is $4 and $6, respectively. Buy your pass on the bus, paying in cash only with exact change, or at the Alvarado Transportation Center, where you can pay by cash or with a credit/debit card. All ABQ Ride buses are wheelchair accessible. Only service animals are permitted to board ABQ Ride vehicles.

ALVARADO TRANSPORTATION CENTER
100 First Street SW

Alvarado Transportation Center (ATC), on the corner of First and Central, is Albuquerque's Downtown transit hub. Here you can make connections with Amtrak, Greyhound Bus, New Mexico Rail Runner Express, and ABQ Ride services. This good-looking Mission Revival–style building complex with a clock tower on the corner is designed to pay homage to the old Alvarado railroad hotel, which used to stand on the same site. There are many cafés and restaurants close at hand, especially on Central Avenue and on Gold, which lies opposite the west exit.

i **Taking the bus with a child? Look for the books on your ABQ Ride to keep the young 'uns occupied. Over 20,000 kids' books have been put in city buses as part of the Discover A Book program.**

Rapid Ride

There are three Rapid Ride routes that, as the name suggests, provide speedy service with fewer stops between key destinations. The 60-foot-long articulated Rapid Ride buses are fitted with a signal priority system, so bus drivers on approach to a traffic light can hold a green light or shorten a red one. On board automatic announcements notify passengers when the next station is approaching.

The Rapid Ride Red Line (route 766) runs frequently along Central Avenue, connecting points of interest, including the Bio Park, Old Town, Downtown, University of New Mexico, Nob Hill, NM Expo at the State Fairgrounds, and the Uptown shopping area. There are approximately six buses an hour on weekdays, four an hour on Saturday. They run a little less often on Sunday. Most stops are attractive Pueblo Deco–inspired sheltered "stations" with neon accents in keeping with historic Route 66. These stations have LED displays showing when the next bus is due. On board the Red Line, passengers have free wireless Internet access for laptops and other devices.

The Rapid Ride Blue Line (route 790) connects Albuquerque's Westside with the University of New Mexico campus. Key stops include Cottonwood Mall and Old Town. There are about three Blue Line buses an hour on weekdays, with less-frequent service on Saturday. There's no service on Sunday.

A third Rapid Ride Green Line opened in late summer of 2009, traveling between Downtown and the Four Hills area at Central and Tramway via Central Avenue.

Fares and conditions for Rapid Ride buses are the same as other ABQ Ride buses above. They are wheelchair accessible, only service animals permitted, and a one-way adult fare is $1, exact change required.

D-Ride

This free shuttle whips you on a loop around Downtown, with stops that include the Alvarado Transportation Center, Civic Plaza, City Hall, and the Convention Center. The D-Ride, or route 40, runs every seven minutes, Monday to Friday, from 6:30 a.m. to 6 p.m. The buses are swathed in a graphic wrap illustrating downtown landmarks.

Park & Ride

There are Park & Ride lots for ABQ Ride passengers, and these are free during transit service hours. City lots are located at Southwest Mesa Park & Ride on West Central and Unser; Uptown Transit Center at 2121 Indiana NE, and Montgomery/Tramway Park & Ride at 12600 Montgomery NE. There are over a dozen more free private Park & Ride lots. Dedicated Park & Ride lots are also provided for special events, with a shuttle at a fee to events such as the state fair, and there's a Rock Star Shuttle to select Journal Pavilion concerts. Find all locations for free Park & Ride and special events at www.cabq.gov/transit/park-ride.

Trolley

In summer months a Downtown to Old Town Trolley (route 21) runs between the Alvarado Transportation Center and Old Town Plaza. It usually operates from Memorial Day weekend through Labor Day weekend. There is no service on Monday or Tuesday. Stops include the New Mexico Museum of Natural History and the Albuquerque Museum of Art and History. Trolleys run every 35 minutes in each direction, from around 10 a.m. to 7 p.m., and the full journey is under 15 minutes. Adult fare is $1, and it's 35 cents for children. You can also use an ABQ Ride pass. (Note that this public transit trolley is not the same as the trolley from ABQ Trolley Co., which also runs from Old Town but is a sightseeing tour. Details on ABQ Trolley Co. tours are in the Attractions chapter.) See the schedule at www.cabq.gov/transit/services or call (505) 243-7433.

NEW MEXICO RAIL RUNNER EXPRESS
(866) 795-RAIL, (866) 795-7245
www.nmrailrunner.com

The New Mexico Rail Runner Express made its inaugural trip in 2006, between Downtown Albuquerque and Bernalillo, and has since been extended. It started serving Santa Fe in December 2008, and more stops are in construction along the north/south Rio Grande corridor. A new station is expected to open at Sandia Pueblo in early 2010. The full New Mexico Rail Runner route map and schedule are at the Web site. The main Albuquerque Downtown station is in the Alvarado Transportation Center, and currently, there are two other Albuquerque stations at Los Ranchos/Journal Center in the north of the city and at 113 Rio Bravo Boulevard SE. The latter stop is alternately called Rio Bravo/Airport or Bernalillo County/International Sunport, depending on which map you look at and whom you're talking to! But in either case be warned that the Rio Bravo stop is not actually at the airport. You need to take a bus or taxi from the train to reach Albuquerque International Sunport. The New Mexico Rail Runner Express runs south to Isleta Pueblo, Los Lunas, and Belen and north to Bernalillo and Santa Fe.

Intended as a commuter service, the New Mexico Rail Runner Express has proven extremely popular. Seats are on a first-come, first-served basis, plus standing room in the aisles. Trains are limited in number, and as we go to press, there are only two Sunday trains in each direction and no regular service on holidays. Fares are calculated by zone, according to how many zones you will travel through on your journey. The three Albuquerque stations are within one zone, and a one-way adult weekday fare is currently $1, with a day pass for $2. Albuquerque to Santa Fe is five zones, and a one-way adult weekday fare is $6, or $8 for a day pass. Children under 10 ride free. Saturday fares are reduced, and reduced fares are also available to seniors 65 and over, students with ID, and people with disabilities if they have certain documentation. Details are at the Web site. Buy tickets on board by cash or credit card; ticket agents wear a yellow vest. Or purchase tickets online in advance to print out; there are discounts for online purchases of day, monthly, and annual passes. You can't bring your pet on board; only service animals are allowed. Rail Runner passengers travel free on connecting ABQ Ride buses, when they show their Rail Runner receipt or pass.

i **The Greater Roadrunner is the official State Bird of New Mexico and is often seen along the sides of roads and trails. A member of the cuckoo family, it can fly but prefers to run, at speeds of 15 or even 20 miles per hour. Like many human New Mexicans, it uses solar energy in cool weather: The roadrunner spreads its wings and lifts its colored top feathers, exposing the black "solar panel" beneath that soaks up the sun. Dusty Roadrunner, sporting a broom to keep New Mexico clean, is the state's litter-control mascot. Some Native American peoples believe the roadrunner's spirit has supernatural powers, because of its speed and stamina and also the bird's X-shaped track that makes it hard to tell which direction it's heading. Pueblo peoples sometimes reproduce the footprint X to confuse evil spirits and keep them away.**

The New Mexico Rail Runner Express trains are extremely handsome beasts! Look out for them dashing across the landscape decorated with a splendid red roadrunner bird motif. The diesel-electric locomotives are painted with the roadrunner head, and the bilevel passenger cars flaunt the bird's tail feathers.

Taxis

ALBUQUERQUE CAB COMPANY
(505) 883-4888
www.albuquerquecab.com

Rates as we go to press are $2.95 for the first mile and $2.60 for every mile thereafter; $1 is added to the final fare for each additional passenger. Tax is charged on these rates. Cash only. Reservations accepted.

YELLOW CAB COMPANY
(505) 247-8888

Rates as we go to press, including tax, are $5.54 for the first mile and $2.60 for every mile thereafter; $1.07 is added to the final fare for each additional passenger. Most Yellow Cabs only take cash, but some take credit cards—check before you start your ride. No reservations.

Limousines

Albuquerque loves its limos deluxe, and with the movie industry hitting town, there's even more call for chauffeured services. Take your pick of cool-cruising Cadillacs, superstretch Hummers, stylish vintage wheels, and of course sedate sedans.

El Camino Real

El Camino Real de Tierra Adentro, the "Royal Road of the Interior Land," is the historic trading route between colonial Spain's new world capital at Mexico City and Santa Fe, which became the Spanish Empire's seat of power north of the Rio Grande.

Over 1,500 miles long, the Camino Real followed indigenous footpaths between what is now Mexico and North America, as portions of the route, if not the whole, were in use long before the Spanish conquest. After Juan de Oñate's trailblazing 1598 expedition from Mexico, the Camino Real was the main trading route for three centuries, until the arrival of the railroad system in the late 1800s. It brought settlers north on their wagons, plus goods, livestock, and supplies. The arduous trip across rugged terrain took six months, and in the early days supply wagons arrived from Mexico City only once every three to four years. Later, the frequency increased to once a year, to meet the northern frontier's demand for scarce necessities and luxury items such as chocolate, sugar, and tobacco. As can be imagined, the isolated settlers greeted supply wagons with much festivity and dancing.

The Royal Road from Mexico City passed through Querétaro, Zacatecas, Durango, Chihuahua City, Juárez, El Paso, Las Cruces, and Socorro, before arriving in Albuquerque. It continued north to Santa Fe, and although Santa Fe is assumed by many to be the Camino Real's ultimate destination, it actually went on to Ohkay Owingeh (San Juan Pueblo), about 30 miles north near Espanola. This appears to be the official end point, according to the route designated by the federal government when it added the Camino Real to the Natural Historic Trails system in 2000. However, many argue that it extended up to Taos Pueblo via the long-standing trading routes that were in use at the time.

In Albuquerque the Camino Real took two paths. The original ran directly north by what is now Broadway and Edith Boulevard. The other swung west a little and followed the curve of the river through Old Town Plaza and up along 4th Street.

The Camino Real is also designated in the National Scenic Byways Program and can be driven from the border at El Paso, Texas, along the Rio Grande valley north through Albuquerque and beyond, totaling over 400 miles.

National Scenic Byways Program information about the Camino Real can be found at www.byways.org. The National Park Service information about El Camino Real de Tierra Adentro National Historic Trail is at www.nps.gov/elca.

CAREY OF ALBUQUERQUE/SOUTHWEST CARRIAGE, INC

(505) 766-5466, (888) 644-4514

www.careylimo.com

A division of Carey Elite Limousine Service, serving 400 cities worldwide, with chauffeured options from sedans to stretch Cadillacs to minibuses

IMPERIAL LIMOUSINE SERVICE

(505) 286-5466

Chauffeur-driven service in classic antique limos from the '40s and '50s. Most popular? A 1956 Chrysler Crown Imperial C70 division-glass model, the same model Presidents Eisenhower and Truman used.

LUCKY BOYZ LIMOUSINE
(505) 836-4035
www.luckyboyzlimos.com
The fleet ranges from the party favorite H2 Hummer Luxury Limousine seating 20 to executive town cars.

STAR LIMO
(505) 848-9999
www.505starlimo.com
A respected livery service that offers luxury sedans and SUVs, stretch SUV limousines, and even a limo jet. Specializes in Albuquerque airport travel.

Cycling

A comprehensive street-bike system connects with over 100 miles of paved multiuse trails in the Albuquerque metro area, plus hundreds more miles of unpaved trails. This makes cycling a good alternative to driving around town, for practical commuting as well as for leisure. Albuquerque has been selected to host the 2010 League of American Bicyclists bike rally.

The City has been encouraging commuters to get out of their cars and on their bikes and provides a free bicycling map, showing bike lanes, multiuse trails, bicycle routes, and roads with wide shoulders, to help bikers plan their journeys and get the most out of their two wheels. Download or request a bike map at the City's Web site, www.cabq.gov/bike, or call (505) 768-2526 to be sent a bike map.

Make sure to check out the 16-mile paved Paseo del Bosque Trail, which runs north to south along the Rio Grande to the west of Albuquerque's urban area. *Sunset Magazine* ranked the Paseo del Bosque Trail number 1 in its top 10 city bike rides of 2008, and as well as being a beautiful ride, it's a good way to travel north/south while avoiding roads.

A new Bicycle Boulevard runs approximately 7 miles, mainly along Silver Avenue, from San Mateo to Paseo del Bosque, with road markings and 18-mph speed limits designed to give road priority to cyclists. A smart new multiuse bridge across the Rio Grande by I-40 is also due to open in spring 2010, intended to provide a safe river crossing for cyclists as an alternative to the busy highways.

All ABQ Ride buses and the New Mexico Rail Runner Express train are equipped with bike racks, so you can bring your bike on board.

For more information visit www.cabq.gov/bike or call (505) 768-BIKE, (505) 768-2453

i Albuquerque's first bridge across the Rio Grande was built in 1876, where the Central Avenue bridge now stands. A floating pontoon bridge, it was destroyed by floods 15 years later.

On Foot

Aside from the many green and open spaces in and around the city, the main areas that are really comfortable for a pedestrian to browse around are in Downtown, in Old Town Plaza, and around University/Nob Hill. Otherwise, it's very much a driving city. When walking, take the same security precautions as in any urban center, and avoid unpopulated areas, especially at night.

HISTORY

It is impossible to separate the history of Albuquerque from the history of New Mexico as a whole. New Mexico is a fairly young state, due to celebrate its 100th anniversary as part of the United States of America in 2012, yet it has been a nourishing heartland to Indian ancestors since at least 10,000 BC. The state capital of Santa Fe is the oldest capital in North America, settled by the Spanish in 1609–1610, a decade before the Mayflower brought the English pilgrims to land at Plymouth Rock. The area around Albuquerque has been home to the families of Spanish settlers since the same period, even before the city was formally founded in 1706. Since then, the flags of Spain, Mexico, the Confederate States, and the USA have flown here. This chapter focuses on the history of Albuquerque but also gives a brief overview of New Mexico's history where relevant as a context for the city's unique story.

ANCESTRAL LANDS

Evidence found in New Mexico of Clovis Man shows there were already people here around 12,000 years ago, but some researchers speculate the true date could be much earlier than that, perhaps over 20,000 years ago. The first inhabitants of what is now New Mexico were the Paleo-Indians, nomadic hunters and gatherers who hunted large game such as mammoths, mastodons, and giant bison. They used a device called an atlatl, a long throwing stick that launched a spear, to bring down their huge prey. Anyone today who is startled by the midnight howl of a coyote might note that predatory beasts once roaming the region included saber-toothed tigers and the ferocious dire wolf, with its massive bone-crunching jaws. The environment at this time, through to the end of the last Ice Age, was much different from today's, with a wetter, cooler climate; lakes scattering the forested and grassy landscapes; and glaciers on the mountain tops. At the end of the Ice Age, 10,000 years ago, the climate became drier, and around this time the exotic big game began to die out.

Later indigenous cultures in the New Mexico region hunted smaller game, such as deer, elk, antelope, turkey, and rabbit, and they also began to actively cultivate corn, beans, and squash, rather than rely on what they could forage. With this shift to farming came a switch away from the nomadic lifestyle, as the people themselves put down roots along with their crops! The first dwellings were rounded pit houses, dug into the earth and covered over. Examples of pit houses from before 600 AD have been found in Bernalillo, just north of Albuquerque, around the site that is now the Coronado State Monument. Later came the expansive cave dwellings high in cliff faces, which were more defensible, and then freestanding multistoried apartment-style structures, built with rocks and mud. These complex villages were home to Indian civilizations that were sophisticated in their self-governance and culture, which established tribal codes for how to live in community that were handed on through generations. They also featured ceremonial kivas—group chambers used for ritual—usually built under or into the ground, reminiscent of the earlier pit houses.

Although there were people living along the Rio Grande valley, the majority of the region's population until the 1300s was based in the north and west, in what is now the Four Corners, embracing New Mexico, Colorado, Utah, and Arizona, and south in the Mogollon Mountains. The Indians had a strong trading network in place by the 12th century, and trading and bartering is known to have taken place between people from Chaco Canyon in the north and those as far south as today's Mexico. As the northern parts of the region grew drier, there was a gradual migration to find more promising lands to cultivate, and between the 13th and 15th centuries more indigenous peoples settled in the Rio Grande valley. The peoples of both Sandia Pueblo and Isleta Pueblo, bordering today's Albuquerque city to the north and south, respectively, date their settlements here back to at least the 1300s. These pueblos were not originally called by these names, as the words are of Spanish origin. The word pueblo itself means "town" in Spanish, isleta means "little island," and sandia means "watermelon." The village of Kuaua, meaning "evergreen," was established in the early 1300s just north of Albuquerque in today's Bernalillo and was constructed from the adobe mix of orange-brown mud and golden straw. The remains of this site, which consisted of 1,200 rooms by the 1500s, can be seen at the Coronado State Monument. The peoples of the nearby Santa Ana Pueblo—the Native name is Tamaya—have lived in this area since at least the late 1500s, and their traditional stories tell that their ancestors came from a subterranean world to the north. Most of the 20,000-plus petroglyphs on the rocks at the Petroglyph National Monument on Albuquerque's west mesa were created by Native peoples from around the 1300s through to the 1600s, but some may be up to 3,000 years old.

i Although you often see reference to the Anasazi Indians in New Mexico, there was no actual tribe called Anasazi, and the term is offensive to some Native Americans. The word Anasazi was adopted by archaeologists to refer to the ancient ancestors of today's pueblo peoples, but in the language of the Navajo or Diné peoples, it actually denotes "ancient enemies" or "enemy ancestors." Consequently, it's preferable today to skip that word and use instead the term "ancestral Puebloans."

SPANISH COLONIAL ERA—FIRST EUROPEAN CONTACT

In 1536 a small party of survivors from a Spanish shipwreck off the Texan gulf coast arrived in Mexico, then called Nueva España or New Spain since being conquered by the Spanish 15 years earlier. The group of four included the leader Cabeza de Vaca, and Esteban the Moor, a black slave from Morocco. Their descriptions of their journey through what is now New Mexico on their long and haphazard journey to safety started rumors about the Seven Cities of Cibola (buffalo). These coincided with existing Aztec and European legends about the Seven Cities of Gold with their great wealth of treasures, rumored to lie in the lands farther north. The Spanish missionary priest Marcos de Niza was sent off to investigate further, guided by Esteban the Moor. In 1539 Esteban, who was accustomed to acting as an intermediary with the natives on his various travels under his Spanish masters, was killed in the Zuni village of Hawikuh while scouting ahead for Fray Marcos. According to Joe S. Sando's report in the book *Pueblo Nations,* the Zunis gave Esteban fair warning to retreat, but instead he showed disrespect, demanding gifts and women, and threatened that a large armed party was behind him. Fearing that Esteban would reveal their location, the Zunis killed him. However, Sando writes: "The Pueblos often say, 'The first white man our people saw was a black man.'"

Marcos de Niza returned to Mexico after Esteban's death, confirming the stories of the Seven Cities of Gold. These early rumors were highly elaborated, although the Indians did wear turquoise and other gems, and in considering the legendary reports of the Cities of Gold over the years, it's worth noting that when viewed from a distance, the sun shining on adobe pueblos does indeed make them gleam like gold.

In 1540 a larger expedition led by General Francisco Vázquez de Coronado arrived in the Zuni lands about 150 miles west of present-day Albuquerque. Coronado identified this area as Cibola, and a battle ensued, but he found no riches. Coronado sent his Captain Hernando de Alvarado ahead up the Rio Grande Valley, where Alvarado appeared to have been struck by the mountains and lush riverside lands in the area that is now Albuquerque. At that time, at least a dozen native Tiwa or Tiguex communities made their home in this area, known as the province of Tiguex. Alvarado sent for Coronado to join him, and Coronado moved the headquarters of his expedition to the vicinity of the Kuaua Pueblo in Bernalillo, wintering over among the Tiguex pueblos during the following two years. It's hard to overstate what an imposing sight those armed and mounted troops must have been to the native residents, who were unfamiliar with horses. Records are not adequate to specify exact locations and details, but it appears that although initial relations were cordial enough, after the Europeans occupied a pueblo (its residents seeking shelter elsewhere) and commandeered food and supplies to survive the winter of 1540–41, combined with their high-handed treatment of complaints of assaults on Indian women, some of the Indian "hosts"' struck back, stealing and killing European horses. The newcomers retaliated with force, and with vastly superior weaponry, leading to the hostilities known as the Tiguex war and further abandonment of some of the pueblos as the villagers fled for safety. (Kuaua Pueblo is now the site of the Coronado Monument, although there is no evidence that Kuaua was the pueblo forcibly ocupied by Coronado; it was probably a pueblo in the area of today's Rio Rancho.) Over his two years of explorations Coronado failed to find the fabled Cities of Gold, discovering instead only villages of mud dwellings, and he returned to New Spain in 1542 with no treasures to show for his pains.

Nevertheless, the Spanish conquistadors were not ready to give up yet. Juan de Oñate received permission to establish a Spanish colony in the province, and in 1598 he founded the first permanent settlement for Spain, about 25 miles north of today's Santa Fe, at the Tewa Indian village of Ohke. Oñate christened his new capital San Juan de los Caballeros, and the Indian village was still known as San Juan Pueblo until 2005, when it reverted to its original name and is now Ohkay Owingeh Pueblo.

Oñate became the first governor of the province and continued to look for gold and establish other settlements. In 1610 Gaspar Pérez de Villagrá would publish his epic poem history of Oñate's conquest, *La Historia de la Nueva México.* Meanwhile, Oñate's treatment of the Indians, especially his brutality at Acoma Pueblo in 1599, set a pattern of repression with long-term ramifications. In 1607 Oñate resigned as governor and was later tried in Mexico City for his abuses of power and mistreatments of the native Indians. He was fined and barred from ever returning to New Mexico.

Despite unpromising beginnings, the Spanish Crown decided to continue settling the region as a royal province, and in 1609 Don Pedro de Peralta was appointed as the new governor. By 1610 Peralta had shifted the capital to Santa Fe under the Sangre de Cristo Mountains, building the Palace of the Governors and laying out the plaza area much as we see it today. Sante Fe—meaning Holy Faith—became the seat of power for the Spanish Empire in the New World north of the Rio Grande and remains the state capital today, although it has been overtaken in size by its younger sibling city of Albuquerque. At this time Albuquerque was not yet a formal town, just families farming their estates along the banks of the Rio Grande, in an area that became known as Bosque Grande de Doña Luisa.

The Spanish brought with them a rich heritage that remains intrinsic to life in Albuquerque today, including the Arab Moorish influence that's shaped some of New Mexico's distinctive personality. The Moors had occupied Spain for nearly 800 years before being driven out in 1492, and elements of that culture were firmly embedded by the time the Spanish explorers made their way through the New World. Words like *adobe, acequia,* and *horno* are Arabic in origin, and the Spanish imported the Moorish acequia irrigation system to New Mexico. Although the Indians already built adobe mud structures, the Spanish introduced the adobe brick construction and other elements of architectural style. The compound structures with the "torreon" watch towers of early Spanish architecture in New Mexico are resonant of the Moorish style, and the famous blue-painted doors and window frames now traditional in the state are also said to owe a nod to the Arabic habit of blue doors as protection against the "evil eye." Others say that the use of the color blue was a Spanish tribute to the Virgin Mary. Some of the designs we associate with New Mexico silver jewelry may be attributed to Moorish influences on the Spaniards who introduced them to the New World. These include filigree, crescent moon shapes, and the squash blossom necklaces resonant of Moorish pomegranate-flower motifs.

New Mexican cuisine also bears Moorish traces, and the Spanish are often credited with introducing the chile pepper (native to South America) up into New Mexico, as well as wheat, orchard fruits, and European grapes. Naturally, the New Mexico wines that we now enjoy owe their provenance to the Spanish, who brought winemaking here. The first grapevines planted in New Mexico in 1629 were introduced by men of the cloth, to make sacramental wine. The Spanish also brought horses and sheep, both animals becoming key to life in the American West.

The early colonists also tried to import their religion through Catholic missions to convert the indigenous population. Indians were also used as virtual slaves to build churches and perform agricultural and other work for the colonists; were subject to compulsory taxes and tithings of their precious harvest; and endured other forms of dominance, mistreatment, and violence. Of course, the colonists did not have an easy time surviving in this new, wild, and often inhospitable land, cut off at the far northern reaches of their empire. Systems of government were confusing between the civil authorities and the religious missionaries, and it seems fair to say that often the left hand didn't know what the right hand was doing.

However, after more than a century since first contact with the Europeans, and growing tired of religious intolerance and harsh treatment, the pueblos united and rose up. Drought was a catalyst, as the Indians were forbidden to practice their traditional spiritual ceremonies, including kachina dances for the spirits who are bringers of rain. Their sacred kivas, kachina masks, and other ceremonial items were destroyed, and in 1675 forty-seven medicine men were arrested on charges of sorcery. Four were hanged, and the rest publically flogged. In tandem with this religious repression, ruinous drought arrived, and the pueblo people feared that the interference with their religious customs meant that the rain would never return. Enough was finally enough. The Spanish had successfully squashed a number of previous native rebellions, but in the Pueblo Revolt of 1680 a concerted uprising by New Mexico's pueblos, co-ordinated with the aid of runners who covered hundreds of miles between outlying Indian communities, the Europeans were overthrown. The Pueblo Revolt drove the surviving Spanish colonialists out of New Mexico for twelve years and is the only example of a successful native uprising against the Spanish colonialists in the New World. In the process of destroying Spanish settlements and churches in an effort to wipe out the traces of the Europeans, many written historical records by the Spanish were burned. Indian repossession of the region lasted until 1692–93, when Don Diego de Vargas took Santa Fe back and reclaimed the territory for Spain. This was a bloody era in history, with suffering and violence on all sides, but by the early 1700s an alliance of sorts was reached, and the Indians were given more freedom to pursue their native religion and culture. The Pueblo peoples also united with the Spanish to defend against raiding Apache, Navajo, and Comanche tribes.

i **New Mexico's Pueblo peoples often refer to themselves as Indians, and talk about Indian Country, although the more formal term Native American is used, too.**

THE FOUNDING OF ALBUQUERQUE

Albuquerque was formally established in 1706 as the Villa de Alburquerque. It was named after the Viceroy of New Spain, the 10th Duke of Alburquerque—that first "r" was later dropped. The original Alburquerque is in the Badajoz province of Western Spain, near the Portuguese border. Its new-world namesake offered settlers water, good fertile pastures, and plenty of timber and firewood. The villa—meaning an administrative center and the second-highest classification available for a town—was established by Acting Governor Francisco Cuervo y Valdéz (Governor de Vargas had died in 1704 in Bernalillo while on a sortie to punish raiding Apache tribes). It appears that Cuervo somewhat overstepped the bounds of his authority initially in designating the villa, both in his capacity as a temporary governor and in not requesting permission from the viceroy (who would then ask permission of the king). Nor did Cuervo obtain a land grant first. (His decision to name the villa after the Viceroy Duke de Alburquerque was clearly a political move to butter the Duke up!) It also turned out in a 1712 inquiry, ordered by the Duke, that Cuervo had exaggerated the population of the settlement and the number and type of buildings it contained, to make it qualify as a formal villa. For example, he claimed thirty-five families inhabited the settlement, totaling 252 people, when later evidence revealed there were 19 original founding families in the Villa, plus some soldiers and their families, comprising 129 people. The viceroy had already replaced the temporary Governor Cuervo with another, permanent governor, but even after the inquiry that revealed the true background of the villa's establishment, the decision on the founding of Albuquerque was not overturned. Albuquerque retained the villa designation, as an administrative center was needed in the region. Still, it's interesting to consider that, in true wild west style, between 1706 and 1712 Albuquerque was effectively an outlaw villa.

Also in 1706 construction began on Albuquerque's first church to serve the devout Catholic citizenry in what is now Old Town. Originally named San Francisco Xavier church, but later changed to San Felipe de Neri, the church was finished by 1719, and it stood on the west side of the plaza until its collapse in 1792. The following year the "new" San Felipe de Neri church was built, the one we see today on the north side of the plaza. Through the rest of the 1700s the Spanish settlers built out around the church area, staying close together for mutual protection and establishing the plaza as a trading center. Many Hispanic families in Albuquerque can still trace their lineage back to these early settlers, who overcame great hardships to establish a new life and support their families by raising their crops and livestock in the middle Rio Grande region.

In these early years the isolated colonists at the northern edge of the Spanish empire relied heavily on El Camino Real de Tierra Adentro, the "Royal Road of the Interior Land." This trading route was firmly established after Juan de Oñate's expedition as the link between Mexico City and the new capital Santa Fe, with Albuquerque as a major stop en route. The Camino Real was over 1,500 miles long, a grueling six-month journey for traders bringing goods, supplies, and livestock, as well as for new settlers traveling north on their wagons. See the Close-up on the Camino Real in the Getting Here, Getting Around chapter for more background on the historic Camino Real and its route through Albuquerque.

THE 1800S—AN ERA OF CHANGE

The Spanish flag flew over Albuquerque until 1821, when, following the Mexican War of Independence, Spain surrendered the new Republic of Mexico and the province of New Mexico came under Mexican rule. The Mexican government didn't have the resources to make much investment in their northern province, and there were tensions as Mexico's constitution provided equal citizen rights to all and prohibited slavery, but some New Mexicans still owned slaves. However, unlike the Spanish, Mexico encouraged open trade with the United States, and by 1822 the

Santa Fe Trail from Missouri to Santa Fe was a burgeoning (if primitive and tough) commercial thoroughfare. The Santa Fe Trail connected with the Camino Real south to Albuquerque, bringing new merchants and prospectors from the East. It was the first toehold into New Mexico for the U.S. and proved to be an indication of things to come.

In 1846, at the beginning of the two-year Mexican-American War, the American government annexed New Mexico, and in 1848 Mexico yielded its northern territories, including New Mexico, to the United States of America under the Treaty of Guadalupe Hidalgo; New Mexico officially became a United States territory in 1850. It was to change hands only once again and briefly, during the American Civil War.

In 1862 Confederate forces came up the Rio Grande Valley from Texas. They entered and occupied Albuquerque on March 2, and after Albuquerque and then Santa Fe were surrendered by the Union Army, the Confederates continued north, seeking to claim not only New Mexico but the gold mines of Colorado. The tables turned on March 26 through 28 at the Battle of Glorietta Pass, just southeast of Santa Fe on the Santa Fe Trail, when Union forces routed the Confederates in what has been called the "Gettsyburg of the West." The two howitzer cannons we see today in Albuquerque's Old Town Plaza are replicas of those buried nearby by retreating Confederate troops. The originals are in the Albuquerque Museum of Art and History.

Following this decisive moment in the Civil War's western theater, as well as in the history of New Mexico, the territory returned to United States control, where it has, of course, remained ever since. Anglo settlers from the middle of the century began to drop the first "r" of Alburquerque, as they couldn't pronounce it, and over following decades, Alburquerque was reborn as Albuquerque. Even earlier, when the explorer Zebulon Montgomery Pike, for whom Colorado's Pike's Peak is named, was mapping out the western territories between 1805 and 1807 under the instruction of the U.S. government, his subsequent map of his trip omitted the first "r" in the city's name.

Plenty of challenges still lay ahead for everyone in the state under American rule. There was early resistance against the U.S. government, most notably in the infamous 1847 Taos Rebellion, shortly after the original annexation of the territory, when the new governor, Charles Bent, and other officials and supporters of the incoming administration were murdered.

The citizenship rights granted at least in principle to Indians under Mexican law were no longer in effect under the U.S. government, and efforts to assimilate Natives by stamping out their own culture included Indian schools, where children were boarded away from their families and forbidden to speak their native language. Indians also saw their ancestral lands encroached upon, and some endured forced relocations. From 1862 New Mexico's Mescalero Apaches were relocated to Fort Sumner southeast of Albuquerque, as were the Navajos, who called this deathly journey the "Long Walk." Almost a third died in captivity. (Many Apaches escaped by 1865, and the Navajos were freed to return to their homelands in 1868.)

The Spanish settlers also found themselves struggling to defend their traditional way of life and their property. The Treaty of Guadalupe Hidalgo protected their land grants in theory, but not all titleholders could validate their ownership under the rather different American legal system. There were also language barriers with the English-speaking administration and judiciary. Ultimately, many families with original Spanish land grants were cheated out of their holdings, either deliberately by crafty newcomers or simply by dint of an alien system that they found impenetrable to navigate. Common lands that had been relied upon for grazing cattle or collecting firewood were also gradually reduced from public access.

i **"Every calculation based on experience elsewhere fails in New Mexico," said Lew Wallace, the territorial governor of New Mexico between 1878 and 1881. Although Wallace had his hands full with the challenges of the job, he also completed the best-selling novel *Ben-Hur* while in office.**

Amid the bigger-picture changes, Albuquerque became a key center for supply to the network of U.S. forts established in the Southwest in the years between 1850 and 1875. But it was the coming of the railway that proved the most important influence on Albuquerque's growth and upon the geographical shape of the city. In 1880 the Atchison, Topeka and Santa Fe Railway arrived in Albuquerque. The tracks were 2 miles east of Old Town, and commercial activity shifted accordingly to this "New Town," which became a shipping center for lumber, livestock, and wool. Shops and saloons sprang up to serve the new arrivals and the railroad workers. At that time today's Central Avenue was known as Railroad Avenue, connecting the railroad depot to Old Town. Plentiful goods arrived that had only been available by long wagon and mule train journeys before, and the old Camino Real and Santa Fe Trail became redundant. The railroad turned Albuquerque into an exotic destination, and numerous Anglo settlers moved to the Wild West to seek their fortunes. The boom was further encouraged by gold strikes in nearby Golden on the Turquoise Trail, which was home to the first gold rush west of the Mississippi after gold was discovered in 1825. Mining companies established themselves there in 1880, although gold production ultimately proved unsatisfactory. In 1885 Albuquerque incorporated as a town and then incorporated as a city just six years later, in 1891, with a population of 3,785. The University of New Mexico was founded in 1889 and would become the state's biggest university, with its main campus still in Albuquerque today.

By the turn of the 1900s, health seekers joined the throngs arriving in Albuquerque by rail, especially tuberculosis patients seeking a cure in the high elevations and sunny dry climate that had proven beneficial for respiratory ailments. A number of sanitoria opened their doors to tend them, including St. Joseph Sanatorium in 1902, run by the Sisters of Charity, and the Southwestern Presbyterian Sanitorium in 1908. From these early hospitals under the wing of the churches, Albuquerque would grow its medical services over the following century, and today the health-care sector remains a major contributor to the city's economy.

BECOMING AMERICA—THE EARLY 20TH CENTURY

On January 6, 1912, New Mexico achieved statehood. President William H. Taft signed the proclamation admitting New Mexico to the United States of America as the 47th state in the Union.

New Mexico's reputation as an exciting destination continued to grow, spurred on by the railroad. In 1902 the Fred Harvey Company opened the Alvarado Hotel in Albuquerque, named for Captain Hernando de Alvarado from Coronado's 1540 expedition. The $200,000 Alvarado Hotel was designed by Charles F. Whittlesey, who also designed El Tovar at the Grand Canyon, another Harvey hotel. The Alvarado assured a glamorous experience for visitors, with its Spanish mission-style architecture, superb service, and Indian building designed to look like a Pueblo interior, containing Native American pottery, rugs, and other arts and crafts for sale. Tourists could watch Native craftspeople weaving blankets and making jewelry. While we appreciate watching Indian artisans at work today, at the beginning of the 20th century, this could only have seemed thoroughly exotic to travelers from afar and an irresistible temptation to their souvenir dollars.

The Alvarado became a hub of Albuquerque's social life too. It was the venue for the Territorial Fair's Montezuma Ball, and it was in the Alvarado's banquet hall in 1911 that the New Mexico constitution was approved by voters, a year prior to statehood. The Alvarado Hotel would be demolished in 1970, but the new Alvarado Transportation Center stands on the site today, modeled after its namesake building, a fitting tribute to the entrepreneurial Fred Harvey, who was instrumental in popularizing tourism to the Southwest. His string of Harvey House restaurants and Harvey hotels served train passengers along the Atchison, Topeka and Santa Fe Railway, providing travelers to the frontier with quality food at reasonable prices in reputable establishments. His string of eateries, from Topeka to California, were effectively the first chain restaurants. Harvey was also famous for his Harvey Girls waitresses, a professional workforce of respectable and efficient young women. Harvey hired his first Harvey Girls in Raton, New Mexico, in 1883, having become infuriated with his rather less-reliable male waiters. Although employing genteel, if attractive, young women as waitstaff was unconventional at the time, the Harvey Girls were such a popular success that Harvey expanded the concept to all his Harvey Houses.

Harvey died in 1901, a year before the Alvarado Hotel opened, but the Fred Harvey Company, along with the Santa Fe Railway, continued to promote cultural tourism in New Mexico. In 1926 they began offering Indian Detours—multiday bus tours from the train station in Albuquerque and other cities to Native American pueblos.

In that same year of 1926, however, Route 66 was commissioned, and although nobody knew it yet, the reign of the railroad was already under threat. Route 66 ran 2,448 miles from Chicago to the Pacific Ocean, and it brought still more travelers through Albuquerque, especially after 1937, when the route was realigned along Central Avenue and the road was fully paved. Some came from necessity, as families migrated west to seek their fortunes in the Great Depression or to escape the Dust Bowl. Others came for pleasure and adventure, mostly after World War II, when Route 66's glory days as the Main Street of America were at their peak. Transportation once again changed the face of the city, as motels, restaurants, and retailers flourished along Route 66 to serve the motorists. The Route 66 Close-up in the Getting Here, Getting Around chapter tells you more about the history and influence of this iconic highway. It was finally decommissioned in 1985.

In 1928 Albuquerque's first private airport opened, and the city was selected as a stop on the first transcontinental air route in 1929. As planes didn't fly at night in those days, passengers with Transcontinental Air Transport (which later became TWA) flew by day and switched to trains at night to make the two-day journey from New York to Los Angeles. The city's first municipal airport would open in 1939, featuring one of the longest runways in the country. By now Albuquerque was firmly on the tourist map, and New Mexico's reputation continued to grow as an arts colony. Throughout the first half of the 20th century, visitors also continued to arrive in Albuquerque seeking health cures.

During the 1930s New Mexico was one of the greatest beneficiaries of the New Deal. Governor Clyde Tingley had a good relationship with President Franklin D. Roosevelt, and lobbied hard for Works Project Administration (WPA) funds to assuage the economic stresses and unemployment created by the Great Depression. In Albuquerque WPA funding was responsible for the Coronado State Monument excavations and the Visitor Center, the Albuquerque Little Theater, the Monte Vista Fire Station (in Nob Hill, now home to a bar), as well as several schools and improved city infrastructure. Numerous WPA art projects can be seen in the Albuquerque Museum, UNM's Art Museum and Jonson Gallery, and in federal buildings; for example, the Gold Avenue Courthouse murals. The New Mexico State Fair was revived with $500,000 of WPA funding, and at the city's EXPO New Mexico State Fairgrounds, you can still see buildings constructed at this time, as well as old elm trees planted as part of the project. The University of New Mexico campus especially benefitted from WPA contributions, with new buildings that included the Zimmerman Library and Scholes Hall, and UNM's student enrollment during the 1930s saw a large increase as a result. Noted New Mexico architect John Gaw Meem designed many of the WPA projects.

In 1939 an entrepreneurial son of New Mexico opened a new 10-story hotel called the Albuquerque Hilton. It was Conrad Hilton's first hotel in his home state, the tallest building in New Mexico at the time and the state's first hotel to sport air-conditioning. Over the following decades that hotel shifted name and ownership, and in the fall of 2009, the historic hotel reopened, after $30 million renovations, in yet another new incarnation as the trendy Hotel Andaluz.

Albuquerque History: Recommended Reading

Bryan, Howard. *Albuquerque Remembered.* Albuquerque: University of New Mexico Press, 2006.

Garcia, Nasario, with Richard McCord. *Albuquerque, ¡Feliz Cumpleaños!: Three Centuries to Remember.* Santa Fe: La Herencia, 2005.

Julyan, Robert. *The Place Names of New Mexico.* Albuquerque: University of New Mexico Press, 1996.

Kessell, John L. *Pueblos, Spaniards, and the Kingdom of New Mexico.* University of Oklahoma Press, 2008.

Mortensen Diecker, Mary. *Roadrunner Tales: 366 Stories About New Mexico.* Albuquerque: the electric bear, 2001.

Palmer, Mo. *Albuquerque Then and Now.* San Diego, CA: Thunder Bay Press, 2006.

Price, V. B. Photographs by Kirk Gittings. *Albuquerque: City at the End of the World.* Albuquerque: University of New Mexico Press, 2003.

Sando, Joe S. *Pueblo Nations: Eight Centuries of Pueblo Indian History.* Santa Fe: Clear Light Publishers, 1992.

Simmons, Marc. *Hispanic Albuquerque, 1706–1846.* Albuquerque: University of New Mexico Press, 2003.

Taylor, Quintard. *In Search of the Racial Frontier: African Americans in the West, 1528–1990.* New York: W. W. Norton & Co., 1998.

The Albuquerque Historical Society has an interesting and easy-to-reference online resource of city history in its Tricentennial Matrix archive: www.albuqhistsoc.org.

A WORLD INFLUENCE—FROM WORLD WAR II

Albuquerque's high-tech era began with the founding of Kirtland Air Force Base in 1940 and Sandia National Laboratories in 1949. Both became, and have remained, major employers and vital to the local economy. Over subsequent decades they have also been instrumental in establishing a culture of science, engineering, and technology in Albuquerque, bringing professionals to the area and resulting in entrepreneurial spin-offs and technology transfer in the private sector. Sandia National Laboratories grew out of the Z Division of Los Alamos National Laboratory, as the lab's weapons design, testing, and assembly branch. Z Division moved to Albuquerque to be closer to an airfield and the military base. Los Alamos, high on a mesa about 95 miles north of Albuquerque, was one of the primary sites for the top-secret Manhattan Project in World War II. Fearing that Germany would produce a nuclear weapon, scientists at Los Alamos National Laboratory—founded in 1943 and then called Project Y—worked under the direction of J. Robert Oppenheimer to develop an atomic bomb. The resulting device was tested at the Trinity site in southern New Mexico in July 1945, and less than a month later two atomic bombs dropped on Hiroshima and Nagasaki quickly brought an end to the war with Japan.

i **War correspondent and Pulitzer Prize–winning journalist Ernie Pyle, who lived in Albuquerque, died by gunfire in 1945 while reporting on the war in the Pacific arena. Pyle's house was later donated to the City of Albuquerque and is now a public library with displays of Pyle memorabilia (Ernie Pyle Library, 900 Girard SE, 505-256-2065).**

Native Americans finally won the right to vote in New Mexico state elections in 1948. By this time Indians from New Mexico had already served their country in the military during World War II, including Navajo Code Talkers. But even though Congress had passed the Indian Citizenship Act in 1924, conferring U.S. citizen's rights on Native Americans and technically giving them the right to vote, actual voting privileges fell under the jurisdiction of the individual states.

Old Town—the place where the current Duke City was born—was formally incorporated into the City of Albuquerque in 1949. Urban development after the war spread to the west and east mesas as the population increased dramatically, with the northeastern heights at the foot of the Sandias being especially attractive to Anglos. In New Mexico "Anglo" is a term used for anyone who isn't from the two earliest cultures—either Native American or Hispanic—or from the later Mexican immigrant populations. These broad-brush terms to divvy up the ethnic pie don't take into account the fact that there are also long-standing populations of African Americans and Asian Americans in Albuquerque who have contributed to the city's history, culture, and growth. There is also a history of crypto-Jews throughout New Mexico, who fled to the New World during the Spanish Inquisition, first to Mexico, and then migrated to the northern territories.

In 1952 the Albuquerque Civil Rights Ordinance was passed, prohibiting discrimination in public places on the basis of race, creed, or ancestry. The ordinance was achieved through the campaigning efforts of Albuquerque's relatively small African-American community, after a student at the University of New Mexico was refused service at a local café. A coalition of UNM students, the black and Hispanic populations, the National Association for the Advancement of Colored People, and others in support of civil liberties fought hard to win this endorsement of equality, which is considered a groundbreaking municipal ordinance of its time.

In 1956 the 18th Duke of Alburquerque in Spain visited modern-day Albuquerque to celebrate the city's 250th birthday. As a descendant of the 10th duke, for whom the city was named, he gave to the citizens of Albuquerque a Repostero, a 300-year-old wall hanging embroidered with the family coat-of-arms in gold and silver thread. The Repostero can be seen today in the Albuquerque Museum of Art and History.

In 1966 the Sandia Peak Tramway made its debut trip. The longest aerial passenger tramway in the world, it has now carried over nine million passengers, rising 3,819 feet in a 2.7-mile-long journey to the top of Sandia Peak, in a snappy 15 minutes. In the same year the Big I Interchange was completed to connect I-25 and I-40.

Albuquerque's iconic International Balloon Fiesta has its roots in a 1972 balloon rally, when a mere 13 balloons launched from the parking lot of the Coronado Shopping Mall. Now it's the world's largest balloon festival, a showcase for over 700 balloons, with a Balloon Fiesta Park launch site comparable to 56 football fields in size. In August 1978 three Albuquerque balloon pilots—Ben Abruzzo, Maxie Anderson, and Larry Newman—made the first balloon crossing of the Atlantic Ocean.

Meanwhile, in 1975 two young men named Bill Gates and Paul Allen came to Albuquerque. They'd developed BASIC—the first computer language program for a personal computer—and provided the program to a company called MITS (Micro Instrumentation and Telemetry Systems), which was based in Albuquerque and which had designed Altair, the first commercially successful

i **Albuquerque was put on the map in a more lighthearted way when Bugs Bunny went off the map in the opening minutes of the 1945 Warner Bros. cartoon *Herr Meets Hare*. In this World War II story, Bugs Bunny heads for Las Vegas but burrows his way to Germany's Black Forest instead. The baffled bunny studies his map and announces, "I knew I shoulda made a left toin at Albukoykee." The rabbit's wrong turn at Albuquerque became a running joke in subsequent Bugs Bunny cartoons.**

microcomputer. Bill Gates and Paul Allen founded Microsoft in Albuquerque, where the youthful pair were apparently known as the "microkids," and they remained in the city, developing their software, until the end of 1978, when they moved their then small company up to Seattle.

The terrific STARTUP gallery at the New Mexico Museum of Natural History and Science shows Albuquerque's role in the personal computer revolution, including fun interactive exhibits and colorful stories of key players Paul Allen, Bill Gates, and Ed Roberts, the head of MITS (1801 Mountain Road NW, 505- 841-2800).

21ST CENTURY WITH A GOLDEN FUTURE

Although the Spanish who first settled Albuquerque never found their cities of gold, perhaps their descendants did, just not in the way they expected. Albuquerque itself has continued to flourish in the early years of the 21st century and shows all the signs of a glittering future.

In 2000 a $350 million revitalization of Downtown began, resulting in a spruced-up business, entertainment, and residential center, ready for Albuquerque to celebrate its 300-year birthday in 2006. The historic Pueblo Deco–style KiMo Theatre, built in 1927, reopened to the public in 2000 after $2 million of renovations. The National Hispanic Cultural Center opened in the same year in Barelas, one of the oldest neighborhoods.

The Big I intersection between I-40 and I-25 received a $291 million reconstruction, completed in 2002. It was New Mexico's largest public works project ever, and one of the nation's 10 biggest highway projects. It set a record at the time for the world's fastest completion of a major interchange that continued to support traffic through the works period.

In April 2006 Spain's current Duke of Alburquerque, Ioannes Osorio y Beltrán de Lis, and his wife, the Duchess Blanca Suelves Figueroa, joined the city's tricentennial festivities, even taking to a hot-air balloon with Mayor Martin Chávez.

Although Albuquerque has a long tradition of movie making, its film industry has especially come under the spotlight since the State of New Mexico initiated powerful economic incentives to attract filmmakers in 2002. The Albuquerque Studios complex, opened in 2007, has been the venue for major Hollywood productions, including *Terminator Salvation,* and in 2008 both *Forbes* and *MovieMaker* magazines cited Albuquerque amongst the country's top movie cities.

The city has also grown its technological industries and has found a role in the renewable energy sector, especially as New Mexico's climate and inclination toward alternative and sustainable living gave it a head start on solar technology. With good employment opportunities, affordable housing, and a high quality of life including terrific arts and outdoor leisure options, Albuquerque has grown its reputation as a relocation destination for both young families and retirees heading for the Sunbelt. Duke City and its facilities and businesses have been acknowledged with high rankings in many national city surveys published by media and other organizations.

In 2012 citizens of Albuquerque, along with the population throughout the state, will celebrate the centenary of New Mexico's statehood.

i **New Mexico's state flag was introduced in 1925, replacing the more generic flag that had flown since 1912. It features a red and yellow Zia sun inspired by a design found on a 19th-century Zia Pueblo water jar, symbolizing the sacred four compass points, the four seasons, and the circle of life. Red and gold also traditionally represent Old Spain and were the colors of Queen Isabel of Castilla. As an image of harmony and brotherhood, the Zia flag brings together the tempestuous history of New Mexico, bonding cultures that once were at odds. The official state salute is: "I salute the flag of the state of New Mexico, the Zia symbol of perfect friendship among united cultures."**

ACCOMMODATIONS

Albuquerque has over 16,000 rooms to sleep in, from charming bed-and-breakfast inns to ultrasmart city hotels. There are also two resort hotels listed in this chapter, both owned by local pueblos, which offer not only excellent accommodation but also a taste of Native American culture. As the city receives a good mix of leisure and business visitors, including a healthy dose of convention travelers, most hotels are geared up to serve families coming for fun and folk in town to work. Many business visitors choose one of the local B&Bs for a home away from home to return to after a long day of labor.

The major areas for hotels are Downtown, Old Town, Uptown, Balloon Fiesta Park/North I-25, and of course around the airport. We've also added choices in the Midtown/University and North Valley areas and in nearby Corrales, Rio Rancho, and Bernalillo.

You won't have trouble finding a bed for the night, and there are plenty of chain hotels strung along I-25 and I-40 as you drive in, plus hotel courtesy phones at the airport. The exception is during major events such as Balloon Fiesta in October, when you really might have trouble finding room at the inn if you haven't planned ahead,

Many older properties have been renovated in recent years, and some are in the process of renovation, with hoteliers upgrading their rooms to keep pace in this competitive market. Still, standards can vary substantially, even among hotels of the same franchise or branded chain in different locations across the city. While there are plenty of terrific hotels and adorable B&Bs to hunt out, there are also a fair number of bland ones. You don't want to waste your time in New Mexico on anything less than a terrific stay, so the accommodations featured here are selected for factors that take into account amenities, customer service, convenient location, and local character, with choices to suit all price points. On the whole, room rates are very reasonable in Albuquerque, and though the price code is a guide to average rates, there are often specials and discounts available to make them even friendlier on the pocket.

There are definitely some accommodations and small pockets of town where the clientele is less than desirable. We've steered you away from those in the following recommendations, of course. But without being alarmist, if you draw up for a pit stop and wonder to yourself if staying here is an entirely wise idea, then trust your instincts and move on. If a hotel or motel room rate is exceptionally cheap, there's probably a reason for that. It's perfectly acceptable to ask to see your room—at any price point—before handing over your credit card.

The listings are organized alphabetically by geographical area, showing the hotels, motels, and B&Bs in the most popular areas to stay. Separate sections follow on extended-stay accommodations, resorts, and RV parks and campgrounds.

As in-room coffee/tea makers, iron, ironing board, and hairdryer are standard equipment in the hotels listed here, these items are not specified in the room amenities. Assume free parking, unless otherwise noted here. Most of these are smoke-free hotels. We've noted where smoking rooms are offered, although these are sometimes limited to just a handful of rooms. Assume no pets are allowed, except service animals, unless otherwise indicated. Some hotels charge a flat-rate cleaning fee for visiting pets; others charge by the night. We give current free details to help you choose the best option, but policies change, so check ahead. All hotels have wheelchair accessible rooms unless otherwise stated.

If you haven't booked a room in advance, pick up the coupon booklets at the visitor service area near baggage claim at the airport. These give good discounts to walk-in guests, and they are also available in some gas stations, especially the bigger travel service centers on I-25 and I-40.

Price Code

The price code is a guideline on the cost per night of a standard room for two adults in peak season, excluding taxes (currently 12.875 percent). Expect to pay more during Albuquerque International Balloon Fiesta weeks, when accommodations usually charge a higher rate. Suites or premier rooms will also cost more. Lower rates are offered during off-peak months, and rates also vary substantially by day of the week—in Albuquerque weekend nights are usually cheaper than weekdays. These hotels, motels, and B&Bs accept all major credit cards.

$.................... under $90
$$ $90–130
$$$ $131–175
$$$$ .... over $175

OLD TOWN

BÖTTGER MANSION OF OLD TOWN BED & BREAKFAST $$–$$$
110 San Felipe Street NW
(505) 243-3639, (800) 758-3639
www.bottger.com

The Böttger Mansion was built in 1910, and the property's history goes back to the Conquistadors. Just a 250-foot stroll from Old Town Plaza, the fine western Victorian house has eight guest rooms with twin, queen, and king beds and a two-bedroom suite. Rooms are named for historical family members, and have private bathrooms, cable TV, phone, and wireless Internet access. Each is individually decorated with Victorian-style detail. The Stephanie Lynn room has a mahogany four-poster canopy queen bed, antique claw-foot tub, and chandelier, and the king-bed Rebecca Leah room has a Jacuzzi bathtub. A typical breakfast starts with a fresh-fruit course, plus an entrée such as Southwest crustless quiche, blueberry-stuffed French toast, or omelette with green chile, plus breakfast meats and such treats as cinnamon scones. Tea is always available, along with snacks in the afternoons. Guests can relax in the parlor or in the floral courtyard under century-old elms. Innkeepers are Steve and Kathy Hiatt, and children 10 and over are welcome. This property is not wheelchair accessible.

CASAS DE SUENOS $$$–$$$$
310 Rio Grande Boulevard SW
(505) 247-4560, (800) 665-7002
www.casasdesuenos.com

There are 21 casitas in this adobe compound, built in the 1930s and '40s as an artists' colony. These include studios and one- and two-bedroom suites and two hot-tub suites. Details vary according to the accommodations, but all have private bathrooms, private entrances, cable TV, and Wi-Fi Internet access. Some have private Jacuzzis, full kitchens or kitchenettes, kiva (or beehive) fireplaces, and private courtyards. A couple of rooms feature wall murals by artist Amado Pena. Decor is southwestern style, and courtyards and gardens ramble between the casitas. There are no phones in the casitas, but there's a phone in the lobby and business center, as well as a computer with printer. Complimentary hot breakfast in the sunroom is cooked to order and might include eggs, bacon, omelettes, pancakes, French toast, burritos, along with fresh fruit, breads, bagels, yogurt, and cereal. This property is not wheelchair accessible.

When leaving your car in an Albuquerque hotel parking lot—including the well-lit and busy ones—remove all valuables, and don't leave anything visible in the car that looks tempting, even if it's worthless, such as an empty bag.

HOLIDAY INN EXPRESS HOTEL & SUITES **$$**
2300 12th Street NW
(505) 842-5000, (877) 863-4780
www.hiexpress.com

A stylish four-story hotel opened in January 2009, the Holiday Inn Express is built on Native American–owned land, opposite the Indian Pueblo Cultural Center. The hotel's chic lobby area feels more designer Mexico than corporate chain, and there's a comfortable lounge. The 108 guest rooms and 27 suites have a sleekly elegant 1930s look, and all rooms are furnished with flat-screen TV, refrigerator, microwave, and free wireless Internet access. Three of the suites feature whirlpool baths. Complimentary breakfast is served in a spacious breakfast room, and amenities include a fitness center, indoor swimming pool and whirlpool, laundry room, and business center for e-mail, Internet, printing, and copying. A neighboring retail and restaurant development is due to be built, but meanwhile there's a good restaurant just a few steps away at the Indian Pueblo Cultural Center (see Restaurants chapter). The hotel is about 1.5 miles from Old Town Plaza. If you have a car, these smart and reasonably priced accommodations are conveniently located to access the areas and attractions of interest to a visitor, and it's quick to hop onto I-40. The Bureau of Indian Affairs lies next door, too, making the hotel a convenient stop for business travelers to the BIA.

i **Some people book their hotel for Albuquerque International Balloon Fiesta in October a year or more in advance. The overflow of visitors means hotels get busy as far away as Santa Fe. If you plan to visit during that time, or during events such as the New Mexico State Fair (September) or Gathering of Nations (April), make reservations as early as possible to guarantee your hotel of choice.**

HOTEL ALBUQUERQUE AT OLD TOWN **$$$**
800 Rio Grande Boulevard NW
(505) 843-6300, (800) 237-2133
www.hotelabq.com

A Heritage Hotel and Resort just a few minutes' walk from the Old Town Plaza and museums, Hotel Albuquerque blends Pueblo, Spanish Territorial, and Western style for a uniquely Albuquerque experience. The impressive lobby sets the tone—a grand hall with tile floor, huge wooden corbels, iron chandeliers, and ample couches. There are 168 guest rooms and 20 suites decorated in southwestern tones, with Navajo rug carpets, colonial-style carved wood and red willow furniture. Rooms have a dressing area with vanity, work table, sofa and coffee table, and free Internet access, and many have a balcony. All accommodations are in one 11-story wing, looking toward either the mountains or Downtown. The hacienda-style building features attractive courtyards and tables under the portals. A seasonal Olympic-size heated pool and deck with shaded tables and loungers is a pleasant spot to relax, and there's also an outdoor Jacuzzi open year-round. There are two restaurants on site—the candlelit Cristobal's for fine dining and the more casual and colorful Café Plazuela Cantina for breakfast, lunch, and dinner. The hotel's Q-Bar is a chic destination lounge, especially popular at happy hour, with a piano bar and other entertainment. See the Q-Bar listing in the Nightlife chapter. Other amenities include a fitness center, a business center, concierge services, and a gift shop. The 19th-century chapel on the grounds and the Spanish Garden and pavilion area are a favorite for weddings.

DOWNTOWN

BRITTANIA & W. E. MAUGER ESTATE BED & BREAKFAST INN **$$–$$$**
701 Roma Avenue NW
(505) 242-8755, (800) 719-9189
www.maugerbb.com

More informally known as the Mauger (pronounced "major") Bed & Breakfast Inn, this 1897

Queen Anne–style house is listed on the National Register of Historic Places.

It's located on a quiet street within walking distance of the Downtown plaza and about a mile from Old Town. There are eight tastefully appointed guest rooms, each with an individual stamp. Some are dramatically contemporary and streamlined, others more classically styled with antiques. All have private bathrooms, phones, Internet access, cable TV, and a minifridge. Two rooms have either a verandah or a patio, and guests may also sit on the front porch, which overlooks the pretty garden. The comfortable lounge area features period antiques, and there's a bright breakfast room with breezy white cotton drapes. Two 1,000-square-foot two-bedroom townhouses are also available in a separate building. A typical full buffet-style breakfast might feature fruit, yogurt, granola, cereals, and a hot sweet or savory dish such as quiche or green chile, with breakfast meats and freshbaked breads. Innkeepers Tammy and Mike Ross also offer a daily wine and cheese reception, at which it's not unknown for guests to get on so well they go out for dinner afterward and stay in touch beyond their visit. However, it's also fine to grab a glass of wine and cozy up in your room. Tea and sweets are always available, and rooms have their own coffeepots. This conveniently located B&B is popular with business guests as well as leisure visitors. A computer is available for e-mail and to print out boarding passes, and guests receive a discount at a local fitness center with a pool. Children are welcome, and families with younger tots are often made comfortable in one of the townhouses. Dogs are accepted by arrangement at a charge of $20 per stay. A ground-floor queen room has a doggy door to the yard. This property is not wheelchair accessible.

i **Hotels often change hands in Albuquerque, with a change of name as a property is taken over by a new chain. If you've stayed somewhere you liked before, but now it's apparently disappeared, see if you can find it by the address or area. It's probably still there under a new guise.**

i **Albuquerque accommodations are subject to gross receipts tax (or sales tax) of currently 6.875 percent, plus a 6 percent lodgers tax. Hotels quote rates without taxes, so add on 12.875 percent to know what you'll really pay.**

EMBASSY SUITES ALBUQUERQUE HOTEL & SPA **$$$$**
1000 Woodward Place NE
(505) 245-7100
www.embassysuites.com

The full-service Embassy Suites hotel opened in 2005 but feels brand-new, with nine floors of impeccable suites built around an attractive leafy atrium. Every suite faces either the mountains or toward the lights of Downtown and the west mesa beyond. Executive suites on the top floor have private balconies. The room rate includes a full cooked-to-order breakfast and substantial breakfast buffet, plus an evening cocktail reception with appetizers. Each comfortable two-room suite is smartly decorated in soft neutral tones and has a 27-inch TV in both the bedroom and living room, plus a wet bar with fridge and microwave, two telephones with data ports, and a sizeable work desk. The sitting room area has a parlor chair and a sofa that converts to a queen-size sleeper. Suites have either a king bed or two double beds, dressed with 200-thread-count sheets. There are also two hospitality suites and a 2,300-square-foot Presidential Suite overlooking the Sandias. The hub of activity is the spacious atrium, which features a waterfall and glass-fronted elevator. Complimentary breakfast and evening reception are served here, and lunch and dinner are available in the atrium's Cyprus Grille. There is also a pleasant lounge-style bar, and Caffeina's Internet café, with Starbucks coffee, snacks, and gifts for sale. Other amenities include a business center, an indoor swimming pool, a fitness center, and a 24-hour video games room. The hotel's Spa Botanica offers a full range of massages, facials, beauty treatments, and day spa packages. Wireless (and wired) Internet access requires a daily fee of $9.95. Smoking suites are available. Embassy Suites is close to I-25, six blocks from the Downtown Civic Plaza, and also handy for UNM and midtown.

HOTEL ANDALUZ **$$$$**
125 2nd Street NW
(505) 242-9090
www.hotelandaluz.com

Hotel Andaluz, which opened in fall of 2009, is the result of a $30 million–plus renovation of the former La Posada de Albuquerque. This property has a long history; it was built in 1939 as Conrad Hilton's first hotel in his home state, and it is on the National Register of Historic Places. The new Andaluz is a stylish boutique hotel with Moroccan and Spanish colonial influences and has 107 guest rooms and suites in the 10-story building, including a penthouse suite. Design throughout is sensual and sophisticated and the super-comfy and finely-detailed rooms feature luxurious beds, large LCD HD flatscreen TVs, work station, free Internet access, and mini bar. The hotel has a strong eco ethos, including allergen-free carpets, sustainable and recycled materials used in furnishing, and energy efficient measures such as solar heated water. The large lobby lounge and bar is dotted with art and sculptures, and six individually decorated alcove rooms along one side give it a casbah feel—draw the curtains for seclusion while you sip a cocktail and listen to the live music offered on some nights. The Lucia restaurant serves breakfast, lunch, and dinner (see Restaurants chapter). There's also a peaceful and well-stocked library room, and a mezzanine level display of art and cultural artefacts, plus interactive touch-screen monitors to find out what's going on in town. A second-floor rooftop lounge bar overlooks Downtown and the mountains. Hotel Andaluz is located centrally, just a block from Downtown's Harry E. Kinney Civic Plaza, and the Albuquerque Convention Center. You can park and walk around Downtown easily; both self parking ($10) and valet parking ($16) are available, with in/out privileges. Pets are welcome for a nominal fee; inquire for details.

i **Obviously, the higher the floor, the better the view, and although many Albuquerque hotels are naturally oriented toward the mountains to the east, the downtown city lights, or the west mesa for spectacular sunsets, lower-level rooms might not give quite such an expansive vista. If the picture outside your window matters to you, consult with the reservations desk, and request a room on a higher story.**

HOTEL BLUE **$**
717 Central Avenue NW
(505) 924-2400, (877) 878-4868
www.thehotelblue.com

This good-value, friendly hotel on Downtown's Route 66 has 140 king and double-queen rooms, each with 40-inch HDTV, Tempur-Pedic beds, and a microwave and fridge. Five suites with a separate living room and bedroom also have a kitchen area with a stove top, microwave, and fridge. Guests enjoy a complimentary continental breakfast that includes fresh fruit, waffles, cereals, and muffins. Coffee, tea, and juice are available at the breakfast bar round the clock. Hotel Blue has six floors, with external corridor entry to rooms, and there's a pleasant courtyard with seating and a seasonal outdoor pool. Free Wi-Fi is available in the lobby, and hardwired high-speed Internet connection in the guest rooms (the front desk will loan you a wire if needed). This is not a hotel for design mavens, but accommodations are spotlessly clean, and the price for the location is hard to beat, with the bars and restaurants of Downtown's Central Avenue on your doorstep in one direction (six blocks from Albuquerque Convention Center), and Old Town about a mile away in the other. Parking is free in the secured parking area, with 90 spaces available on a first-come, first-served basis, and a shuttle between 7 a.m. and 10 p.m. takes you to the airport, convention center, and Old Town. Same-day laundry service is available. There are five smoking rooms on request. Pets are permitted at a fee of $15 per night.

HYATT REGENCY ALBUQUERQUE **$$$**
330 Tijeras NW
(505) 842-1234
www.albuquerque.hyatt.com

A smart AAA Four Diamond–rated hotel in the heart of Downtown, the Hyatt Regency has 395 guest rooms with city or mountain views. The pyramid top of the 20-story tower is an Albuquerque landmark over Harry E. Kinney Civic Plaza, and the hotel is adjacent to the Albuquerque Convention Center. Guest rooms have something of a glamorous and streamlined updated art deco look and feature Hyatt Grand Beds with fine linens, 25-inch or larger TVs with cable/satellite and video on demand, Hyatt iPod stereo, armchair with ottoman, a good-size work desk, cordless phones, and Portico bathroom products. There are also chic suites and a presidential suite. An elegant atrium lobby has a light and airy palm court feeling, with a comfortable seating area that's great for casual meetings or people watching. Around the lobby are gift stores, a Starbucks, and the hotel lounge bar Bolo's Saloon with beautiful stained glass panels. Breakfast, lunch, and dinner are served in McGrath's Bar And Grill (although the restaurant is quite refined, it's named for one Lizzie McGrath, who presided over a bordello near here in the city's wilder west days). There is a year-round rooftop pool with hot tubs and great views and a well-equipped 24-hour gym and sauna. Other amenities include a full-service business center and concierge services. There are four smoking rooms. Wireless Internet access is $9.95 a day. Valet parking is $16 per night, and self-parking is $12, both with in/out privileges.

i **The Hyatt Regency Albuquerque is one of only two AAA Four Diamond hotels in the Albuquerque area. The other is its sister Hyatt Regency Tamaya Resort and Spa on the Santa Ana Pueblo, Bernalillo.**

UNIVERSITY/ MIDTOWN

CLUBHOUSE INN & SUITES **$**
1315 Menaul Boulevard NE
(505) 345-0010, (866) 345-0010
albuquerque.clubhouseinn.com

The courtyard is popular with guests here; it's landscaped, with two gazebos, patios with shaded tables, and barbecue grills with flatwear provided—all you have to bring is the food! There's also a large seasonal outdoor heated pool and an indoor Jacuzzi. Accommodations are in 137 rooms, including 14 suites, and room renovations underway include new carpets, granite vanities, new bedding, and flat-screen TVs. Most of these should be in place by the end of 2009, but check on booking. The room rate includes a hot breakfast buffet, with such offerings as eggs, bacon, pancakes, and waffles, and an evening cocktail hour with two cocktails per adult and light nibbles, excluding Sunday evening. Rooms offer free Internet access, full cable TV, and a work desk. Suites also have a kitchen area. Guests receive a pass to a nearby gym. The hotel is located right by I-25 (on the west side) for easy access around town, although if you have a room overlooking the oasis of a courtyard, you could easily forget how close you are to the bustle of the city! Pets are accepted with a fee of $10 per pet per day. Note that this two-story hotel does not have an elevator.

LA QUINTA INN & SUITES **$$**
2011 Menaul Boulevard NE
(505) 761-5600, (800) 531-5900
www.lq.com

There are 72 suites in this very comfortable all-suites property, opened in 2004. Open-plan suites have king or two double beds, a microwave and fridge, smart dark-wood furniture, large work desk, full-size sofa sleeper in the living area, TV with premium cable channels, free wireless Internet, good lighting with plenty of lamps, and quality towels in the roomy bathroom. Overall, the spotless and spacious accommodations read as from a higher price range. A complimentary hot breakfast buffet includes scrambled and boiled eggs, waffles, sausages, fresh fruit salad, cereals, yogurt, and muffins, served in a dining area off the lounge-style lobby. Coffee is available all day. There is an indoor pool and whirlpool and a fitness room, and the business center offers two computers with Internet access and free printing. Laundry facilities are also available. Service is especially friendly, and front-desk staff are quick to recognize guest preferences among their repeat clients, including many business travelers. The pleasant courtyard out back has a gazebo and table. Pets stay free, and next to the cookies that are often available on the front desk for human visitors, the staff keeps a jar of doggie treats. A few smoking rooms are available on one floor. The three-story hotel is set back behind a Village Inn, and the Range Cafe is a couple of hundred yards away on the opposite side of Menaul.

i Pets stay for free at La Quinta Inn & Suites in Midtown and at the Sheraton Albuquerque Uptown.

SUBURBAN EXTENDED STAY **$**
2401 Wellesley Drive NE
(505) 883-8888
www.suburbanhotels.com

Despite the name, one-night and short-stay visitors are welcome here, and it's a good budget option at just under $50 a night, with rates dropping the longer you stay. Standard "efficiency" rooms are fairly compact but include a kitchen area with microwave, large fridge, stovetop burners and dishes, pans, and utensils. A bar counter with chairs serves as a dining table and doubles as a work desk if needed. The 136 king or double-queen rooms have free WiFi Internet access, phone with voicemail and free local calls, and a 27-inch TV with premium cable and movie channels. There are on-site laundry facilities and a business room with a computer and fax and copy services. Housekeeping takes place twice a week, but you can obtain room supplies at the front desk if needed. There are two floors, and smoking rooms are available. Pets up to 30 pounds stay with a one-time fee of $25 for up to five nights. Wellesley is off Menaul a block west of Carlisle.

i Many hotels give AAA or AARP discounts. Even if they don't advertise discounts, it's worth asking.

UPTOWN

HOMEWOOD SUITES BY HILTON **$$$**
7101 Arvada Avenue NE
(505) 881-7300, (800) 225-5466
homewoodsuites1.hilton.com

There are 100 one-bedroom and 6 two-bedroom suites in this six-story hotel, renovated in 2008. All suites have a separate living area and a full kitchen equipped with microwave, fridge, dishwasher, two-burner stove, and dishes, pans, and utensils. Suites are furnished with king beds or two double beds with Serta Sweet Dreams Mattresses, and the separate living area has a full-size sleeper sofa, chair, and work space with free high-speed Internet access. There are two TVs with premium channels and phones with voicemail in the living room and bedroom. MP3 players can be plugged into the alarm clock. Homewood Suites offers a complimentary hot breakfast and a Welcome Home Reception on Monday through Thursday evenings with a meal and salad bar, featuring such hot dishes as chicken Parmesan and barbecue burgers. Other amenities include a fitness center, an outdoor pool, and a business center. Pets up to 50 pounds stay for a $50 flat fee. Smoking suites are available. Guests on longer stays receive a discount on room rates.

HYATT PLACE **$$**
6901 Arvada, NE
(505) 872-9000, (888) 492-8847
www.hyattplace.com

Formerly an AmeriSuites hotel, this property has recently been extensively remodeled into the Hyatt Place modern clean-lined style. King and double rooms are divided into living and sleeping areas and furnished with the Hyatt Grand Bed, 42" flat-screen HDTV, plush sofa, wet bar with fridge, work desk and two phones including a cordless, and granite vanity units in the bathroom. Wi-Fi Internet access is free. A continental breakfast is included, and there is also a Bakery Café selling beer, wine, and Starbucks coffees, and the guest kitchen offers 24-hour freshly made meals and snacks. Business services include a computer and printer room. An outdoor swimming pool and fitness room complete the package. There are 126 rooms in this six-story hotel.

MARRIOTT ALBUQUERQUE $$$$
2101 Louisiana Boulevard NE
(505) 881-6800, (800) 228-9290
www.marriott.com/abqnm

The 17-story Marriott towers over the Uptown restaurant and shopping district and has 405 rooms and 6 suites. Recently renovated guest rooms are tastefully decorated, with floor-to-ceiling windows looking toward the city or mountains. Furnishings include 32" LCD HDTVs with connectivity boxes and cotton-rich linens and down comforters. There's a lobby bar, and the Cielo Sandia restaurant is open for breakfast, lunch, and dinner, serving American and regional cuisine, including steak and fish from the grill. You can lounge peacefully by the sleek indoor and outdoor pool areas or get more energetic in the fitness center. The Marriott has a full-service business center. In-room Internet access is available for a fee of $11.95 per day but is complimentary in concierge-level rooms and for gold and platinum members. Concierge rooms, at a slightly higher rate, also include access to a lounge with complimentary continental breakfast and other snacks and benefits. Weekend room rates at the Marriott are steeply reduced. While booking it's worth comparing the price of standard and concierge-level rooms, as the higher rates may work in your favor if you take advantage of the concierge extras.

i **Room rates at a hotel's own Web site often match those found at online travel sites or even go one better with special discounts, such as three nights for the price of two, or other promotions and benefits. In addition, booking directly with the hotel usually offers greater flexibility for cancellations or date changes without incurring a penalty.**

SHERATON ALBUQUERQUE UPTOWN $$$
2600 Louisiana Boulevard NE
(505) 881-0000, (800) 252-7772
sheratonabq.com

A $20 million facelift in 2008 gave the Sheraton Albuquerque Uptown a chichi boutique hotel look, with bold contemporary decor in the 295 guest rooms and public areas. Accommodations feature Sheraton Sweet Sleeper beds, 37" LCD flat-screen TVs, work desks with ergonomic chairs, generously sized bathrooms, and Starbucks coffee in the room. Internet access costs $9.99 a day. Sheraton Club guest rooms are located on the top (eighth) floor of the hotel, with a Club Lounge and other upgraded amenities and benefits. The ABQ Grill serves breakfast, lunch, and dinner; the Sol Café is a hot spot for snacks; and there's a convivial lobby lounge bar with TVs. Amenities include a stylish indoor pool, a hot tub, and a workout center. The new Jacuzzi suites are a popular pick since the renovations. Pets are permitted here with no fee, but alert them in advance if you're bringing a pooch or puss. If your dog is over 80 pounds, contact the management first for approval.

BALLOON PARK / NORTH I-25

COURTYARD BY MARRIOTT $$$
5151 Journal Center Boulevard NE
(505) 823-1919, (877) 905-4496
www.courtyard-abq.com

This southwestern adobe-style hotel was renovated in 2009, and each of the 150 rooms has its own balcony or patio. The comfortable lobby is traditionally decorated with hand-carved furniture and a fireplace, and the landscaped courtyard has benches to relax around the fountain. Rooms are furnished with king or double-queen beds, a chair with ottoman, and flat-screen TVs with cable channels, including HBO, ESPN, and CNN and pay-per-view movies. The work desk has a speakerphone with voicemail, and an ergonomic chair. High-speed Internet access is free, and there's also a business center in the hotel. For on-site dining, Pepper's of Albuquerque restaurant serves breakfast, lunch, and dinner, and other amenities include a fitness center, an indoor pool and whirlpool, and a gift shop and convenience store. The viga-studded building has four floors on the east wing and two on the west wing, with views to the Sandia Mountains. As this hotel is handy for the Journal Center, it's popular with business travelers, so weekends have lower rates.

HACIENDA ANTIGUA INN **$$$–$$$$**
6708 Tierra Drive NW
(505) 345-5399, (800) 201-2986
www.haciendantigua.com

Built in 1790 by a Spanish rancher and soldier, this historic adobe hacienda has served over the centuries as a trading post, wagon stop, stagecoach stop, and railroad stop. Now visitors stop there to enjoy the serenity of the bed-and-breakfast inn, with its four guest rooms and four suites. Guest rooms have queen beds, while suites have king beds plus a single bed, sitting areas, and cable TV. All accommodations have private bathrooms with robes, phone, and wireless Internet access and are furnished with antiques. Each room has its own character and details—one was originally the hacienda chapel—and features include original vigas, kiva fireplaces, and claw-foot bathtubs, and some rooms have their own Jacuzzi. The U-shaped building surrounds a central courtyard, and there is an outdoor swimming pool, hot tub, and lovely gardens. Innkeepers Robert and Susan Thompson serve a full buffet breakfast, which might include an egg dish, bread pudding, meat dish, fruit, yogurt, homemade granola, and juice. There are also evening snacks. Some rooms are wheelchair accessible, but check with the inn to confirm details. Pets may stay for a fee of $35 a visit.

MARRIOTT PYRAMID **$$$$**
5151 San Francisco Road NE
(505) 821-3333, (800) 262-2043
www.marriott.com/abqmc

The Marriott Pyramid has 256 guest rooms and 54 suites arranged around a 10-story-high central atrium. Southwestern-style rooms are fitted with down comforters and designer duvets on the beds, 32" LCD flat-screen TVs, and executive desks. Internet access is $9.95 a day. First-floor rooms have small patios. The ninth and tenth floors are concierge-level rooms, offering guaranteed quiet and access to the concierge lounge with complimentary breakfast and other light snacks. For leisure there's an indoor/outdoor connecting pool, sauna, whirlpool, and fitness center. The hotel has a lounge bar and restaurant serving breakfast, lunch, and dinner. The name comes from the stepped design of the stories on either side of the central building, reminiscent of a Mayan pyramid.

NATIVO LODGE **$$**
6000 Pan American Freeway NE
(505) 798-4300, (888) 628-4861
www.hhandr.com

Easy to spot from I-25 with its vibrant zigzag-design exterior, lit up by red and blue neon at night, Nativo Lodge has a strong Native American theme and stands out as something a little different from the chain hotels. It also feels quite opulent for the price range. The colorful lobby atrium sports Indian rugs hanging against the terra-cotta walls, a huge warrior sculpture, striking chandeliers, giant carved butterflies, and a glass-front elevator. Large circular sofas and canopied seating make it an exotic place to hang out, and there's a smart lobby lounge bar for cocktails. Nativo Lodge is part of the Heritage Hotels & Resorts group and has 145 guest rooms and 2 suites in five stories. All rooms have balconies or patios. Decor is in warm tones of red, brown, and gold, and the very plush beds feature sueded comforters. Carpets replicate a Navajo chief's blanket design, and art includes framed dreamcatchers. Bathroom products are by Aveda.

Rooms also have a work desk, comfortable chair and free Internet access. The lighting is perfect for a romantic stay. If you're working, you might find it a little on the low side, but you can take your laptop into the lobby, where there are power sockets and Wi-Fi. Leisure facilities include a spa tub and an indoor/outdoor pool with spa tub, and the pool is surrounded by pleasant lounging areas and an outdoor teepee (kids will love it!). There's also a fitness center, a business center, and guest laundry facilities. Spirit Wind's Cafe serves breakfast and dinner (evening opening hours have been known to be unpredictable, so check in advance). Next door is a Starbucks, and there are many restaurants nearby. Smoking rooms are available, and dogs are permitted for a $50 flat fee for up to two weeks.

i Some colorful old Route 66 motels are still in business, and it's worth driving past for a look. Always check out smaller motels, though, before you check in, or the experience might be more colorful than expected.

AIRPORT

HILTON GARDEN INN **$$$**
2601 Yale Boulevard SE
(505) 765-1000
www.hiltongardeninn.com

One of the more handsome hotels near the airport, the Hilton Garden Inn has 107 rooms on four floors. King or double-queen rooms all have a fridge and microwave, cable TV, an armchair with ottoman, clock radios featuring an MP3 jack, 250-thread-count sheets, and granite vanity units in the bathroom. Business travelers will appreciate the large work desk, two phones, and free high-speed Internet access. The hotel's business center is open 24 hours. The Great American Grill restaurant offers a breakfast and dinner menu, and has a full service bar. Snacks and microwavable dishes are available at the 24-hour Pavilion Pantry. Other amenities include a fitness center and an indoor swimming pool and whirlpool. There are also self-service laundry facilities and valet laundry. The hotel has a free airport shuttle. Smoking rooms are available.

HOMEWOOD SUITES BY HILTON **$$**
1520 Sunport Place SE
(505) 944-4663, (800) 225-5466
homewoodsuites1.hilton.com

This all-suites hotel opened in 2007 and has 94 rooms on four floors. Most are open-plan studio suites, but there are about 10 two-room suites with separate living area. All have full kitchens with a stove, fridge, microwave, and dishes, cookwear, and utensils. Studios feature a desk, TV with premium channels, phones with data ports, an alarm clock with MP3 player, and free high-speed Internet access. Guests enjoy a complimentary hot breakfast and an evening "Welcome Home Reception" Monday through Thursday with a light meal. There is a business center, a fitness center, and an outdoor pool and whirlpool. Coin-operated and valet laundry are available. Pets up to 60 pounds are allowed with a $100 flat fee. A few smoking rooms are available. Homewood Suites has a 24-hour airport shuttle, and long-stay visitors receive a discounted room rate.

HYATT PLACE **$$**
1400 Sunport Place SE
(505) 242-9300, (888) 492-8847
www.hyattplace.com

The trendy and high-tech Hyatt Place has 125 rooms on six floors. It was extensively converted from the former AmeriSuites hotel in 2008, and the king- and double-bed accommodations have divided living and sleeping areas. The design is

i Ask if your hotel offers a free shuttle. In addition to airport shuttles, some will drop you at local area attractions. If you have an early or a late flight, check your hotel's shuttle hours of operation to make sure you're not left in the lurch. Or call a taxi from Albuquerque Cab Company (505-883-4888) or Yellow Cab Company (505-247-8888).

contemporary and streamlined, with Hyatt Grand Beds, a media center, 42" flat-panel HDTV, wet bar with minifridge, comfy couch, large work desk, two phones with voicemail (including a cordless phone), granite bathroom vanity, and free high-speed Internet access. Continental breakfast is included in the room rate, or hot breakfast is available to order. A self-serve café is open 24 hours with touch-screen ordering for appetizers, entrées, salads, pizza, and sandwiches. Beer, wine, and Starbucks specialty coffees are also available. There is an outdoor heated pool and 24-hour fitness center. A free shuttle between 5 a.m. and 11 p.m. operates on a 3-mile radius, which is plenty for the airport but also means guests can be taken to and collected from nearby points of interest such as Nob Hill.

STAYBRIDGE SUITES $$
1350 Sunport Place SE
(505) 338-3900, (800) 225-1237
www.staybridge.com/abqairport

New in 2009, this four-story property offers 100 studio, one-bedroom, and two-bed/two-bath suites. All feature full kitchens with a microwave, fridge, dishwasher, stove, and all dishes, pans, and utensils. The TV has premium cable channels, and there's also a DVD player. Business travelers have a work desk and speakerphone with voicemail, as well as free Wi-Fi Internet access. Hotel facilities include a 24-hour fitness center, heated outdoor pool, whirlpool, putting green, and barbecue grills if you fancy a cookout. A complimentary hot breakfast buffet is served daily, and evening receptions from Tuesday through Thursday offer drinks and light snacks. There's a business center, ATM, and self-service laundry as well as valet laundry and dry cleaning. Service is friendly, and the hotel is popular with guests on extended stays. A one-time $75 charge applies to pets for up to six nights, but check with the hotel in advance regarding requirements for your pooch. Located a mile from the airport, Staybridge Suites offers a complimentary shuttle to any destination within a 3-mile radius.

i **The Sheraton Albuquerque Airport Hotel is scheduled to open in July 2010, after extensive renovations to the Albuquerque Grand Airport Hotel (which remains open for business while the changeover is completed). The fifteen-story property is a familiar sight to travelers arriving by air, as it stands right at the entrance to the Albuquerque International Sunport. Amenities include a fitness center, outdoor swimming pool, restaurant and bar. (2910 Yale Boulevard SE. The current phone number 505-843-7000 will remain, and online reservations for the Sheraton Albuquerque Airport Hotel will be at www.starwoodhotels.com.)**

NORTH VALLEY

ADOBE NIDO BED & BREAKFAST $$
1124 Major Avenue NW
(505) 344-1310, (866) 435-6436
www.adobenido.com

Nido means "nest," and this authentic adobe home designed by Hap Crawford with 10" thick walls has two queen rooms and one suite for up to six people, all named to follow the bird theme. Each has a private bathroom with a jetted tub big enough for two and a shower. Decor is in colorful country style, and rooms have satellite TV with a DVD player (a DVD library is available), hair dryer, robes, and Wi-Fi. There's no phone in the rooms, but guests can use the house phone, fax, and computer. Amenities include an outdoor Finnish sauna, darts, and pool table, as well as a patio and gardens featuring a pond, waterfall, banco seating, and tables for a take-out lunch or dinner. There is also an aviary. Family-style breakfast includes a hot entrée such as a casserole or pancakes, with breakfast meats, fresh fruit, and sweet breads or pastries. B&B hosts Rol & Sarah Dolk will accommodate special diets. Coffee and tea are always available. Guests receive a 10 percent discount at a day spa a half mile from Adobe Nido, and Sarah is a certified aromatherapist, offering custom blends of essential oils for misting sprays, diffusers, and body oils. Although Adobe Nido has a rural atmosphere, Major Avenue is off 12th Street north of the Indian Pueblo Cultural Center and is about a mile north of I-40. Children are welcome, but one of the resident dogs is scared of small children, so check beforehand. This property is not wheelchair accessible.

LOS POBLANOS HISTORIC INN & CULTURAL CENTER **$$$–$$$$**
4803 Rio Grande Boulevard NW
(505) 344-9297
www.lospoblanos.com

This ranch house was designed in 1934 by renowned southwestern architect John Gaw Meem, and it lies on 25 gorgeous acres in pastoral Los Ranchos de Albuquerque. Nine acres are occupied by a working organic farm growing fruit, vegetables, and lavender, and Los Poblanos hosts an annual lavender festival. The bed-and-breakfast inn is very family friendly, and guests have the choice of three standard rooms with king, queen, or twin beds, plus three suites and a casita. All have private bathrooms, phones, Wi-Fi, and kiva fireplaces laid with fragrant piñon wood. Cable TV is available in some rooms and in the shared library. Several rooms open directly onto the large hacienda-style courtyard. Decor is traditional New Mexican, including antique furnishings, and many well-known artists have contributed to the ranch's architectural details. Bathroom toiletries are made with the farm's own lavender. The beautiful tree-studded grounds with formal gardens offer a seasonal swimming pool, lots of wildlife, and easy access to walking trails, and guests can borrow bikes. There is a gift shop, and the inn hosts such events as cooking classes. Gourmet breakfasts feature the farm's own seasonal produce, and snacks at 5 p.m. might include fresh-baked pastries, cheese, crackers, and fruit. Innkeepers Armin and Penny Rembe are adding extra guest rooms over the 2009–10 winter. All major credit cards except Discover are accepted. Rooms are not wheelchair accessible. Los Poblanos is located on Rio Grande Boulevard south of Alameda Boulevard and north of Griegos Boulevard.

i **If you want a hotel with easy access to the North Valley area, Holiday Inn Express Hotel & Suites in the Old Town section is on the border of Old Town and North Valley.**

SURROUNDING NEIGHBORHOODS

Corrales

CHOCOLATE TURTLE BED & BREAKFAST **$$**
1098 West Meadowlark Lane
Corrales
(505) 898-1800, (877) 298-1800
www.chocolateturtlebb.com

The four rooms at this charming rural retreat are named Road Runner, Quail, and Bunny, for the wildlife you're likely to see in the gardens, and Sandia for the mountain views. The adobe-style home has a comfortable great room with a TV and a fireplace in the winter. The spacious patio with portale overlooks the lovely gardens to the mountains and is candlelit in the evening. There are always fresh flowers and chocolate turtles in the bedrooms, which are colorfully decorated with such details as cowboy hats and quilts hanging on the walls. All rooms have private bathrooms with Cedar Mountain products; if you want a tub rather than a shower, ask for the queen-bed Quail Room. The Sandia king-bed room has a private walled patio and also an antique Taos-style bed, which serves as a sofa or could sleep a child. There's also a twin-bed room and another queen. Rooms don't have Internet access, but you can use the computer in the great room. Breakfast always includes fresh fruit such as melon and pineapple, and hot entrées might be French toast with sausage and sauteed apple, frittata, New Mexican casserole, eggs con *queso,* and blintzes, plus scones and specialty breads.

Innkeepers Dallas and Nancy Renner accommodate special diets with notice. Eat breakfast on the patio or in the dining room, where local arts and crafts are for sale. Coffee, tea, and sodas are on hand all day, plus chips, cookies, energy bars, and popcorn. The peaceful one-and-a-half-acre grounds are beautifully cultivated, with benches amongst mimosa trees, lavender, salvia, and penstemon. Rooms here are not wheelchair accessible. Children 6 and over are welcome. In the village of Corrales, Chocolate Turtle is 1.5 miles from Rio Rancho, with its many restaurants and shops, and is an easy drive of about 25 minutes to downtown Albuquerque. North Valley attractions and restaurants are a little closer.

Rio Rancho

HILTON GARDEN INN **$$$**
1771 Rio Rancho Boulevard
Rio Rancho
(505) 896-1111
www.hiltongardeninn.com

There are 129 rooms in this light and bright four-story hotel. Rooms feature the hotel's Garden Sleep System beds, a microwave and refrigerator, high-definition LCD TV, free high-speed Internet access, and clock radios with MP3 jacks. There's a large work desk with Herman Miller ergonomic desk chair for business travelers and a two-line speakerphone. Bathrooms have granite vanity units, and 10 rooms sport a jetted bathtub. These rooms are available on request at no extra charge. The on-site Great American Grill is open for breakfast and dinner, and beer and wine are served with dinner. The Pavilion Pantry sells snacks and microwavable dishes round the clock. There is an indoor swimming pool, a fitness center, a 24-hour business center, and a self-service and valet laundry. Smoking rooms are available.

SUPER 8 **$**
4100 Barbara Loop SE
Rio Rancho
(505) 896-8888
www.super8.com

A nicer-than-average motel for the price, Super 8 is on a quiet street just off the main strip but is still within walking distance of restaurants. Rabbits hop around the grass by the parking lot, and 48 rooms over two floors are accessed by interior corridors. Spacious rooms have king or two queen beds, a TV, a microwave and fridge, and free Internet access. Complimentary continental breakfast is served in the kitchen area of the bright and well-kept lobby, and coffee, tea, and juice are available all day. Although the immediate area isn't picturesque, rooms on the east/mountain side have a long view across the valley to the Sandias. Smoking rooms are available. Pets are allowed for a $10 fee.

Bernalillo

HOLIDAY INN EXPRESS **$**
119 Bell Lane
Bernalillo
(505) 867-1600, (877) 863-4780
www.hiexpress.com

There are 63 king and double queen guest rooms with 27-inch flat screen TVs with cable including HBO, a work desk, two phones, and free Internet access. Six suites also have a fridge and microwave. A complimentary hot breakfast buffet is served, and the Holiday Inn Express has an indoor swimming pool and a hot tub, two treadmills, and one recumbent bike. Guests can also use a nearby fitness center for a fee. There are laundry facilities, and business services, including a computer and printer. The hotel is close to the Coronado State Monument, and handy for the Santa Ana and Twin Warrior golf clubs, and the Santa Ana Star Casino. Nearby dining includes the Range Cafe and the Flying Star Cafe, and there's fine dining at the Prairie Star at the Santa Ana Golf Course. From I-25, take exit 242 one block west and turn right (north) onto Camino del Pueblo. Bell Lane is immediately on the left.

i **If you're looking for a hotel in Bernalillo, also check out the Hyatt Regency Tamaya Resort & Spa in the resorts section.**

EXTENDED-STAY ACCOMMODATIONS

ROXBURY SUITES **$**
1604–1616 Carlisle Boulevard NE
(888) 210-8549
www.roxburysuites.com

Roxbury Suites has 22 fully furnished one-bedroom apartment suites in Midtown. The minimum rental period is one month, and there is no maximum-stay limit. Standard 650-square-foot suites have a separate living room and bedroom and fully equipped kitchen and bathroom and are well kitted out with contemporary IKEA-style furnishing, plenty of storage space, satellite TV, and a DVD and CD player. There are also bungalow-style casitas and suites with a 300-square-foot private garden. Utilities, Wi-Fi, laundry-room facilities, a private mailbox, and dedicated parking space are included. This is a good option for visitors on work contracts or other long-stay trips, who want to arrive to an already setup "home." Guests can usually be accommodated with two to three weeks' notice. Smaller, well-behaved dogs are accepted. Rates at time of writing are between $925 and $1,050 per month, all inclusive.

SUBURBAN EXTENDED STAY **$**
2401 Wellesley Drive NE
(505) 883-8888
www.suburbanhotels.com

The 136 king- and double-bed efficiencies are quite compact but are conveniently located in Midtown for access around the city, and the price is hard to beat—under $50 a night, and it drops below $40 for month-long stays. There is no minimum stay, and the hotel also takes one-night bookings. The clean and modern two-story buildings look like suburban housing from the outside. Inside, each open-plan room has a full kitchen equipped with microwave, large fridge, two-burner cooktop, and dishes, pans, and utensils. A bar counter with chairs serves as both a dining table and work desk. Rooms have free Wi-Fi Internet access, phone with voicemail and free local calls, and a 27-inch TV with premium cable and movie channels. Decor is functional but reasonably bright. There is no sitting-room area as such, but some rooms are available with sofa sleepers. Housekeeping takes place twice a week, with a quick service followed by full service after seven days. Towels and other room supplies are always available at the front desk. Facilities include an on-site laundry and valet laundry and a business center with computers and fax and copy services. Smoking rooms are available. Pets up to 30 pounds stay with a one-time fee of $25 for up to five nights. For business or leisure travelers who are busy around Albuquerque and need a good-value self-catering base to return to, this can make an excellent choice. Wellesley is off Menaul a block west of Carlisle.

RESORTS

HYATT REGENCY TAMAYA RESORT & SPA **$$$$**
1300 Tuyuna Trail
Santa Ana Pueblo
(505) 867-1234
tamaya.hyatt.com

Set on 500 gorgeous acres of the 73,000-acre Santa Ana Pueblo reservation, this AAA Four Diamond hotel and resort feels a world away from the city, although it's only about 30 minutes' drive from the airport. It overlooks the cottonwood bosque along the banks of the Rio Grande, with excellent views to the mountains, and the resort itself is a visual treat, beautifully designed in adobe pueblo-style architecture. Numerous accolades from travel magazines include *Travel + Leisure's* naming it one of the top five best-value hotels in the continental United States and Canada in 2009. Enter the grand lobby lounge with viga ceiling and Sandia views; it's a cozy place to relax on a couch by the fireplace or play at one of the tables set with chess and backgammon. Original art and artifacts are in evidence throughout the resort, including native crafts, pots, and rugs. There are 350 rooms, mostly with private patios or balconies, including standard kings and doubles and suites from executive through to presidential. Rooms are very comfortably appointed with traditional Santa Ana pueblo designs and natural materials and each features a plush Hyatt Grand Bed, a fridge, a work desk, and a deluxe bathroom.

Three swimming pools include the centerpiece circular walled pool inspired by a ceremonial kiva, a fun pool for children with water sprays and a water slide hidden inside a faux adobe pueblo "house," and the shallower Oxbow pool. There's a poolside bar and grill and an outdoor hot tub under a rock waterfall. Other leisure facilities include the resort's 18-hole championship Twin Warriors Golf Course designed by Gary Panks, a fitness center with yoga and water aerobics classes, two tennis courts, and on-site balloon rides. The Stables at Tamaya offer trail rides into the shady bosque and a weekly rodeo in summer. There are also easy walking and bike trails from the hotel.

The Tamaya Mist Spa & Salon's delicious signature treatments use indigenous ingredients such as piñon-scented oil, blue corn, Jemez mountain mud, lavender flower, and red chile. The spa is divided into men's and women's areas, and each has an outdoor whirlpool and deck and a sauna and steam room (clothing optional). For kids Camp Tamaya's recreational children's activities run in morning, afternoon, and evening sessions. Babysitting services are also available. The Srai-Wi family program (it means "to gather children together and share with them" in the native language) includes Native American storytelling, archery, and guided walks, and you can make drums or pottery and bake bread in a traditional hurana oven. Srai-Wi activities are led by people from the Santa Ana Pueblo (the actual village is 9 miles west of the resort). Kids love these unique programs, but they're just as fun for parents, too.

Fine dining is in the Corn Maiden restaurant (see Restaurant chapter), while the more casual Santa Ana Cafe serves breakfast, lunch, and dinner with tables on the courtyard under *chitalpa* trees. The Rio Grande Lounge is a super sunset spot for cocktails on the terrace with broad views of the Sandia mountains, and it also has a bar menu. A shuttle is available to the nearby Santa Ana Star casino in Bernalillo. Other amenities include a full-service business center, concierge services, and an on-site cultural museum. There is also a deli and convenience store for snacks and gifts.

Guests enjoy excellent (and unstuffy) service, and the tranquil resort is equally suitable for families and business travelers and makes a romantic destination for couples.

Special offers and packages are often available, including golf and spa packages and girlfriend getaways such as a dude ranch Saddle Up and Spa trip. Guests in Regency Club rooms have VIP privileges in the Regency Club lounge, including complimentary continental breakfast, evening cocktails, and other benefits. The House of the Hummingbird amphitheater and a Cottonwoods Pavilion in the bosque are popular choices for weddings. Pets up to 30 pounds are allowed for a $50 fee. High-speed Internet access is $9.95 a day. Choose valet parking or free self-parking. Four smoking rooms are available. Take I-25 north of Albuquerque to exit 242, then west onto Highway 550 toward Bernalillo. The resort signage is on your right after about 2.4 miles.

i **New Mexico residents often receive discounts on golf, spa, and dining at Tamaya—ask if there are any current discounts available.**

SANDIA RESORT & CASINO **$$$$**
30 Rainbow Road NE
(505) 796-7500, (800) 526-9366
www.sandiacasino.com

Owned and operated by the Pueblo of Sandia, this hotel and resort lies on 692 acres beneath the Sandia Mountains, and the adobe glow of this handsome nine-story building is visible from many parts of town. It opened in 2005 with 228 guest rooms, including 30 suites, and terrific views of the mountains and across the city and Rio Grande valley. Southwestern-designed 477-square-foot rooms offer king or two queen beds, a 32" LCD flat-screen TV with pay-per-view movies, a fridge, a desk, high-speed Internet access, desktop and cordless phones, comfortable chairs, large picture windows, and a generous bathroom with both a walk-in shower and a tub.

As you enter the resort, you'll find the expansive casino on the first floor, with over 2,100 slot machines, table gaming, and a poker room. Outside, the seasonal heated pool is surrounded by lounging chairs, cabanas, a year-round hot tub, and a bar. Golfers will love the 18-hole championship golf course designed by Scott Miller, which covers spectacular terrain and has a very attractive clubhouse and restaurant overlooking the greens. The resort also offers a 12,000-square-foot spa and fitness center. The Green Reed Spa offers massages, facials, and body treatments such as the Green Reed Clay Wrap and Hot River Stone Massage and has a full-service salon. The Bien Shur rooftop restaurant on the ninth floor is the resort's signature fine-dining restaurant, with a rooftop bar and lounge, enclosed and outdoor patios, and a separate bar menu. Other restaurants include the Council Room Restaurant and Bar, the Thur Shan Buffet, and several casual eateries, including a sports bar and a coffee shop. The splendid open-air amphitheater hosts major name musicians and bands, and there is regular music and entertainment in the lounges. There is a gift and convenience store, and although the resort doesn't have an official business center, services such as printing and faxing are available at the front desk. Valet parking is free. Smoking rooms are available, and there are both smoking and smoke-free areas within the casino. Take I-25 north to exit 234; head east on Tramway.

RV PARKS & CAMPING

ALBUQUERQUE NORTH / BERNALILLO KOA
555 South Hill Road
Bernalillo
(505) 867-5227
www.koa.com

There are 62 full-hookup RV sites and 10 tent sites at this pleasant tree-lined location, plus six one- or two-room cabins for rent. Enjoy free cable TV and Wi-Fi, and free breakfast pancakes, tea, and coffee. Facilities include a seasonal swimming pool and patio, a playground, volleyball and basketball courts, horseshoes, a games arcade, showers and restrooms, laundry, phones, an outdoor covered cafe, a gift shop, and video rental. The site is 1 (walkable) mile from the Bernalillo Rail Runner Express station, which takes you to central Albuquerque or Santa Fe. RV sites cost $34.95 to $38.95 a night, tent camping is $21.95, and cabins are $37.95 to $47.95.

AMERICAN RV PARK
13500 Central Avenue SW
(505) 831-3545, (800) 282-8885
www.americanrvpark.com

This RV park is west of the river, convenient to I-40, and about 11 miles from downtown. There are 213 full-hookup RV sites for $32 to $41 but no tent sites. Cable TV and Wi-Fi are included for each RV and a free continental breakfast. The site is landscaped, and facilities include a seasonal heated pool, a covered spa tub that's open year-round, a playground, picnic areas and barbecue grills, laundry facilities, hot showers and restrooms, and a convenience store. Two lodges are for rent ($109 and $119), both sleeping eight, each with a fully equipped kitchen, living area with TV, bathroom, and either a porch or a deck. You can also rent a clubhouse with a large kitchen if you're coming for a group event.

TURQUOISE TRAIL CAMPGROUND AND RV PARK
22 Calvary Road
Cedar Crest
(505) 281-2005
www.turquoisetrail.org

This is real mountain camping on the Turquoise Trail to the east side of the Sandias. There are 43 full-hookup RV sites and 12 partial hookups (electricity and water), plus 25 tent sites. Three rustic cabins are also available with minimal furnishings, designed purely for sleeping. One has its own restroom. Facilities at the campground include hot showers and restrooms, picnic tables, a playground, a laundry, and fire pits and grills, although at certain times the Forest Service prohibits fires. There is a gift shop and a phone for emergency use only. Take your own food, as there's nowhere to buy supplies on-site. Wi-Fi is available but not cable TV. Drive to trails into the Cibola National Forest a few miles away. RV sites cost $27 a night; tent camping is $16 for one person, one tent, and one vehicle, plus an additional $2 per additional person over the age of 4, up to four people per site. Cabins are $36 for two people in the small cabins, $58 for the larger cabin.

HOSTEL

SANDIA MOUNTAIN HOSTEL
12234 Highway 14 North
Cedar Crest
(505) 281-4117
www.hostelz.com/hostel/26631

For budget accommodations in beautiful scenery, this tranquil hostel has eight bunks in each of two dorms and a house with two private rooms. There is a shower in each dorm and one in the house. Guests share a well-equipped kitchen with fridge, stove, and microwave, and the common lounge area has a woodstove and trail maps. There's no TV here, and it's not a partying kind of hostel. The owner has donkeys on the grounds, and if you ask, he'll take you on a donkey ride. Lockers are available, and the hostel is wheelchair accessible. It's near restaurants and a gas station, and a supermarket is a quarter mile away. Rates are $20 for a bunk, $40 for a private room. Call ahead to ensure there's space. Take I-40 east and go north on Highway 14 from the Tijeras/Cedar Crest exit, along the Turquoise trail. The hostel is about 4 miles from I-40, after mile marker 3, on the right (east) side of the road, marked by a sign showing a donkey.

i During Albuquerque International Balloon Fiesta, there's an RV park on-site within walking distance (or a quick shuttle ride) from the launch field. Reservation information is at 888-422-7277 or www.balloonfiesta.com.

RESTAURANTS

Food is a major passion in Albuquerque, and city dining provides a wide range of options from small mom-and-pop-type eateries, to stylish contemporary cafés, to swanky upscale restaurants. There are plenty of national chains to be found, but as you're already familiar with those, we're focusing on the places that will give you real local flavor in both food and atmosphere. Highlights include authentic New Mexican restaurants, of course, and visitors on their debut trip to the state have a treat in store as they discover our local specialties for the first time. New Mexican cuisine has a very specific character and is quite different from Mexican or Tex-Mex food. The regional cuisine has developed over centuries, combing traditional Native American foods with ingredients brought by the early Spanish settlers from Europe and Mexico. New Mexican dishes typically feature corn and blue corn, squash, beans, cheese, and—of course—the all-important chile pepper! Even restaurants that focus on American, European, or other international cuisines often incorporate New Mexican culinary elements for a unique twist. See the Close-ups on Chile and What's on the Menu? for more background on the ingredients and dishes you'll have the opportunity to taste in Albuquerque. We also give recommendations for cafés serving traditional and updated American diner classics, plus restaurants specializing in French, Italian, Greek, Mexican, and Asian cuisine. We list gourmet pizza joints, steakhouses, and a vegetarian restaurant (Annapurna's in the University area and the North Valley)—although vegetarians are also well catered to in most of the restaurants in this chapter. Many eateries offer patio dining, and some host live music. Some of the best food is hidden behind humble facades or even tucked away inside storefronts, such as Duran's Central Pharmacy and Model Pharmacy.

On the whole, Duke City dining is fairly casual. Nobody gets too hung up about formal mealtimes. All-day menus mean you can eat breakfast at dusk, and there are plenty of places you can stop in for a full meal or a quick snack. Prices are competitive compared to other American cities, and even the smartest establishments tend to offer a broad and flexible menu to suit all appetites and pockets. These include smaller plates and lighter fare and sometimes a separate bar menu. Restaurants are also generally receptive to diners dropping in for an appetizer or two and a dessert. While our price codes indicate average prices for a substantial meat-based dinner entrée, it's perfectly possible to eat in even the most upscale places for less. Lunch menus (where available) are targeted to a lower price point and are a very accessible way to get a taste of our best fine-dining establishments.

Restaurants are wheelchair accessible unless otherwise stated. Smoking is not permitted in New Mexico restaurants, although sometimes there is smoking on the patio. Some restaurants are only licensed to serve beer and wine, and others offer a full bar; these are indicated in the listings.

Reservations are generally accepted, although often unnecessary. We'll let you know where you can't reserve or if reservations are recommended. Even where reservations are recommended, restaurants will usually fit you in if you're prepared to wait a little, although it's always wise to make reservations during major events and festivals.

Plenty of places are open all day, and guidelines are given for opening hours at the time of

AIRPORT EATS

If you're staying near the airport, there are several chain restaurants on Yale Boulevard; many are open late so you can grab a quick and easy bite. Or it's a short drive up Yale away from the airport to Central Avenue. Turn right to the University and Nob Hill areas or left to EDo (East Downtown) and on to Downtown. For late-night airport arrivals, the Village Inn is open 24 hours, with the exception of Sunday, when it closes at midnight, to reopen at 5 a.m. on Monday morning (2340 Yale Boulevard; 505-243-5476). Eateries around University/Nob Hill also tend to keep longer hours, including Frontier Restaurant, open from 5 a.m. to 1 a.m daily (2400 Central Avenue; 505-266-0550) and the Zinc Cellar Bar, open till 1 a.m. (3009 Central Avenue; 505-254-9462).

writing, but as with everything in unpredictable New Mexico, hours may change. There are sometimes changes of policy or seasonal alterations, and restaurants are likely to be closed on major holidays, so it's best to check before setting off. Albuquerque diners also often eat earlier than in other cities, and it's not unknown for a restaurant to close early if it's a quiet night. If you want to eat later in the evening, it's advisable to call ahead and book a table, because if you show up unannounced at the last minute, you may find darkened doors. And that would be a shame, as there is some truly excellent food in Albuquerque, just waiting for your knife and fork.

Restaurant listings are organized alphabetically by geographic area, covering the main city areas, followed by the surrounding neighborhoods of Bernalillo and Santa Ana Pueblo, Corrales, Rio Rancho, and Sandia Pueblo.

Price Code

The code key indicates the average price of a meat entrée for dinner (or lunch, if the restaurant doesn't serve dinner). This does not include tax or tip. You can expect to pay less for lunch and breakfast, where applicable. In most restaurants listed there are also entrées available in a lower price bracket. Restaurants accept all major credit cards unless otherwise indicated.

$	**under $10**
$$	**$10–20**
$$$	**$21–30**
$$$$	**over $30**

OLD TOWN

CHURCH STREET CAFÉ **$$**
2111 Church Street NW
(505) 247-8522
www.churchstreetcafe.com

The charming old adobe Casa de Ruiz was built in the early 1700s and now houses the Church Street Café, tucked in a quiet street a block north of Old Town Plaza, behind San Felipe de Neri church. Enjoy breakfast, lunch, or dinner here, either in the cozy indoor dining rooms or on the patios—the front patio overlooks the street, the flowery back patio is a shady haven with a pond and fountain. There's a full range of New Mexican dishes, plus burgers served on Indian fry bread, tortilla, or a regular bun and specialty sandwiches in a choice of breads, including baguettes, croissants, and tortillas. Entrées such as Carne Adovada al Horno and Old Fashioned Chile Rellenos come with sopaipillas, beans, and a choice of *calabacitas,* rice, or spinach. As we

i **Hatch, New Mexico, less than 200 miles south of Albuquerque, has been dubbed the chile capital of the world and is home to a chile festival each Labor Day weekend. Albuquerque's own Fiery Foods and Barbecue Show takes place each March, and visitors can sample and buy chile products from all over the world and watch chef demonstrations.**

Chile

Chile is the heart and soul of New Mexican cuisine. Note that we're talking chile, not chili. While the chili con carne confection of meat and beans in tomato sauce is delicious, if you order chile in New Mexico, that's not what you'll get. Here, chile means both the chile pepper itself and the rich sauce made from red or green chiles, which can be smothered over burritos, enchiladas, and other delicacies or served in a bowl as a stew dish with a few tortillas to mop it up. You'll also find fresh chopped or dried and ground chile in everything from breads and pizzas to chocolate, jams, apple pie, coffee, and even beer. When New Mexicans are not eating chiles, we like looking at them: Chile ristras are a string of red chiles hung to dry, and they make cheerful and festive decorations.

The chile is the official state vegetable, and it's responsible for New Mexico's state question: Red or green? The red chile pepper is just the ripened form of the green chile, and color is no indication of heat—either can bring tears to the eyes or be relatively mild. In dishes with a choice of red or green chile sauce, there's no way to predict which will be spiciest, because much depends on the variety and the specific batch. The best thing is to ask the server which is hottest today and make your choice. You can also answer "Christmas" to get a taste of both red and green. If you aren't sure how much you'll like a chile-smothered dish, it's fine to order your chile on the side.

go to press, Church Street Café is building a new garden room extension. Serves wine and beer. Open daily, closed on Sunday evening.

DURAN'S CENTRAL PHARMACY $
1815 Central Avenue NW
(505) 247-4141

Burqueños rightly wax lyrical over the freshly made tortillas in this drugstore and pharmacy diner that serves breakfast and lunch, and on weekdays dinner, too, if you don't mind dining early before the shop closes. Walk through the drugstore, which also sells imported soaps, kitchen gadgets, and jewelry, to the dining area with a dozen tables, a patio with additional tables, and a full counter where you can watch the progress of your tortillas as they're rolled out, tossed on the griddle, and served deliciously hot and soft on your plate. There are usually about twenty goodies on the New Mexican menu, including chicken enchiladas and stuffed sopaipillas on certain days of the week, and the excellent red chile is a popular pick here. For dessert try buttermilk pie or various fruit pies. Milkshakes are made from scratch with ice cream. No alcohol is served, no reservations are needed, and Duran's takes cash only, no credit cards. Monday to Friday hours are currently 9 a.m. to 6:20 p.m., Saturday's are 9 a.m. to 2 p.m., and Duran's is closed on Sunday.

LA CRÊPE MICHEL $$
400 San Felipe Drive, Suite C2
(505) 242-1251
lacrepemichel.com

This intimate café tucked in a charming Old Town adobe delights the taste buds with classic French cuisine and superb savory and sweet crêpes. Crêpe selections might include salmon, fruits de mer, chicken in a Madeira wine sauce, or ratatouille—there are always vegetarian dishes available. At lunch the menu includes salads, daily quiches, soups, and sandwiches such as Croque Monsieur. Dinner entrées change nightly, all as well seasoned and sauced as you'd expect of traditional French country fare, with fish and meat specials, including treats like filet mignon. La Crêpe Michel serves wine and beer and is open for lunch and dinner from Tuesday to Saturday and for lunch only on Sunday. Closed Monday.

MONICA'S EL PORTAL **$**
321 Rio Grande NW
(505) 247 9625
Monica Baca is always in the kitchen at this friendly family restaurant, serving the traditional dishes that her family has enjoyed here in Old Town for generations. Breakfast is served all day, or come for lunch or dinner. Everything is cooked from scratch, and specialties include enchilada ranchera, beef tripe menudo, and *chicharrones*. Monica's sopaipillas are superbly light and flaky, and try to save room for the *natillas* vanilla pudding. Everyone orders green chile in late summer, when Monica roasts her own chiles in the back of the restaurant. Burgers, sandwiches, and salads are also on the menu, and as Monica's sister is a vegetarian, there's a good selection of vegetarian plates. There's also a children's menu. Dine on the front porch enclosed by attractive blue wrought iron screens or in a series of brightly welcoming dining rooms decorated with Mexican tiles and southwestern art. (Note that, although the patio and dining area are wheelchair accessible, at the time of going to press, the bathroom is not yet accessible.) You don't tend to find many tourists here, but if you want to join the locals, Monica's is just a block south of the Mountain Road and Rio Grande Boulevard intersection, and there's plenty of parking. Wine and beer are available. Reservations are accepted, and large parties must book in advance. Closed Monday; only breakfast and lunch served on Saturday and Sunday.

i **Agua Fresca is a traditional Mexican drink, but you'll find it served in some New Mexican restaurants, too, where it's just as refreshing! The fresh-fruit waters quench the thirst in flavors that include watermelon, cantaloupe, and pineapple.**

RESTAURANT ANTIQUITY **$$$**
112 Romero NW
(505) 247-3545
Step into Antiquity's warren of dining spaces and booths, warmly lamp-lit to make the red walls glow, and you quickly see why it has a reputation for romantic dining. Set in a century-old adobe house, Antiquity seats around 60 diners but feels much more intimate, with its cellarlike coziness under old vigas. Aside from romance, diners come here with beef on their minds! (There's not much here for vegetarians, except for some starters.) One popular choice is the Henry IV filet mignon on a bed of artichoke leaves, topped with an artichoke heart and béarnaise sauce. The Chateaubriand for Two is another signature dish, carved at the table. Nightly specials might include veal and lamb, and there are also seafood dishes. You can finish off your meal with a dessert of Polyczenta: ground walnuts with cream wrapped in a crêpe, with chocolate drizzled over the top. The wine list is strong on French wines and champagnes, including a Dom Perignon at $220 a bottle if you really want to splurge. But the selection of domestic and international wines is broad in style and price, and you can also find New Mexico's own very good fizz, Gruet Blanc de Noir, for $28. Old Town parking is around Romero Street and the plaza, and there's a nearby city parking lot. Restaurant Antiquity serves dinner only, seven nights a week, and reservations are recommended, especially for weekends or special-occasion dates.

SEASONS ROTISSERIE & GRILL **$$$**
2031 Mountain Road NW
(505) 766-5100
www.seasonsabq.com
This sophisticated restaurant serves American cuisine with seasonal ingredients and a dash of cosmopolitan style. Signature dishes include calamari with fire-roasted tomato salsa and lemon aioli, and center-cut beef sirloin with roasted garlic mashed potatoes, julienne vegetables, crispy-fried onion strings, and rosemary-portobello demi-glace. The lunch menu has inventive sandwiches, salads, and burgers, at prices around half of those of the dinner entrées. The light-wood and harvest-toned dining room reflects Seasons' family ties to California wine country, and there's a wide selection of international wines, plus a full bar. You can also dine on the patio of the lively

rooftop Cantina, open in the evenings only, with great views. A separate Cantina menu has more casual fare, and you can also come to the Cantina just for a glass of wine or a Seasons' original margarita and listen to live jazz on summer weekends. The rooftop (as well as the restaurant) is fully wheelchair accessible, served by an elevator. Free parking is in the adjacent parking structure. It's advisable to make dining reservations here. Seasons Rotisserie & Grill is open for lunch on weekdays and for dinner every day.

ST CLAIR WINERY & BISTRO **$$**
901 Rio Grand Boulevard NW
(505) 243-9916
www.stclairvineyards.com

This bistro is owned by New Mexico's St Clair vineyard, so the Bistro's chef naturally cooks with a splash of homegrown vintage in dishes like Cabernet braised pot roast or pasta with shrimp sautéed in Pinot Grigio. The menu offers salads; Kobe burger on a sourdough bun; and pasta, fish, and steak dishes; and there's a tasty selection of panini at lunch. The large front room of the Bistro is also the wine retail store, with tables between the bottle-stacked shelves, or you can take a seat at the bar for a glass of wine and a snack or to taste a wine flight. The softly lit and quietly elegant dining room at the back has intimate booth seating and more freestanding tables. The atmosphere throughout is relaxed, and regulars come for the well-priced wines and food and for the mellow live jazz, usually from Thursday to Sunday. In summer music is on the patio. St Clair Winery & Bistro takes reservations, and large parties or private functions might be seated in the cryptlike Rio Grande room, behind a red velvet curtain. Open daily for lunch and dinner.

DOWNTOWN AND EDO

FLYING STAR CAFE **$**
723 Silver Avenue SW
(505) 244-8099
www.flyingstarcafe.com

This building was designed by renowned architect John Gaw Meem and was originally the Southern Union Gas Co. Revamped into the stylish Downtown branch of the local Flying Star chain, with a space-age-sleek glass façade on Silver, it's an impressive space to drop in to for coffee and a snack or for all-day breakfast and dinner. See the Nob Hill listing for menu details. No reservations; serves beer and wine and is open from breakfast through dinner every day.

GOLD STREET CAFFÈ **$$**
218 Gold Street SW
(505) 765-1677

Despite Gold Street Caffè's hip reputation and its role as a major player in the Downtown revival, it's easy to feel at home there in minutes, even if you aren't one of the cool Q gang. The understated decor in tones of mellow golds and browns is soothing, and it's pleasing to note that solo diners are not steered away from the prime window seats or the larger tables at the front of the restaurant. With the exception of bread from Sage Bakehouse and chocolate torte from a chocolatier, everything is made in-house to the personal recipes of Chef Matt Nichols, and his unusual touches give a new spin to New Mexican classics. For example, Gold Street Enchiladas with chicken or veggies, in a divinely intense mole sauce, are served with coconut rice and black beans drizzled with cinnamon crema. The seafood stew is famous, and other favorites are herb-crusted salmon salad; fish tacos; and grilled marinated chicken breast on sautéed spinach with raisins, pine nuts, and vegetables. If you're a BLT fan, try their version with award-winning thickly sliced bacon in a red chile glaze. Among the homemade desserts and baked goods, white chocolate raspberry scones are a knockout. While business people are the main daytime clientele, the ambience changes at night and becomes more softly lit and romantic. Chef Nichols likes to serve wines "with a lot of kick for the dollar"; rather than bottles being priced individually, wines are priced by tier. There's a good selection at $26 a bottle or $7 a glass, plus some reserve wines only by the bottle at $31 or $36. A long-running promotion, in addition to Happy Hour, is Half Off Tuesday for bottles of house wine. Serves breakfast, lunch and dinner and takes reservations, except for weekend brunch. Closed for dinner on Sunday and Monday.

LUCIA **$$$**
125 2nd Street NW
(505) 242-9090
www.hotelandaluz.com
Located in Hotel Andaluz and serving breakfast, lunch, and dinner, Lucia retains the Moroccan and Spanish colonial style influences of this chic boutique hotel opened in fall 2009. The spacious dining room with its open kitchen is soothingly sleek, and the menu offers an innovative take on Mediterranean classics such as Mezze Platter, baked flatbread pizzas, roasted Greek chicken with falafel cake, and an absolutely knockout Catalonian herb crusted rack of lamb with oil poached tomato, chickpea compote, and roasted garlic asparagus. The price code reflects the majority of dinner entrees. The lunch menu is modestly priced at around half the dinner rate for downtown business folk looking to catch a bite of something a little different in elegant surroundings. Breakfast might include lemon ricotta pancakes or steak and eggs with rosemary skillet potatoes. Lucia's wine menu is well-chosen and reasonably priced for the fine-dining atmosphere, although there are several splurge bottles on the list, too, and there are plenty of interesting options for wine by the glass. Friendly service and the beautifully designed Hotel Andaluz lobby bar (or the seasonal second-floor rooftop lounge bar) for pre- or post-dinner drinks top off the experience. Open daily.

SLATE STREET CAFÉ **$$**
515 Slate Avenue NW
(505) 243-2210
www.slatestreetcafe.com
Cool in every sense, the spacious Slate Street Café is set on a quiet side street, and the clean-cut loft-style interior, with its high ceiling and peppy lime, red, and orange accents is a revitalizing antidote to the Downtown bustle. Breakfasts include wholesome American fare such as steak and eggs or pancakes, plus New Mexican classics. Lunch and dinner menus offer Slate Street's slant on comfort food, such as fish and chips of salmon with a beer batter and lemon basil tartar sauce served in a brown bag, Auntie May's meatloaf wrapped in prosciutto with porcini gravy, and mac and cheese with pancetta bacon and parmesan brittle. A few dishes offer Asian flavors, and there's a wide selection of bruschettas, gourmet burgers, and sandwiches, including bacon, lettuce, and fried green tomato. Solo diners might opt to sit at the curved counter featuring Albuquerque postcards and memorabilia under its glass top. There's also shaded patio seating. The café has a comprehensive beer and wine list, and on Tuesday through Saturday evenings the smart upstairs wine loft serves 25 wines by the glass along with accompanying snacks. Slate Street Café is open for breakfast and lunch Monday through Friday, for dinner on Tuesday through Saturday, and for brunch on Saturday and Sunday.

THAI CRYSTAL **$**
109 Gold Avenue SW
(505) 244-3344
Thai Crystal's floor-to-ceiling windows along Gold Street make this a great spot for people watching as you tuck into classic Thai curries, Pad Thai, Tom Kah Gai chicken coconut soup, and Tom Yum hot-and-sour soup. The dining room setup is fairly no-frills, but seating is spacious enough that you aren't an unwilling witness to the conversation at the next table, and the waitstaff is efficient and helpful. Colorful Thoong flags hang from the high ceiling, turquoise and gold mythical art sprinkles the walls, and there's a raised Sala Thai seating section, based on an old-fashioned Thai living room and looking much like an indoor gazebo to Western eyes. Thai Crystal is a popular lunch choice for downtown workers, but it's also handy for Rail Runner Express travelers, as it's just steps from the Alvarado Transportation Center. In the evening it's busy pre- and postscreenings at the movie theater around the corner. Thai Crystal specialties include scallops with basil leaf and Drunken Noodles with pork, beef, chicken or shrimp. Spicy dishes are clearly labeled, although they'll hold back on the heat if requested, but

What's on the Menu?

You'll see these ingredients and dishes on Albuquerque menus, although different restaurants have their own variations on dishes, often based on traditional family recipes handed down over generations.

Atole: A cooked cornmeal porridge, often blue corn, served for breakfast; also a sweetened and spiced cornstarch-based hot drink

Biscochito: New Mexico's official state cookie, flavored with anise

Blue corn: Native blue corn is popular in blue corn pancakes, tortillas, tortilla chips, and posole.

Burrito: A flour tortilla rolled up and filled with some combination of meat, beans, rice, vegetables, and cheese. On the plate it's usually smothered with chile. A typical breakfast burrito filling is scrambled eggs, bacon or sausage, potatoes, chile, and cheese. A breakfast burrito-to-go is the ultimate portable fast food—wrapped in foil to keep it hot so you can eat it on the move!

Calabacitas: Casserole of squashes and corn

Carne adovada: Red chile-marinated pork, a New Mexico specialty

Chalupa: Corn tortilla shaped into a bowl and deep fried until crisp, filled with vegetables, shredded meat, beans, lettuce, and/or guacamole

Chicharrones: Pork rinds seasoned and deep fried into crackling

Chile: Green or red chile peppers, made into a sauce to dress burritos, enchiladas, or other regional foods. A bowl of chile means a bowl of red or green chile stew (not the quite different chili con carne dish with beans). Chiles can range from relatively mild to spicy hot.

Chile relleno: A whole green chile pepper, stuffed with cheese (and sometimes other ingredients) and fried in batter

Chimichanga: A burrito, deep fried till crispy

Chipotle: A rich smoked red chile sauce

Chorizo: Extra-spicy pork sausage

Enchiladas: Corn tortillas, often of blue corn, usually rolled but sometimes served flat and stacked in New Mexico, filled with cheese, meat, vegetables, beans, baked in chile sauce

Fajitas: A grilled platter of chicken, meat, or seafood, cooked with onions, peppers and other vegetables, served with tortillas to make your own wraps and usually accompanied by guacamole and sour cream

Flauta: Deep-fried corn tortillas, tightly rolled into a flute shape, filled with meat, beans, chile, or other fillings

Frijoles: Beans—usually referring to pinto beans or black beans (frijoles negros)

Guacamole: The Southwest's favorite dip, made of avocado mashed with lime, garlic, onions, and chile

Huevos rancheros: a southwestern breakfast specialty, a tortilla topped with eggs, beans, and cheese and swimming in chile

Jicama: A crunchy, sweet, and refreshing root vegetable, often shredded raw in salads

Menudo: Tripe soup or stew seasoned with chile

Natillas: Vanilla- and cinnamon-flavored custard dessert

Mole: A spicy savory sauce of chocolate and red chile

Pico de gallo: A thick salsa of fresh chopped tomatoes, chiles, onions, and cilantro

Piñon: Pine nuts, used to flavor pancakes, coffee, and savory and sweet dishes

Posole: A hominy stew, cooked with pork and chile

Quesadilla: Quesa is cheese, the primary ingredient in a flour tortilla, which is folded over and grilled or fried with a variety of other fillings.

Salsa: Spicy sauce made of red chile, onions, tomatoes, garlic, and spices, usually served as a condiment, especially for dipping tortilla chips

Sopaipilla: Puffy pillows of deep-fried dough, sopaipillas may be stuffed as an entrée in themselves. However, they're often served as an accompaniment to a savory dish, with a pot of honey. Drizzle the honey over the delicious sopaipilla while it's still warm, and eat it with your main course to take the edge off spicy dishes!

Taco: A tortilla, usually corn, either folded, then deep fried till crispy, and filled with meat, beans, lettuce and tomato, guacamole, and so on or lightly fried and served soft and flat with a variety of toppings

Tamale: Cornhusk filled with cornmeal and meat or vegetables, then baked or steamed

Tortilla: Traditional unleavened flat bread made of corn or wheat flour, shaped into rounds and served as accompaniment to a meal or filled with meat, beans, rice, or other fillings

if you prefer a milder yellow coconut curry, opt for the Kang-Ka-Ree-Chicken. Beverages include beers, a short wine list, and wine-based cocktails, plus a good range of sake, served hot, cold, or at room temperature. There's free parking with validation if you park in the multilevel parking structure just around the corner, south on 2nd Street. Open for lunch and dinner Monday through Saturday; Sunday is dinner only.

TUCANOS BRAZILIAN GRILL **$$**
110 Central Avenue SW
(505) 246-9900
www.tucanos.com

It's all about the meat at this Brazilian-themed restaurant that's part of a small western chain. Pay a flat rate for a *churrasco* meal of seasoned and skewered meats and vegetables cooked over open-flame grills, and the server brings selections to your table until you indicate with a nifty color-coded "cue" that you've had enough. Entrées include breads, fried banana, and a substantial salad bar, and skewers are laden with beef, poultry, pork, seafood, and grilled vegetables and pineapple. Despite the meaty emphasis, vegetarians will find plenty to be happy about, including roasted vegetable and pineapple skewers, the extensive salad bar, soups, appetizers, and pasta with a completely vegetarian sauce. Cocktails from the full bar naturally include the Brazilian caipirinha. Children under 12 pay a reduced rate, and kids 6 and under eat free with a paying adult. The atmosphere is lively, and it's a fashionable pick for parties. Reservations are recommended, especially on weekends. Open for lunch Monday to Saturday, for brunch on Sunday, and for dinner every day.

EAST DOWNTOWN (EDo)

ARTICHOKE CAFE **$$$**
424 Central Avenue SE
(505) 243-0200
www.artichokecafe.com

Offering fine dining with a menu of French, Italian, and American cuisine, Artichoke Cafe is a consistent star in the firmament for Duke City foodies. The menu changes seasonally, but dinner options might include grilled rack of lamb chops with spinach, Yukon Gold potato quiche, leek fondue, and a fig-brandy demi-sauce; or steak frites, house-made ravioli, scallops, and fresh fish-market catches, all prepared with a creative edge. The elegant modern dining room displays changing art exhibits, and the sleek and intimately lit bar area serves a more casual bar menu and cocktails. In addition to full bar service, there's a phenomenal wine list, plus a list of classic cocktails including the Sidecar, Bellinis, and the evocative Blood and Sand. Artichoke Cafe suggests making a reservation, as they like to know who's coming, but in typical Duke City laidback style, even at this top-notch establishment reservations aren't necessary. Open for lunch on weekdays and for dinner every night.

FARINA PIZZERIA **$$**
510 Central Avenue SE
(505) 243-0130
www.farinapizzeria.com

The young and buzzy offspring of the neighboring Artichoke Cafe, Farina Pizzeria and wine bar delights hip Burqueños with its artisan thin-crust pizzas showcasing out-of-the-ordinary toppings like sweet fennel sausage, roasted onion, and mozzarella or goat cheese, leeks, scallions, and pancetta. The Bianco, with its fresh sage and truffle oil, makes a definite impression on the taste buds. There's also a substantial antipasto platter, salads, and calzone and knee-weakening Butterscotch Budino for dessert. The exposed brick interior adds to the urban vibe, and there is some patio seating. Farina Pizzeria serves a well-chosen wine and beer menu, including local brews, and doesn't take reservations. Open for lunch on weekdays and for dinner every night.

THE GROVE CAFE AND MARKET **$**
600 Central Avenue SE
(505) 248-9800
www.thegrovecafemarket.com

Serving all-day breakfast/brunch plus lunch, this airy cafe is refreshing in every sense, with super-fresh dishes featuring organic and locally produced ingredients, beautifully presented. The trendy warehouse-style interior has a gourmet food market up front, selling artisan breads, cheeses, chocolates, and other culinary treats, and after ordering at the counter you take your seat indoors or on the patio. Brunch is a knockout, including highly recommended pancakes and French toast with seasonal fruit and crème fraîche, and lunch offers salads and hot and cold sandwiches with interesting combination fillings. It's also worth treating yourself to a signature cupcake. There's a full range of teas and coffees, including espressos, and beer and wine. No reservations. Closed Monday.

New Mexico state law prohibits the sale of alcohol in restaurants (and everywhere else!) before noon on Sunday.

STANDARD DINER **$$**
320 Central Avenue SE
(505) 243-1440
www.standarddiner.com

Not at all your standard diner, this restaurant serves upmarket comfort food in a smart Art Deco environment in a renovated 1938 Texaco station. There are two dining rooms joined by a long bar area. The higher of the two, to your left as you enter, featuring brick walls and black circular booths, is probably the more characterful of the two, but both are comfortable spaces to enjoy dishes like Bulldog Burger with roasted green chile and cheese, Lobster Caesar salad, Country Fried Tuna with wasabi guacamole, Chicken Fried Steak, or Standard Mac & Cheese in a Guinness and Irish Cheddar sauce. The menu offers lighter snacks through to substantial entrées and decadent desserts, and Sunday brunch is also popular here. The atmosphere is relaxed and family friendly (a lighthearted sign reads "Unattended children will be given an espresso and a free puppy"), and since opening in 2006 Standard Diner has built a loyal following. Beer and wine are available, including wine-based cocktails, and there's a small (dog-friendly) patio. Reservations recommended. Open seven days for lunch through dinner; Sunday brunch is served.

City population swells during the Albuquerque International Balloon Fiesta in October and the New Mexico State Fair in September. Everyone heads to the best restaurants, so make restaurant reservations well in advance for these busy weeks and during other major events such as the Gathering of Nations in April.

UNIVERSITY/MIDTOWN

ANNAPURNA'S **$**
2201 Silver Avenue SE
(505) 262-2424
www.chaishoppe.com

Vegetarian and vegan food following Ayurvedic principles is on the menu here, in world food featuring organic ingredients and many wheat-free and gluten-free options. Well-being considerations aside, Annapurna's is named for the Hindu goddess of food and abundance, and her name is not taken in vain as this warm-hearted café dishes up deliciously nourishing East Indian dishes, including a Thali Plate with daily specials. Other options include shepherd's pie, Malaysian stir-fry, Greek and Lebanese wraps, and pizza on a wheat-free herb crust. Cardamom breakfast pancakes are served with mango sauce. The scent of spices greets you as you enter, and the soothing dining room is adorned with flourishing hanging plants, vibrantly painted tables, and hanging banners. You might even get a quick diagnosis on your dosha balance. There's no alcohol, but the chai is terrific, and you'll find a wide selection of teas, specialty hot chocolates, and cold drinks, including coconut water and mango lassi. Window tables look over the corner of Silver and Yale, and the pleasant patio area is a couple of buildings along on Silver—order at the counter, and a server will bring your food to you. Accepts Visa and MasterCard, and reservations are only necessary for the patio. Open Monday to Saturday for breakfast through dinner and for Sunday brunch. In 2009 Annapurna's opened a second Albuquerque location at 7520 4th Street NW; (505) 254-2424.

EL PATIO DE ALBUQUERQUE **$**
142 Harvard Drive SE
(505) 268-4245

At this busy little restaurant in an old house in the university district, the attractive blue-fenced patio is popular with locals, and the authentic New Mexican cooking is very good. The restaurant opened in 1978, and the green chile chicken enchiladas are a perennial favorite. There's a strong selection of vegetarian plates, including spinach enchiladas. Serves beer and wine and takes cash only, no credit cards, but there's a handy ATM on-site. Open seven days a week, from lunch through dinner.

FRONTIER RESTAURANT **$**
2400 Central Avenue SE
(505) 266-0550
www.frontierrestaurant.com

A quirky Burque institution since opening in 1971, this all-American classic serves breakfast all day, plus lunch and dinner, and it closes late. In keeping with the Western frontier theme, portraits of cowboy hero John Wayne grace the walls, and the large restaurant has booth seating along the big windows overlooking Route 66. Frontier is renowned for its cinnamon sweet rolls, green chile stew, huevos rancheros, hash browns, homemade flour tortillas, and carne adovada burritos, but you'll also find sandwiches, burgers, and steaks on the menu. It's a self-service place—you order at the counter and then collect your food when your number comes up. Prices are low, and there's no alcohol. Open seven days from early till late (currently 5 a.m. to 1 a.m.).

JENNIFER JAMES 101 **$$$**
4615-A Menaul Boulevard NE
(505) 884-3860
www.jenniferjames101.com

Something of a darling of the Duke City dining scene and a familiar name on the "best of" lists, Chef Jennifer James excels with a short and frequently changing menu of locally sourced dishes offering her original takes on contemporary cuisine. The streamlined restaurant in glowing pumpkin hues is smallish and has an open kitchen, giving a personal, almost "at home" feel as Chef James works. A community table night on Tuesday and Wednesday features a one-sitting family-style meal of three courses or more, including wine on the table, at a very reasonable set price. There are no options on the family meal, and the menu is finalized close to the day as it's driven by current market produce; seating is limited, so book in advance. The à la carte menu is available on those nights, too. Wine and beer are available. Reservations are strongly recommended, and Jennifer James 101 is open for dinner only, from Tuesday to Saturday.

OLYMPIA CAFE **$$**
2210 Central Avenue SE
(505) 266-5222
www.olympiacafeabq.com

Directly opposite UNM, this authentic Greek café has fed hungry students since the 1970s. Order at the bustling counter, where the delicious smells are likely to tempt your taste buds if you weren't hungry already, and take your number to a table in the spacious dining room. Decor is basic, although earthily charming with its Greek pictures dotting the walls, and the small tables are often occupied by diners having intense intellectual conversations while filling up on excellent gyros, falafel, spanakopita, and Grecian herbed chicken. You can order à la carte, or the generous meat and vegetarian combo platters help make the decision for you. (The price code reflects dinner platters—individual dishes cost less.) The stuffed grapevine leaf Dolmathes are good here, too. Desserts include baklava and the family-recipe *rizogalo* (rice pudding). Food is usually served pretty quickly. There's no alcohol and no reservations, and Olympia Cafe is closed on Sunday.

THE RANCHERS CLUB OF NEW MEXICO **$$$$**
Inside the Hilton Albuquerque
1901 University Boulevard NE
(505) 889-8071
www.theranchersclubofnm.com

This august establishment in the Hilton hotel has a AAA Four Diamond rating and is renowned for its prime steaks grilled over aromatic woods. Beef buffs are partial to the Filet Mignon, Kobe Filet, and the Cowboy Cut Bone-In Ribeye. Fine seafood and lamb and elk chops are also on the menu. The wood-paneled dining room evokes the atmosphere of an exclusive club with a western flavor, including hunting trophies on the wall. Service is attentive, and there's a full-service bar and an extensive award-winning list of fine wines. The elegant Ranchers Club bar is home to live piano music from Wednesday through Saturday. Reservations are recommended, and the dress code is business casual. The restaurant serves dinner only, seven days a week.

THE RANGE CAFÉ **$$**
2200 Menaul Boulevard NE
(505) 888-1660
www.rangecafe.com

One of three Range Cafés in Albuquerque, this location serves the same hearty home cooking as the original restaurant in Bernalillo. See that entry for menu details. The Menaul branch has a classic diner feel, with booths along the windows and additional seating at a long counter. Overhead, a funky 3-D cow and desert roads mural stretches the length of the kitchen. Although often busy, the tone is pretty laid back, and the staff doesn't rush you even if you're just nursing a coffee and a pie. Open for breakfast, lunch, and dinner every day.

SAGGIO'S **$**
107 Cornell Drive SE
(505) 255-5454
www.saggios.com

Neapolitan-style pizza is the default order at this pizza palace, but you can also choose Sicilian pan baked or New York thin crust. The restaurant is resplendent with murals inside and out, portraying stars from John Wayne to the Beatles, and a Mercedes Benz taxi serves as a dessert station. Order at the counter, and find a spot in the sports-oriented dining room with 20 big-screen TVs or in the quieter family room. Choose a supersized slice, or opt for calzone, pasta including spaghetti with meatballs and build-your-own lasagne, panini, and salads. New York cheesecake or cannoli are good for dessert. The price code is for pizza; other entrées cost a little more. Serving beer and wine, Saggio's is open for lunch through dinner every day.

i **Save dollars by buying discounted dining certificates at www.999dine.com and www.restaurant.com. Participating Albuquerque restaurants range from small mom-and-pop places to chains and fancy dining establishments. The discounted price can save you over 50 percent on the face value of a certificate. Some restrictions apply regarding valid days and times or minimum purchase, so check before punching in your credit card number. You'll also find the latest news on Duke City dining deals and discounts, from "kids eat free" to happy-hour specials and restaurant promotions, at the local blog Albuquerque on the Cheap (www.abqonthecheap.com).**

NOB HILL

BRASSERIE LA PROVENCE **$$**
3001 Central Avenue NE
(505) 254-7644
www.laprovencenobhill.com

Come here for traditional French cuisine in an unpretentious atmosphere. It's hard to miss the rounded pink frontage and inviting neon signs of Brasserie La Provence, and pedestrians strolling by tend to glance enviously at diners on the attractive patio, enjoying specialties such as mussels, soupe à l'oignon gratinée, canard à l'orange, and roasted quail stuffed with wild mushrooms and pears, served over Boursin polenta cake. There's a tasty selection of salads and sandwiches, all with a soupçon of French magic, plus vegetarian dishes and a much-praised crème brûlée. Brasserie La Provence serves beer and wine and is open for lunch and dinner daily, with a brunch on Sunday. Reservations are recommended and are pretty much necessary on weekends.

CRAZY FISH **$$**
3015 Central Avenue NE
(505) 232-3474

The restaurant is not currently signed Crazy Fish (it's a bit of a slippery fish), but when you see a fish symbol and a sign saying Sushi, that's the place, and it's worth looking out for. Inside you'll find a spare and chic interior in neutrals and black, punctuated with lacquer-look red tabletops and Japanese manga images decorating the walls. Local Nob Hill yuppies and the younger university bunch are frequent diners here for the good value and easy location, but you won't feel out of place if you don't fit into one of those crowds. Despite the shiny, hard-edged aesthetic, the mood is pretty mellow and the service accommodating. Most people come here for the sushi, the signature garlic sashimi, and the California dynamite rolls topped with baked scallops and dynamite sauce of Japanese mayo, green onion, and smelt egg *masago*. But the menu also includes teriyaki dishes, crisp and light veggie or shrimp tempura, vegetable *gyoza* pot stickers, and a bunch of salads with an amazingly good ginger-soy dressing. They also serve a pretty mean miso soup. For lunch try the spicy salmon bowl. Wash it all down with beer, wine, or sake as you sit by the window to watch the cruising Central Avenue scene. Or perch at the bar to watch the sushi chef at work—he's the restaurant owner, and the waitstaff rather sweetly and reverently refer to him as Ono San. No reservations—it's strictly first come, first served. Lunch Tuesday to Friday, dinner Tuesday to Sunday. Closed Monday.

FLYING STAR CAFE **$**
3416 Central Avenue SE
(505) 255-6633
www.flyingstarcafe.com

A local chain with nine New Mexico locations, Flying Star Cafes are a cool choice for good casual food, whether you want a full meal or just a latte and a muffin from the bakery. Breakfast and dinner are served all day, and the newsstand has a diverse array of arty and mainstream magazines. Design in all locations is urban coffeehouse hip—if *Friends* had been filmed in Albuquerque, Flying Star would be the café set—but you'll see all ages here and plenty of families. There's also a kid's menu. Food is freshly made and wholesome, including organic, fair trade, and local produce with no trans fats. Order at the counter from a menu of local and American blue plates such as chicken pot pie and pastas, plus weekly specials, burgers, salads, and sandwiches. A couple of Asian dishes include the satisfying Buddha Bowl of stir-fried veggies and rice in lemongrass-ginger sauce, with shrimp, chicken, or tofu. The Nob Hill Flying Star is the original location and is a busy hangout for the university crowd. Wine and beer are available. The price code is for an average adult dish, although you can pay slightly more for some dinner entrées. No reservations. Open daily for breakfast through dinner.

i **Flying Star Cafe's coffee drinks are made with locally roasted Satellite Coffee, and Flying Star owns eight Satellite Coffee houses in Albuquerque, with a lighter food menu. The "Frequent Flyer" customer loyalty card can be used in either chain to earn rewards.**

IL VICINO **$**
3403 Central Avenue NE
(505) 266-7855
www.ilvicino.com

Superb wood-oven pizzas, a charming staff, and a buzzy trattoria atmosphere are the recipe for Il Vicino's success. The Nob Hill branch is the original Il Vicino (the restaurant has expanded to several other cities) and is easily recognizable by its stylish graphic façade. Il Vicino's extensive selection of pizza toppings ranges from the classic to the more adventurous to tempt a jaded palate; for example, the Bianca, with spicy oil, mozzarella, *capocollo* ham, portobello mushrooms, caramelized onions, goat cheese, Gorgonzola, tomatoes, and rosemary. (The long list of extras you can add to customize your pizza includes green chile, of course.) There are also plump calzones, panini served with a side salad, hearty meat or vegetarian lasagnes, and a handful of salads, including the highly praised Caesar salad. Order at the counter, and waitstaff delivers your drinks and meal and takes any subsequent drinks or dessert order. A well-chosen selection of wines is available by the bottle or glass, including their own private-label wines, or try Il Vicino's own microbrewed ales. In summer you can eat at one of the few sidewalk tables, but there's more outside seating at Il Vicino's second Albuquerque location, at 11225 Montgomery NE (see Eastside listing). A Corrales branch is also scheduled to open as we go to press. Open seven days for lunch through dinner. No reservations.

LOS EQUIPALES **$$$**
4500 Silver Avenue SE
(505) 265-1300
www.losequipales.com

At the eastern edge of the Nob Hill district, Los Equipales is known for its fine Mexican seafood. Note that we're talking authentic Mexican cuisine here, not New Mexican, and the restaurant is named for its traditional Mexican equipale chairs made of leather and crisscrossed wood slats. Camarones al Tequila is a favorite dish here; large grilled shrimp with a mildly spiced tequila cream sauce are served with poblano rice and vegetables. Along with flavorful seafood, Los Equipales serves fajitas, chicken mole, and desserts, including Pastel De Tres Leches—a sweet, moist three-milk cake. The restaurant's Mexican blues and warm oranges, terra-cotta tile floor, and atmospheric touches like a portrait of Frida Kahlo fit the food, and there's a seasonal patio and year-round live music on Friday and Saturday evenings. Los Equipales serves wine and beer and is open for lunch and dinner. Reservations are suggested. The restaurant closes early at 8 p.m. on Sunday nights and is closed all day Monday. Find it one block south of Central, east of Washington.

MODEL PHARMACY **$**
3636 Monte Vista Boulevard NE
(505) 255-8686

In this vintage lunch spot you can browse the pharmacy's range of European bath products, fragrances, hair accessories, jewelry, and a super selection of cards, before chowing down on a bowl of the highly recommended green chile stew with pork, plus fresh soups, quiches, and sandwiches from grilled ham with melted Brie and roasted peppers on a baguette to hot brisket on a French roll and a classic deli Reuben. Everything is made on the premises; even the turkey is baked in-house, and desserts include scrumptious fruit cobblers. Model Pharmacy has a full soda fountain with floats, malts, shakes, and old-fashioned phosphate sodas. The fountain's classic pastel-tiled counter with its row of pink stools adds an extra dose of charm. There's no alcohol, no reservations, and only Visa and MasterCard are accepted. Although the store is open for regular shop hours, food service stops at 4 p.m., and from 3 p.m. on, the menu is limited to cold sandwiches. Closed Sunday.

NOB HILL BAR & GRILL **$$**
3128 Central Avenue SE
(505) 266-4455
www.upscalejoint.com

At this cozy but polished neighborhood place dishing up casual fare with a gourmet twist, the menu offers turf, surf, and veggie options. A top pick is the Dirty Burger with Kobe beef, cheddar cheese, Nob Hill steak sauce, frizzled onions, bacon, a fried egg, beeronnaise, and red chile oil. The Caesar salad, fire-roasted tomato bisque, and mac and cheese skillet with grilled vegetable salad and roasted portobello are also hits. You can't miss the 500-gallon saltwater fish tank, and the large garage-style doors separating the patio and dining room are opened in good weather to add to the convivial atmosphere. There's a full bar and a wine menu, and the bar is a prime destination for its imaginative cocktails featuring house-made syrups and classic cocktails such as the Sidecar. Serves lunch and dinner daily, and reservations are recommended in the evenings, especially on weekends and for parties greater than six.

SCALO NORTHERN ITALIAN GRILL $$$
3500 Central Avenue SE
(505) 255-8781
www.scalonobhill.com

As the name suggests, Scalo focuses on Northern Italian cuisine using local organic produce. It serves house-made pasta, inspired wood-fired pizzas with a special handmade thin crust, meat and fish entrées, and a changing list of specials. There are also soups, salads, panini, and a tempting choice of appetizers. For dessert check out the tiramisu, chocolate torte, and homemade gelato. Scalo has long won the hearts of locals and is usually pretty bustling. The streamlined dining room with a mezzanine level is casually classy, and there's patio dining to watch the passing action on Nob Hill. Scalo hosts regular live jazz, serves a full bar, and has an extensive list of Italian and international wines. Reservations recommended. Open for lunch through dinner every day.

VIVACE $$
3118 Central Avenue SE
(505) 268-5965
www.vivacenobhill.com

Owner and chef Joey Minarsich stays true to the restaurant's Italian roots with authentic recipes from Italy, freshly made from scratch. You might try a daily special or Vivace's signature dish Farfalle al Salmone Affumicato—smoked salmon with a cream sauce, asparagus, and bell pepper. In addition to pastas you'll find steak, chicken, and fish entrées and at lunchtime an assortment of panini. Finish off with their Diplomatico pound cake soaked in coffee and layered with chocolate mousse. The wine list, representing mainly Italian regions with some American, too, offers a strong selection of fairly priced bottles. Customers, ranging from those on romantic dates to families, business people, and larger parties, all add to the happy atmosphere. Reservations are recommended for Friday and Saturday night and for large parties. Open for lunch Monday to Saturday and for dinner every night.

YANNI'S MEDITERRANEAN GRILL AND OPA BAR $$$
3109 Central Avenue NE
(505) 268-9250
www.yannisandopabar.com

You could almost imagine you're in the Med in the cool sea-blue and white dining room, complete with Greek columns and tiled bar. The menu offers contemporary fine dining with popular items, including choice steaks; rack of lamb; fresh fish dishes, such as Grilled Yellow Fin Sole Encrusted with Parmesan Cheese; pasta dishes; and traditional Greek platters. Vegetarians are spoiled for choices, too. There's a full bar and wine list, and the Opa Bar in refined dark red tones also serves food and has live music on Friday and Saturday nights. Open daily for lunch and dinner, with ample free private parking behind the restaurant. Reservations recommended.

ZINC WINE BAR & BISTRO $$$
3009 Central Avenue NE
(505) 254-9462
www.zincabq.com

Mixing urban edge and bistro style, Zinc serves mainly American food with a little French influence. The spacious restaurant sports a long zinc bar, wood floors, and a mezzanine level overlooking the main room, and you can also take a stool at the exhibition kitchen bar. Perhaps start with Crispy Duck Confit Eggrolls with peanut curry and chile-lime dipping sauces, followed

i **Some restaurants with only a wine and beer license serve margaritas made with agave wine instead of tequila. Be warned: These tasty margaritas still pack a pretty potent punch!**

by a rotisserie tenderloin of beef with Maytag blue mashed potatoes. There is also a selection of entrées under $20. Service is friendly and efficient, and there's a full bar, substantial wine list, and accessible wine flights. The downstairs Cellar Bar is open late and has its own small-bites menu, with live music or a DJ from Thursday to Saturday night. The restaurant is open for lunch Tuesday to Friday, plus Saturday and Sunday brunch, and dinner every night except Sunday. The Cellar Bar is open every night till 1 a.m., with the exception of Sunday when it closes at 11 p.m.

i **Central Avenue divides North from South in city addresses, so Nob Hill restaurants on the north side of the road on Central have an NE address; on the south side they'll be SE.**

UPTOWN

FLYING STAR CAFE **$**
8001 Menaul Boulevard NE
(505) 293-6911
www.flyingstarcafe.com
The smallest branch of the popular Flying Star local chain keeps the modern ambience and good-food-fast philosophy and serves breakfast and dinner all day. There's an in-house newsstand and regular dining specials, and Flying Star sells beer and wine as well as locally roasted coffee. See the main listing for the Nob Hill location. No reservations. Open daily for breakfast through dinner.

MARCELLO'S CHOPHOUSE **$$$$**
2201 Q Street NE
(505) 837-2467
www.marcelloschophouse.com
A fine-dining steakhouse serving à la carte chops and steaks, Marcello's Chophouse is an elegant destination in the Uptown district. Kobe beef is a top pick here, and other options include Buffalo Tenderloin crusted with ancho chile and veal, pork, and lamb chops. You might start with the lobster bisque, and there are grilled fresh fish entrées and surf-and-turf dishes. Budget-conscious diners will find a good selection of lower-dollar dishes, including "Range Classics." Business people and shoppers on the go are offered a lunch menu of lighter entrees and burgers. The fine wine list has earned Marcello's Chophouse the Wine Spectator Award of Excellence. There's also patio dining, and reservations for the restaurant are highly recommended. You can also come for cocktails or to eat in the Chophouse Piano Bar, where there's live music from Wednesday to Saturday night. Serves lunch and dinner; closed Sunday.

i **The free monthly *Local Flavor* magazine is dedicated to dining in New Mexico and includes interviews with chefs and news on restaurant openings. The daily *Albuquerque Journal* and weekly *Alibi* newspapers also have restaurant reviews and updates on local cuisine. See Gil Garduno's thoughtful reviews of restaurants in Albuquerque and other New Mexico towns at the blog www.nmgastronome.com.**

EASTSIDE

FLYING STAR CAFE **$**
8000 Paseo del Norte NE
(505) 923-4211

4501 Juan Tabo NE
(505) 275-8311
www.flyingstarcafe.com
Both branches of this local chain serve the fresh-made, wholesome fare that Flying Star is known for, in colorful and contemporary surroundings. See the Nob Hill entry for menu details. Both have dog-friendly patios. The Paseo del Norte location is on the southeast corner of the Wyoming intersection, just east of the I-25 North corridor. It has an in-house bakery, mountain views from the ceiling-high windows, and a patio with umbrellas shading the tables. The Juan Tabo café has a large mural and two patios with pretty landscaping. Wine and beer are available. No reservations. Open daily for breakfast through dinner.

HIGH FINANCE RESTAURANT AND TAVERN **$$$**
via Sandia Peak Tramway
East end of Tramway Road NE
(505) 243-9742
www.sandiapeakrestaurants.com

The magnificent view is the compelling attraction here, as the restaurant perches on top of Sandia Peak, with views over the city below and across 11,000 square miles to the far horizon. Unless you're extremely energetic and want to tackle the 10,378 foot Sandia Peak to work up an appetite, access to the restaurant is by riding up on the Sandia Peak Tramway, and tram tickets are discounted if you have dinner reservations in the High Finance restaurant (see the Attractions chapter for Tramway details). The restaurant specializes in steaks, prime rib, seafood, and pasta for dinner, and at lunch there are pastas, burgers, sandwiches, soups, and salads. A full bar is available, and it's also fine to pop in just for a drink at the bar. Reservations are recommended for dinner. There are no reservations for lunch, except for parties of 20 or more. Open daily.

i **Take a jacket or other warm layer up with you to eat at High Finance, as the high-elevation peak is always cooler than the city. After sundown, temperatures chill down further.**

IL VICINO **$**
11225 Montgomery Boulevard NE
(505) 271-0882
www.ilvicino.com

A spin-off from the popular Il Vicino in Nob Hill, this trattoria-style restaurant serves the same great wood-oven pizzas and calzones, washed down with wines, including Il Vicino's private-label wines, and their own microbrews. See the full listing under Nob Hill. The Montgomery branch is bigger than the original Nob Hill restaurant, and the advantage here is the patio with views of the Sandias. It's located on the corner of Montgomery and Juan Tabo, in the Heights Village Shopping Center. No reservations. Open seven days for lunch through dinner.

PAISANO'S **$$**
1935 Eubank Boulevard NE
(505) 814-6802
www.paisanosabq.com

Paisano's fresh pastas are truly fresh—the pasta is rolled, cut, and cooked once you've placed your order. In addition to pasta favorites like richly layered meat and vegetarian lasagnas, and linguine with herby white clam sauce, there are fresh-made pizzas, salads, veal and chicken dishes, and seasonal weekly specials. Finish off with desserts that include Sicilian cannoli and Italian wedding cake. Paisano's has also grown a reputation for offering gluten-free versions of many of their traditional Italian dishes, including pastas, pizzas, breads, and desserts. The restaurant serves wine and beer—gluten-free beer, too!—and you can buy their marinara sauce by the jar. Entrées include soup or salad, and the price code shown is for pasta entrées; half orders are available on many dishes. Several smaller rooms with tables off the main dining room lend the place an intimate atmosphere. On your way in, don't miss a fragrant sniff of the enormous rosemary bush by the front entrance! Reservations are taken only for parties over six people, and Paisano's only accepts MasterCard and Visa. Lunch is served Monday to Friday; dinner is seven days a week.

SAVOY BAR & GRILL **$$$**
10601 Montgomery Boulevard NE
(505) 294-9463
www.savoyabq.com

A sunny, city-smart restaurant with a big wine leaning, Savoy is the sibling restaurant to Nob Hill's Zinc Wine Bar & Bistro and Seasons Rotisserie & Grill in Old Town. The dining room has an upscale, contemporary California feel, and the very fine food follows the same direction, focusing on fresh organic produce, much of it sourced locally. Check out the lamb and steaks from the wood-fired oven, and though menus change four times a year, the herb-roasted prime rib and the filet mignon with sour cream mashed potatoes and black truffle butter are constants. Cedar Plank Salmon and Ravioli with New Mexican Goat Cheese are also favorites. There's a full bar and a comprehensive wine list, including the family's own-label Roessler wines from California, and Savoy hosts wine-tasting events. The chic patio with fire pits is a big draw, especially at happy hour; a patio lounge menu offers lighter snacks and appetizers, and you can order oysters individually. Restaurant reservations are recommended on the weekend. Open daily for dinner; lunch is served on weekdays only. The patio bar and lounge opens at 3 every day.

BALLOON FIESTA PARK/ NORTH I-25

CHAMA RIVER BREWING COMPANY $$

4939 Pan American Freeway NE
(505) 342-1800
www.chamariverbrewery.com

Superior brewpub fare includes steaks, ribs, pastas, seafood such as Maple Brown Sugar Salmon on a sweet potato purée, gourmet burgers, and toothsome appetizers. The Green Chile and Ale Fondue and the Truffled Bleu Cheese Fries get everyone hooked. The obvious accompaniment to a meal here is one of Chama River's award-winning ales and lagers, but you can also opt for a glass of wine. There's outdoor seating, and lunch and dinner are served daily.

THE RANGE CAFÉ $$

4401 Wyoming Boulevard NE
(505) 293-2633
www.rangecafe.com

This is the newest addition to the area's three Range Cafés, and details on its "ordinary food, made extraordinarily well" menu is in the listing for the original restaurant in Bernalillo. The light and airy diner on Wyoming continues the funky cowboy-art theme with a fabulous 3-D Western mural/installation and flying cows! Open for breakfast, lunch, and dinner every day.

SIAM CAFÉ $

5500 San Mateo Boulevard NE, Suite 101
(505) 883-7334

The modest Siam Café has a loyal following for its knockout Thai food, including pad Thai, red curry, and stir-fry hot basil. Go for lunch or dinner, and on weekdays a combo lunch special gives a choice of either rice or noodles and two stir-fry dishes. No alcohol is available, and in this small restaurant reservations are only recommended for groups of six or more. Closed Sunday.

i **New Mexico was the first state to designate an official state cookie. The anise-flavored *biscochito* was given the honor in 1989 and is a traditional Spanish cookie baked for weddings, baptisms, and other festive events. Although available year-round, it's especially popular as a sweet Christmas treat.**

BARELAS AND SOUTH VALLEY

BARELAS COFFEE HOUSE $

1502 4th Street SW
(505) 843-7577

A real local gem serving authentic New Mexican cooking, Barelas Coffee House opened in the historic Barelas neighborhood in 1978, and the cheery front-of-house staff has been here for at least a decade, some of the cooks for much longer. Patrons are a sociable mix of neighborhood residents, Downtown professionals, and politicos. President Clinton ate here—before he was president—as did John McCain. The inside is extensive and family-friendly, and specialties include huevos rancheros, chicharrones, *menudo,* posole, and peppy red chile. Portions are large, and no alcohol is served. There are no reservations, and despite lines in peak times, the wait for a table is usually not long. Large groups are advised to send someone ahead, and they'll set up a special table or area for you. Barelas Coffee House is open for breakfast and lunch only and closed on Sunday. It's just down the road from the National Hispanic Cultural Center and makes a good stop for breakfast en route to see the center's terrific art museum.

i For terrific Mexican take-out, drop by El Modelo in Barelas, justifiably famous among Burqueños for its fabulous pork tamales. Other options include burritos, enchiladas, and breakfast Huevos Rancheros, all cooked up in the enormous kitchen visible behind the counter, which also supplies dozen packs of tortillas and sopaipillas, and prepared masa dough if you want to take them home for your own cooking. El Modelo Mexican Foods ($) is off the beaten tourist track, but the genuine local flavor is part of the appeal. Note that it is take-out only, with a few tables around the parking lot if you can't wait long enough to head for a more picturesque picnic spot! It's busy during peak times, but you can also phone your order in ahead to collect. Accepts Visa and MasterCard. Open daily. 1715 2nd Street SW, just south of Bridge Boulevard. (505) 242-1843.

NORTH VALLEY AND LOS RANCHOS

EL PINTO **$$**
10500 4th Street NW
(505) 898-1771
www.elpinto.com

The lovely leafy patios are a big draw at this pastoral location along the Rio Grande bosque. El Pinto was established in 1962, and out-of-town visitors are pleasantly surprised to find such a verdant spot in the desert, complete with fountains, shady floral porches, and festive chile ristras hanging around the hacienda. El Pinto's is famous for its salsa, made to a family recipe, and it produces 15,000 jars of salsa or green chile sauce every day, to be sold all over the country. Sip a margarita with some nachos while soaking up the atmosphere, and choose from an extensive menu of New Mexican dishes, steaks and grilled entrées, and a selection of low-fat dishes. There's also a children's menu, a weekday lunch buffet, and a short wine list. The price code represents New Mexican plates and grilled entrées; steaks cost more. Open for lunch and dinner daily and also for Sunday brunch.

EZRA'S PLACE **$$**
6132 4th Street NW
(505) 344-1917

An offspring of Sophia's Place just up the road, Ezra's is tucked around the side of Lucky 66 Bowl, the same bowling alley where Sadie's (see listing on page 79) was once located. Look for Ezra's Place in big graffiti across the wall, directing you up the ramp and into the spacious restaurant, with windows overlooking the bowling lanes. The restaurant interior is modest in appearance, but the food has won the same kind of rave reviews as the parent restaurant, with highlights that include a Kobe beef burger with blue cheese and caramelized onions, duck confit with French lentils and mustard sauce, and duck enchiladas and quesadillas. There are nightly specials, and Ezra's Place serves wine, beer, and tequila margaritas but not a full bar. The popular brunch on Saturday and Sunday offers dishes like huevos rancheros, eggs Benedict, and mixed berry or special pancakes. Open for lunch and dinner from Tuesday through Saturday, with brunch on Saturday and Sunday. Closed Monday.

FLYING STAR CAFE **$**
4026 Rio Grande Boulevard NW
(505) 344-6714
www.flyingstarcafe.com

A city-style café in the pastoral North Valley, this Flying Star location, part of the small regional chain, is next door to the Bookworks independent bookstore, and it's not unusual to see patrons dining with their head in a book. Place your order at the counter for coffee and bakery goods or a full fresh-cooked meal, including beer and wine. See the main Nob Hill entry for more menu information. There is outside seating, and no reservations are taken. Flying Star is open daily for breakfast through dinner.

MARY & TITO'S **$**
2711 4th Street NW
(505) 344-6266

You'll still find Mary behind the cash register at this family-run establishment that's grown a loyal local following since 1963. It's a no-frills, down-home-type eaterie, where family photos dot the walls and the juke box features tunes like "Boot Scootin' Boogie" and "Amor Como Mi Amor." Mexican turnovers are specialties here: sopaipillas stuffed with fillings such as *carne adovada* (pork marinated in red chile and baked) or beef, beans, rice, and cheese. The burritos filled with guacamole, beans, and rice and smothered with red or green chile won't leave you hungry either. Mary & Tito's is famous for its intensely flavorful red chile, made from chile pods, rather than powder. The restaurant buys it from a farmer in Hatch and credits the chile's alive-on-the-tongue sparkle to the fact that the chile is sun-dried, not machine-dried. Even though that's a slower process, the cooks clearly believe that good things are worth waiting for, and customers seem to agree. It gets very busy at lunchtime, from Monday through Saturday. Opening hours are slightly quirky: Although they serve breakfast six days, too, the opening time as we go to press is 9 a.m. Closing time Monday to Thursday is 6 p.m., and on Friday and Saturday is 8 p.m. As with any New Mexico eaterie, it's always worth calling ahead to check hours if you're making a special trip. Reservations are accepted, especially for large groups, and are essential for lunch parties of five or more, or you could have a long wait during their packed peak hours! You can also buy ready-made chile by the pint or quart. There is no alcohol license; soft beverages only. Closed on Sunday.

PUEBLO HARVEST CAFE AND BAKERY **$$$**
Indian Pueblo Cultural Center
2401 12th Street NW
(505) 724-3510
www.indianpueblo.org

Set inside the Indian Pueblo Cultural Center (no admission fee for the restaurant alone), the Pueblo Harvest Cafe and Bakery serves Native-Fusion food, using the traditional cooking techniques and ingredients of New Mexico's Pueblo peoples. This leads to unique spins on familiar food—such as the Zia Burger, served on Native frybread, or the Ohkay Owingeh Ovenbread Pudding with caramel sauce. The restaurant is set over two floors, spanned by a two-story flagstone fireplace, with views of the Sandia Mountains from the upstairs dining room and balcony. There is also outside seating on the downstairs patio. Request a Spirit Bowl for your table if you want to follow the Pueblo tradition of offering food to ancestral spirits as a mark of respect. Break off a small piece of your meal and breathe on it, then place it in the bowl. The Sunrise over the Sandias breakfast menu is available until 11 a.m. on weekdays, and all day on weekends; it includes Zuni Blue Corn Pancakes, cooked on the hot rock and served with piñon butter and sausage, bacon, or ham. Or try Blue Corn Atole with raisins and pecans. The price code reflects the cost of the Chef's Selection dinner entrées, but lunch and dinner menus are broad and adaptable to most budgets; offerings include salads, pastas, sandwiches, burgers, and vegetarian options. You might plump for a hearty bowl of mutton stew, or try bison short ribs, braised in red wine with ancho chile and plums. Or splash out on the Oop Ka Waan, a 32-ounce rib eye steak for two. Beer and wine are available. Open daily for breakfast and lunch; dinner is served from Monday to Saturday.

i **Corn, beans, and squash are principal ingredients in Native American food and have been called the Three Sisters.**

SADIE'S OF NEW MEXICO **$$**
6230 4th Street NW
(505) 345-5339
www.sadiessalsa.com

Sadie's *cocinita* has been satisfying Burqueños' appetites since the 1950s, when founder Sadie Koury started cooking in a tiny nine-seater establishment, little knowing that 50 years later the restaurant bearing her name would be one of the most popular dining places in the city. Sadie's has moved through various locations, including a stint in the same bowling alley that now houses Ezra's Place, but today Sadie's of New Mexico occupies a big adobe building with a main dining room, bar lounge, sunroom, and covered patio. Choose from best-selling dishes like carne adovada (pork marinated in red chile, slow-cooked till tender) and the Roberto Special—a grilled hamburger steak covered with Sadie's chile con *queso* and with frijoles and *papitas*. If you can't make up your mind, there are also combination plates so you can sample an array of favorite dishes. Either way, don't miss the melt-in-your-mouth sopaipillas, drizzled with honey, which helps tone down the heat! Sadie's does not throttle back on the chiles—you get the full authentic flavor here, but if piquant doesn't pique your taste buds, opt for a grilled pork chop, rib eye steak, or burgers and sandwiches. The fried ice cream dessert is also worth a taste. Sadie's has a full bar, with a selection of premium tequilas, and is known for its excellent margaritas, which you can order in various quantities from a small glass to a full carafe. The Grand Gold Margarita with Grand Marnier is especially velvety smooth. This is a bustling fiesta of a restaurant, adorned with Indian rugs hanging from the ceiling, a retro street-scene mural of the original Sadie's, and old photos and memorabilia, and with a contagiously cheerful atmosphere, where you immediately feel like one of the family. Indeed, lots of families come here, to celebrate a daughter's Quinceañera or just for an everyday dinner. There is a short "para los niños" children's menu. Sadie's takes reservations only for parties of eight or more. Otherwise, there is often a short wait, especially on weekends, but their wait system is well organized with electronic beepers to alert you when your table is ready, so the best thing is to chill out, grab a drink in the bar, and help yourself to complimentary salsa and chips. You can also eat in the bar area, ordering from the same menu. The sheltered patio, with its decorative water feature and ivy covered adobe walls, is a serene spot and can be less noisy than the main dining room. Sadie's sells its own salsa, sopaipilla mix, and other food and souvenir clothing items in the restaurant's small shop and through the Web site. Serves lunch and dinner every day.

i **The Quinceañera is a traditional Hispanic coming-of-age ritual on a girl's fifteenth birthday, marking her transition from childhood to womanhood–a little like a sweet sixteen celebration but including a church ceremony, where the young woman renews her commitment to God and receives a blessing.**

SOPHIA'S PLACE **$**
6313 4th Street NW
(505) 345-3935

You could easily drive by Sophia's Place and barely notice it's there, but that would be a pity as, despite its humble exterior, this is a favorite Albuquerque haunt for breakfast and lunch. Nursing a big round cup of coffee in this colorful and cozy dining room feels like you're hanging out at a friend's place, with old vigas, quirky art, and corn dolls hanging on the walls. Order at the counter from the menu on a blackboard over the bustling kitchen, and servers bring the freshly cooked food to your table. Breakfast is served all day, including exceptional breakfast burritos smothered with homemade smoked red chile. The veggie burrito is supercheesy and might be stuffed with celery, zucchini, yellow squash, red cabbage, and potatoes. There are also tacos, quesadillas, salads, sandwiches on Sage Bakehouse bread with popular shoestring potato fries, and daily specials. Weekend brunch sees the Sophia's Place famous pancakes on the menu with homemade piñon butter. Outside seating is not the most picturesque, but it serves as an overspill for the dining room. There's no alcohol here, and Sophia's Place doesn't usually take reservations, except for large parties. (Sophia's Place owns the nearby Ezra's Place, which serves dinner.) Sophia's Place is open weekdays for breakfast and lunch and on Saturday and Sunday for brunch.

Albuquerque Wine Country

New Mexico is the oldest wine-producing region in the country. The first vines were planted in 1629 by Spanish missionaries and are believed to be a European variety called Monica that still grows here and is commonly known as the "mission grape" because, initially, wine was produced for the sacrament. In 2007 wine sales by New Mexico wineries totaled nearly $20 million. Wineries around Albuquerque today produce award-winning wines, including Cabernet Sauvignon, Merlot, Pinot Noir, Chardonnay, Riesling, Sauvignon Blanc, Zinfandel, and fruit wines. Many of these wines appear on local restaurant menus. Here are some highlights among Albuquerque area wineries, all of which have tasting rooms to test the fruits of the vine and buy direct from the vintner. Call ahead to confirm current opening times before setting off. Other local wineries can be found at the **New Mexico Wine Growers Association** Web site: www.nmwine.com.

Anasazi Fields Winery in Placitas is between Albuquerque and Santa Fe, and it produces dry fruit, berry, and grape wines, and off-dry cranberry wine for the holiday season. Open for free tours and tasting from noon to 5 p.m., Wednesday through Sunday. January through March, Anasazi Fields is open on the weekend and by appointment only during the week (26 Camino de los Pueblitos, Placitas, 505-867-3062, www.anasazifieldswinery.com).

Casa Rondeña Winery is set on a beautiful estate in rural Los Ranchos de Albuquerque, and the elegant tasting room is open every day for trying award-winning wines from the Casa Rondeña and Calvin labels. Wines include a Meritage red; Cabernet Sauvignon; Viognier; a Spanish-style blend of Syrah, Tempranillo, and Cabernet Sauvignon; and a port. There is also a gift shop, and visitors may enjoy the grounds, complete with a pond and fountain. Tasting room hours are 10 a.m. to 6 p.m. Monday to Saturday and noon to 6 p.m. on Sunday (733 Chavez Road NW, 505-344-5911 or 800-706-1699, www.casarondena.com).

Corrales Winery offers free tours and tastings from noon to 5 p.m., Wednesday through Sunday, of its handcrafted red and white wines, including award-winning Muscat Canelli dessert wine (6275 Corrales Road, Corrales, 505-898-5165, www.corraleswinery.com).

Gruet Winery is the highest-producing winery in the state, with over 100,000 cases a year. The Gruet family was originally from France's Champagne region, and the winery is renowned for its very reasonably priced Methode Champenoise sparkling wines. These are distributed in 49 states and are a festive favorite in many Albuquerque restaurants. The Gruet Winery tasting room is open Monday to Friday between 10 a.m. and 5 p.m. and from noon to 5 p.m. on Saturday. For $6 visitors may taste five wines and receive a souvenir wine glass. Tours take place daily at 2 p.m. or by appointment for groups of 10 or more (8400 Pan American Freeway NE, 505-821-0055 or 888-57-9463, www.gruetwinery.com).

St Clair Winery has its vineyard near Deming in southern New Mexico, where wines are produced under the labels of Blue Teal, DH Lescombes, San Felipe, and St Clair. The St Clair Winery and Bistro in Albuquerque serves as a tasting room as well as a restaurant (901 Rio Grand Boulevard NW, 505-243-9916, www.stclairvineyards.com; see the main restaurant listing). With a $6 wine flight, you can choose six wines and have a one-ounce taste of each. If you don't want to eat a full meal, then choose the artisan nosh plate ($9.95) to accompany the tasting. A generous platter of cheeses, olives, nuts, grapes, mango chutney, crostinis, and chocolate provides enough for two to share.

Vegetarians will find plenty to savor in New Mexican cuisine, but note that some apparently meat-free dishes may be prepared with lard, pork, or other meat products. These include chile, beans, rice, posole, soups, fry bread, tamales, and bizcochito cookies. Check with your server when ordering. You'll often find that a restaurant offers both a meat-based and a vegetarian version of their chile.

SURROUNDING NEIGHBORHOODS

Corrales

CASA VIEJA $$
4541 Corrales Road
(505) 508-3244
www.casaviejanm.com

The current Casa Vieja restaurant opened in March 2009, although other restaurants have occupied this delightful 300-year-old adobe building, which has also served in the past as a courthouse, a chapel, and a stagecoach stop. Casa Vieja's inviting courtyard evokes a true sense of tranquillity as you sit at one of the painted wooden tables in the shade of the mulberry trees or beneath the portal, listening to birdsong and soaking up the atmosphere of old Corrales. The menu is described as world cuisine with a New Mexico twist and with an emphasis on local produce, and the restaurant makes its own pasta, bread, red and green chile, and sausages. For lunch roasted mushroom soup with truffle oil and thyme crostini is a popular choice by the cup or bowl, and there are daily burrito specials. The calabacitas here is a rich and complex treat, or try the Ensalada de Tres Patos, which combines duck confit, duck pate, and a poached duck egg. The menu changes seasonally, but for dinner you might choose Red Chile Coffee Braised Lamb Shank or New Mexican Cassoulet, followed by Green Chile Chocolate Soufflé. Chef Josh Gerwin's signature green chile chicken enchilada has so many devotees, it's guaranteed to stay on the menu. There is a rather chic bar serving cocktails, wines, and beers, and the three comfortable dining rooms are full of southwestern charm, with tile floors, vigas, kiva fireplaces, and art. There are also three patios. Open for lunch and dinner daily and Sunday brunch.

FLYING STAR CAFE $
10700 Corrales Road
Corrales
(505) 938-4717
www.flyingstarcafe.com

Immediately on the right after the Alameda Boulevard junction, before entering the main village of Corrales, this restaurant is part of the local chain of family-friendly Flying Star Cafes. For the menu see the main listing for the Nob Hill location. In Corrales the colorful decor features comfortable booths, and the tiered seating keeps an intimate feel in the large modern space. Huge windows give an indoor/outdoor feel in the rural setting with mountain views. On the patio out back, there's a rock fountain in summer and a fire pit in winter. No reservations, serves beer and wine, and is open for breakfast through dinner every day.

New Mexican cooks are creative in their interpretations of even the most classic dishes, so if you have a food allergy or sensitivity or are vegetarian, check the exact contents before ordering.

Rio Rancho

BANANA LEAF $$
355 Highway 528 SE
(505) 892-6119

Asian food lovers should find what they want on the Banana Leaf's menu of Thai, Vietnamese, and Chinese cuisine. Dine in the cool yellow and lavender restaurant decorated with calligraphy art or order takeout and maybe have a drink at the bar, beneath an altar dedicated by the Taiwanese owner to Guan Gong. Honoring Guan Gong is supposed to bring good fortune, and certainly the food here is a fortunate find, including excellent Thai coconut and basil curries (they'll scale back the heat if you ask) and specials such as Spicy Garlic Golden Scallop, and Tama Orange Roughy Filet, cooked with cilantro, scallion, broccoli, and onion, in a garlic ginger sauce. Some people make a special visit just for the salad rolls, either vegetarian or with shrimp and pork. Banana Leaf serves wine, beer, and sake and is open for lunch and dinner daily. Only accepts Visa and MasterCard.

FAT SQUIRREL PUB & GRILLE $$
3755 Southern Boulevard SE
(505) 994-9004
www.fatsquirrelpub.com

Although the Fat Squirrel only opened in 2008, it feels as if it has been a part of the Rio Rancho scene for years. The upholstered booths welcome you in, and if you sit at the communal high-top island bars, it's easy to get chatting with your neighbor. The owner of the nearby Turtle Mountain Brewing Company is a part owner in Fat Squirrel, and the unusual name follows in the tradition of English pubs, which are famous for their quirky names. Why Fat Squirrel? The story goes that one of the brewers at Turtle Mountain noticed a squirrel stealing grain from the dumpster after brewing was finished. The squirrel grew so fat, she could only lie around the parking lot, but when she had babies, she brought those round for the free feast, too! As Fat Squirrel is just around the corner from Turtle Mountain, they say that the original squirrel's grandchildren still live in the trees nearby. Despite the name, Fat Squirrel is much sleeker than the average English pub, with polished black granite counter tops and brushed steel chairs, mixed with dark-wood tables and booths. Check out the bar, made of 20,000 freshly minted copper pennies under glass. Behind the bar there are Turtle Mountain brews, of course, as well as a wide range of other draft and bottled beers and a modest selection of wines. The menu offers such traditional pub fare as bangers and mash and shepherd's pie, plus appetizers, salads, steaks, sandwiches, and burgers. Fish and chips are a favorite, and so is the Monte Cristo sandwich: Turkey, ham, and Swiss cheese are piled between three pieces of bread, then beer-battered and fried, served with raspberry jam for dipping. Fat Squirrel has nine TVs for sports and other events and also offers patio seating. The price code is for the pub-grub entrées; burgers are less, and steak meals cost more. It is open seven days, lunch through dinner, and has a late-night bar menu.

NODA'S JAPANESE CUISINE $$
2704 Southern Boulevard SE
(505) 891-4378

The Nodas are welcoming hosts at this family-run neighborhood place that lures Japanese-food fans from the city for excellent sushi and other specialties such as teriyaki and tempura noodles. Entrées are served with good miso soup and a salad. The restaurant seats 46 and doesn't take reservations, so sometimes there's a short wait. Wine, sake, and beer are served in the evening only. Open for lunch and dinner, Tuesday through Saturday.

TURTLE MOUNTAIN BREWING CO. $$
905 36th Place SE
(505) 994-9497
www.turtlemountainbrewing.com

A busy haunt even at lunchtime, when people come for meetings or to sit at the bar with their laptops, this neighborhood brewpub serves its own beers, including an award-winning India Pale Ale, and the steel and copper fermenters are visible behind the bar. Wood-fired pizzas and calzones form the backbone of the menu—the Adam Bomb pizza is a favorite, with pepperoni, Italian sausage, green chile, spinach, pine nuts, and mozzarella—but you'll also find a good range of burgers, salads, and rugged grinder sandwiches. The caramelized Carrizozo Apple Calzone is a big hit for dessert. Vintage beer trays, signs, and tankards decorate the walls, and one table features an overhead dome with witty beer-themed takes on classic paintings. There are TVs inside, and a patio set beside the parking area is probably best enjoyed at sunset to watch the sky change colors. Turtle Mountain Brewing Co. is named after the Tewa name for Sandia Peak, in honor of the owner's father, who was born on one of the Tewa-speaking pueblos, and the company also supplies beer to other Albuquerque-area restaurants. Parking space is limited, but there is also street parking and a paved lot one block to the west, by the library and park, with a fenced walkway connecting to 36th Place. Open seven days for lunch and dinner.

VIET RICE $
1340 Rio Rancho Boulevard
(505) 892-7423
Viet Rice's clean-lined decor in chartreuse and burgundy, plus its elegant lighting and art, immediately set a cool Asian tone for this stylish restaurant. The bamboo awning around the counter adds to the atmosphere, too! The restaurant's motto is "We Know Rice," and that becomes evident with their terrific rice noodle bowls and other rice dishes, although they also offer egg noodles. The menu looks fairly short at first glance, but that's deceptive, as many of the dishes are customizable: You choose your protein, perhaps grilled pork, chicken, beef, shrimp, or tofu, and then select your saucy seasoning, maybe spicy lemongrass, chili pepper, or ginger. The flavors are strong and fresh, and there are also some refreshingly different options, including papaya salad with shrimp, chicken, or tofu and a Grilled Beef Wrap with Grape Leaf. Or try the rice crepes with shrimp, chicken, or tofu, pan fried with bean sprouts and served with lettuce, basil, mint, cilantro, and a side of sweet fish sauce. Besides wine and beer, beverages include Vietnamese iced or hot coffee and exotic fruit shakes. Open for lunch and dinner but closes early on Sunday, so check in advance.

Bernalillo

FLYING STAR CAFE $
200 South Camino del Pueblo
(505) 404-2100
www.flyingstarcafe.com
The relaxed Flying Star Cafe is part of a local chain; see the main listing under Nob Hill. The spacious Bernalillo location features a bakery that produces artisan breads and pastries, plus fireplaces, raised seating for wide mountain views, and a mural depicting Bernalillo's history. You can also eat on the attractive patio. Beer and wine are available. No reservations are taken at this casual spot; Flying Star serves breakfast through dinner, seven days a week.

THE RANGE CAFÉ $$
925 Camino del Pueblo
(505) 867-1700
www.rangecafe.com
The Range Café describes its cooking as "ordinary food, made extraordinarily well," and obviously, it's doing something right; since the first restaurant opened in Bernalillo in 1992, another two have followed suit in central Albuquerque (a fourth is said to be scheduled at the airport terminal as we go to press). The long menu is pretty diverse. Home on the range dishes include breakfasts from huevos rancheros to fresh granola to the hearty Wagon Train—eggs, bacon, sausages, pinto beans, cheese, tasty Range fries, and pancakes. Lunch and dinner offer burgers, sandwiches, New Mexican plates, the favorite Tom's Meatloaf with mashed potatoes and mushroom gravy, Chicken Fried Steak, and Gramma's Spaghetti-n-Meatballs. Vegetarians are well catered for with the rich Portabella Artichoke & Spinach Ravioli at dinner. Desserts are indulgent, and the respectable wine list includes selections from the Milagro Vineyards and Winery in Corrales. The Bernalillo Range Café is located in a former drugstore with an original tin ceiling and cowboy-artsy decor. There's regular live music in the café's Lizard Rodeo Lounge. Open for breakfast, lunch, and dinner every day.

Sandia Pueblo

BIEN SHUR ROOF TOP RESTAURANT & LOUNGE $$$
Sandia Resort and Casino
30 Rainbow Road NE
(505) 798-3700

On the ninth and top floor of the Sandia Resort and Casino, Bien Shur is a dinner-only spot and perfect for sunset watching, with terrific views from the big windows and the enclosed and outdoor rooftop patio areas. The international menu includes seafood such as Maine lobster and Chilean sea bass, Angus beefsteaks, and double-cut New Mexico lamb chops, and the popular 20-ounce Bone-In Prime Rib Eye is served with a choice of sauces, including green peppercorn and caramelized shallot jus. À la carte side dishes offer options such as green chili goat cheese au gratin potatoes and baked mac 'n' cheese. There's a full bar service, and you can also just come for a cocktail at the rooftop bar, where a separate appetizer patio menu is available. Reservations are recommended, and Bien Shur is open for dinner only from Tuesday to Saturday.

Santa Ana Pueblo

CORN MAIDEN **$$$$**
Hyatt Regency Tamaya Resort and Spa
1300 Tuyuna Trail
(505) 771-6037

Imaginative cuisine and first-class service in a beautiful setting make the Corn Maiden a top pick for Duke City gourmets. Part of the AAA Four Diamond Hyatt Regency Tamaya Resort and Spa on the Santa Ana Pueblo, the restaurant is in a separate adobe-style building, looking out to the Rio Grande bosque and the Sandia Mountains beyond. The menu takes a "foods on fire" approach, with skewered, slow-cooked, and spit-fired meats and fish. Signature rotisserie are served tableside "from sword to plate," which adds a nice dramatic flourish to dishes like the Ocean, comprising glazed ahi tuna, lavender-salted swordfish, monkfish loin seasoned with alderwood smoked salt, and lavender-salted shrimp, all served with a green curry-coconut beurre blanc. The menu ranges from tapas-style plates for sharing to Chateaubriand for two carved at the table. Seared jumbo scallops wrapped in prosciutto and sweet chile shrimp make a delectable starter, and the rack of Colorado lamb encrusted with pine nuts with a red chile demi-glace is also spectacular. Vegetarian highlights include pan-seared hazelnut-crusted chevre crostini, and a marinated portabella mushroom with red pepper polenta and lemon-seared tofu brochette. Traditional local flavors punctuate the menu, and attention to detail is superb. Fine homemade breads are served with a tangy tapenade of Nopalitos cactus, roasted peppers, sun-dried tomatoes and olives. Handmade truffles are included in the dessert choices, although it's hard to pass up the trio of crème brûlées, where flavors may include raspberry, mango, and vanilla. Reserve a seat at the Chef's Counter for a prix fixe three-course menu, including wine pairings, and watch the French chef de cuisine Bruno Gras as he works and sometimes offers tastings of other items. The very reasonably priced prix fixe menu is also available at a table. There's a full bar and comprehensive wine list, and the intimate and warmly toned restaurant with a fireplace is elegantly comfortable and intimate. There's also patio dining, or it's worth arriving a little early to enjoy cocktails on the resort's Rio Grande Lounge patio with equally fabulous mountain views at sunset. Dress code at the Corn Maiden is business casual, reservations are required, and the restaurant is open for dinner from Tuesday to Saturday. Take exit 242 from I-25 north of Albuquerque, west onto Highway 550 toward Bernalillo. The resort is signed after about 2.4 miles on your right.

NIGHTLIFE

Route 66 really is the place you're likely to get your kicks in Albuquerque, as many bars and nightlife venues are strung along Central Avenue. Many bars, pubs, and lounges also offer an eclectic mix of pleasures to while away the night, including live music from jazz to rock, DJs, dancing, pool tables, or other games and events. Duke City also has some terrific artisan breweries, with brewpubs attached, which are popular gathering places with the commuting crowd. Most bars feature happy hours, and in a city where food is taken seriously, nightspots also provide plenty of options to grab a better-than-average bite. Some of the eateries in our Restaurants chapter also have lively bars that are popular destinations for nondiners.

If you want to try your luck at the slots or the poker table, gaming is permitted on Indian lands, and there are several large casinos at the local pueblos of Sandia, Santa Ana, and Isleta. If you're looking for theater, ballet, opera, or other performance arts and cultural nightlife, including classical, jazz, pop, and general music concerts, see the detailed listings in our Arts chapter.

There is no indoor smoking in Albuquerque, with the exception of the casinos and the cigar bar listed in this chapter. Many bars do, however, permit smoking on their patios. New Mexico state law prohibits anyone under 21 from purchasing or consuming alcohol, and minors are not permitted inside lounges. Always carry your picture ID as evidence of date of birth, as establishments are stringent on the age laws. Bars and lounges can close as late as 2 a.m. and at midnight on Sunday. There are no alcohol sales before noon on Sunday.

BARS & LOUNGES

ATOMIC CANTINA
315 Gold Avenue SW
(505) 242-2200
www.atomiccantina.com

This popular Downtown haunt has a well-stocked jukebox, plus pool table, foosball, and pinball. You can hear live music at least three nights a week, including punk, rock, and indie from local and touring bands, and there's a swing dance and rockabilly evening on Thursday. Crooners can join in the Tuesday night karaoke. The atmosphere is very low key and casual, and there's no cover charge for music or events. Open seven nights.

i Don't forget to take picture ID to prove you're over 21—you will be carded!

BLACKBIRD BUVETTE
509 Central Avenue NW
(505) 243-0878
blackbirdbuvette.com

Owned by partners from the Albuquerque rock band the Dirty Novels, the Blackbird Buvette is a European-style haunt where you can drop in for good coffee, drinks, or food from lunchtime through late night, with some kind of entertainment usually taking place six evenings a week. Expect live music in a range of styles on two or three nights, plus regular DJs and dance parties and events such as art openings, ongoing art exhibits, and a monthly Poetry and Beer poetry night. The high-quality food menu is diverse, and breakfast is served all day. The bar serves plenty of local beers on tap and interesting cocktails. There are two patios. Open seven days.

BURT'S TIKI LOUNGE
313 Gold Avenue SW
(505) 247-2878
burtstikilounge.com
A colorful hangout with live music later on most nights, playing everything from bluegrass to punk, Burt's Tiki Lounge is something of a Duke City legend. The intimate space is packed with kitschy tiki decor and an eclectic clientele. With a DJ dance party on Thursday, no cover charge for music and events, and plenty of specials on drinks, it's where locals come to loosen up. Closed Sunday.

NOB HILL BAR & GRILL
3128 Central Avenue SE
(505) 266-4455
www.upscalejoint.com
You can tell yourself it's purely historical research when you sip one of Nob Hill Bar & Grill's classic "lost" cocktails, including the Sazerac, the Aviation, and the Sidecar. The bar specializes in handcrafted cocktails using fresh fruit, herbs, and house-made syrups, resulting in mojitos with moxie, the healthy-sounding Green Tea Lemon Drop, and the aptly named New Mexico Sunset Punch. On Friday nights only, try their acclaimed and (literally) smoking Berries & Bubbles, with different berries every week, a flavored vodka, champagne float, lime juice, and a house-made syrup, finished off with a dash of dry ice for dramatic effect. Open seven days.

ONE UP ELEVATED LOUNGE
301 Central Avenue NW
(505) 242-1966
oneupabq.com
This sleek but comfortable new Downtown lounge is set on the second floor with floor-to-ceiling windows and a balcony overlooking Central Avenue. There's an extensive cocktail menu, and the food offering focuses on inventive tapas, many with an Asian or Southwestern spin, plus a selection of entrées, including the popular Buffalo Bacon Burger with spicy mango ketchup. Regular entertainment includes live music and DJs, and in addition to the comfortable bar and lounge areas, an equally smart billiard lounge has 11 tables. Closed Sunday.

i **Please don't drink and drive. DUI is a major contributor to deaths in the state of New Mexico, and law enforcement officers are rigorous in catching offenders. Call a cab to carry you home safely: Albuquerque Cab Company (505-883-4888) or Yellow Cab Company (505-247-8888).**

Q-BAR
Hotel Albuquerque
800 Rio Grande Boulevard NW
(505) 222-8718
www.QbarABQ.com
A stylish destination bar at the Hotel Albuquerque in Old Town, Q-Bar is all the rage for its plush decor, live jazz and piano music, DJ nights, and pack-a-punch cocktails. Q-Bar has a series of low-lit, warm-hued lounges with comfy couches, including a piano lounge, a wine room with curtained booths, a billiard lounge, a more minimalist gallery bar with sculptures, and a VIP room. The food menu offers small plates and appetizers with Asian, New Mexican, and French fusion cuisine. Live music plays Wednesday through Saturday. Closed Sunday.

BREWPUBS

CHAMA RIVER BREWING COMPANY
4939 Pan American Freeway NE
(505) 342-1800
www.chamariverbrewery.com
Serving award-winning ales and lagers from its large copper bar, Chama River is a favorite with brew buffs and also popular as a comfortable dining spot with its fine food menu. There are six house beers on tap, including the popular Rio Chama Amber Ale, plus various seasonal and specialty beers. Lunch and dinner menus offer a culinary edge over normal brewpub fare, ranging from signature steaks to upscale burgers and appetizers such as Truffled Bleu Cheese Fries, plus pasta and seafood, including Maple Brown Sugar Salmon. The Green Chile and Ale Fondue is popular as an appetizer. Open daily.

KELLY'S BREW PUB
3222 Central Avenue SE
(505) 262-2739
www.kellysbrewpub.com

In the renovated Jones Motor Company building and gas station on old Route 66, Kelly's striking neon-light exterior retains a touch of retro glamour, while playing host to a very contemporary crowd. You'll find over 20 Kelly brews to suit all palates, and these beers are only sold at the pub. Broad-ranging breakfast, lunch, and dinner pub-grub menus include build-your-own burgers and breakfast burritos. The large and dog-friendly patio is especially popular for watching the Nob Hill passersby, and inside there's a sports bar with pool table and TVs. Open seven days.

i **Il Vicino trattoria and pizza restaurant also serves its own highly regarded microbrews at two locations. See the Restaurants chapter.**

MARBLE BREWERY
111 Marble Avenue NW
(505) 243-2739
www.marblebrewery.com

Although it only opened in 2008, the Marble Brewery pub has quickly grown a following of beer-loving trendsetters and media folk, although the place itself is utterly unpretentious. The indoor space, with a long bar looking through to the brewery, is low-lit and cozy, in contrast to the bright patio out front with umbrella-shaded tables. The patio is more urban than picturesque, tucked on a backstreet dotted with auto body shops, but the authentic Downtown feel is part of the charm, and it's a convenient and relaxed spot for thirsty city workers to pop in when they clock off. There's seasonal live music on the patio on Saturday evenings. The pub serves 10 beers on tap, including Wildflower Wheat, made with New Mexico wildflowers, and a fragrant India Pale Ale, and tours of the brewery are often available. A short but quality food menu includes sandwiches and Texas-style chili. Customers are also welcome to bring their own food to enjoy with a beer or order in from local restaurants on request. Open seven days.

TURTLE MOUNTAIN BREWING CO.
905 36th Place SE
Rio Rancho
(505) 994-9497
www.turtlemountainbrewing.com

This neighborhood brewpub is all about the beer. You can see through to the steel and copper fermenters from the bar, and collections of vintage beer trays, towels, signs, and tankards stud the walls. A fun dome over one table shows classic paintings adapted to the beer theme. Mona Lisa is depicted with a foamy lip from her pint of stout, and Munch's "The Scream" finally resolves the question of why he's screaming—he's spilled his ale. Staple Turtle Mountain brews include Steam, a pale ale from Northern Brewer; Cascade hops; and the award-winning TMBC India Pale Ale. There's a big-screen TV, plus more TVs behind the bar, and the patio can get quite lively as people spill out to enjoy the sunset skies. There's a good menu of wood-fired pizzas and calzones, burgers, salads, and sandwiches. Open seven days.

i **Hopheads look out for beers from local breweries sold in other bars, pubs, and restaurants around town.**

CASINOS

HARD ROCK HOTEL & CASINO ALBUQUERQUE
11000 Broadway SE
(505) 724-3800
isleta-casino.com

Over 1,600 slots and 30 table games are in play at this 300,000-square-foot casino inside the resort on Isleta Pueblo, about seven minutes' drive south of the airport. Previously the Isleta Casino & Resort, this property is changing to a Hard Rock Hotel & Casino in spring 2010, with major renovations to the casino, and the addition of rock memorabilia and high energy music. Slot wager ranges are from a penny to $5. Table games include blackjack, craps, and roulette, and wager ranges vary, but blackjack has a table limit of $3 to $2,000. The poker room with daily tournaments is nonsmoking, and alcohol and food are served to the table here. The casino also has high-stakes bingo with various buy-in levels. The 777's Sports Bar features live music at the weekend. Smoking is permitted in the casino, with some smoke-free areas. Alcohol is served only in the bar and is not allowed on the gaming floor.

SANDIA RESORT & CASINO
30 Rainbow Road NE
(505) 796-7500, (800) 526-9366

The extensive casino inside the crescent-curved Sandia Resort and Casino has more than 2,100 slot machines playing from 1 cent upward, plus table gaming that includes blackjack, minibaccarat, craps, pai gow, roulette, Caribbean stud, and three-card poker. Sandia claims the largest poker room in New Mexico. There is also live bingo and keno. The southwestern-designed high-limit room, with a $25 to $3,000 wager range on table games, includes five blackjack tables and two minibaccarat tables, plus 114 slot machines for $1 to $100 wagers. It also features the sleekly modern Governor's Room VIP Lounge. This resort under the mountains is owned and operated by the Pueblo of Sandia. There are bars in the casino, but if you fancy a break from the action to enjoy terrific views over the city, pop up to Bien Shur rooftop bar and restaurant. Smoking is permitted in most of the casino, with a smoke-free area offering table games and slots. Alcohol is available in the bars but is not allowed on the gaming floor, only in designated areas. Open daily.

SANTA ANA STAR CASINO
54 Jemez Canyon Dam Road
Santa Ana Pueblo, Bernalillo
(505) 867-0000
www.santaanastar.com

On the Santa Ana Pueblo just north of Albuquerque, the Santa Ana Star Casino has around 1,500 slot machines and 28 table games, including blackjack, craps, let it ride, four-card poker, and both American roulette and European-style single-zero roulette. The poker room offers Texas Hold 'Em, Omaha Hi-Low, or High/Low and Stud, with wager ranges from $1 to no limit. There's often live entertainment, or you can pop into the 36-lane Starlight Bowling Center with computerized scorekeeping, giant video screens, and "cosmic bowling" on weekends, with special-effects lighting and fog machines. The bowling center also has its own 1,000-square-foot arcade. Among the casino's seven restaurants and lounges, the Feast Buffet has quite a following among locals. Santa Ana Star is undergoing renovations as we go to press and adding more slot machines, although business is as usual, and work is due to be completed around the end of 2010 or early 2011. The casino is hot on special promotions, and the Web site includes a blog that posts deals and events. Liquor is served in the bars, but there's no alcohol on the gaming floor. This is a smoking facility. Open daily. The casino is off Hwy 550, 2 miles west of the I-25 Bernalillo exit 242, north of Albuquerque.

CIGAR BARS

IMBIBE
3101 Central Avenue NE
(505) 255-4200
www.imbibenobhill.com

Imbibe's rooftop patio overlooking Nob Hill is a big attraction on fine evenings, with fire pits set into the low tables to keep patrons warm once the sun goes down. Downstairs there's a lounge with a full bar, a large humidor, and a wide array of fine cigars for sale, and smoking is permitted indoors. An adjoining sleek cave of a room is the venue for live music and other events. There are regular jazz and DJ nights here. Open seven days.

GLBT

EXHALE NIGHTCLUB & GRILL
6132 4th Street NW
(505) 342-0049
www.exhaleabq.com

Although open to all, Exhale is popular with lesbian lasses looking to dance in this spacious club over several floors. There's a patio, lounges, food and bar specials, and live acts and shows, plus regular karaoke. Opening days vary.

SIDEWINDERS
8900 Central Avenue SE
(505) 275-1616
www.sidewindersbar.com

Open seven days a week from noon, Sidewinders serves the GLBT community and has a strong country-western influence. There are country-and-western and club dance nights, retro and other theme nights, dance lessons and karaoke, plus pool tables, bar food, and drinks specials, such as Sunday beer blasts with free burgers and dogs.

IRISH PUBS

O'NIELL'S IRISH PUB
4310 Central Avenue SE
(505) 255-6782
www.oniells.com

A down-to-earth pub with a touch of the Old Country, O'Niell's has a good selection of beers, including some unusual bottled microbrews. You'll hear live music each Sunday, from folk to bluegrass, and Monday is open-mic night, including Celtic music. Join in the pub quiz for prizes on Wednesday and Sunday nights. Less typical for an Irish pub is the art display that changes every month. The food menu offers hearty Irish dishes, such as Beef and Boxty, plus a tasty shepherd's pie, pastas, sandwiches, soups, and weekly specials. The Burger in Paradise with cheese, bacon, and green chile is something of a legend! Food is served late till midnight (Sunday, 11 p.m.). There's also a patio.

TWO FOOLS TAVERN
3211 Central Avenue NE
(505) 265-7447
www.2foolstavern.com

Pick up a pint of Guinness at the long wooden bar of this traditional Irish pub, whose catchphrase, "where the craic is mighty," tells you what to expect (craic, pronounced "crack", loosely translated, means fun or having a good time). Steeped in the atmosphere of the Emerald Isle, the pub is cozy with wood-planked floors, paneled walls, and decorative stained glass. There's no evening entertainment, but it's a friendly place for a bit of blarney over an aged malt whiskey, and you can fill up on bangers and mash, corned beef and cabbage with a whisky mustard sauce, fish and chips, sandwiches, burgers, and melts, and homemade Bailey's Irish Cream bread pudding. Food is served till 11 p.m. They also serve an Irish Sunday Brunch, sometimes with Celtic music.

SALSA NIGHTS

The Cooperage restaurant is a steakhouse that's also popular for its seafood, but on weekends it's a hot spot for salsa dancing to live bands (7220 Lomas Boulevard NE, 505-255-1657). If you eat first, there's no cover charge; otherwise there's a cover of $7, and you can hang out at the bar. You'll recognize the Cooperage for its exterior, which looks like a wooden barrel. Once inside, the round interior is intimate and softly lit. From September to May salsa is on Friday and Saturday nights from around 9:30 pm. In the summer it's on Saturday night only. However, the Cooperage sponsors Salsa Under the Stars on summer Fridays, at the amphitheatre of the Albuquerque Museum of Art and History, so you can salsa there instead. The Summer Salsa Under the Stars schedule and ticket information is at www.cabq.gov/museum or www.nmjazz.org, or call (505) 255-9798.

Albuquerque Swing and Country Dance Club

You don't have to be a club member or even have a dance partner to join the party with this friendly group. All are welcome at their regular events and one-off outings to various venues around town, which often include lessons. There are nearly 700 members, making it the largest social dance club in New Mexico. Ongoing dates include a Wednesday social dance night to a DJ at the Central Cabana (7915 Central Avenue NE), with a $2 cover. The club also meets on the second and fourth Saturday evening of the month at the Albuquerque Square Dance Center (4909–15 Hawkins NE) for dance styles that include swing, country and western, two-step, cha-cha, waltz, and hustle. This is a no-alcohol event, with a fee of $7. You'll find the latest schedule at www.nmdance.com or call (505) 299-3737. Susan Kellogg, founder of the Albuquerque Swing and Country Dance Club, also publishes the free monthly Local DanceNews e-mail newsletter, with information on activities in all forms of dance throughout New Mexico but mostly in Albuquerque and Santa Fe. To get on the list, contact Ms. Kellogg at the number above, or e-mail glkello@nmia.com.

In addition to the AS&CDC events, the Albuquerque Square Dance Center hosts regular square dance nights and lessons in its two dance halls and is home to several square dance clubs, including a club for singles and a club for lesbian and gay dancers. Find it at 4909–15 Hawkins NE; (505) 345-9797; asdc.org.

LIVE MUSIC

LAUNCHPAD

618 Central Avenue SW
(505) 764-8887
www.launchpadrocks.com

Consistently ranked a top spot for live music, Launchpad hosts regional acts and national touring bands playing rock, hip-hop, R&B, punk, and metal, and it also has dance-club DJs. There's plenty of space for dancing in this rocket-ship-themed venue, and the full bar has earned its own loyal clientele. Usually, you'll find shows here seven nights a week, and while most are for over-21s, some shows are for all ages. Tickets can be purchased in advance on the Web site.

i Fans of folk, world, acoustic, and Americana music should check out the AMP Concerts schedule to find shows to tap their toes. AMP Concerts (standing for Albuquerque Music Presenters) hosts nationally acclaimed performers in various venues around town; previous music stars have included Arlo Guthrie, Joan Baez, Lyle Lovett, and Suzanne Vega. Information on forthcoming shows is at ampconcerts.org.

NIGHTCLUBS

GRAHAM CENTRAL STATION

4770 Montgomery Boulevard NE
(505) 883-3041
www.grahamcentralstationalbuquerque.com

You'll find several dance floors, each dedicated to a different style of music, and one or another should suit you, whatever your idea is of a good time! The South Beach Club plays chart hits, hip-hop, and techno, while Denim & Diamonds is for country fans and two-steppers. There's also a retro club with hits from the '70s, '80s, and '90s. The Alley Cats room features live performers and karaoke. Wednesday is Ladies' Night (no cover for women), and there are drink or buffet specials on other nights. Over-21s only. Open Wednesday through Saturday.

LOTUS NIGHTCLUB & VIP ULTRALOUNGE
211 Gold Avenue SW
(505) 243-0955
www.lotusabq.com
DJs mix an eclectic cocktail of music on the two dance floors at this Downtown club, including hip-hop, R&B, salsa, merengue, reggae, electro, house, and techno. There are also special events and promotion nights. The intimate bar and lounge spaces are hot red and Asian influenced. Mainly an over-21s venue, Lotus also hosts regular nights for over-18s. Open Wednesday through Saturday.

POOL HALLS

ANODYNE POOL HALL & COCKTAILS
409 Central Avenue NW
(505) 244-1820
This is a fun and laid-back spot with a huge range of beers and great cocktails, and people often just drop in for a drink here. Or you can play on eight full-size pool tables, one snooker table, and two quarter-size tables, and there's also pinball. There's no food menu. Open daily.

SPORTS BARS

COACHES SPORTS GRILL
1414 Central Avenue SE
(505) 242-7111
www.coachessportsgrill.net
A favorite sports bar with many locals and a conveniently short drive from the game venues of Isotopes Park, UNM's football stadium, and UNM's The Pit basketball arena, Coaches Sport Grill boasts 20 TVs, including 8 big screens. The bar serves 22 beers, with 12 on tap, plus a good range of wines and liquors. Food isn't sidelined here, and the tasty menu offers appetizers, burgers, sandwiches, and salads, plus a few entrées, including steak, ribs, and barbecue. There are regular food and drink specials, a patio, and events that include karaoke and trivia quizzes. Open seven days.

FOX AND HOUND PUB & GRILL
4301 The Lane at 25 NE
(505) 344-9430
fhrg.com
Fox and Hound is part of a national chain of entertainment pubs, and there are over 50 TVs here, including high-definition large screens, plus eight pool tables, two darts areas, and arcade games. The pub hosts Ultimate Fight Championship TV nights and a hospitality party on the first Monday of the month, with staff dressed to a theme and costume contests. A full menu features burgers, pizzas, sandwiches, entrées, and combo platters. There is a patio. Open seven days.

UPTOWN SPORTS BAR & GRILL
6601 Uptown Boulevard NE
(505) 884-4714
www.uptown-sportsbar.com
This lively bar has 26 TVs, including five 52" high-definition flat screens, and when you're not watching, you can play pool, foosball, darts, and video games. There's a good range of draft and bottled beers, a raunchy cocktail list, and daily specials on drinks and food. The menu includes appetizers, burgers, sandwiches, and fajitas. Uptown Sports Bar & Grill hosts darts leagues, is the home bar for New Mexico's Los Brujos rugby club, and Pittsburgh Steeler fans in Duke City gather here to watch Steeler games. There's an outdoor patio and also an enclosed glass patio. Open seven days.

WINE BARS

PRAIRIE STAR WINE BAR
Santa Ana Golf Club
288 Prairie Star Road
Santa Ana Pueblo
(505) 867-3327
If you're in the Bernalillo area to the north of Albuquerque or you fancy a short drive to get some country air, it's well worth dropping in to

this wine bar in the Prairie Star restaurant at the Santa Ana Golf Club. It's a charming old adobe mansion, complete with fireplaces and viga ceilings and with a recently expanded patio offering peaceful views over the golf course to the Sandia Mountains, making this an excellent spot at sunset. Over 50 wines by the full or half glass are available, including premium and rare wines by the glass, kept in perfectly fresh condition by their large Cruvinet. Peckish wine buffs can order from the tapas menu. In summer there's weekly music on the patio, usually on Friday. Take I-25 north to the Bernalillo exit 242, then head west on Hwy 550 about 2.5 miles to Tamaya Boulevard on your right. Almost immediately, the turnoff for Prairie Star Road and the Santa Ana Golf Club are clearly signed. Closed Monday.

SLATE STREET CAFÉ WINE LOFT
515 Slate Avenue NW
(505) 243-2210
www.slatestreetcafe.com
Climb the staircase in this airy Downtown restaurant to the smart wine loft with leopard-print stools, club chairs, and sofas. Twenty-five wines are served by the glass, or choose a bottle from the longer list. Snacks include fried olives stuffed with Boursin cheese and bruschettas with a selection of toppings. The loft hosts wine tastings with appetizer pairings on the first Tuesday and last Thursday of the month. Open evenings from Tuesday to Saturday.

ST CLAIR WINERY & BISTRO
901 Rio Grand Boulevard NW
(505) 243-9916
www.stclairvineyards.com
The Albuquerque bistro of New Mexico's largest vineyard has a bar in the front room that doubles as the retail store, and there's also a flowery patio. It's a friendly place to relax with a glass of one of the winery's own offerings, or try a wine flight. You can also order food at the bar, and the artisan nosh plate with cheeses, olives, nuts, and other nibbles is generous enough for two to share. There's live jazz, too, usually from Thursday to Sunday, although nights may vary. Open seven days.

ZINC WINE BAR & BISTRO
3009 Central Avenue NE
(505) 254- 9462
www.zincabq.com
There are two bars at this supersmooth Nob Hill bistro to enjoy wines by the glass or bottle from the extensive wine list. Draw up a stool at the long zinc bar of the main dining room, which is a good place to people watch (closed Sunday night). Or head downstairs to the Cellar Bar, a cozy hideaway with live or DJ music from Thursday to Saturday night. The Cellar Bar offers a menu of appetizers, sandwiches, and salads and opens late to 1 a.m., Monday to Saturday, and 11 p.m. on Sunday. Despite the "wine bar" name, both bars are full service.

ATTRACTIONS

Albuquerque has a host of attractions and museums sure to please all ages and all interests. Many focus on the outdoors, as you'd expect in a city where the land itself is a big part of the area's character and history. The Albuquerque Biological Park is a must-see for many visitors, and it includes a zoo, an aquarium, and a botanic garden. The Sandia Peak Tramway is an adventure, giving you the chance to boast that you've ridden the longest aerial tramway in the world, even if you just zip straight up and come immediately down again. Nobody does, though, of course! The tram's destination is part two of this unique experience—the heights of Sandia Mountain, where you can hit the trails into Cibola National Forest or head onto the ski slopes, eat at the restaurant on the peak, or just take in the view of thousands of square miles of glorious New Mexico. On hotter summer days, higher-elevation and out-of-town attractions like the tramway and the Tinkertown Museum on the east side of the mountain are especially welcome to those who feel the heat. Visitors interested in the history and peoples of New Mexico will want to check out Albuquerque's two terrific cultural centers—the National Hispanic Cultural Center and the Indian Pueblo Cultural Center—while the Albuquerque Museum of Art and History gives a superb cross-cultural overview of the area's history. Petroglyph National Monument and Coronado State Monument offer an intriguing glimpse into the past, reflecting the worlds of the indigenous ancestors in this region. At the same time both monuments get you out into the land, to enjoy vistas of spectacular beauty. For all outdoor attractions remember that we're at high altitude and the sun is strong. Take your sunscreen, sunglasses, sun hat, and a bottle of water. Sensible walking shoes are also a must. Even at indoor attractions you can cover a lot of ground, so pick your footwear wisely, and you'll be smiling all day!

Many of the local museums showcase subjects that we especially associate with Albuquerque and New Mexico, so we have museums focusing on balloons, dinosaurs and natural history, nuclear science, and even a couple of museums dedicated to rattlesnakes and the state gem, turquoise! Other attractions are destination areas such as Old Town, the University of New Mexico campus, and the village of Corrales. Each of these brings a different aspect of local history to life, as well as being aesthetically lovely, with superb architecture, and lots of things to see or do. They are all free for you to wander and spend a few hours soaking up the ambience.

Times for museum docent tours and other special events at attractions are shown as guidelines and are correct at the time of writing, but they may change. So if you want to join a tour or see Indian dances, call ahead to make sure you're there at the right time. Museums and attractions usually close for some or all major holidays, although specifics vary, so check with the individual venue. (A child's-eye view of attractions can be found in the Kidstuff chapter.)

Price Code

Admissions to attractions and museums are reasonable and sometimes free, so it's easy on the pocket to take in several of the options offered. The following price codes are based on admission for one adult, but bear in mind that children's admission is generally lower or even free for the very young. There are also often discounted admission fees for senior citizens, students, or New Mexico residents and in some cases for military personnel. We've noted where museums offer free admission days.

$ .... Less than $5
$$ .... $5 to $10
$$$ .... $11 to $20
$$$$ .... More than $20

ALBUQUERQUE BIOLOGICAL PARK

ALBUQUERQUE BIOLOGICAL PARK
(505) 768-2000
www.cabq.gov/biopark

Albuquerque BioPark is an environmental park that includes four attractions: the Albuquerque Aquarium, the Rio Grande Botanic Garden, the Rio Grande Zoo, and Tingley Beach. The aquarium and botanic garden are on the same property, and one fee covers entry to both. The nearby zoo has a separate admission fee. Tingley Beach is free. There is plenty of free parking at all the facilities.

Information on each attraction is below. You can buy a combo ticket for same-day admission to the aquarium, the botanic garden, and the zoo. This costs a little less than buying separate tickets for each and includes unlimited rides on all trains (the Rio Line connecting the BioPark attractions and the Thunderbird Express tour at the zoo). Combo tickets are only valid until noon on Tuesday through Sunday. The reason for the morning-only limitation on combo tickets is that if you enter the BioPark after noon you won't have time to visit all three attractions. Combo tickets aren't valid on Monday because there is no Rio Line train service that day.

The narrow-gauge Rio Line train travels between all the facilities; it's a 1.5-mile journey along the Rio Grande bosque connecting the aquarium, the botanic garden, and the zoo, with a stop at the Tingley Beach train station. This is a great way to get around and save tired feet, as there is already quite a lot of walking within each of these large attractions. If you don't have a combo ticket, you can still ride the train for fun around the BioPark ($2 for adults, $1 for children 3–12), although there are some restrictions. Note that during the summer, only visitors who have purchased a combo ticket can travel on the Rio Line on Saturday and Sunday. As previously mentioned, there are no Rio Line trains on Monday. BioPark summer and winter opening hours vary, and there are different times for summer weekends, weekdays, and holidays, so check the current schedule. In all cases last admission is 30 minutes before closure.

Albuquerque Biological Park was the leading attraction in New Mexico in 2008, with 1,123,000 visitors, according to the New Mexico Tourism Department. It's a popular part of city life for locals as well as tourists, and City research shows that in 2006–2007 62 percent of Albuquerque's citizens came to the BioPark. It was ranked eighth in *Sunset* magazine's 2008 list of "Top 10 Urban Parks." The BioPark is a division of the City of Albuquerque's Cultural Services Department.

i **Look out for the new Insectarium at the Aquarium and Botanic Garden, starting with preliminary exhibits from fall 2009, followed by the main opening in 2010. See native bugs such as scorpions, tarantulas, millipedes, and beetles alongside their exotic cousins from other climates, including foot-long African millipedes, tropical beetles, and emperor scorpions up to 8 inches long!**

ALBUQUERQUE AQUARIUM $$
2601 Central Avenue NW
(505) 768-2000
www.cabq.gov/biopark

The aquarium is on the same property as the Rio Grande Botanic Garden, and admission to both is included in the entry fee. Take an exciting adventure down the Rio Grande as the aquarium leads visitors through the story of the river, following a single drop of water from the Colorado headwaters to the Gulf of Mexico. You'll see exhibits reflecting the various environments on the way, from fresh-water riverines to coral reefs and out into the deep ocean. There are around 3,000 salt- and freshwater aquatic animals. Walk through the eel tunnel; watch seahorses, stingrays, and luminous jellyfish; and come face to face with a shark at the 285,000-gallon ocean tank sporting a floor-to-ceiling 38-foot-wide viewing window. The aquarium opened in 1996 and has become a popular attraction that also educates about the vital mountain-to-desert-to-gulf watery lifeline of the Rio Grande. Activities at different times of the day include a seasonal touch pool, plus regular shark feedings and the opportunity to watch divers in the coral reef tank and the shark tank. There is an aquarium gift shop; the Wildflower Snack Bar with drinks, ice cream, and nibbles; and the Shark Reef Cafe (505-848-7182), which serves full breakfast and lunch. The Albuquerque Aquarium entry fee includes admission to the Rio Grande Botanic Garden. It is part of the Albuquerque Biological Park; see that entry for details on money-saving combo tickets for the Rio Grande Zoo as well and the train service connecting the facilities. Open seven days.

i If you join the New Mexico BioPark Society, you get free unlimited entry to all BioPark facilities, plus certain train privileges, half-price tickets for Summer Nights and Zoo Music concerts, discounts at BioPark gift stores, members-only events, discounts at partnering national zoos and aquariums, and other benefits. There are membership plans for individuals, couples, families, and senior citizens. Information from (505) 764-6280 or at www.biopark society.org.

RIO GRANDE BOTANIC GARDEN $$
2601 Central Avenue NW
(505) 768-2000
www.cabq.gov/biopark

The Rio Grande Botanic Garden is a gorgeous haven covering 36 developed acres of land beside the Rio Grande and the Albuquerque Aquarium, and admission to the aquarium is included in the botanic garden entry fee. Open since 1996, the garden illustrates the horticultural and agricultural history of the Rio Grande Valley with a series of themed gardens and a 10-acre Heritage Farm complete with farmhouse, vineyards, orchards, and farm animals such as horses, goats, pigs, and cows. A 10,000-square-foot conservatory contains Sonoran and Chihuahuan desert plants in one wing and Mediterranean species in the other. The Curandera garden introduces you to the herbs of the Curanderos, traditional Spanish healers, and features a bas-relief sculpture by Diego Rivera. The old-world gardens include a walled Spanish-Moorish garden with water features, beautiful tiling, and aromatic plants. This style from the deserts of North Africa, carried to Spain by the Moors and then by the Spanish to New Mexico, harmonizes perfectly with this "new world" desert landscape. There is also a walled Ceremonial Rose Garden, and in 2010 a new rose garden with glass conservatory is scheduled to open. The Pollinator's Garden attracts bees, butterflies, and birds, and the Camino de Colores boasts seasonal color year-round. The Sasebo Garden—named in honor of Albuquerque's twin city in Japan—is a recent addition to the biopark, opened in 2007. The four-acre classic Japanese garden designed by Toru Tanaka includes a koi pond and elegant Japanese landscaping and architecture. The PNM Butterfly Pavilion, sponsored by the PNM utility company, is open in summer months, when visitors can walk among hundreds of butterflies fluttering around thousands of nectar plants. Other attractions include a Fantasy Garden for children and a lake. A series of once-a-week Summer Nights music concerts playing blues to funk takes place in the botanic garden between June and August. On evenings from the end of November through December you can walk through the glittering River of Lights holiday light show and light sculptures, with a display of fiber-optic lit snowmen, too. On some nights you can skate on an outdoor ice rink in the botanic garden plaza.

Drinks, ice cream, and quick bites are available in the Wildflower Snack Bar. For a full meal, go to the Shark Reef Cafe in the aquarium. The Garden Gift Shop sells souvenirs, garden tools, and books. No pets are allowed at the botanic garden, except service animals, although kennels are available. The entry fee for the Rio Grande Botanic Garden includes admission to the Albuquerque Aquarium on the same property. It is part of the Albuquerque Biological Park; see that entry for details on money-saving combo tickets for the Rio Grande Zoo as well, and the train service connecting the facilities. Open seven days.

i **If children grow tired on the 1.5 mile walk through the botanic garden and aquarium or while in the Rio Grande Zoo, you can rent wagon-style strollers and also carry-all wagons for your belongings. Find them at the visitor service center in the main plaza between the gardens and aquarium, or at the zoo's Gazebo Plaza.**

RIO GRANDE ZOO **$$**
903 Tenth Street SW
(505) 764-6200
www.cabq.gov/biopark

Over 250 species of exotic and native animals live in naturalistic habitats in the 64-acre Rio Grande Zoo. The zoo is home to such creatures as gorillas and chimpanzees, cheetahs and jaguars, hippos, rhinos, elephants, giraffes, zebras, koalas, camels, hyenas, Komodo dragons, Mexican wolves, mountain lions, storks, warthogs, alligators in the Gator Swamp, and the ever-popular polar bears, seals, and sea lions. A globe-trotting 2.25-mile walk through the zoo introduces you to wildlife from Africa, Asia, Indonesia, Australia, and the Americas. A good way to get an overview is to chug around on the narrow-gauge Thunderbird Express train ride for a 20-minute tour of the grounds. Conductors tell the background story on the animals you're seeing, point out what's new at the zoo, and answer any questions. Thunderbird Express tickets are $2 for adults and $1 for children 3 through 12, unless you have a combo ticket for the BioPark, which includes the tour. Catch the train from the Africa area depot, which leaves at 30-minute intervals from Tuesday to Sunday (it also runs on some holiday Mondays). The train is wheelchair accessible. Activities at the zoo include bird shows and camel rides for a small fee (currently $3.50), and you can watch daily feedings of polar bears, seals, and sea lions. The Zoo Music summer concert series is a two-decade-long tradition presenting folk, roots, and ethnic music, previously scheduled on Friday nights in June and July. The New Mexico Symphony Orchestra has also previously held a spring series of Symphony Under the Stars at the zoo, playing a program of popular family favorites (505-881-8999; www.nmso.org). Other special events each month introduce you to new members of the family at the zoo or focus on seasonal activities. You can eat inside or at an outdoor table at the Cottonwood Cafe (505-764-6215) near the duck pond, which is open all year, and in the summer season at the Matunda Cafe in the Africa exhibit area or the Phoenix Plaza Snackbar. Buy souvenirs, books, and film at Critter Outfitters and the Jungle Shop or exotic gifts at the Out of Africa shop in the Africa exhibit. No pets are allowed in the zoo except service animals, but kennels are available. It is part of the Albuquerque Biological Park; see that entry for details on money-saving combo tickets for the Rio Grande Botanic Garden and Albuquerque Aquarium and the train service connecting the facilities. Open seven days.

TINGLEY BEACH
1800 Tingley Drive SW
(505) 768-2000
www.cabq.gov/biopark

Visiting Tingley Beach is a lovely way to get out of the city, within the city. There are three fishing lakes and a model boat pond to float your own boat or "rent" one to test your skills at sailing a miniature yacht—buy tokens inside Tingley Beach Station. You can also rent pedal boats and bicycles in the summer. The beach links into the 16-mile paved Paseo del Bosque bike trail. Or just come to stroll and feed the ducks or relax at the picnic tables. There's a great statue of Clyde and Carrie Tingley, as part of Albuquerque's public art program. Clyde Tingley was the governor of New Mexico for whom the beach and other places around Albuquerque are named, including Tingley Stadium at EXPO New Mexico. You can grab a snack at the Tingley Café, and Tingley Beach Outfitters sells fishing licenses, gear, and also Rio Line train tickets when available. You can take your pet on a leash to Tingley Beach. The beach is free and is open seven days, from sunrise to sunset.

HISTORICAL SITES AND OUTDOOR ATTRACTIONS

CORONADO STATE MONUMENT $
485 Kuaua Road
Bernalillo
(505) 867-5351
www.nmmonuments.org

On this historical site you can see the partially reconstructed ruins of the Kuaua Pueblo, which was occupied from 1300 AD until it was abandoned toward the end of the 16th century. Kuaua means "evergreen" in the Tiwa language, and in the 1500s the original pueblo had some 1,200 rooms. The site is named for Francisco Vásquez de Coronado, who came to the valley with his soldiers in 1540 searching for the legendary Seven Cities of Gold. It is believed that Coronado camped near here. Kuaua's earthen pueblo was excavated in the 1930s, uncovering an 18-square-foot kiva with murals showing hundreds of figures of dancers, animals, and other ceremonial symbols. The excavation was carried out by New Deal WPA workers, and rather than risk damage and erosion to the pueblo's old adobe walls, the archaeologists had reconstructed walls built over the ruins, to show the outline of the pueblo. Today you can take an interpretive trail through the architectural remains of the village and climb down a ladder into the reconstructed square kiva with reproductions of the murals. The handsome Coronado Visitor Center, designed by the renowned New Mexico architect John Gaw Meem and opened in 1940, houses fifteen of the original mural sections, plus Indian and Spanish colonial artifacts. Outside are shaded picnic tables with superb views of the Rio Grande and across the valley to the mountains and trails down to the river. It's a beautiful place to take in the scenery and imagine the flourishing life of the Kuaua village here, half a millennium ago. Closed on Tuesday.

Bernalillo is 17 miles north of Albuquerque. From I-25, take exit 242 to State Highway 550/44 heading west. Follow for 1.7 miles to Kuaua Road on your right.

PETROGLYPH NATIONAL MONUMENT
Las Imágenes Visitor Center
Unser Boulevard NW at Western Trail
(505) 899-0205
www.nps.gov/petr

New Mexico has been big on art from the start, and at Petroglyph National Monument there are over 20,000 petroglyphs, mostly made between 400 and 700 years ago, but some may be up to 3,000 years old. Petroglyphs are images pecked or carved into the boulders using a rock or a stone chisel and a hammer stone. The monument is on Albuquerque's 17-mile-long West Mesa escarpment and covers over 7,000 acres; it is one of the largest petroglyph sites in North America. The escarpment began to be created around 150,000 years ago, when a series of volcanic eruptions forced flows of lava from a large crack in the earth's crust. The resulting black basalt rocks, with a patina created by natural cycles over time, later proved to be a natural canvas for Indian ancestors. By painstakingly pecking off the thin top layers of "desert varnish" or patina to reveal the lighter rock beneath, they created the high-contrast petroglyphs we can see today. Images are of animals and birds, human figures, mythological creatures, tribal symbols, geometric symbols, and many other cultural and religious symbols that clearly had great significance to the makers, considering the labor required to create them. The full meaning of some of the symbols remains unknown. The geographic positioning of each petroglyph in relationship to the landscape, the horizon, and other petroglyphs is also considered to have significance. While most petroglyphs were created by Pueblo, Apache, and Navajo peoples, some were made by early Spanish settlers. The escarpment is on the National Register of Historic Places, and the Petroglyph National Monument was established in 1990 to protect this culturally important site. It is operated in a partnership between the National Park Service and the City of Albuquerque.

There are four areas to explore in the monument. I recommend Boca Negra Canyon for first-time visitors who are mainly coming to see petroglyphs rather than for hiking opportunities, especially if you are coming as a family. Boca Negra Canyon has three trails from easy to moderately strenuous, all designed to lead you past some excellent and varied petroglyphs, with signs to explain the images. Round-trip times to walk these three trails are approximately 5, 15, or 30 minutes, respectively. If you take the 30-minute Mesa Point Trail to the top of the lava flow, you're likely to want to pause for a while and take in the terrific views across Albuquerque to the Sandias and north to the Sangre de Cristo and Jemez mountains. Trails are partially paved but not level and a bit bumpy or narrow in places. They are not recommended for wheelchairs or strollers, and walkers are advised to wear hiking shoes. With that caveat these trails offer an accessible way for visitors of various ages and physical abilities to take a close look at some wonderful petroglyphs. You could well see lizards, hawks, roadrunners, snakes, millipedes, and other wildlife in this and the other areas of the monument. At Boca Negra Canyon there are restrooms, a shaded picnic area, and a water fountain. It is 2 miles north of the Visitor Center on Unser Boulevard, a quarter mile north of Montaño.

Pets are not allowed in Boca Negra Canyon, except services animals on a leash. Pets are permitted in other parts of the park, also on a leash. As with any outdoor activity in Albuquerque, take sunscreen, hat, sunglasses, and water, and heed advice provided by park officials at their Web site and in trail guides. Information on other areas to hike in the Petroglyph National Monument can be found in the Parks and Recreation chapter.

Although you can head directly to any of the park trails, I recommend dropping by the Las Imágenes Visitor Center first. Here you can pick up detailed trail guides and other information, and the center has reconstructed petroglyphs that you can touch to discover how they feel. There are also books and other items for sale. The visitor center and park is open year-round for day use only, except on major holidays. Some park areas may be closed in bad weather. There is no fee to visit, but there is a car-parking fee at Boca Negra Canyon of $1 durng the week and $2 on weekends.

The monument is sacred land to American Indians. In the interests of preservation, it is prohibited to touch the petroglyphs, and it is illegal to remove or in any way alter the petroglyphs or any objects in the monument.

i Wheelchair accessibility at Petroglyph National Monument varies. Las Imágenes Visitor Center is wheelchair accessible. The trails at Boca Negra Canyon are not, although you can see petroglyphs from the shady ramada here, at the foot of the Macaw and Cliff Base trails, and restrooms are accessible. Rinconada Canyon is largely inaccessible. A trail on the Volcanoes area is partially prepared for wheelchair access, and at the time of writing there are plans to extend it to a full half mile of accessibility. The restrooms and shade structure are accessible. Wheelchair users are advised to call (505) 899-0205 for the latest information and advice on each area.

SANDIA PEAK TRAMWAY $$$
East end of Tramway Road, NE
(505) 856-7325
www.sandiapeak.com

The world's longest aerial tramway lifts you to the top of 10,378-foot Sandia Peak, passing through four climate zones and past dramatic granite spires and cliffs. On the ride you might spot mule deer, black bear, bobcats, and other wildlife in the mountain and canyons below or fly alongside a golden eagle, a hawk, or ravens. Once you're at the summit, enjoy top-of-the-world views

Albuquerque Old Town

A must-see for all visitors, historic Old Town is where the city of Albuquerque began. Despite the city's sprawling expansion since its foundation over 300 years ago, Old Town remains both its emotional heart and a center of community for holiday celebrations and fiestas, art, culture, shopping, and dining. The only way to really get acquainted with Old Town is the old-fashioned way—on foot. Park your car, take your camera, and wander the narrow streets, where you'll find beautiful adobe architecture, art galleries, and flowery courtyards and patios around every corner.

The historic Old Town area is centered between Mountain Road on the north, Central Avenue on the south, Rio Grande Boulevard on the west, and 19th Street on the east.

The hub of activity is the Old Town Plaza, with the landmark San Felipe de Neri church. Construction on the first Old Town church began in 1706, under the direction of a Franciscan priest, Fray Manuel Moreno. It was originally called San Francisco Xavier church, but the Duke of Alburquerque changed the name to San Felipe de Neri to honor King Philip of Spain. This church stood on the west side of the plaza and was completed by 1718–19. It collapsed following the heavy rains of 1792, and the church we see now was constructed on the north side of the plaza a year later. Its adobe walls are 5 feet thick. Around 1853 the church received a new roof, altar, and pulpit. The two bell towers, now white-painted and easily recognizable from a distance, were added in 1861. The church is listed on the National Register of Historic Places, and a parish museum and gift shop are in the former Sisters of Charity convent adjacent to the church. You might notice the grapevines growing in the back courtyard. You can go inside the church, but bear in mind that it is an active place of worship. Mass is held here daily, include Mass in Spanish on Sunday morning.

The Old Town Plaza took shape in the 1700s as Spanish settlers built their dwellings close together for mutual protection against the native peoples, and in the early days the plaza was used as a corral for livestock at night. The architecture around the plaza is mainly in traditional Pueblo Spanish style, with rounded adobe walls and flat roofs supported by log beam vigas. Some of these old buildings are still homes; others have become galleries and restaurants. There are over 100 boutiques and galleries around Old Town, selling fine art, jewelry, pottery, and other southwestern and specialty items. Restaurants and cafés serve food, with cuisine ranging from authentic New Mexican to French.

The charming gazebo in the center of the plaza, looking like an old-time bandstand, is a popular spot for weddings and is the venue for outdoor entertainments. It's surrounded by mature cottonwoods shading painted wrought iron benches and grassy areas that make a sweet spot to stop and watch the world go by. The plaza has been a center for trading since its earliest

from the observation deck, where you can gaze over 11,000 square miles of gorgeous Land of Enchantment scenery. There are hiking and bike trails in the Cibola National Forest, and you can rent mountain bikes at the top. In winter ride the tramway to the Sandia Peak ski area. The High Finance restaurant on the peak serves lunch and dinner, with spectacular vistas. Reservations are recommended to dine here (505-243-9742, www.sandiapeakrestaurants.com), although you can also just pop in for a drink. The Sandia Peak Tramway has taken more than 9 million passengers up the mountain since its debut trip in 1966. The journey is 2.7 miles long diagonally, rising 3,819 feet from the base station, and takes about 15 minutes each way. Normal speed is 12 miles per hour, which works out to nearly 18 feet per second. Two towers support the tram cables between the base terminal and the top terminal. The 232-foot tall Tower One is built to lean at an

outdoor markets, and the tradition continues today. Beneath the old portal lining the eastern edge of the square, artisans spread out blankets to display their handmade silver and turquoise jewelry and other crafts.

Five different flags have flown over this plaza, starting with the Spanish flag from 1598 to 1821, followed by the flags of Mexico (1821–1846), the United States (1846 to present), the Confederate States (1862), and the state of New Mexico (1912–present). The two cannons in the plaza are replicas of those buried nearby by retreating Confederate troops in 1862. The originals are in the Albuquerque Museum of Art and History.

Leading up to Christmas, luminarias light the soft adobe curves of Old Town, and in summer there are outdoor salsa parties, flamenco and tango dances and other music events at the gazebo; strolling mariachis; and block parties and patio parties in the streets winding around the plaza.

Don't miss the gorgeous and colorful mosaic flourishing across the east gate by the Albuquerque Museum of Art and History parking lot, welcoming you to Old Town Plaza Vieja! Also check out the candlelit Chapel of our Lady of Guadalupe nestled away in the Patio Escondido, 404 San Felipe NW.

The New Mexico Gunfighters Association performs dramatic—and often funny—Old West plays featuring lively gunfights around the plaza on most Sunday afternoons from April to October (the gunshots are of course blanks). The gunfights have most recently been held on S. San Felipe Street, near the Rattlesnake Museum.

Museums in and around Old Town are the Albuquerque Museum of Art and History, New Mexico Museum of Natural History and Science, Explora, Rattlesnake Museum, and Turquoise Museum. You can take a guided walking tour of the history and legends of Old Town or a spooky nighttime ghost tour with Tours of Old Town, (505) 246-TOUR, www.toursofoldtown.com. Or save your feet and take a guided tour on a Segway around the historic quarter. Call Segway New Mexico at (505) 244-1420, www.segwaynm.com.

The Visitors Information Center is a little hidden away on Plaza Don Luis on Romero NW. To find it turn right outside San Felipe de Neri church to Romero at the end of the block. Plaza Don Luis is on the opposite side of the road, a little to the right. The Visitor Center is at the back of the plaza on the left. It is open daily, although hours vary by season. Plaza Don Luis is also the departure point for the Tours of Old Town walking tours and ABQ Trolley Co. city tour. The Old Town Web site, with a map and information, is www.albuquerqueoldtown.com. Comprehensive information on the Old Town current events calendar is kept up to date at the City of Albuquerque Web site: www.cabq.gov/crs.

18-degree angle, so if you notice that small tilt, don't worry! The maximum clean span between Tower Two and the top terminal is 1.5 miles, making this the third longest clear span in the world. There are two tramcars, and when they pass each other at the midway point, they are nearly 1,000 feet above the ground. This feat of engineering was manufactured by Bell Engineering of Lucerne in Switzerland. Tram cars depart every 20 or 30 minutes, and each carries up to 50 passengers.

Even if you don't have a head for heights or don't have time for a tramway trip, it's well worth making a visit to the base terminal, which at 6,559 feet still has terrific views over the city and across the valley to the west. In the terminal building Sandiago's Mexican Grill (505-856-6692, www.sandiapeakrestaurants.com) is a colorful cantina-style restaurant serving lunch and dinner with a full bar, and you can look out through the windows running the length of the restaurant or from the deck. Sandiago's Deli is also here, where you can grab a snack or drinks either to take up the tramway or to hang out at one of the picnic tables outside. Note that drinks taken on the tramway must have a screw-on lid. The Sandia Tram Gift Store, also in the base terminal, sells southwestern souvenirs and other items. The New Mexico Ski Museum is a one-room collection of the state's ski memorabilia, vintage pictures, and other exhibits showing the history of skiing in New Mexico and highlighting important individuals in the Ski Hall of Fame. Although the museum is small, it is free to drop in here, and the displays have a certain charm in showing just how far the ski industry has come, thanks to early pioneers of the sport.

No pets or bikes are allowed on the tramway. Tram tickets are discounted if you have dinner reservations in the High Finance Restaurant or Sandiago's Mexican Grill. See more information on High Finance in the Restaurant chapter. A fee of $1 is charged to cars at the entrance to the tramway base terminal, whatever your purpose in coming here. The entrance is manned between 8:30 a.m. and 5 p.m. There is no charge after 5 p.m. when the attendant goes home!

The tramway is open 7 days year-round, except for two 10-day maintenance periods in April and November. The tramway also stops on a handful of occasions each year for bad weather or high winds. If in doubt, check before setting off.

The Sandia Peak Tramway is at the east end of Tramway Road, where it dead-ends in the parking lot. Tramway Road intersects at the north end of Tramway Boulevard and the turnoff from Tramway Boulevard is clearly signed. By interstate it's approximately 9 miles north from I-40 exit 167, or from exit 234 on I-25 follow Tramway Road east.

i **Get the best of all worlds by riding up the Sandia Peak Tramway during daylight hours for the full scenic view, have a meal or a drink in the High Finance Restaurant to watch the sunset, and return back down the mountain after dark with the city lights sparkling below.**

MUSEUMS & CULTURAL CENTERS

ALBUQUERQUE MUSEUM OF ART AND HISTORY $

2000 Mountain Road NW
(505) 243-7255
www.cabq.gov/museum

The museum takes you through four centuries of life in Albuquerque and the Middle Rio Grande Valley, including exhibits of crafts and decorative arts, textiles, maps, armor, photographs, and artifacts. On the way you pick up all kinds of interesting tidbits, from finding out what was the greatest compliment you could pay a 16th-century caballero to learning that planked wood floor boards weren't used in New Mexico till the 1850s. Before that interior floors were packed earth, often hardened with ox blood. The art collection presents historical and contemporary regional paintings in chronological order from the late 1800s. These include works from the influential Transcendental Painting Group, Los Cinco Pintores, and the Taos Society of Artists. A portrait collection of notable New Mexicans introduces you to figures from the arts and politics. There are also art pieces in all media by contemporary regional, national, and international artists. The museum hosts temporary historical and arts exhibits curated around regional themes. The Gem Theater has a daily schedule of films about Albuquerque's history. Outside is the fine Sculpture Garden with more than 60 pieces in a range of styles and media. Docent tours of the sculpture garden are offered from April through November, at 10 a.m. on Tuesday to Saturday. Or take a self-guided tour using the sculpture garden map available at the front desk. Docent tours of the gallery itself are at 2 p.m. daily. This handsome and modern museum is in Old Town, and the museum offers a free daily walking tour of Old Town to museum patrons with the price of admission, from mid-March to mid-December, at 11 a.m. The Gallery Store sells books, videos, glass, jewelry, and arts and crafts. The City Treats Museum Cafe is open for lunch, beverages, and pastries. The museum hosts music and other performance events on summer evenings in the amphitheater, with separate admission fees. By the way, the greatest compliment you could pay a 16th-century caballero was to tell him he rode well *en ambas sillas*—in both saddles and styles; that is, in both the *a la jineta* light and fast cavalry style introduced to Spain by the Moors, and the *a la brida* traditional style of heavily armored European knights. Closed Monday. Admission is free on Sunday from 9 a.m. to 1 p.m. and free all day on the first Wednesday of the month.

AMERICAN INTERNATIONAL RATTLESNAKE MUSEUM **$$**
202 San Felipe NW
(505) 242-6569
www.rattlesnakes.com

In the back rooms behind a shop front in Old Town, you'll find 34 different varieties of rattlesnake in what is said to be the largest collection of different species of live rattlesnakes in the world. The museum also educates visitors with plenty of myth-busting facts and tidbits about rattlesnakes, reminding us of their value in the ecosystem and their influence in Native American culture and the arts. Besides rattlesnakes, you can see other snakes and creatures such as vipers, pythons, scorpions, salamander, tortoise, poisonous Mexican beaded lizard, and tropical spiders. You're in quite close quarters with the critters behind glass, so you see them up close and personal. There is often the opportunity to touch a nonvenomous snake. A collection of snakey memorabilia includes rattler-inspired auto license plates, beers, and other products; an exhibit of clippings showing reptiles in the news; and a 1910 snake-skull opium casket. On the way out you'll receive a certificate of bravery. The gift store up front sells T-shirts, jewelry, pottery, and shed rattlesnake fangs and skin. Open seven days.

ANDERSON-ABRUZZO ALBUQUERQUE INTERNATIONAL BALLOON MUSEUM **$**
9201 Balloon Museum Drive NE
(505) 768-6020
www.cabq.gov/balloon

Opened in 2005 adjacent to Balloon Fiesta Park, this appropriately light, bright, and airy museum takes you through the history of ballooning from the first manned flight in 1783 and explains how and why balloons fly, including interactive exhibits. Fly in the balloon ride simulator—you don't leave the ground, but standing in a balloon gondola (the basket part) you steer your craft by tugging on the pulleys to ascend and descend, catching the breezes to navigate toward a target on the huge screen in front of you. Or practice your ballooning knots—an essential skill for mooring and tethering craft, while quick-release knots are needed for changing flight conditions. The balloon museum has a collection of gondolas, some from record-setting flights, such as the Double Eagle V gondola that made the first successful manned crossing of the Pacific Ocean in 1981, piloted by Ben Abruzzo, Larry Newman, Ron Clark, and Rocky Aoki, in a voyage that took over 84 hours. An array of colorful balloons and airships hang from the ceiling of the 59,000-square-foot space. There are exhibits on women and balloons (women took to the skies as early as 1784), the uses of balloons in science, and recreational ballooning for barnstorming, competition, and of course the Albuquerque International Balloon Fiesta. See how balloons have been used in war—for example, Germany's zeppelins that bombed England—Japanese Fugo balloon bombs, and the role of balloons in the 1870 Siege of Paris. Displays of balloon-related decorative arts and memorabilia round out a visit, from jewelry and balloon pins to a handmade quilt made of commemorative T-shirts from balloon fiestas between 1973 and 1990. The gift store is packed with more balloon-themed items. The striking exterior of the award-winning building is designed to look like a balloon lying on its side before inflation. There are good views of the Sandias from here. To reach the balloon museum, take the Alameda Boulevard exit 233 from I-25 and go about 1 mile west on Alameda to Balloon Museum Drive (on the north side of Alameda). Closed Monday. Admission is free on Sunday from 9 a.m. to 1 p.m. and free all day on the first Friday of the month.

EXPLORA $$
1701 Mountain Road NW
(505) 224-8300
www.explora.us
Although not a museum in the strict sense of the word, Albuquerque considers this innovative children's discover-and-learn center as one of its museums, and it's located near the New Mexico Museum of Natural History and Science and the Albuquerque Museum of Art and History. Explora is a paradise for kids, but adults love it, too, with hands-on educational fun in the fields of science, technology and art. Make your way around the activity tables to try your hand at experiments including Moving Air, Strange Light (light and optics), Shapes of Sound to create your own music, and My Chain Reaction, where you invent and build a moving contraption. You can also build a motor or gearshift or run experiments in the Water Lab. A great place for families to play together and make their own discoveries among the 250 exhibits, Explora also holds adults-only nights every other month, with live entertainment. The Kidstuff chapter tells you more about what's here for children. Open seven days.

INDIAN PUEBLO CULTURAL CENTER $$
2401 12th Street NW
(505) 843-7270, (866) 855-7902
www.indianpueblo.org
Owned and operated by the nineteen Pueblo tribes of New Mexico, the Indian Pueblo Cultural Center serves as an excellent introduction to the history, arts, and lives of the state's native peoples. The handsome building is modeled after Pueblo Bonito in Chaco Canyon and encloses a circular inner plaza where Indian dances are held every weekend. The center underwent a $2 million expansion in 2008. Don't miss the museum on the lower level with the permanent exhibition "Our Land, Our Culture, Our Story." This leads you through the history of the Pueblo peoples from long before the arrival of the Europeans through early contact with the Spanish to the Pueblo Revolt of 1680 and up to the current day. Pick up the museum's self-guided tour pamphlet for the story behind the exhibits. A small theater screens short films on San Ildefonso potter Maria Martinez and painter Pablita Velarde of Santa Clara. The museum also houses contemporary arts and crafts from all of the 19 pueblos, showing the distinctive designs and craft traditions of each. Both indoors and outside in the courtyard, large murals by Native artists similarly illustrate varying artistic styles. The Indian Pueblo Cultural Center has a collection of over 2,000 artifacts, including pottery, jewelry, textiles, paintings, archeological objects, and photographs. South-wing galleries present changing Native American arts and educational exhibits, curated around various themes. From summer 2009 a new permanent installation shows the Saints of the Pueblos, a collection of 23 retablos by santero Charles Carrillo, representing the patron saints of the nineteen current pueblos and four extinct pueblos and exploring the role of Catholicism in Native history and contemporary life.

Native American dances are held every weekend, twice a day on Saturday and Sunday, from the first weekend of April through the last weekend of October. Between June and September there is also a daily dance on Thursday and Friday. From November through March there is one dance a day on Saturday and Sunday. Check with the center for current times. There is also a monthly art demonstration workshop. The Pueblo House is an activity center for children, open for specific sessions only. See the Kidstuff chapter for more information. The gift shop sells authentic handcrafts and arts by Native artisans, including jewelry, pottery, rugs, sculptures, paintings, and kachina dolls. There are also books on history and other subjects written from an Indian perspective, cards, and Native American music. It's worth dropping in to the Pueblo Harvest Café and Bakery for a cup of Starbucks coffee; a

i **The Indian Pueblo Cultural Center's *avanyu* logo (*avanyu* is a Tewa word meaning "water serpent") draws on imagery from San Ildefonso and Santa Clara Pueblo pottery and symbolizes the importance of water to desert dwellers.**

quick snack; or a full breakfast, lunch, or dinner of authentic Native-Fusion cuisine. See the listing in the Restaurants section for more information. Or just pick up some salsa or fresh oven bread to take home. Café hours vary, so call the restaurant at (505) 724-3510 to check opening hours and for reservations. The Indian Pueblo Cultural Center is open seven days a week.

i **Santeros are literally saint-makers! These artists craft santos–carved and painted images of saints. Santos may be in the form of a *retablo,* with the saint, religious icon, or scene carved and painted on a flat wood panel, or as a *bulto,* a sculpture of the saint often carved from cottonwood and then hand-painted. Santos are familiar sights in New Mexico's churches, on home altars, or tucked in a *nicho,* which is an alcove or recess in an adobe wall.**

MAXWELL MUSEUM OF ANTHROPOLOGY
University of New Mexico
Main Campus
(505) 277-4405
http://maxwellmuseum.unm.edu

One of the country's most highly acclaimed anthropological museums, the Maxwell Museum holds over 10 million items, including a superb collection of art and artifacts from the Southwest and extensive holdings from throughout the American continent, Africa, Asia, Australia, and the Pacific Islands. The emphasis here is on the Southwest's cultural heritage, leading visitors through 11,000 years of the region's history and the lives of Native peoples, including a reconstruction of a room at Chaco Canyon. An "Ancestors" exhibit travels still further back in time, tracing evolution through 4 million years to the origins of man, via "Lucy," the Neanderthals, and *Homo habilis.* There is also a reconstructed cave with Ice Age drawings. Don't miss the courtyard at the back of the museum through the gift shop, with an adobe horno oven and a splendid 46-foot-high totem pole. The totem pole comes from British Columbia and dates back to circa 1903, carved and painted on cedar by artist Charlie James. The totem pole depicts faces of ancestors and animals including a bird, a wolf, a whale, and a bear with a salmon. Even if the museum is closed, you can see the totem pole from the back gate of the courtyard. In the gift shop there are books, pottery, jewelry, and fetishes. The Maxwell Museum was the first public museum in Albuquerque, founded in 1932 as the Museum of Anthropology of the University of New Mexico. Closed Sunday and Monday. Admission is free. The Maxwell Museum is on the University of New Mexico main campus, on Redondo Drive east of University Boulevard between Las Lomas and Dr. M. L. King Jr. Avenue. Limited parking is available in the lot off Redondo, parallel to University, on the west side of the museum. Park here, and ask in the museum for a parking permit to leave visible in your car.

NATIONAL HISPANIC CULTURAL CENTER ART MUSEUM **$**
1701 4th Street SW
(505) 246-2261
www.nhccnm.org

The Art Museum at the National Hispanic Cultural Center holds over 2,000 pieces of Hispanic and Latino art in its permanent collection, from traditional crafts and art styles to cutting-edge contemporary works in all media imaginable. It also presents themed temporary exhibitions by leading artists. The History & Literary Arts building, a renovated Works Progress Administration schoolhouse, documents Hispanic history, culture, and literature and features changing exhibitions. The center opened in 2000, on 50 acres of land in the Barelas district, one of the oldest neighborhoods in Albuquerque along the Camino Real. Its mission is to preserve, promote, and advance Hispanic culture, arts, and humanities, and in 2008 it received 225,000 visitors. The campus includes the Roy E. Disney Center for the Performing Arts, which hosts music, theater, dance, literary readings, and other cultural events and programs.

The center is well worth a visit, not only to check out the exhibits but to see the stunning

Village of Corrales

A pretty and pastoral village just north of Albuquerque but a world away in atmosphere, Corrales holds on to its rural roots and makes a charming destination for lunch, shopping, and a little cool air on hot city days. It is also home to the historic San Ysidro Church and Casa San Ysidro. As you drive from Albuquerque along the Scenic Byway into Corrales, tucked between high-tech Rio Rancho and the rolling Rio Grande, you're welcomed by a sign reading, THIS IS AN ANIMAL-FRIENDLY VILLAGE—DRIVE WITH CARE. That sign sets the tone perfectly for your visit to this community of 7,300 people, with its pink and white blossoming chitalpa trees, grand old cottonwoods, and adobe homes and galleries surrounded by rounded adobe walls and flowering shrubs lining the length of the main street. The village name comes from the historic corrals—enclosures to hold horses and cattle—and locals still wax nostalgic about the Lewie Wickham song "What Is Corrales," with lyrics about how the village's human population was vastly outnumbered by dogs and horses!

Although there is evidence that Corrales Valley was inhabited from around 500 AD, Spanish settlers started to make their home in this fertile area in 1712, and French and Italian farmers arrived in the 19th century, bringing knowledge of viniculture that grew Corrales's reputation as a wine producer. You'll see vines growing along the side of the road, and you can visit Corrales Winery for free tours and tastings Wednesday through Sunday, from noon to 5 p.m. (6275 Corrales Road, 505-898-5165, www.corraleswinery.com). Contact Milagro Vineyards in advance to make an appointment for tours and tastings and to buy wine (985 West Ella, 505-898-3998, www.milagrovineyardsandwinery.com).

Casa San Ysidro is part of the Albuquerque Museum of Art and History, a partially reconstructed 18th- and 19th-century hacienda, with a chapel, central plazuela, and enclosed corral. Inside you'll see Spanish colonial furniture and Hispanic New Mexican artifacts, including a loom from the late 1700s. The house is not open for drop-in visits, but there are one-hour public tours from Wednesday through Sunday ($4 for adults, no reservation needed). Times vary by day and season, so check for current details. There are no tours in December and January, although there is usually a holiday open house in early December. Casa San Ysidro is located at 973 Old Church Road, and you can get visitor information at (505) 898-3915 or www.cabq.gov/museum.

The Old San Ysidro Church (966 Old Church Road) is a sweet old adobe that now serves as

architecture inside and out, which combines Mesoamerican and traditional Spanish styles both from old Europe and colonial New Mexico. Some of the barrel-vaulted ceilings and majestically high doors could make you believe you are in a 16th-century Spanish castle. Details include a tin and mica ceiling in the Bank of America Atrium, burned copper doors, and copper and mica chandeliers. The exterior of the Roy E. Disney Center for Performing Arts resembles a stylized Mayan pyramid. The leafy Barbara Richardson Plazuela, featuring a pool and fountains, is a serene spot to pause between sightseeing activities.

Outside the main building the round El Torreón tower replicates the watchtowers built by Spanish settlers. The interior of the Torreón is expected to be open to the public in fall 2010, featuring a fresco painting by artist Frederico Vigil that will cover 4,000 square feet, including the ceiling and 45-foot-high walls, and depict Hispanic cultural heritage from prehistory to the present day.

La Tiendita gift store has a beautiful selection of Latin American and New Mexican arts, crafts, books, jewelry, accessories, decorative objects, and music. La Fonda del Bosque restaurant serves local dishes for breakfast, lunch, and a set-price

a community center and venue for music concerts. It was built after L'Iglesia Jesus, Maria y Jose, the first colonial church in Corrales, which dates back to the mid-1700s, was destroyed in floods in 1868. Timbers, lintels, and vigas were salvaged from the flood and used to build the Old San Ysidro Church, which was constructed on higher ground! The church was deconsecrated in the 1960s and used as a performance space for a while by the Adobe Theater. In 1973–74, the Archdiocese of Santa Fe sold the church to the Corrales Historical Society, which later deeded it to the Village of Corrales. The historical society still manages the property and has made extensive renovations. The church is open to the public on weekends from June through October, between 1 p.m. and 4 p.m. It is wheelchair accessible, and docents are on hand. For information on the concerts held here, seating 175 patrons to hear music from classical to jazz to Native American with terrific acoustics inside the church's nearly 3-foot-thick adobe walls, call (877) 287-0082 or go to www.musicincorrales.org.

San Ysidro is the patron saint of farmers, and the Corrales Growers' Market is held on Sunday morning and Wednesday afternoon seasonally, just south of the post office.

The village has a flourishing arts community, and galleries and studios along Corrales Road show fine art paintings, drawings, and photography, jewelry, rugs, pottery, baskets, masks, furniture, fiber art, glass, and more. Art in the Park events are held from May through October on the third Sunday of the month in La Entrada Park (www.corralesartists.org).

Shops, restaurants, and galleries are stretched along both sides of the one leafy main street through Corrales, and the country road can get busy during peak times. Park and take a walk along the road to shop or window-shop in the galleries. Or eat in the pretty courtyard patio of the Casa Vieja restaurant, admiring this 300-year-old adobe building that's had a colorful history, including a stint as a stagecoach stop. In the winter cozy up by the kiva fireplaces in the arty dining rooms or sit at the bar for cocktails or a glass of wine, including selections from New Mexico winemakers (4541 Corrales Road, 505-508-3244, www.casaviejanm.com).

The Village of Corrales incorporated in 1971, and it lies within Sandoval County. (Until 2005, the southern part of the incorporated area rested in Bernalillo County.) Drive to Corrales by crossing the Rio Grande via Alameda Boulevard, then turn right onto Corrales Road, Highway 448. Or cross the river on Paseo del Norte, turn right onto Coors Boulevard, and continue to the junction with Corrales Road, Highway 448, where you'll bear right. The drive takes about 25 minutes from Downtown Albuquerque. Find details on seasonal events and village information at www.visitcorrales.com.

Sunday brunch. The restaurant is closed on Monday, and opening hours differ from the center's opening times; call the restaurant at (505) 247-9480. The National Hispanic Cultural Center is free to visit just to look around the building and grounds or to go to the gift store or restaurant, but there is an admission fee for the art museum. Closed on Monday.

NATIONAL MUSEUM OF NUCLEAR SCIENCE & HISTORY **$$**
601 Eubank Boulevard SE
(505) 245-2137
www.nuclearmuseum.org

With the tagline "reactions welcome," the museum explores every aspect of nuclear science, from the past to the present and looking ahead to the future. Exhibits cover the history of the Atomic Age, including the top-secret World War II Manhattan Project to develop the first atomic bomb and the Trinity test site in New Mexico. Visitors also learn about the factors informing the decision to drop two atomic bombs on Hiroshima and Nagasaki and the aftereffects of that world-changing event. Other exhibits examine what radiation is and how it occurs in our world; relate the story of X-ray technology; and introduce visitors to pioneers in nuclear physics, medicine, and quantum mechanics, including Albert Einstein and Marie Curie. Interactive exhibits include Energy Encounter, exploring the role of nuclear power amid the range of alternative energies available for the future. Kids will get a kick out of cranking a handle to launch a Ping-Pong ball; a chemical reaction produces gases that ignite, and the heat energy propels the ball. You can also take a look inside a re-created family fallout shelter from the Cold War era and learn about the Cold War nuclear arms race. An area on the cultural influences of the Atomic Age focuses on music, movies, and TV, as well as products from toys to food and appliances. Outside, the nine-acre Heritage Park displays planes, rockets, and missiles, with such historic aircraft as a B52-B Stratofortress used in Operation Dominic in 1962 for the last atmospheric tests, including the airdrop of a nuclear device. Friendly and informed volunteer docents who have worked in related fields are on hand to talk to you about the exhibits. The museum store sells books, DVDs, gifts, and other merchandise inspired by the science themes. This is the nation's only congressionally chartered museum in its field, housed in a recently constructed 30,000-square-foot building. Formerly the National Atomic Museum, the museum changed its name and moved to the new Eubank Boulevard location in 2009. (Note that some older maps will still show its previous Old Town address.) Open seven days a week.

NEW MEXICO MUSEUM OF NATURAL HISTORY AND SCIENCE **$$**
1801 Mountain Road NW
(505) 841-2800
www.nmnaturalhistory.org

Take a fascinating stroll through 12 billion years of natural history, and discover New Mexico's heritage from dinosaurs to space exploration. The TimeTracks permanent exhibit over two floors of the museum leads you on a journey from the very formation of the universe and the origins of planet Earth, through the "dawn of the dinosaurs" into the period when much of New Mexico was covered by an inland sea, on to the later volcanic era, up to the Ice Age, and into the present day. This breathtaking tour introduces you to marvels that include the Seismosaurus dinosaur, a 30-ton Jurassic giant known only in New Mexico. At 110 feet in length, it is the longest land animal of all time. Dinosaur fossils at the museum include a T. rex jawbone with teeth, and you can see a 40-foot-long replica skeleton of Stan, the second largest Tyrannosaurus rex ever found, poised for attack. Science exhibits include a full-size model of the Mars Rover—and you can move the model camera and track results on a monitor. The StartUp gallery describes Albuquerque's place in the history of personal computers, including Altair, the first commercially successful PC, and the early work of whiz kids Bill Gates and Paul Allen in their Duke City days, which led to the establishment of Microsoft. There are fun, interactive exhibits here (for example, design your own computer program) as there are throughout the museum. A Space Frontiers exhibit will run through 2011 or longer and features the heritage and future of space exploration in New Mexico, from the earliest Native American observatories at Chaco Canyon. The museum also includes a planetarium with daily child-friendly shows, and the Lockheed Martin DynaTheater, with a five-story-high screen showing natural history films. The DynaTheater and the planetarium require separate entrance fees. The NatureWorks Discovery Store sells dinosaur- and science-related gifts and books, and the M Cafe (505-841-2804) serves breakfast and lunch and has been voted "Best Undiscovered Gem" by the weekly *Alibi* newspaper. Catch a breather here during your museum visit, sitting along the counter by the window to watch the world go by. No admission fee is required to go into the NatureWorks store or M Cafe. Museum entry is free on these dates: the second Tuesday in January; second Tuesday in February; September 11; Veterans Day, November 11; and Christmas Eve day. These free days do not include entry to the DynaTheater or planetarium. Residents of some New Mexico counties receive free entry for specific months each year; check the Web site for details. New Mexico seniors over 60 are admitted free every Wednesday. Open seven days but closed on all Mondays in September and January.

Coelophysis is New Mexico's State Fossil and has only been found here. Coelophysis was one of the first dinosaurs, and it roamed New Mexico 205 to 210 million years ago. A biped up to 9.8 feet in length and weighing up to 100 pounds, it had a long neck and tail, and it moved fast. It had over 100 pointed and serrated teeth and ate meat, including cannibalized smaller Coelophysis. You can see Coelophysis at the New Mexico Museum of Natural History and Science.

TINKERTOWN MUSEUM **$**
121 Sandia Crest Road / Highway 536
Sandia Park
(505) 281-5233
www.tinkertown.com

This extraordinary museum centers around the wood-carved figures and scenes created by Ross J. Ward, including an animated and incredibly detailed miniature 1880s Western town and a three-ring circus. Press a button and the miniatures move, in settings meticulously furnished with antique toys. That's only the half of it, though, as you wander through a maze of 22 rooms literally packed to the rafters with folk art, memorabilia, and curiosities of all kinds. Esmerelda, a 1940s arcade-style automated fortune-teller, reveals your fate when you pop in a quarter. Otto, an automatic one-man band plays a tune on accordion, drums, and xylophone. There's a collection of wedding figurines, from 1840s wax figures to a bride and groom carved in a nutshell. See the size 22 shoes that belonged to 8'4" Big Louie Moilanew, "the largest man in the world," and step into his footprint to compare your own feet to his. The building itself is a magical warren, constructed with over 50,000 glass bottles studding the concrete walls, horseshoes set in the floor, signs with philosophical or funny messages, and every surface covered with collections of Americana, Western memorabilia, and whatever took Ward's fancy, from antique tools to bullet pencils. Outside there's a 35-foot boat that sailed around the world, old wagons and buggies, and an art-car Jeep Cherokee, painted and decorated with coins, shells, toys, and models. The gift store sells an equally diverse and fascinating collection of souvenirs, games, toys, trinkets, and curios, all fairly low-dollar items. Tinkertown began as a hobby when Ward carved a miniature general store in 1962, the only thing he intended to make at the time. The hobby took over for the rest of his life (Ward died in 2002), and as Ward said, "I did all this while you were watching TV!" The private museum is now run by Ward's wife. You will want a few quarters for the antique arcade-style machines, but if you don't have any, the counter staff will make change. This museum is just off the Turquoise Trail, so you may want to combine it with a day trip, or it's about 25 miles from Downtown Albuquerque. Take I-40 east to exit 175, then north on Highway 14 for 6 miles through Cedar Crest, and turn left on Highway 536/Sandia Crest Road, the road that leads to the Sandia Peak ski area. Tinkertown is 1.5 miles on the left. Tinkertown Museum is open seven days a week from April 1 through November 1.

It's worth pausing to chat with the friendly staff on the Tinkertown Museum ticket desk. They are all friends of the Ward family or people who know the museum well, so they will give you lots of insider background and stories on the history and can answer any questions.

TURQUOISE MUSEUM **$**
2107 Central Avenue NW
(505) 247-8650
www.turquoisemuseum.com

Explore the history and mystery of turquoise in this privately owned museum that houses turquoise specimens from over 100 mines. Discover how the gemstone is mined, walk through a mock mine, and learn about the value of turquoise, with advice on how to choose the gem when buying and how to care for it once you have it home. A lapidary display and daily demonstrations show how the stone is polished and shaped. If you take a piece of turquoise to the museum (one piece!) you'll receive an evaluation of its worth and identification of the mine source. Once you've learned all there is to know about turquoise, you can stop off in the gift store and treat yourself. Closed Sunday.

Turquoise has been New Mexico's State Gem since 1967.

UNM GEOLOGY MUSEUM
Northrop Hall
UNM Main Campus
(505) 277-4204
epswww.unm.edu/museum.htm

Here you can see minerals, fossils, and rocks from the 20,000 catalogued specimens in the University of New Mexico's geological collections. A highlight is the femur of a hadrosaur found in Farmington, New Mexico. It is estimated to be from one of the last dinosaurs to have lived in New Mexico before their extinction around 66 million years ago. The thigh bone is not under glass, so you can inspect it closely. An exhibit on the 15-million-year-long "age of elephants" in New Mexico includes the right femur of a mammoth, found near Deming. There are colorful displays of outstanding minerals and gems and corals from the former seabeds of New Mexico.

Visitor parking for an hourly fee is on the UNM campus in the Cornell Parking Structure on Redondo Drive; the entry is just east of Stanford Drive. Go into the Welcome Center on the ground floor in the southwest corner of the parking structure to pick up a campus map for the short walk to Northrop Hall. Basic directions: Walk north from the parking structure, between the Welcome Center and the Center for the Arts, then turn left between the Center for the Arts and the Student Union Building. Continue directly ahead to the circular Homage to Grandmother Earth sculpture, and on the far side of that sculpture lies Northrop Hall. The UNM Geology Museum is open Monday through Friday, except UNM holidays. It closes for lunch. Admission is free.

UNM METEORITE MUSEUM
Northrop Hall
UNM Main Campus
epswww.unm.edu/meteoritemuseum/

This one-room museum is packed with meteorites from the 600-piece collection of the University of New Mexico's Institute of Meteoritics. Expecially of interest is the Norton County meteorite, the world's largest single piece of an achondrite meteorite, weighing approximately 2,200 pounds, which fell on Kansas in 1948. The Navajo iron meteorite, found in Apache County, Arizona, in 1921, also has an interesting story, which is told in the display. Native American Indians had known about this meteorite since around 1600 and named it Pish le gin e gin, meaning "black iron." The meteorite was found buried with Indian beads. Documentation includes a 1922 photo of the Navajo meteorite being loaded on the railroad, when 20-year-old Marvin Porter, who helped load it, described the experience as "the first time I had my foot on a star."

Visitor parking for an hourly fee is on the UNM campus in the Cornell Parking Structure on Redondo Drive; the entry is just east of Stanford Drive. Go into the Welcome Center on the ground floor in the southwest corner of the parking structure to pick up a campus map for the short walk to Northrop Hall. Basic directions: Walk north from the parking structure, between the Welcome Center and the Center for the Arts, then turn left between the Center for the Arts and the Student Union Building. Continue directly ahead to the circular Homage to Grandmother Earth sculpture, and on the far side of that sculpture lies Northrop Hall. The UNM Meteorite Museum is open Monday through Friday, except UNM holidays. Admission is free.

UNSER RACING MUSEUM **$$**
1776 Montano Road NW
(505) 341-1776
www.unserracingmuseum.com

Honoring the Albuquerque Unser family racing dynasty and the sport itself, the museum features classic race cars and memorabilia from racing history. The family has won the Indy 500 nine times, four of which Al Unser Sr. won. The museum is organized in six sections around a central "winner's circle" hub, with exhibits showcasing four generations of Unser drivers and their cars, the changing technologies in design and engineering, plus a Nascar simulator and interactive kiosks and videos. The museum store stocks books, clothing, collectibles, and gifts with a motoring theme. Open seven days.

i Sometimes you'll see a "chautauqua" advertised in Albuquerque or nearby. A chautauqua is a themed event combining education and entertainment, including music, performance, lectures, or other cultural offerings, sometimes with audience participation. Traveling chautauqua shows and assemblies were popular in the late 19th and early 20th centuries. They were originally a form of religious training, based on the activities of New York's Chautauqua Institution. Free chautauquas in Albuquerque have recently included an Old-Time Traveling Medicine Show and a Living History Chautauqua in Old Town.

SIGHTSEEING TOURS

ABQ TROLLEY CO. $$$$
Plaza Don Luis
303 Romero Street NW
(505) 240-8000
www.abqtrolley.com

The Best of ABQ trolley tour runs several times a day between April and November and is a good way to get acquainted with the lay of the land, escorted by a local guide who tells you the history and interesting tidbits on all the sights. It follows an 18-mile route for a 66-minute journey around key city destinations, including Old Town and the nearby museums, Downtown, Route 66, Nob Hill, sports stadiums such as Isotopes Park and the Pit, the National Hispanic Cultural Center and the historic Barelas neighborhood, the Rio Grande River, the Rio Grande Zoo, the Albuquerque Aquarium, the Rio Grande Botanic Gardens, Tingley Beach, and other areas. This is not a hop-on, hop-off tour—there are no stops en route. It starts and ends at Old Town, and you ride on an open-air trolley that seats up to 34 passengers. The specially constructed customized trolley offers its own flavor of Albuquerque, with wrought iron rails, stucco paneling, turquoise trim, and mosaic tile art. The open-air trolley has a roof shade to protect passengers from the sun, and drop-down rain curtains if needed, but with no windows it's easier to take photos of the landmarks you pass. Each tour has a driver and a separate tour guide. The guides are all Burqueños who know the city inside out and tell you about their favorite places.

This new city-tour trolley company took its debut trip in 2009, and it also runs occasional sunset tours. There is no assigned seating on the trolley—it's first-come, first-served—and you can't take food or drink on board. Buy tickets at the trolley boarding point beside Plaza Don Luis or on the company's Web site. Tours leave several times a day except Monday, and times vary according to the day and season. The trolley arrives at the departure point 20 to 30 minutes before each tour. The ABQ Trolley Co. regular service runs from April 1 to November 1. Over winter months, there may be some service and special event tours; for example, to see the holiday lights.

i Buy ABQ Trolley Co. tickets online for a $2 discount. This also guarantees your spot on your preferred tour and saves you from waiting in line to buy tickets, so you can hop aboard first and nab your favorite seat!

FOLLOW THE SUN $$$$
Building D-3, Suite 314
8201 Golf Course Road NW
(505) 897-2886, (866) 428-4786
www.ftstours.com

Follow the Sun offers a driving tour of Albuquerque that in two-and-a-half hours takes you on

University of New Mexico

Although one might not normally think of a seat of learning as an attraction for visitors, the University of New Mexico campus is worth exploring for its historic architecture, free museums, and gorgeous leafy grounds complete with duck pond. The university was founded in 1889 and currently occupies 600 acres in Albuquerque, with branch campuses around the state.

The main points of interest for a first visit are contained with an easily strollable section of the main campus on the north side of Central Avenue, where there is parking and a Welcome Center for visitors. Pick up a walking tour map in the Welcome Center and a map of the public art, and you're off!

Thirty UNM buildings were designed by the important southwestern architect John Gaw Meem in Pueblo Revival style, many as part of the New Deal's Works Progress Administration. Some of the most notable John Gaw Meem buildings you'll see include the Zimmerman Library, named by the American Institute of Architects as the New Mexico building of the 20th century, and Scholes Hall, listed on the National Historic Register and with two towers and other details inspired by Acoma Pueblo's San Esteban del Rey Church. The Alumni Memorial Chapel recalls Franciscan mission pueblo churches with its broad curving buttresses.

The university's public art collection features more than 200 sculptures, murals, and paintings, dating back to UNM's first commissions of public art in the 1930s. Among the many outdoor artworks, look out for the Homage to Grandmother Earth granite sculpture by Youn Ja Johnson outside Northrop Hall museums; the 21-foot-high wind-powered angular stainless steel kinetic sculpture by George Rickey near the duck pond; and the superb 46-foot Kwakiutl Totem pole from British Columbia by Charlie James on the patio of the Maxwell Museum of Anthropology. An almost-alive wolf statue, *Lobo,* by John Tatschl guards the Stanford Avenue entrance to the university. The lobo (Spanish for "wolf") is the UNM mascot, and there are several wolf statues around the campus. More than 300 species of trees flourish on the grounds, including flowering fruit trees and lilacs, mature cottonwoods, Japanese maple, honey locusts with their distinctive dark brown "bean pods," and dapple-barked London Plane trees.

All UNM museums are free, and they include the Maxwell Museum of Anthropology, with a shady picnic table outside. This northwest area of the campus over to the duck pond, with the picturesque Alumni Memorial Chapel in between, has long been considered an oasis by UNM students and faculty. The duck pond and fountain, surrounded by western catalpa, pines, and weeping willow trees, makes a perfect picnic spot. The UNM Meteorite Museum and Geology Museum are both in Northrop Hall. The UNM Art Museum, with the state's largest fine art collection and also housing the Jonson Gallery, is in the Center for the Arts, next door to Popejoy Hall, the city's distinguished performance venue and home to the New Mexico Symphony Orchestra. The UNM Bookstore, just opposite the Center for the Arts, stocks a huge selection of books and is a good place to hunt for books on the Southwest. It's also worth dropping by UNM's nearby Tamarind Institute, with its gallery of fine art lithography. (The institute is in the process of moving a short distance at press time; check the Arts chapter for details.)

The UNM Welcome Center is opposite the UNM Bookstore, in the southwest corner of the university's Cornell Parking Structure on Redondo Drive, between Cornell Drive and Stanford Drive (this section of Redondo lies parallel to and a short block north of Central). Entry to the parking is just east of Stanford. Visitor parking costs $1.75 an hour. There is also metered parking around the campus, but it can be tricky to find a space, with limitations on stays. The Welcome Center is open 8 a.m. to 5 p.m. on weekdays. Contact the center on 505-277-1989 or go to www.unm.edu/welcome/welcomecenter.html.

a trip around highlights that include Old Town, Downtown, the Rio Grande Botanic Garden, the National Hispanic Cultural Center, the Rio Grande, Rio Grande Boulevard, the Balloon Park, and a local winery, plus other areas and landmarks. The Albuquerque City Tour doesn't run to a regular timetable, and a minimum of three people is needed to make a tour group. So if you have three or more in your party, call them to arrange a trip. Individuals and couples should call to find out if a group is scheduled that they can join or to get on the list for a new group. There is no departure point; Follow the Sun will pick you up at your hotel.

NEW MEXICO JEEP TOURS **$$$$**
9950 Florence Avenue NE
(505) 252-0112
www.nmjeeptours.com

Explore the mountains, mesas, extinct volcanos, petroglyphs, pueblo ruins, and wildernesses around Albuquerque in these tours by Jeep. Tours run from a quarter day to a full day, in open or covered vehicles, with off-road adventures and opportunities for hikes. Hotel pickup is included in the tour price, plus drinks and snacks or sandwich lunches for longer tours. Jeep tours run year-round, and customized trips are also available.

i **If your eye skipped over our listing on the Sandia Peak Tramway because you get giddy standing on a chair, then please reconsider! You don't have to ride up in the tram to visit the base terminal, which is a lovely spot for views across the city with seating outside. You can watch the tramcars rise serenely up the mountain face, and eat at Sandiago's Mexican Grill. See the tramway listing for full details.**

SEGWAY NEW MEXICO **$$$$**
Ste. B, 1816 Lomas Boulevard NW
(505) 244-1420
www.segwaynm.com

Hop on a Segway for a guided tour around Old Town (1.5 hours), from Old Town to Downtown (two hours), or Tingley Beach and the Rio Grande bosque (1.5 hours). Training on the Segway is provided before the tour. There are also fishing tours, and customized tours can be designed for a family or group. The daily tours run year-round, in the morning and afternoon, but check with the company for exact times. Gliding along on the two-wheeler Segway is a fun way to see the sights and to cover more ground than a walking tour. Wear closed shoes or boots, not open-toed sandals, and bring your own helmet or one will be provided for you. You'll also need a driver's license or ID. Riders must weigh between 75 and 260 pounds, and under-18-year-olds must be accompanied by a parent or guardian during training. Reservations are required. Parties of five people or more may receive a discount, and there may be a discount for reservations booked online in advance. Tours leave from 1816 Lomas Boulevard NW, on the south side of Old Town where Central meets Lomas.

TOURS OF OLD TOWN **$$–$$$**
Plaza Don Luis
303 Romero Street NW
(505) 246-TOUR, (505) 246-8687
www.toursofoldtown.com

Choose from a host of guided walking tours with experienced guides who know Old Town back to front and who share the stories, secrets, and spooks of this historic quarter. The daily History, Legends & Lore walk takes 75 minutes and usually starts at 10 a.m., noon, 2 p.m., and 4 p.m. every day except Thursday (Thursday tours can be arranged in advance for groups of four or more people). The nightly Ghost Tour starts at 8 p.m. for a 90-minute lantern-lit trek around the haunted buildings and backstreets of Old Town. Both of these tours are suitable for all ages.

Moonlight Ghost Tours are held each month at 10 p.m. on the nights of the full moon. If you're a really keen ghost buster, then you might want to try the (more expensive) Ghost Hunting Tours, held once or twice a month, when you get the chance to take part in paranormal investigations, using electromagnetic field detectors, dousing rods, and other special equipment. Moonlight Ghost and Ghost Hunting tours are not recommended for children under 13. Advance reservations are recommended for the History, Legends & Lore tour, but if you haven't booked in advance, it's worth checking to see if they can fit you in. Advance reservations are required for the Ghost Tour and all other tours.

Tours are held year-round and proceed as scheduled no matter the weather. Minors must be accompanied by an adult. The tour routes cover around a mile and are all on the flat in Old Town. There are places you can sit down and listen along the way, and the routes are wheelchair accessible. It's fine to take photos, but video and audio recording are prohibited. The departure point is the ticket window at Space N-120, Plaza Don Luis, 303 Romero Street NW. The ticket window opens 15 minutes before tours, or you can book online or by phone.

i **The Albuquerque Convention & Visitors Bureau has free self-guided walking tours available on its Web site, www.itsatrip.org. These include city neighborhoods such as Nob Hill, a Downtown Plaza to Old Town Plaza walk, and a tour of Pueblo Deco architecture. Just print out the tour maps plus interesting information about the sights along the way.**

THE ARTS

Artists, writers, and photographers have long been drawn to New Mexico. The light, the landscapes, and a certain sense of magic in the air—the sense that anything is possible here—seem to fuel creativity. Artist Georgia O'Keeffe, photographer Ansel Adams, and writer D. H. Lawrence are some of the more famous names who found inspiration here. For them, as for so many local artists and performers, their creative work was born out of a sense of place, and the sense of place here is unique. It's partly defined by the wide-open spaces under enormous blue skies, the wild sunsets, and natural beauty from mountain to desert. But the geography can't be separated from the history of the place—the combination of cultures that have informed today's New Mexico, from the architecture to the way of life.

The Pueblo and Hispanic societies that first populated New Mexico have long traditions of art and culture, often inextricably entwined with their spiritual beliefs. Consider the Native American dances, which are not a performance but a sacred ceremony expressed through music and movement. Consider the beautifully carved and painted Catholic santos—images of saints—found in churches and homes. People here have always understood and experienced the arts as an everyday part of life. And so it continues in Albuquerque, as the city's arts scene flourishes with visual arts and crafts, music, dance, theater, literature, and all manner of performances from the classic to the folkloric, contemporary, and avant-garde.

In 2009 *AmericanStyle* magazine placed Albuquerque fifth in its rankings of top big-city arts destinations, after New York (#1); Chicago; Washington, D.C.; and San Francisco. *U.S. News & World Report* highlighted Albuquerque's "diverse options for theater buffs" when ranking the city in its "Best Places to Live 2009."

These credits may come as news to people who haven't spent much time in Albuquerque and who associate the arts more with Santa Fe or Taos, Albuquerque's close cousins to the north in the Rio Grande corridor. It's no news, though, to Duke City residents, who are active and enthusiastic participants in the host of arts experiences the city has to offer.

According to the Albuquerque Theatre Guild, there is more live theater per capita in Albuquerque than in almost any other U.S. city of comparable size. In 1978 Albuquerque established the first public art collection (now worth $10 million) in the state, There are over 100 galleries and studios in town, and monthly gallery ARTScrawls have been a popular tradition since 1990.

Although the arts here often reflect the traditional roots of the area, a thriving arts scene needs interaction with the outside world to keep it from stagnating from insularity and also for economic reasons, so there is access to new patrons. UNM's student population of 25,000 helps bring fresh energy to the arts, providing an audience for more avant-garde or experimental performance companies. UNM's arts students also contribute to the creative culture, bringing new ideas to the Duke City melting pot from wherever they call home. Albuquerque International Sunport is only a few minutes' drive from the citys' major venues, and Albuquerque is often the only New Mexico stopping point for national performers on tour. It's also easy for visitors from out of state to fly in for the weekend and take in a couple of performances and the latest art exhibitions.

A 2007 report by the University of New Mexico Bureau of Business & Economic Research

(BBER) found that the arts and cultural industries in Albuquerque and Bernalillo Counties generated receipts of nearly $1.2 billion in 2004, making it a major contributor to the area's economy. The arts and cultural industries sector was responsible for 6 percent of the county's employment, with 19,500 jobs and $413 million in wages. Half of that was funded by dollars from outside the region. Cultural tourism brought in an estimated $213.3 million in 2004. These are the most recent figures available

Ticket prices can be surprisingly low for such high-quality opera, ballet and contemporary dance, music, and theater—often much lower than their equivalents elsewhere; anyone accustomed to paying "big city" box office rates might wonder if someone's misprinted the price. In keeping with the generally relaxed vibe in Albuquerque, dress can be less formal than in other cities for evening events. You can leave your tux or tiara at home.

PERFORMING ARTS

ARTS ALLIANCE
1100 San Mateo Boulevard NE
(505) 268-1920
www.abqarts.org

The Arts Alliance is a nonprofit organization promoting and serving the arts in the Albuquerque metropolitan area. It focuses on dance, theater, visual arts, music, and literary arts, as these are the area's five main disciplines. The Arts Alliance provides information, programs, services, and advocacy for the arts and since 1985 has presented the annual Arts Alliance Bravos Awards to acknowledge excellence in the arts community. The organization is a great resource to find out about local arts groups, artist studio tours, workshops, and just about anything else related to the arts in the Albuquerque area. The Web site is a wealth of information and has online newsletters, calendars, and directories of artists and arts organizations.

Arts Centers and Venues

AFRICAN AMERICAN PERFORMING ARTS CENTER
310 San Pedro NE
(505) 222-0785
www.aapacnm.org

The African American Performing Arts Center and Exhibit Hall opened in 2007 as a venue to express African-American history and culture through performance, exhibits, and education. The award-winning $4.3 million center is on the edge of the EXPO New Mexico grounds, and it's a stately looking building, with a hint of updated Pueblo Revival in its clean-lined architecture. It contains a 300-seat performance hall that hosts local and national touring companies for music, drama, and dance. The stage here has seen productions by Musical Theatre Southwest and concerts by Grammy Award nominee Nnenna Freelon and the Albuquerque Jazz Orchestra. The Exhibit Hall features changing shows of art and photography. The center is closed on Sunday and Monday.

KIVA AUDITORIUM
Albuquerque Convention Center
401 2nd Street NW
(505) 768-4975
www.albuquerquecc.com

It's worth keeping an eye on forthcoming events here, as although the Kiva Auditorium can fall under the radar in comparison with other arts venues in town, it hosts national artists for music concerts, comedy, speaking tours, and other acts. Author David Sedaris and comedians Kathy Griffin and Jerry Seinfeld have appeared here, and concert performers have ranged from Norah Jones and Duran Duran to Country Music Hall of Famer Vince Gill. Local groups such as the Duke City Chorus also perform here. Seating for an audience of 2,300 is in the half-round with a proscenium stage.

POPEJOY HALL
UNM Center for the Arts
Redondo and Cornell
(505) 277-4569
www.popejoyhall.com

Popejoy Hall is Albuquerque's premier performing arts venue, home to the New Mexico Symphony Orchestra and to the Popejoy Presents series of touring international theater, music, and dance performances, ranging from Broadway musicals to ballet. Named for former University of New Mexico president Tom Popejoy, this venerable Albuquerque institution opened in 1966 and seats nearly 2,000 patrons. Known for its naturally fine acoustics, the hall was renovated in 1996, had new seating in 2007, and was fitted with a new sound system in 2009. Performances here include everything from Shakespeare's *A Comedy of Errors* to Cirque Le Masque and from the Martha Graham Dance Company to a Mariachi Christmas. Popejoy Hall is located on the University of New Mexico main campus at UNM Center for the Arts, directly north of the University Bookstore, at Redondo and Cornell. For stress-free parking you're encouraged to use the free shuttle service that runs from the university's nearby special events parking lot every 10 minutes and drops you right in front of Popejoy Hall. Shuttles start 90 minutes before a show and continue for an hour afterward. Shuttle buses are wheelchair accessible. The special event lot (University G lot) is north of Lomas on University. Alternatively, you can pay for parking in the on-campus parking structure just east of Stanford and Redondo, which is a brief walk from the performance center.

ROY E. DISNEY CENTER FOR THE PERFORMING ARTS
National Hispanic Cultural Center
1701 4th Street SW
(505) 246-2261
www.nhccnm.org

This beautiful venue opened in 2004, and it's worth taking a look around when you're at the National Hispanic Cultural Center, even if you don't have time to see a production. You can't miss the impressive exterior, inspired by a Mayan pyramid, but also check out the graceful and airy award-winning interior drawn from Romanesque architecture. There are three stages in the center. The largest is the Albuquerque Journal Theatre, a proscenium theater with a curving interior that not only looks great but enhances the superb acoustics. The 691-seat theater features one of the largest indoor stages in New Mexico, with 1,700 square feet of performing space for dance, theater, music, and other events. The Bank of America Theatre is used mainly for film and video, with top-notch digital equipment as well as projectors for both 16mm and 35mm films. The removable film screen reveals a small thrust stage for performances and readings that require more intimate staging to the 291-capacity audience. The Wells Fargo Auditorium is cozier still, with a dark red interior and seating for 97 patrons. The Roy E. Disney Center hosts Albuquerque performing arts companies, as well as national and international performers, and the packed schedule of events can be found on the National Hispanic Cultural Center's Web site.

Some people who've worked at the Roy E. Disney Center are convinced that the backstage area is haunted by the ghost of Mrs. Adela Martinez, who refused to sell her childhood home and land to the state when the center was being planned. As a result, the layout of the center was turned around (for the better, according to the architect!) and designed around Mrs. Martinez's house, which still sits on the north end of the campus and is now occupied by her family members.

SOUTH BROADWAY CULTURAL CENTER
1025 Broadway SE
(505) 848-1320
www.cabq.gov/sbcc

A multicultural center for visual, performing, and literary arts, the South Broadway Cultural Center is a little tucked away from the main tourist areas but is worth a trip to check out the striking building, as well as its contents. Completed in 1994, the center's architecture manages to appear both classical and futuristic at the same time. The art gallery's silver columns and airy arched ceiling set off contemporary art exhibits reflecting the cultures and ethnicities that define Albuquerque. These have included Day of the Dead and Virgin of Guadalupe themes, visual interpretations of Rudolfo Anaya's acclaimed novel *Bless Me, Ultima,* and fantastic and surreal images from Los Fantasticos, an ensemble of four Albuquerque artists. The center's John Lewis Theater, seating just over 300 people, has been host to the New Mexico Ballet Company, Alma Flamenca, Ballet en Fuego, and Finland's Tero Saarinen dance company. Concerts have included Grammy nominee folk singer–songwriter John McCutcheon, New York klezmer music band The Klezmatics, and jazz and Irish bands. The center also houses an attractive library. Public art pieces here include vibrant murals and a large silver sculpture called *Marquee* by Robert Woltman, outside the front corner. The South Broadway Cultural Center is closed on Saturday and Sunday.

VSA NORTH FOURTH ART CENTER
4904 Fourth Street NW
(505) 345-2872
www.vsartsnm.org

North Fourth is a contemporary arts center, housing the N4th Theater, which stages an assortment of contemporary dance and drama performances, plus music, multimedia productions, and poetry readings. Following building renovations, the 99-seat state-of-the-art black-box performance space opened in 2006. N4th Theater steps outside the mainstream, and its eclectic and adventurous programming includes a lively lineup of festivals, usually spread over a series of weekends. Global Dancefest brings cutting-edge performers from all over the world, and Wild Dancing West presents contemporary dance from New Mexican and Californian companies. The Two Worlds program features original Native American plays, film, and photography, and starting in 2010, Two Worlds will also include dance. Year-round productions range from lighthearted musicals to satire to edgier works with a strong social message. The N4th Gallery displays an equally diverse variety of art by emerging and established artists, including juried shows, invitationals, and touring work. The gallery is open on Saturday from noon to 4 p.m., and during N4th Theater performances. The North Fourth Art Center offers educational arts programs to individuals with disabilities. The center is operated by VSA arts of New Mexico, a nonprofit organization affiliated with the John F. Kennedy Center for the Performing Arts and the national VSA arts network. It is dedicated to full accessibility in the arts for people of all abilities, ages, cultures, and income levels.

Dance

BALLET REPERTORY THEATRE OF NEW MEXICO
6913 Natalie NE
(505) 888-1054
www.btnm.org

Formerly the Ballet Theatre of New Mexico, Ballet Repertory Theatre performs several times a year at the KiMo Theatre. This classical ballet company's repertoire includes both traditional and innovative contemporary works. Artistic Director Katherine Giese has worked or performed with the Joffrey Ballet Workshop, the New Mexico Ballet Company, the Contemporary Dance Ensemble, the Canyon Movement Company, and the Incarnate Word College Ballet Company. As a child she performed in *La Sylphide* with the Berlin Ballet, which featured Rudolf Nureyev and Eva Evdokimova. The company includes Jackson Stewart, who dances professionally with the State Street Ballet of Santa Barbara, and Dominic Guerra, who has performed professionally with American Repertory Ballet and danced with Luis Fuentes Ballet, the Alvin Ailey Showcase Group, Connecticut Ballet, and Zig Zag Ballet. Female dancers include Cristal Segura, who has performed with the Martha Graham Company, and Sabrina Lord-Linde, who danced for two years with Vladimir Issaev's company, performed in St. Petersburg, Russia, in the 2005 International Dance Open, and trained with Mme. Alla Osipenko (former prima ballerina of the Kirov Ballet) at Arts Ballet Theatre of Florida, where she received the Osipenko Award of Outstanding Achievement.

KESHET DANCE COMPANY
214 Coal Avenue SW
(505) 224-9808
www.keshetdance.org
Keshet (which means "rainbow" in Hebrew) was founded by Artistic Director Shira Greenberg, and the company has built a strong reputation for creating and performing innovative and experimental dance works. The company performs at various city venues. Guest artists invited to create original works with Keshet's dancers have included Henning Rübsam of New York City's SENSEDANCE and Maggie Bergeron of Shapiro and Smith Dance in Minneapolis. The company's annual Choreographers' Showcase (in August) puts the spotlight on the works and works-in-progress of local choreographers and dancers. Keshet's professional dancers also serve as mentors and instructors in educational community programs, including preprofessional and youth classes and classes for dancers with physical or developmental disabilities. Keshet Dance Company's popular annual show of *Nutcracker on the Rocks* puts a rock-and-roll twist on the classical holiday ballet, featuring a Harley-Davidson; music by James Brown, Aretha Franklin, and the Rolling Stones; and dancers of different physical abilities performing with Keshet's professional artists. At the time of writing, plans have been announced for Keshet to move into a new space adjacent to the KiMo Theatre as the KiMo's resident dance company. The City of Albuquerque has also approved an agreement for Keshet to operate the KiMo Theatre, where it intends to increase the frequency and breadth of the theater's programming. Keshet Dance Company's contact information should remain as above through 2010. Construction on the KiMo space is anticipated to be completed in 2011, at which point the company will move to its new headquarters.

NATIONAL INSTITUTE OF FLAMENCO
214 Gold Avenue SW
(505) 242-7600
www.nationalinstituteofflamenco.org
Founded in 1987 by Director Eva Encinias-Sandoval, the National Institute of Flamenco (NIF) is devoted to preserving the art, culture, and history of flamenco. Classes in flamenco dance, music, and song are taught in the Conservatory for Flamenco Arts, and the NIF has three performing groups. Yjastros, the American Flamenco Repertory Company, is directed by Joaquin Encinias and is a national touring company. Alma Flamenca is a preprofessional company featuring advanced dance students from the Conservatory of Flamenco Arts and the University of New Mexico. Niños Flamencos presents some of the best young students ages 5 to 14 from the Conservatory. Additionally, NIF hosts leading international flamenco artists. National Institute of Flamenco performances can be seen at various city venues and festivals, including productions at the National Hispanic Cultural Center and the Rodey Theater. NIF also presents the annual Festival Flamenco Internacional de Alburquerque (the extra "r" is in honor of the city's original name). Claimed as the largest flamenco event of its kind in North America,

i **Church of Beethoven is a favorite of locals in the know—not a church, but a Sunday morning series of classical music concerts, with occasional variations such as opera and flamenco. The self-dubbed "church without the religion" events celebrate community and culture with a one hour program of music including a short reading by a regional poet and a two minute "celebration of silence." The season runs from September through May, and suggested admission for adults is $15. Arrive early for complimentary coffee from the baristas; the program itself starts at 10:30 a.m. at the Kosmos performance space in a renovated factory. 1715 5th St NW. www.churchofbeethoven.org.**

this 10-day festival in June is usually held at the University of New Mexico, and it brings leading artists and students from around the world to Albuquerque for workshops and public performances at various city venues. Many flamenco fans were disappointed when the 23rd annual festival in 2009 was suspended for economic reasons. Director Eva Encinias-Sandoval intends to bring the festival back in 2010.

NEW MEXICO BALLET COMPANY
PO Box 21518
Albuquerque, NM 87154-1518
(505) 292-4245
www.nmballet.org

New Mexico Ballet Company was formed in 1972 by Suzanne Johnston and partners and was originally a touring company as a member of the Southwest Regional Ballet Association. The company performs two major productions a year at venues that have included Popejoy Hall, the National Hispanic Cultural Center, the South Broadway Cultural Center, and the KiMo Theatre. The repertoire for this classical ballet company includes both traditional and contemporary works, including an exciting program called 20th Century Composers—21st Century Choreographers. Patricia Dickinson has been the artistic director since 1997. Dickinson studied at the Graham Conservatory in New York and with Madame Valentina Belova and Nikita Talin of Ballet Russe de Monte Carlo. She danced with the Dallas Opera and the Dallas Ballet. The New Mexico Ballet Company is now based at Dickinson's dance training academy, Dance Theatre Southwest (4200 Wyoming NE, 505-296-9465, www.dtsw.com).

Music

CHAMBER MUSIC ALBUQUERQUE
4407 Menaul Boulevard NE
(505) 268-1990
www.cma-abq.org

Chamber Music Albuquerque has been a performing arts force in the city since 1942. Originally the "June Music Festival," it changed its name in 1997 to present its position more accurately in Albuquerque's musical scene. Chamber Music Albuquerque presents a series of international performers and composers that draw not only from the European classical tradition but from jazz and folkloric roots as well, expanding the usual vision of what constitutes "chamber music." Diverse programming has featured artists such as the Alexander String Quartet, pianist Joel Fan from Yo-Yo Ma's Silk Road Ensemble, the Music from Copland House ensemble, and the flamboyant baroque interpretations of Red Priest. Chamber Music Albuquerque still sponsors the June Music Festival, which has featured groups like the Takács Quartet, the Lark Chamber Artists, and the Calder String Quartet. The organization hosts free family concerts and educational programs as part of its outreach program. Most performances take place at the Simms Performing Arts Center at the Albuquerque Academy, 6400 Wyoming Boulevard NE.

JOURNAL PAVILION
5601 University Boulevard SE
(505) 452-5100
www.livenation.com/venue/journal-pavilion-tickets

This is Albuquerque's mega outdoor arena for big-name bands on national tours. The Journal Pavilion has a capacity of 12,000 people and

i **The Southwest Stages radio show, produced in Albuquerque, brings "live" music into your home from festivals and other music events in Albuquerque, around New Mexico, and across the Southwest. The show records live performances of blues, jazz, folk, country, rock, Americana, Native, and world music, plus interviews with the artists. Hosted and produced by John Strader, the hour-long show is broadcast on KUNM 89.9 FM in Albuquerque, on Wednesday at 10 p.m. (at time of writing). Dozens of other stations broadcast the program, too, at different times, in Southwest states and a few farther-flung places. Stations and schedule are at www.southweststages.org.**

Local pueblo resorts and casinos offer great music too, bringing well-known bands and singers to town, often for just one night. At the Sandia Resort and Casino, the Gipsy Kings, James Taylor, Bonnie Raitt, Lynyrd Skynyrd, Chicago, and Earth, Wind & Fire have all appeared on the magnificent outdoor Amphitheater stage (505-796-7778, www.sandiacasino.com). The former Isleta Casino and Resort, due to change its name to Hard Rock Hotel & Casino Albuquerque in spring 2010, has featured such entertainers as Rick Springfield, the B-52s, Pat Benatar, and Blondie (505-244-8191, www.isletaeagle.com).

hosts 20 to 25 concerts a year. Performers have run the gamut from Def Leppard and Iron Maiden to Kanye West, Gwen Stefani, Bob Dylan, John Mellencamp, and Willie Nelson. Most shows offer a family area on the lawn where smoking and alcohol are not allowed. There are ATMs and concessions for food, drink, and merchandise in the venue. Parking fees are included with the ticket price for most shows, but some concertgoers have found access and parking slow, so allow plenty of time to get there before the performance. A limited number of VIP parking spaces are available for $20 per vehicle. A Park & Ride Rock Star Shuttle is sometimes provided for selected Journal Pavilion concerts (www.cabq.gov/transit/park-ride). Driving to the venue along University Boulevard, you'll know you're nearly there when you pass the second of two enormous snake sculptures serving as road dividers.

NEW MEXICO JAZZ WORKSHOP
5500 Lomas Boulevard NE
(505) 255-9798
www.nmjazz.org

For over 30 years New Mexico Jazz Workshop has promoted jazz education and performance, although their musical offerings range broader than solely jazz. Concerts include the summer series Jazz & Blues Under the Stars and Salsa Under the Stars, both running from around May through August. They also present a Father's Day weekend Blues Fest and an annual Women's Voices festival (usually June) to showcase some of the best of New Mexico's female vocalists. All these events have been held in previous years at the Albuquerque Museum of Art and History Amphitheatre. Sunday evening jam sessions, also May through August, are traditionally held on the Seasons Rotisserie & Grill restaurant's rooftop patio, with a house band of professional musicians and others welcome to turn up and join the jam. There is no cover charge, so come to listen or play. New Mexico Jazz Workshop also has a program of jazz classes for adults, youth, and kids.

NEW MEXICO SYMPHONY ORCHESTRA
4407 Menaul NE
(505) 881-8999
www.nmso.org

In 2007 the New Mexico Symphony Orchestra celebrated its 75th anniversary as a major Albuquerque cultural institution. An estimated 130,000 people attend New Mexico Symphony Orchestra performances each year, and the orchestra is the state's largest year-round performing arts organization, with around 100 musicians and staff. Over half of its annual performances are given in and around Albuquerque. The season runs from September to May, and its main home is Popejoy Hall, where most of its Classics Series and Pops Series concerts are performed. Classics matinees are also presented at the National Hispanic Cultural Center's Journal Theatre. The orchestra has been performing pops concerts since 1935; programs include movie music, best of Broadway, jazz, and rock. In the spring the Symphony Under the Stars outdoor concerts at the Rio Grande Zoo are a

Want to get involved in insiders' events, special programs, and social events, while helping to support the New Mexico Symphony Orchestra? Join the New Mexico Symphony Guild to meet other music lovers in this 50-year-old volunteer organization. Membership starts at $45; www.newmexicosymphonyguild.org.

family favorite. The orchestra has evolved since it began as the Albuquerque Civic Symphony in 1932, giving its first concert in UNM's Carlisle Gymnasium. It became the Albuquerque Symphony Orchestra in 1966, growing its reputation and performance quality under Musical Director Maurice Bonney and featuring an increasing number of highly regarded soloists. Finally, after Governor Jerry Apodaca declared it the official orchestra of the State of New Mexico in 1976, it changed its name to New Mexico Symphony Orchestra. It's wise to buy tickets in advance for all performances, at the Web site, by phone, or at the box office at 4407 Menaul NE. However, tickets are available at the door 45 minutes in advance of performances, if there are seats remaining.

i **In 2009, "Under New Mexico Skies" became New Mexico's official State Cowboy Song. The song was written by Syd Masters and selected at a songwriting competition in Albuquerque. To hear Syd Masters and the Swing Riders play in Albuquerque or nearby, check the schedule at sydmasters.com. On the Sound Clips page you can hear a few bars of "Under New Mexico Skies."**

OPERA SOUTHWEST
515 15th Street NW
(505) 243-0591
operasouthwest.org

Since 1972 Opera Southwest has presented both traditional and contemporary opera to Albuquerque audiences. Two to three major operas are performed each year, and the casts feature national and regional performers. Productions in previous seasons have included Bizet's *Carmen,* Donizetti's *Lucia di Lammermoor,* Strauss' *Die Fledermaus* and Rossini's *La Cenerentola.* The season runs from fall through spring at the KiMo Theatre. Anthony Barrese was appointed music director and principal conductor in 2008. Maestro Barrese has worked with the Boston Lyric Opera, the Dallas Opera, New Hampshire's Opera North, and the Sarasota Opera, and he was a 2007 Fellow of the Georg Solti Foundation. Opera Southwest estimates that it has performed over the years for a total audience of around a quarter of a million. It has also staged 23 world premieres of works by local composers. One of the company's strong suits is producing original operas especially for children, to encourage their interest in the art.

As part of its mission to make opera accessible to all, Opera Southwest sells remaining tickets to students at a reduced price of around $10 one hour before curtain.

i **If you fancy some live music (especially jazz) in a relaxed and intimate environment, Outpost Performance Space hosts regular gigs of local and touring artists playing and singing jazz of all flavors, folk, blues, roots, Latin, classical, experimental, and world music. Check out the 1927 Steinway grand piano. There is a beverage bar, but this is an alcohol-free zone. Buy tickets in person or by phone, or just turn up on the night. Box office hours are Monday to Friday, 2 p.m. to 5:30 p.m., and one hour before each show. Outside those hours, upcoming shows are listed on a prerecorded message. The schedule is also on the Web site. Outpost Performance Space is at 210 Yale Boulevard SE, two blocks south of Central (505-268-0044; www.outpostspace.org).**

Theater

ADOBE THEATER
9813 4th Street NW
505-898-9222
www.adobetheater.com

Adobe Theater is based in an intimate venue, seating 90 in a thrust-style performance space, meaning that the audience surrounds the stage on three sides. Productions in this local gem are consistently praised. Adobe Theater has staged works that include Noel Coward's *Private Lives,*

Summer Outdoor Concerts

Summertime, and the living is definitely easy in Duke City, with outdoor summer concerts to suit every musical taste. Here are some picks of places and events to check out if you like to hum along under the heavens. Schedules may vary each year, so do check details before you set off.

The city's free Summerfest concerts on Saturday evenings in June, July, and August at the Downtown Harry E. Kinney Civic Plaza present music from Cajun to country and jazz to Latin. A beer garden, food vendors, an arts and crafts market, and children's activities are also part of the fun. Civic Plaza is at 3rd Street and Marquette NW (www.cabq.gov/crs). You can park ($6) in the garage beneath the plaza. Or avoid the traffic, and for a dollar take Rapid Ride's Rapid After Dark bus (www.cabq.gov/transit).

Albuquerque Biological Park offers several popular concert series each year. Summer Nights Concerts in the Rio Grande Botanic Garden features local and regional artists playing blues to bluegrass, funk to folk. Zoo Music at the Rio Grande Zoo is a long-standing tradition in celebration of folk, roots, and ethnic music. Both series are held on nights in June and July, and people come with blankets or lawn chairs and either bring a picnic or buy food at the event. You can also buy beer and wine at the Biopark, but it's not okay to bring your own. Buy tickets online or at the biopark's botanic garden, aquarium, or zoo (www.cabq.gov/biopark, 505-768-2000).

New Mexico Symphony Orchestra's May series of Symphony Under the Stars concerts at the Rio Grande Zoo are also great for families, with programs including Hollywood's Greatest Hits, tunes from Broadway, or classical favorites like the 1812 Overture (505-881-8999; www.nmso.org)

The Albuquerque Museum of Art and History Amphitheatre hosts an annual summer music festival with the New Mexico Jazz Workshop, on numerous dates from May through August. Events include Jazz & Blues Under the Stars, Salsa Under the Stars, Blues Fest, and the Women's Voices festival. The Cooperage Restaurant provides food and full bar service. Schedule and ticket information is at www.cabq.gov/museum or www.nmjazz.org or call (505) 255-9798.

Rockers and pop music fans head to the Journal Pavilion, a huge, modern outdoor arena that is the choice of many national and international artists during their American tours (505-452-5100, www.livenation.com/venue/journal-pavilion-tickets). In a very different style but also drawing major popular music biz names, the Sandia Resort and Casino Amphitheater is built of warm pink rock with seating in a traditional semicircle, with views of the Sandia Mountains beyond the outdoor stage (505-796-7778; www.sandiacasino.com.)

Harold Pinter's *Betrayal,* and the walk-down-memory-lane musical *Back to the 80's.* The all-volunteer organization has had its home here since 1995, although its roots go back to a community theater created by Corrales folk in 1957. Renovations in 2008 included new seats.

ALBUQUERQUE LITTLE THEATRE
224 San Pasquale SW
(505) 242-4750
www.abqlt.org

Neither too little nor too big, the 480-seat historic Albuquerque Little Theatre is exactly the right size for an intimate evening of live theater. The Albuquerque Little Theatre group was founded in 1930, and after six years based at the KiMo Theatre, it moved to its current location in 1936. The building was designed by southwestern architect John Gaw Meem and was Albuquerque's first Works Progress Administration project, under Franklin D. Roosevelt's New Deal. Productions here range from comedy to musicals to dramas. Shows have included *The Full Monty, Dial "M" For Murder, The Best Little Whorehouse in Texas, Amadeus, La Cage aux Folles, A Child's Christmas in Wales,* and *The Complete Works of William Shakespeare* (abridged). Located just south of Old Town, Albuquerque Little Theatre calls itself a "true community theater" and remains committed to involving Albuquerque residents, from volunteer assistance in all aspects of production to simply attending and enjoying their consistently popular performances. The Family Theater Series introduces young people to the pleasures of live theater performances, including shows such as *101 Dalmatians.*

i **Emmy Award–winning actress Vivian Vance, who played Lucy's sidekick Ethel Mertz in the *I Love Lucy* television series, started her career at the Albuquerque Little Theatre. Vance also performed at the KiMo Theatre.**

BLACKOUT THEATRE COMPANY
PO Box 40153
Albuquerque, NM 87196-0153
(505) 554-1086
blackouttheatre.com

The Blackout Theatre ensemble specializes in creating new, original works, while pushing the limits of established theater, particularly in the realm of comedy. Still a relatively young company, launching in just 2007, Blackout Theatre has carved itself a distinctive niche in the local arts scene. Voted Best Theatre Troupe in the 2009 Weekly *Alibi* Best of Burque picks, they are ensemble-in-residence at the Box. Their work "outside the box" includes guerrilla and environmental theater events.

THE BOX PERFORMANCE SPACE
1025 Lomas Boulevard N.W
(505) 404-1578
www.theboxabq.com

Through its in-house Cardboard Playhouse Productions, the Box hosts a popular series of children's shows as well as being a top venue for improvisational theater and comedy. The comfortable Box Performance Space quickly won local affection when it opened in 2007 and was voted one of the top ten art happenings of the year by the weekly *Alibi.* Recent shows for kids have included Disney's *Cinderella, Beauty and the Beast,* and *Willy Wonka Junior.* Improv events include the furiously fast and funny One Night Stanleys, and for comedy they've hosted local troupes Eat Drink & Be Larry and the Pajama Men. They also present summer camps in comedy, film, and junior theater and host the Duke City Improv Festival in late summer. The Box also hosts the Blackout Theatre Company as its resident ensemble.

THE CELL THEATRE & FUSION THEATRE COMPANY
700 1st Street NW
(505) 766-9412
www.liveatthecell.com
www.fusionabq.org

Known as Albuquerque's boutique performance center, the Cell hosts live theater, music, dance, movie screenings, and special events. This historic Downtown building was home to a brewing company in the late 1800s and later a coal yard. Now converted to an intimate performance space seating 75, it is also home to the FUSION Theatre Company. A professional Equity company, producing work by emerging playwrights as well as classic American theater, FUSION has garnered excellent reviews for its rendition of such plays as John Patrick Shanley's Pulitzer Prize–winning drama *Doubt.* It also sponsors educational programs for disadvantaged youth and produces the Seven, a new-plays festival offering annual opportunities for new voices to take the stage.

KIMO THEATRE
423 Central Avenue NW
(505) 768-3544
www.cabq.gov/kimo

The KiMo Theatre is one of the city's key architectural treasures, listed on the National Register of Historic Places. Built in 1927 in the Pueblo Deco style and lavishly decorated inside and out, the theater has been extensively renovated and is now home to dance, music, drama, festivals, poetry slams, and many other arts events. As much as people come to see the local, national, and international performers on the bill, they also come to enjoy the venue itself. A night out here is a unique experience, with its lively history, exotic decor, and whispers of ghost stories. Read more about the history, the design, and the stories behind the KiMo in the Close-up.

You can take a self-tour of the theater during business hours (below), as long as there are no activities or performances scheduled. See the scheduled events at the KiMo's Web site, but daytime rehearsals might also close the auditorium to the public, so it's worth phoning the KiMo office (505-768-3522) ahead of time to check availability. Guided tours may also be available by appointment. The theater lobby presents exhibits of local and regional art.

The KiMo's comfortable seats are restored Pueblo Deco–style seats, replaced during the theater's $2 million facelift in 2000—the latest in a long series of renovations. The auditorium accommodates 650.

Note that due to the historic nature of this building, there is no elevator to the balcony and upper floors. There are several flights of stairs to access these floors. The theater's main floor, however, is fully compliant with the Americans with Disabilities Act and has four wheelchair and companion seating areas.

At the time of writing, the City of Albuquerque has recently approved an agreement for Keshet Dance Company to operate the KiMo Theatre, as well as to become the theater's resident dance company. Keshet plans to increase the frequency and breadth of the theater's programming. You can find the theater's performance schedule and ticketing information on the Web site or by phone at the event information number, 505-768-3544. The KiMo Theatre is at the corner of Central and 5th Street. Paid parking is in the multilevel parking structure just behind the theater at 5th and Copper NW. Business hours are Tuesday through Friday, 8:30 a.m. to 4:30 p.m. Saturday 11 a.m. to 5 p.m. Closed Sunday, Monday, and city holidays.

MOTHER ROAD THEATRE COMPANY
The Filling Station Arts & Performance Space
1024 4th Street, SW
(505) 243-0596
www.motherroad.org

Under the banner of "Engage, Challenge, Transform," Mother Road Theatre is noted for its innovative ensemble performances, for its devotion to supporting local theater arts professionals, and for hosting youth literacy and playwriting theater education programs for all ages. Operating out of the Filling Station, a vintage 1930s gas station in the Barelas district that has been renovated as a contemporary arts and 1600-square-foot black–box-style performance space, you can't get more "Burque" than this. The Filling Station is on the old Route 66 that ran north-south through Albuquerque along 4th Street, before the road was realigned to run along Central Avenue. Route 66 is known as the Mother Road, hence the theater company's name. Mother Road Theatre Company also sponsors the yearly New Mexico Young Playwrights Festival.

i **Buy a Mother Road Theatre Company season pass ($40) and see the season of three shows for a lot less than you'd pay for a single show on Broadway. For just $5 more you can upgrade to the Page to Stage program, which allows you to attend selected rehearsals and other behind-the-scenes events.**

MUSICAL THEATRE SOUTHWEST
6320B Domingo NE
(505) 265-9119
www.musicaltheatresw.com

Bringing quality musical theater to New Mexico at affordable prices, Musical Theatre Southwest has performed just about every musical you can imagine, from Broadway classics to contemporary, from *Oklahoma!* and *HMS Pinafore* to *The Rocky Horror Picture Show* and *Grease*. Incorporated in 1966, the company's first performances at Popejoy Hall were in 1968, and it has produced

KiMo Theatre

One of Albuquerque's proudest landmarks is the KiMO Theatre on Central Avenue, the old Route 66. Almost every local you talk to about the KiMo can be relied upon to say, "I love that place," at some point in the conversation. It's not surprising that Duke City citizens are so fond of this old movie palace. They saved it from demolition in 1977 by voting to approve a $324,000 bond for the City of Albuquerque to purchase it, and thanks to that initiative, and many subsequent renovations, this historic venue has been restored to its former glory.

One of the best-known examples of the unique regional style called "Pueblo Deco," the KiMo Theatre first opened its doors on September 19, 1927, as a silent movie picture palace and vaudeville house. The Native-meets-deco decor includes buffalo skulls with glowing eyes, funeral canoe chandeliers hanging from the ceiling, air vents camouflaged to look like Navajo rugs, stylized wrought iron birds in the stair railings, and nine large murals by Carl von Hassler, a well-known southwestern artist who used to have a studio on the theater's third floor. The murals, painted in oils, depict pueblos originally thought by Spanish explorers to be the legendary Seven Cities of Cibola or Cities of Gold. Almost all the surfaces in the theater are painted, textured, or decorated in some way.

The theater was originally built by entrepreneur Oreste Bachechi, and he commissioned Carl Boller of the Boller Brothers to design it. The Boller Brothers' midwestern architectural firm specialized in theater design, and they were responsible for numerous classic theaters of that era. Boller's design was inspired by his trips around New Mexico's pueblos and the Navajo Nation. The flamboyant styling of his themes reflected the high spirits of the roaring '20s. The theater cost $150,000 to build.

The name was the idea of the governor of Isleta Pueblo, Pablo Abeita. He was awarded a tidy $50 for naming it KiMo. The word combines two Tiwa words that literally mean "mountain lion" but are broadly translated to mean "king of its kind." The KiMo certainly was a king of its kind, or even a one of a kind. (Once the word was adopted outside its Native culture, it was perceived as a "dead" word in Tiwa and was dropped by Native speakers.)

In its heyday the theater hosted performances by stars such as Gloria Swanson and Ginger Rogers. After a fire in the 1960s destroyed much of the stage area, however, the theater fell

shows at various venues over the years. Currently, Musical Theatre Southwest stages shows at the African American Performing Arts Center (310 San Pedro NE) around the corner from its own rehearsal and costume and prop warehouse facility. Recognized for its lively performances and varied programming, Musical Theatre Southwest offered three productions in 2009, in February, July, and December, but the program changes each year, so check the schedule on the Web site or by phone. Recent musicals have included *The Producers, West Side Story,* and *Little Shop of Horrors.*

TEATRO NUEVO MEXICO
107 Bryn Mawr SE
(505) 362-6567 / 266-2656
www.teatronm.com

This innovative and exciting troupe looks not only to the past, seeking to keep Spain's zarzuela (Spanish operetta) tradition alive in New Mexico by training new generations of performers, but breaks new ground with cutting-edge productions such as *River of Tears.* Playing to sold-out audiences at the National Hispanic Cultural Center and other venues, this trilingual performance incorporated song, dance, and live music on traditional instru-

into disrepair. People were also shifting away from the (now revitalized) Downtown area. The down-at-its-heels theater was due to be demolished, until the 1977 vote by Albuquerque residents rescued it. Years of discussion, planning, and fund-raising followed. A multimillion dollar restoration, its second phase completed in 2000, finally returned it to its rightful place among the classiest venues in the city. The renovations also uncovered old treasures. Beneath the original acoustic materials were sandpaintings and artworks of Navajo Yei figures. Replications of these damaged originals appear on the renovated walls. Decorative tile was also found under the old carpeting and was cleaned up and restored.

Backstage is a shrine dedicated to the memory of a six-year-old boy named Bobby, who was killed in 1951 when a water heater exploded in the lobby. Presenters add small keepsakes and gifts to the shrine to pacify the boy's ghost, which, it is said, still inhabits the theater and occasionally disrupts performances when not paid enough attention. Some of the items on the shrine are quite old, left in a nook on the steps between the dressing rooms and the stage. Although generally thought to be a peaceful ghost, Bobby has been known to appear on the staircase or smiling and waving from the upper floors, occasionally causing doors to swing open and shut by themselves and lightbulbs to explode. He is also said to like doughnuts, which performers and crew hang from a backstage water pipe, only to find them gone the next morning; those left are said to be marked with bites by little teeth. Some people also claim to have seen the ghost of an old lady in a bonnet wandering the halls, although nobody knows who she is. Take a tour of the theater, and you can see the shrine—and perhaps even the ghost—for yourself. See the main KiMo Theatre listing for information.

Note that although the name is commonly "KEE-mo," with a hard "K," the theater says the true pronunciation is with a soft "K," more like an "H" and a clipped "i": "Him-o." So if you hear it said that way, you'll know what they are referring to. Conversely, if you say it that way to be authentic, be warned that not everyone will know what you're talking about!

This living legend now hosts events from chamber music to poetry slams and is a busy venue for the local performing arts community. Many companies perform here, including those from out of state and overseas. The KiMo Theatre is located at 423 Central Avenue NW, at the corner of Central and 5th Street. The event information number is (505) 768-3544; www.cabq.gov/kimo.

ments with computer-generated imagery and spoken word in English, Spanish, and Nahuatal, an official language in Mexico. This is the kind of stimulating Teatro Nuevo México experience you can expect, and it's something you won't find in every city. The volunteer-operated Latino company was formed in 2003 by a group of veteran theater professionals and activists dedicated to positive representation and preservation of Latino cultures, as well as nurturing new Latino talent. Outreach has included sponsoring free master classes for singers and actors and special performances for schoolchildren from Albuquerque and the surrounding area. Most Teatro Nuevo México events are at the National Hispanic Cultural Center.

TRICKLOCK COMPANY
1705 Mesa Vista NE
(505) 254-8393
www.tricklock.com

Founded in 1993, the avant-garde Tricklock Company creates and presents year-round productions of original work, renovated classics, and challenging contemporary theater. The repertoire ranges from Shakespeare's *Cymbeline* to the physical comedy of the company's original play *Catgut Strung Violin*. Albuquerque venues include the University of New Mexico's Rodey Theatre and Theatre X, the National Hispanic Cultural Center, KiMo Theatre, N4th Theatre, and the Box. The ensemble also tours the United States and Canada and has performed widely in Europe. Tricklock sponsors the Manoa Project Teen Playwriting Competition and Ensemble Apprenticeship and hosts the annual Revolutions International Theatre Festival, bringing ground-breaking international theater companies to Albuquerque. In 2006 Tricklock became the first theater company in residence at the University of New Mexico.

UNM THEATRE AND DANCE
The Rodey Theatre & Theatre X
Center for the Arts
UNM Main Campus
UNM Ticketing: (505) 925-5858, (877) 664-8661
theatre.unm.edu

The University of New Mexico's Department of Theatre & Dance produces a mainstage series of five events: three plays, a faculty-choreographed dance concert, and the Words Afire Festival of New Works. The annual spring Words Afire Festival premieres new plays by MFA student playwrights in UNM's Dramatic Writing program, both fully staged and in readings. In 2009 UNM established a partnership with the Drama League of New York City for innovative young Drama League directors to collaborate on the Words Afire Festival productions and readings.

There is also a Theatre X series of student-produced plays and student dance showcases and outreach tours.

The main performance facilities for UNM's Department of Theatre and Dance are the Rodey Theatre and Theatre X. The Rodey Theatre is a 400-seat venue that is convertible from a proscenium to a thrust-theater style, designed by George Izenour. The Theatre X black box experimental theater is a flexible space seating 100 or more, according to the configuration. Other performing companies also stage productions at these venues.

Information on productions is at the UNM Web site above, with links to the UNM ticketing service. This is a fairly quick and easy way to see what's on the calendar. Or you can go directly to www.unmtickets.com to find events there and purchase tickets. The phone number for UNM ticketing is 877-664-8661 or 505-925-5858.

Rodey Theatre and Theatre X are in UNM's Center for the Arts, located directly north of the UNM Bookstore, at Redondo Drive and Cornell.

i Find out what's on at the theater this week at www.abqtheatre.org. The Albuquerque Theatre Guild represents around thirty theater venues and performing companies, and ATG's show listings of current and future productions save you from having to check around at each one to see what's on when. (Theaters that are not members of the ATG are not listed.) If you're a thespian yourself, ATG also posts information on auditions, workshops, and other theater events.

THE VORTEX THEATRE
2004½ Central Avenue SE
(505) 247-8600
vortexabq.org

Offering cutting-edge, dynamic contemporary live theater with a nod to the classics, the Vortex was named Best in Burque by the weekly *Alibi* newspaper for their production of *Hedwig and the Angry Inch*. Recent performances have also included such edgy classics as *Who's Afraid of Virginia Woolf?* and *True West*. The theater also hosts a series of staged readings featuring local playwrights. Located within an easy walk from the University of New Mexico campus and Nob Hill, the Vortex is perfectly situated for a night on the town, before or after the performance. Parking is on the street so allow time and arrive early.

LITERARY ARTS

Albuquerque's literary stars, either as residents or through long association with the city, include Rudolfo Anaya, whose beautiful debut novel *Bless Me, Ultima,* established him as the founder of modern Chicano literature. Anaya's subsequent works include *Alburquerque: A Novel.* Fiction and nonfiction author Tony Hillerman, best known for his Navajo tribal police mysteries featuring Joe Leaphorn and Jim Chee, was a popular figure around town. When Hillerman passed away in 2008, Governor Bill Richardson ordered flags around New Mexico to be lowered to half-staff in his honor, and Albuquerque's Wyoming Library (8205 Apache NE) was renamed Tony Hillerman Library. Jean-Marie Gustave Le Clézio, winner of the 2008 Nobel Prize in Literature, formerly lived in Albuquerque and is now a part-time resident. Other Albuquerque writers are Demetria Martínez, whose widely translated novel *Mother Tongue* won the Western States Book Award for Fiction; Alisa Valdes-Rodriguez, dubbed the godmother of Chica Lit following her debut best-selling novel *The Dirty Girls Social Club;* and poet Levi Romero, author of the acclaimed *A Poetry of Remembrance: New and Rejected Works* and an influential mentor to Albuquerque's new-generation poets and slam poets. Poet and author Jimmy Santiago Baca's powerful work, drawn from his extraordinary real-life story, broke open the door for many young Chicano writers, and his Cedar Tree nonprofit foundation is active in Albuquerque, with an ongoing writing workshop in the Albuquerque Women's Prison and at the South Valley Community Center, plus an internship program providing live-in writing scholarships in the city's South Valley.

Lois Duncan, author of 48 books, is best known for her young adult suspense novels including *I Know What You Did Last Summer.* Judith Van Gieson's mysteries include the Claire Reynier series, with an amateur sleuth heroine who works as an archivist and librarian at UNM Albuquerque.

516 ARTS
516 Central Avenue SW
(505) 242-1445
www.516arts.org

An ongoing series of 516 Words poetry readings takes place here, plus other literary events, book-release parties, and storytellings, with regional and visiting writers. The Treehouse Reading and Open Mic nights start with an hour-long open mic that anyone can sign up for, followed by a half-hour reading from a featured poet. Most events are free with pass-the-hat donations, and the space is gorgeous in the 516 Arts Gallery.

i **Luis Tafoya's poem "A Nuevo Mexico," written in 1911 before New Mexico's statehood, was officially declared New Mexico's State Poem eighty years later, in 1991.**

HARWOOD ART CENTER
1114 7th Street NW
(505) 242-6367
harwoodartcenter.org

Harwood presents a series of literary events under the umbrella of its Sowing Poetry program. These include the quarterly WordStream Poetry Reading Series of free readings from New Mexico poets. In 2008 they presented the first STIR: a Festival of Words poetry festival with other venues, including 516 Arts. The Harwood was a core supporter of Albuquerque's Slam Poetry from the early days, providing space for rehearsals and fund-raising, and worked to bring the National Poetry Slam Championship to the city.

NATIONAL HISPANIC CULTURAL CENTER
1701 4th Street SW
(505) 246-2261
www.nhccnm.org

The NHCC's History and Literary Arts programs include poetry and other readings, author lectures, and book signings. The National Latino Writers Conference has been held here since 2003 and is one of the center's most exciting ini-

Albuquerque Slams!

Spoken word "slam poetry" is a predominant literary art form in Albuquerque, and the city appointed its first Slam Poet Laureate in 2009. In a poetry slam poets compete by performing their work, judges give points for content and performance, and the whole audience is encouraged to give feedback. It makes for a rousing event, with everyone actively involved, rather than a more passive poetry reading. Mayor Martin J. Chávez supported the creation of Albuquerque's laureate position, but unlike most laureates who are appointed, this one had to compete in front of a live audience for his crown. Danny Solis, who was already considered the city's unofficial poet laureate by many, won the title of 2009 Slam Poet Laureate at the finals in the KiMo Theatre after previous qualifying rounds had whittled down the contenders to twelve. Zachary Kluckman, creator of the laureate program and himself a slam poet, says this is the world's first Slam Poet Laureate. The city's annual laureate serves as a spokesperson and liaison for the art and also works on outreach to schools and other groups in the community.

Albuquerque has an active slam poetry circuit, and in 2005 the Albuquerque team won the National Poetry Slam, which is the equivalent of the Superbowl for slammers! The Albuquerque team's poets were Hakim Bellamy, Carlos Contreras, Cuffee, Kenn Rodriguez, and Esme Vaandrager. The University of New Mexico's Lobo Slam team has also earned national honors, winning the College Unions Poetry Slam Invitational twice, in 2006 and 2008.

Albuquerque poet Juliette Torrez started the first poetry slam here in 1994. She'd just returned from the Lollapalooza Third Stage national tour of poets, where she'd been exposed to slam, a form born in Chicago in 1986. There was already an open-mic poetry reading at the former Dingo Bar on Central, where Burt's Tiki Lounge is now. Torrez turned that open-mic night into a slam event. "Slam seemed to galvanize everything," says Kenn Rodriguez, spokesperson for the ABQ Slams organization and a member of the 2005 winning National Poetry Slam team. "The Downtown open mics at that time weren't necessarily as performance driven as slam, but there was kind of a street poetry or guerrilla poetry bent to the scene." Slam quickly took hold, capturing the imagination of the community and giving voice to individuals outside the academic poetry world.

The Southwest Shootout was launched in Albuquerque and is now the leading regional poetry slam in the western United States, involving teams from New Mexico, Texas, Arizona, Colorado, Utah, and sometimes Northern California. The Southwest Shootout is held on alternate years in Albuquerque; the next will be summer 2011, and it rotates to other participating states in the years between.

The book *A Bigger Boat: The Unlikely Success of the Albuquerque Poetry Slam Scene,* edited by Susan McAllister, Don McIver, Mikaela Renz, and Daniel S. Solis, was published by UNM Press in 2008. It gives insider stories, and poems, from those involved in the rise of slam, leading to the city's triumph at the 2005 National Poetry Slam competition.

There are currently three ongoing poetry slams a month, as well as the Firestorm women's quarterly slam. Come and join the audience, or sign up on the night to join the poets! Poetry and Beer, on the first Wednesday of the month, is held at Blackbird Buvette, 509 Central NW. MASPoetry, on the third Wednesday of the month, and the Final Friday event are both held at Winning Coffee Company, 111 Harvard SE. These lively evenings include music and events such as "Haiku Deathmatch." Although these are ongoing slams, details may change, so check for location, date, and timing before setting out. Information on all slams and the Southwest Shootout is at ABQ Slams: www.abqslams.org.

tiatives, with a superb faculty and a record of successes ensuing for attending writers. Writers such as Rudolfo Anaya, Sandra Cisneros, Luis Alberto Urrea, and Jimmy Santiago Baca have presented at the NHCC. The center sponsors events for several days each year around Dia del Libro or World Book Day (April 23). It also mounts literary exhibits and holds a permanent collection of more than 14,000 books and other archives focusing on Hispanic history worldwide, especially in the American Southwest.

i **The Poetry on the Bus program, launched in 2008, gives passengers a few moments of poetic repose as they travel around town on ABQ Ride buses. Poems are selected from submissions by writers in the Albuquerque area.**

SOUTHWEST WRITERS
(505) 265-9485
www.southwestwriters.com
Southwest Writers is an organization with over 600 members writing in all forms and genres. Despite the name, the group is based in Albuquerque, and all events are held here. Southwest Writers hosts an annual writers' contest and conference and a twice-monthly program of workshops and seminars on the craft and business of writing, plus other subjects relevant to aspiring or published writers.

VISUAL ART MUSEUMS AND GALLERIES

Art Museums

ALBUQUERQUE MUSEUM OF ART AND HISTORY
2000 Mountain Road NW
(505) 243-7255
www.cabq.gov/museum
The Albuquerque Museum's art collection focuses on regional works, both historical and contemporary, and this is an excellent place to be introduced to the art of New Mexico. Those familiar with the regional arts will find plenty to be delighted at, too, from fresh perspectives to pieces that haven't been shown before. The museum's collection includes paintings by the members of the Taos Society of Artists, Los Cinco Pintores from the Santa Fe art movement, and the Transcendental Painting Group. The Common Ground: Art in New Mexico permanent collection displays works from the late 1800s to today in chronological order to illustrate the evolution of the region's art. The museum also shows work by contemporary regional, national, and international artists in all media.

Leave time to wander around the museum's terrific Sculpture Garden, featuring more than sixty works by artists such as Luis Jiménez, Fritz Scholder, Donald Duncan, Reynaldo Rivera, Ed Vega, and Ron Cooper. Pick up a Sculpture Garden map in the lobby for a self-guided tour of the grounds, or join a docent-guided tour. Docent tours are available from April through November, at 10 a.m., Tuesday to Saturday. For more information on the Albuquerque Museum of Art and History, see the listing in the Attractions chapter. Closed Monday and city holidays. Adult admission $4, New Mexico residents with ID $3, seniors 65 and over $2. For children 4 to 12, entry is $1. Free for children 3 and under. Admission is free on Sunday from 9 a.m. to 1 p.m. and free all day on the first Wednesday of the month.

i **Lew Wallace, territorial governor of New Mexico between 1878 and 1881, was also the author of the novel *Ben-Hur*, completed while he was in office. The novel's full title is *Ben-Hur: A Tale of the Christ*, and it became a best seller that has never been out of print. The 1959 movie version won eleven Academy Awards.**

NATIONAL HISPANIC CULTURAL CENTER ART MUSEUM
1701 4th Street SW
(505) 246-2261
www.nhccnm.org

Since opening in October 2000, the National Hispanic Culture Center has acquired a growing collection of over 2,000 pieces of Hispanic and Latino art. Displayed in the 10,000-square-foot Art Museum, under the banner of ¡Aquí Estamos! (We are here!), the permanent collection includes major works from New Mexico and throughout the United States, Latin America, Spain, and other regions of Hispanic culture. This exciting collection presents paintings; drawings; sculpture; installations; prints; photographs; fiber arts; furniture; mixed media; and works in metal, wood, and more. You'll see a broad diversity of styles here, ranging from traditional forms and themes to contemporary interpretations of traditional forms and themes to exhilaratingly groundbreaking work. Temporary exhibits focus on influential Hispanic artists or are curated around themes such as Lowriding in New Mexico or the Virgin of Guadalupe. For more information on the National Hispanic Cultural Center, see the listing in the Attractions chapter. Closed Monday. Adult admission $3, seniors $2, free on Sunday, and always free for children under 16.

UNM ART MUSEUM
UNM Center for the Arts
University of New Mexico Main Campus
Redondo and Cornell
(505) 277-4001
unmartmuseum.unm.edu

The University of New Mexico Art Museum has over 30,000 objects in its permanent collection, making it home to the largest fine art collection in the state. This includes paintings, drawings, photographs, prints, and sculpture and treasures from the Old World and the New. European art from the Renaissance forward is found here, including old masters, American 19th- and 20th-century art, and a collection of over 10,000 photographs representing the most famous names in the form. The UNM Art Museum was closed for renovations and expansion in spring 2009; it is expected to reopen in February 2010. The expansion adds 8,000 square feet of space, including a 3,000-square-foot gallery for new media and video-art installations. There is also a new print and photography study room, plus offices and extra storage space to accommodate the permanent collection. The Jonson Gallery is also now housed in the UNM Art Museum, having moved from its former home of over half a century. The Johnson Gallery features the work of modernist painter Raymond Jonson (1891–1982), a UNM faculty member and the founder in 1938 of the influential Transcendental Painting Group. The Jonson Gallery also shows exhibits from emerging and underrecognized artists.

Private collections donated to the UNM Art Museum add to its substantial holdings of superb art. For example, the bequest of UNM alum E. Gerald Meyer, valued at around $6.2 million, includes works by Rembrandt, Picasso, Nicholai Fechin, and Georges Rouault, plus over 100 paintings from Taos School artists and contemporary Western art.

The UNM Art Museum is located on the University of New Mexico main campus at the Center for the Arts, directly north of the UNM Bookstore, at Redondo Drive and Cornell. The UNM Art Museum is closed on Monday; on Saturday and Sunday it is open afternoons only. Weekday opening times don't conform strictly to regular business hours, so it is worth checking opening times with the museum before setting off. Admission is free.

i **Some galleries will open by appointment outside their usual business hours, so if you're considering buying but your schedule doesn't match theirs, give them a call to see.**

Public Art

Albuquerque's Public Art Program is one of the oldest in the country. Since 1978 the city has acquired more than 620 artworks, and about 20 more are added each year. The collection is now worth $10 million, and works include sculptures, murals, mosaics, statues, fountains, paintings, and other decorative installations and architecture, including arted-up bus stops. Public art appears all over the city, but pockets of art, where it's hard to go far without spotting a piece, include Albuquerque International Sunport, Old Town, Downtown and the Civic Plaza area, the biological park, the University of New Mexico main campus, and the Main Library at 501 Copper NW.

Albuquerque's love affair with public art sprang out of the city's 1978 Art in Municipal Places ordinance. This reserved 1 percent of city construction funds derived from the general obligation bond program and certain revenue bonds for purchasing or commissioning works of art. (Santa Fe followed suit in 1985 with its own Art in Public Places Program, and the New Mexico State Legislature took the initiative statewide in 1986.) Commonly known as "One Percent for the Arts," the program aims for a balance between figurative and abstract pieces and between traditional styles and cutting-edge contemporary.

Some of the art is quiet and discreet—you almost have to know it's there to look for it—while other pieces are attention grabbers. The landmark *Cruising San Mateo I* by Barbara Grygutis is a blue-tiled 1957 Chevrolet perched on top of a huge tiled arch, standing at San Mateo and Gibson SE. If art is meant to be a conversation starter, this piece certainly set tongues wagging when it was installed circa 1991 and not always with approval. Now people have grown very fond of it, and its popular nickname is *Chevy On A Stick*. At the City's Public Art Web page, you can find links to images and maps of Albuquerque's art: www.cabq.gov/publicart.

Galleries

ALBUQUERQUE PHOTOGRAPHERS GALLERY

328-C San Felipe Street NW
(505) 244-9195
www.abqphotographersgallery.com

Albuquerque Photographers Gallery was founded in 2003 as a cooperative venture for local photographers to exhibit and sell contemporary fine art photography. Membership in the cooperative is juried and limited to 10 photographers, including founding photographer Marilyn Hunter, Robert Medina Cook, Urey Lemen, Tom Spross, and Pat O'Brien. The gallery aims to promote fine art photography as a major participant in the visual arts, and it hosts themed exhibitions three times a year. This charming Old Town adobe gallery is located on Poco Apoco Patio off San Felipe Street. Closed Tuesdays.

ANDREWS PUEBLO POTTERY AND ART GALLERY

303 Romero Street NW
(505) 243-0414, (877) 606-0543
www.andrewspp.com

Andrews is a family-owned Old Town business selling authentic Native American pottery since 1974. You'll find both contemporary and historic pueblo pottery here, plus Native American basketry, fetish carvings, katsina dolls, beadwork, and jewelry. The gallery offers Doug West's serigraph landscapes and oil paintings and wood sculptures from the award-winning Navajo artist Sheldon Harvey. There is also Mexican pottery from the village of Mata Ortiz in Chihuahua. Open seven days.

ARTScrawl

Twice a month Albuquerque art lovers take off around town on an adventure of aesthetics. The Albuquerque Art Business Association organizes two self-guided gallery tours, but as we all know, self-guided tours are much more fun when you're not doing it by yourself. Hence ARTScrawl and First Friday, which are both great ways to get out and gallery hop and have a good time meeting other people also poring over a map and wondering where to go next.

ARTScrawl has been a Duke City institution since 1990, taking place on the evening of the third Friday of every month. A different neighborhood plays host each month: Downtown, Old Town, Nob Hill, or the Northeast Heights. Once you're there, you'll find special art events, including artist receptions, artist demonstrations, exhibition openings, benefits, and open houses. Maps are provided to show which galleries are taking part, with information on the events at each one.

First Friday, added to the arts menu in 2005, works the same way, but it's on the first Friday of the month with citywide events.

There is art for every taste among the galleries taking part, and these relaxed evenings are an excellent way to meet artists and gallery owners and chat about the art. Both events usually run between 5 p.m. and 8:30 p.m. Maps and information on forthcoming ARTScrawls and First Fridays are on the Albuquerque Art Business Association (AABA) Web site (see below), or you can call the number below or see local media. The Web site also contains details on AABA member galleries. If you haven't yet picked up AABA's latest Albuquerque art brochure, with information on their member galleries, request one by phone or online or download a copy from the Web site; Albuquerque Art Business Association: (505) 244-0362; www.artscrawlabq.org.

ARTS ALLIANCE GALLERY
1100 San Mateo Boulevard NE
(505) 268-1920
www.abqarts.org/gallery.htm

The Arts Alliance organization advocates for the performing, visual, and literary arts in the Albuquerque metropolitan area. Their 1,500-square-foot bright and airy gallery presents monthly shows by regional art groups. Examples include the New Mexico Bead Society, the Albuquerque Fiber Arts Council, New Mexico Potters & Clay Artists, New Mexico Gourd Society, New Mexico Wood Turners, Pastel Society of New Mexico, and Rio Rancho Art Association. The gallery is right next to the offices of the Arts Alliance, at the north end of the Courtyard Shopping Complex at San Mateo and Lomas. Closed Sunday and most Saturdays.

BRIGHT RAIN GALLERY
206½ San Felipe NW
(505) 843-9176
www.brightraingallery.com

Expect strong contemporary work at this relatively young gallery in Old Town. Owner Travis Bruce Black's art is displayed, along with a pleasing variety of about thirty other artists working in disciplines that include painting, printmaking, photography, pottery, jewelry, sculpture, and woodworking.

CORRALES BOSQUE GALLERY
4685 Corrales Road
Corrales
(505) 898-7203
www.corralesbosquegallery.com

Located in Corrales village, this artist-owned gallery represents more than 20 artists working in a mix of fine arts and crafts. The gallery aims to present an eclectic mix of work at reasonable prices. In addition to promoting the work of gallery members, which includes paintings, ceramics, and jewelry, Corrales Bosque Gallery contributes to the development of Corrales as a cultural arts center. A focal point for the local arts community, the gallery hosts receptions four times a year. Open seven days.

DSG FINE ART
510 14th Street SW
(505) 266-7751, (800) 474-7751
www.dsg-art.com
In business since 1982, and formerly the Dartmouth Street Gallery, DSG Fine Art is an elegant gallery owned by John Cacciatore. It presents work by major local artists such as Frank McCulloch, former recipient of the Governors Award in the Arts and recognized by the Albuquerque Arts Alliance as Albuquerque Artist of the Year. Artists include Larry Bell, Kevin Zuckerman, Martin Facey, and Victoria Martinez Rodgers, whose work has been acquired for the permanent collection at the National Hispanic Cultural Center. DSG Fine Art also shows the tapestries of Nancy Kozikowski, vice president and artist in residence.

516 ARTS
516 Central Avenue SW
(505) 242-1445
www.516arts.org
It's hard to miss this museum-style gallery on Downtown Central Avenue with its graphically stylish glass facade. The innovative exhibits cover the gamut of media and disciplines, in styles from traditional through contemporary, with curated shows and collaborative projects from regional, national, and overseas artists. Work from both established and emerging artists can be seen here. Exhibits sometimes feature a combination of installation, video, and performance art. 516 ARTS is an independent nonprofit organization, and the gallery also hosts readings, literary events, and educational programs. Open Tuesday through Saturday.

GOWEN ARTS
Plaza Don Luis, Suite 114N,
303 Romero Street NW
(505) 242-6831, (800) 350-6099
www.galleryg7.com
An Old Town gallery specializing in the vivid metal work and sculptures of Greg Gowen. Gowen's work is influenced by desert, Native American, and New Mexico themes, and his creations include copper plate work and copper canvases "created with fire." Besides Gowen's work, the gallery shows Native American and southwestern jewelry, stone sculpture, watercolors, acrylics, and oil paintings from regional and out-of-state artists. Gowen also owns and exhibits at Copper Tree Gallery in Corrales (4514 Corrales Road, 505-922-8899). Open seven days.

HARWOOD ART CENTER
1114 7th Street NW
(505) 242-6367
www.harwoodartcenter.org
A creative center for community and the arts, the Harwood Art Center is housed in a 1925 neoclassical Revival-style building that was home to the Harwood Girls School between 1925 and 1976 and later to the Albuquerque Urban Indian Center. Harwood Art Center has been here since 1991, and its four galleries host new works every month by local and national artists. The diverse array of art is well balanced between the galleries, mixing disciplines and styles in all 2D and 3D media, including installations. You might also find the work of young talent presented beside that of established artists. There is a lively schedule of programs, arts classes, and events, including literary and performing arts. Harwood Art Center is the community outreach program of the independent nonprofit Montessori school Escuela del Sol. The galleries are closed on Saturday and Sunday.

MARIPOSA GALLERY
3500 Central Avenue SE
(505) 268-6828
www.mariposa-gallery.com

A Nob Hill gallery that's grown a great reputation over more than 30 years, Mariposa focuses on fine contemporary craft by New Mexico artists, including jewelry; functional and decorative clay; ceramics; fiber art; and work in glass, metal, and wood; plus paintings and mixed media. Also known for promoting emerging artists. Open seven days.

MATRIX FINE ART
Suite 100A, 3812 Central Avenue SE
(505) 268-8952
www.matrixfineart.com
A Nob Hill gallery featuring established and emerging New Mexico artists working in painting, ceramic, glass, and sculpture. The 2,000-square-foot contemporary gallery mounts 12 exhibitions each year. The gallery represents artists that include Frank McCulloch, Mark Beck, Marilyn Dillard, and Sara D'Alessandro. Closed Monday.

OPEN MIND SPACE
Suite C-1, 404 San Felipe NW
(505) 259-3566
www.theopenmindspace.com
The Open Mind Space combines a gallery of fine art, a yoga studio, and a meeting place for the creatively inclined. Artist exhibits change monthly and usually showcase the work of one guest artist, although there are group shows, too. Most but not all are New Mexico artists, working in a variety of media from painting and photography to outdoor sculpture and photographic quilts. Featured artists have included Larry Bell, Douglas Kent Hall, Charles Strong, and Kitty Alice Snead. The gallery offers a contemplative atmosphere for the appreciation of art, culture, and spirituality. The Old Town gallery is open to visitors on afternoons only, Wednesday through Sunday. There are also yoga classes on Thursday and Sunday mornings.

RIO GRANDE GALLERY
Plaza Don Luis
303 Romero Street NW
(505) 242 8008, (800) 388-2787
www.riograndegallery.com
Recently relocated to a light and spacious gallery upstairs in Old Town's Plaza Don Luis, the Rio Grande Gallery is a great stop to see some excellent examples of Southwestern paintings and sculpture, including the works of R. C. Gorman; the gallery has represented Gorman and his estate for twenty-five years. Other artists include Frank Howell, Ben Wright, C. J. Wells, and Taos painter Miguel Martinez. Smaller pieces by Pablo Antonio Milan are surprisingly affordable for those starting out a collection. Open seven days.

TAMARIND INSTITUTE
2500 Central Avenue SE (from mid-2010—see note below)
(505) 277-3901
tamarind.unm.edu
Tamarind Institute is a center for fine art lithography, with an international reputation for its contributions to contemporary printmaking. A division of the College of Fine Arts at the University of New Mexico, Tamarind trains master printers and houses a professional collaborative studio for artists. The Gallery at Tamarind Institute is open to visitors. Here you'll see collections of artists' most recent lithographs.

Free tours are also offered on the first Friday of each month. The 90-minute tour includes a visit to the workshop and a printing demonstration, information on Tamarind history and programs, and a screening of *Four Stones for Kanemitsu,* an award-winning video on the collaborative process. The tour is at 1:30 p.m. You must reserve a space on this limited-numbers tour. Call (505) 277-3901.

Tamarind Institute celebrates its 50th anniversary in 2010. At the time of writing, it is breaking ground on a new 14,000-square-foot building at 2500 Central Avenue SE. The scheduled date to move into this building is June 1, 2010, in time for its 50th anniversary celebrations and exhibition. Until the move, the Tamarind Institute Workshop and Gallery remain open at its old home: 108–110 Cornell SE. If you are visiting Tamarind during summer 2010, it is probably wise to call and check on the status of the move before setting out. The phone number should remain the same at both addresses. Opening hours to the public are Monday through Friday, 9 a.m. to 5 p.m., or call for appointment.

i **Plein Air Painters of New Mexico (PAPNM) holds several group "paintouts" every month throughout the year, in a variety of landscapes. Artists visiting Albuquerque are welcome to join one of these plein air painting (in the open air, or outdoors) sessions; see the schedule on the PAPNM Web site. Although paintouts are for PAPNM members, annual membership is $25, so even if you only come for one paintout during your trip, this is a reasonable fee to pay for a day of plein air painting camaraderie, often followed by a social get-together. Bring your own art supplies. Paintouts can number from a couple of artists to 20-plus. You don't need to be a New Mexico resident to join in; PAPNM currently has members from nearby Texas, Colorado, and Arizona too. An annual six-day paintout travels around to various beautiful sites, followed by a gallery exhibition and best-of-show awards; www.pleinairpaintersnm.org.**

WEEMS ART GALLERY

Louisiana Plaza
7200 Montgomery Boulevard NE, Suite D
(505) 293-6133

Plaza Don Luis—Old Town
303 Romero NW
(505) 764-0302
www.weemsgallery.com

This is a popular gallery among locals, in business since 1981. Weems Art Gallery shows work by a couple of hundred artists, in a wide range of forms and styles and an equally broad price range. There are plenty of pieces that are suitable for gifts, and Weems offers a wedding registry service. The gallery sells traditional, Southwestern, and contemporary paintings, prints, sculpture, glass, pottery, jewelry, mixed media, and general home decor objects. The gallery owner, Mary Ann Weems, sponsors the annual Weems International Artfest in Albuquerque in November. Weems Art Gallery is in two locations: The Louisiana Plaza gallery is closed Sunday. The Old Town gallery is open seven days.

WEYRICH GALLERY

2935-D Louisiana NE
(505) 883-7410
www.weyrichgallery.com

Find contemporary fine crafts and fine art in this gallery, which focuses on harmony in art and works from dreams, folklore, myth and the earth. The gallery specializes in porcelain with a traditional Japanese approach. You'll find contemporary Arita-style porcelain, tea bowls, Raku vessels, contemporary Karatsu Japanese stoneware, and woodfired stoneware. They also have Native American pottery, paintings, and works in glass, metal, wood, jewelry, and fiber, plus limited-edition monotypes, collagraphs, mezzotint, etching, photogravure, and serigraphs. Weyrich Gallery contains the Art of Living Center, which offers Reiki sessions, feng shui consultations, nutritional counseling, and other services and is host to seminars on subjects like stress reduction, color and placement of art, and the Japanese tea ceremony. Closed Sunday and Monday.

WOODEN COW GALLERY AND ART SPACE

7400 Montgomery Boulevard NE, Suite 20
(505) 999-1280
www.thewoodencow.com

This young gallery opened in 2008 and quickly drew favorable reviews from the community, including a best art gallery slot in the weekly *Alibi* newspaper's Best of Burque 2009. A cooperative of local artists, it presents an eclectic array of media and styles. You might see more unusual pieces like gourd art, stoneware fountains, metal weaving, assemblage and mosaic, silk painting, raku ceramics, and handturned pens, plus paintings, sculpture, pottery, jewelry, photography, woodcut prints, and mixed media. Open Wednesday through Sunday.

FILM

It might come as a surprise to people outside the movie world to learn that Albuquerque has a flourishing film industry. Movies shot here, at least in part, include *Terminator Salvation, The Book of Eli, Wild Hogs, The Men Who Stare at Goats,* and the Oscar-winning *No Country for Old Men.* As the Albuquerque Film Office folks say, perhaps slightly tongue in cheek: "Albuquerque—who knew?"

The State of New Mexico has worked hard to attract filmmakers and in 2002 was one of the first states to commit to a serious package of economic incentives. The menu of incentives has included a 25 percent tax rebate on eligible direct production costs, including New Mexico crew. There are also exemptions on state gross receipts tax (sales tax) at the point of sale, and a Film Investment Loan Program, offering interest-free loans of up to $15 million for eligible projects. A Film Crew Advancement Program reimburses 50 percent of wages for on-the-job training of New Mexico residents in certain crew positions. These lucrative financing packages have been a big draw for moviemakers, benefiting the entire state in growing its film industry and leading New Mexico to be tagged "Hollywood Southwest."

Albuquerque is a hub of the action, and in 2008 *Forbes* cited Albuquerque among "Hollywood's Favorite Cities." *MovieMaker* magazine ranked Albuquerque number two in its "Top 10 Movie Cities of 2008."

The city's movie muscle has paid dividends to the local economy. In the 2004 fiscal year, direct spend from the film industry to the city of Albuquerque was $11 million. By 2007 spend had leaped to $83 million. A mere year later, in the fiscal year of 2008, the film industry earned the city a rocking $130 million.

Albuquerque is just a 90-minute flight from Los Angeles, and one of its many appeals to movie and TV producers is its easy access to a wide range of locations. These include settings from contemporary urban to suburban to rural. Albuquerque has masqueraded on film as cities as diverse as New York, Dallas, Cincinnati, and Munich. But there are also many open-space and unspoiled areas around the city that can pass for (or be easily transformed to) the Old West, old-world Europe, the Middle East, a sci-fi futuristic Planet Earth, or even another planet altogether. Landscapes on Albuquerque's doorstep range from mountains to deserts, as well as the forests and pastoral and prairie lands in between. Architecture runs the gamut from evocative old adobe neighborhoods to Western ranches to charming Victorian houses and ultramodern Downtown lofts. There is no location fee for filming in state-owned buildings, and few permits are required for filming in the Albuquerque area. Consistent weather patterns help keep shooting on schedule, with a reliable 310 days of sunshine a year. The sun shines in more than 75 percent of daylight hours even during winter months.

There is also an experienced and eager workforce of crew, talent, and production and technical staff. Film pros have chosen to live in New Mexico for years—at times it's seemed like a kind of dormitory community for Hollywood, with crew and actors commuting to California for jobs. Now Hollywood comes to them, and the workforce is growing as colleges step up their professional training. The University of New Mexico's Interdisciplinary Film and Digital Media Program aims to integrate filmmaking and digital media and "build a native New Mexican Hollywood."

The jewel in the crown of Albuquerque's filming facilities is Albuquerque Studios, which opened as a state-of-the-art $74 million complex in 2007 and has since expanded. *Terminator Salvation,* starring Christian Bale, Sam Worthington, and Helena Bonham Carter was shot here, and the filmmakers cited the diversity of nearby locations available as one reason for choosing the venue, as the movie covers mountaintops to deserts. They also needed a studio with plenty of land around to build (and blow up) sets as needed. *Terminator Salvation* is said to be the biggest and most expensive film shot to date in New Mexico.

Albuquerque's reputation as a film hot spot was enhanced further when Sony Pictures Imageworks opened a Downtown facility as a satellite to its Culver City, California, headquarters. Sony Pictures Imageworks is the Academy Award–winning digital production studio, famous for its innovative visual effects and digital character animation. The company's cited criteria for choosing branch locations are that they must be convenient for clients, close to centers of artistic excellence, in areas offering economic and lifestyle incentives, and low operational costs. Sony Pictures Imageworks projects in Albuquerque include Tim Burton's *Alice in Wonderland,* Jerry Bruckheimer's *G-Force,* Brad Peyton's *Cats & Dogs 2,* and Sony Pictures Animation's *Cloudy with a Chance of Meatballs.*

In 2009 ReelzChannel opened production facilities and moved its corporate headquarters to Albuquerque. ReelzChannel is a cable and satellite network and accompanying Web site dedicated to programming about (suitably enough) movies, from behind-the-scenes coverage to new movie reviews. It reaches over 43 million homes nationwide and is the first national TV network based in New Mexico. It is located in 30,000 square feet of office and production space at Albuquerque Studios.

Besides the big names and the blockbusters, Albuquerque also has a thriving independent movie culture and was ranked number five by *MovieMaker* magazine in its list of the "25 best cities in the U.S. to ride it out as an independent moviemaker" in 2009. The nation's economy crunch was hitting home at the time of that report, and *MovieMaker*'s calculations aimed to identify the places offering indie filmmakers the "best all-round chance of finding success with their art."

Of course, it doesn't hurt that even the most glittering screen stars enjoy a visit to the Land of Enchantment. On the whole, Burqueños are pretty cool about the celebrities in their midst, as laid back about Val Kilmer's dropping into a Lobo basketball game as they are about most other things (Kilmer's lived in New Mexico for some years and is rumored to be a possible candidate for governor). And the actors themselves seem fairly relaxed here. The *Washington Post* reported that when *The Book of Eli* was being filmed in Albuquerque, New Mexico governor Bill Richardson dropped by the set and spotted lead actor Denzel Washington. "Hey, Champ, good to see you," said Richardson. To which Washington apparently replied, "Good to be seen by you."

When it comes to VIPs, people in Albuquerque tend to get less excited about Very Important People than Very Important Places. Spotting and identifying home-city locations used in movies is a popular pastime, and Duke City citizens share tips on their favorite places that have cropped up on screen, from car washes to cafés. The *Albuquerque Journal* newspaper Web site started a map of locations used in the Emmy Award–winning TV series *Breaking Bad,* a show that is actually set in Albuquerque as well as being produced here. The drama tells the story of a chemistry teacher in desperate circumstances, who resorts to dealing drugs. That may not be the kind of image the city wants to promote, but it certainly creates a buzz as locals spot familiar locations whizzing by.

ALBUQUERQUE FILM OFFICE
PO Box 1293
Albuquerque, NM 87103
(505) 768-3283, (505) 768-3289
www.cabq.gov/film
Part of the Albuquerque Economic Development Department, the Albuquerque Film Office

offers support to filmmakers; liaison with city agencies; and assistance with locations, equipment, and other logistics. This is the "first-stop shop" for movie makers coming to Duke City. For film buffs and workers in the industry, the Albuquerque Film Office Web site maintains a list of movie and TV productions in the city and posts film-related news, crew calls, and casting calls. It also showcases independent movies shot in or around Duke City. There is information on permits and application forms, a directory of companies providing production services to filmmakers, and hotels and car-rental agencies offering discounts to film-industry professionals. It also has a photo gallery of locations and details on Albuquerque sunrise and sunset times. The Albuquerque Film Office encourages "green" filmmaking and will coordinate the supply of recycling containers to production companies.

i **Even nonactors can get in on the act. Anyone in Albuquerque can turn up at the frequent casting calls for extras, and you'll see casting-call flyers in cafés and bars, or you can keep an eye on the Web sites of the film organizations in these listings. The Albuquerque Film Office Web site has a page explaining the protocol of being an extra and how it all works. You won't earn the down payment for your first yacht, and you're unlikely to become George Clooney's new best friend, but if you have the time and inclination, it's a fun way to sneak a peek inside the workings of the industry and feel a part of Albuquerque's movie scene; www.cabq.gov/film/soyou wanttobeanextra.html.**

ALBUQUERQUE STUDIOS
5650 University Boulevard SE
(505) 227-2000
www.abqstudios.com

This 28-acre purpose-built movie and TV production facility opened in 2007 at a cost of $74 million. It is owned and operated by Pacifica Ventures of Santa Monica, California. It boasts eight soundstages totaling 168,000 square feet and claims to have some of the largest and tallest stages outside of Hollywood. Soundstages in the cutting-edge facility are built in pairs, separated by partition walls that can be opened up to create a mammoth 48,000 square feet of shooting space in the biggest pairs. Close the partition wall off, and a gunshot fired on one stage can't be heard on the other. The studio also has extensive production support and office space. It is located five minutes from Albuquerque International Sunport in the Mesa del Sol area south of the airport. Feature productions at Albuquerque Studios have included the blockbuster *Terminator Salvation* with Christian Bale; *Gamer*, starring Gerard Butler; *The Book of Eli* with Denzel Washington, and *The Spirit,* starring Scarlett Johansson, Samuel L. Jackson, and Eva Mendes, which was entirely produced at Albuquerque Studios. TV series include *In Plain Sight* and two seasons of the Emmy Award–winning drama series *Breaking Bad,* which is set in Duke City.

NEW MEXICO FILM OFFICE
418 Montezuma Avenue
Santa Fe
(505) 476-5600, (800) 545-9871
www.nmfilm.com

The state film office provides full information and assistance to filmmakers regarding New Mexico's tax incentives and resources related to services to movie and TV producers in Albuquerque and throughout the state. Their Web site has information on current projects shooting across New Mexico and a detailed filmography for the state, including information on locations used. At the time of writing, the filmography page is a bit buried away in the layers of information on this comprehensive site but can be found at www.nmfilm.com/filming/filmography. It also has a locations database with photos. Information for locals includes classes and workshops, employment opportunities, crew calls and casting calls, and news on screenings.

RIO RANCHO FILM COMMISSION
Rio Rancho Convention and Visitors Bureau
4011 Barbara Loop, Suite 208
Rio Rancho
(505) 891-7258, (888) 746-7262
www.rioranchonm.org

Productions shot in Rio Rancho include the ABC family series *Wildfire, Jebediah Smith* for the History Channel, *Far Side of Jericho, Dreamland,* and *A Thief of Time.* Commercials have been shot here for GMC, Chevrolet, Renault, Presbyterian Healthcare, the Discovery Channel's *Animal Planet,* and Giant Industries. The Rio Rancho Film Commission offers assistance with locations, permits, equipment, accommodations, and other resources for filmmakers.

i **Movie fans head to the Nob Hill art house Guild Cinema for indie flicks, foreign films, documentaries, cult classics, and weekend midnight movies. This 1966 gem on Route 66 is independently owned and doesn't take credit or debit cards. Tickets are cash only, $7, or $5 for seniors, students, and under-12s. First show of the day matinees are also $5. You can't buy tickets in advance; just turn up at the box office—it opens 15 minutes before the movie; Guild Cinema, 3405 Central Avenue NE, (505) 255-1848; www.guildcinema.com.**

ANNUAL FILM FESTIVALS

ALBUQUERQUE FILM FESTIVAL
Various locations
www.albuquerquefilmfestival.com

The annual Albuquerque Film Festival made its debut in 2009, with an August festival over four days in venues that included the KiMo Theatre, Cell Theatre, and the National Hispanic Cultural Center. In addition to screenings of U.S. and international films, plus panels and workshops, the festival is an event "where the arts collide" and features flamenco, music, and theater.

DUKE CITY SHOOTOUT
Various locations
(505) 255-1991
www.dukecityshootout.org

The world's first script-to-screen filmmaking competition, Duke City Shootout started out in 2000 as Flicks on 66. The competition selects seven winning short film scripts from international submissions and brings the writers to Albuquerque to shoot, edit, and premiere their films in one week (usually in July/August). The organizers provide cast, crew, equipment, mentoring, and all other support needed to shoot the film. There are various events through the week and a gala premiere screening of the finished movies. Festival events have been held at venues including the Kiva Auditorium at the Albuquerque Convention Center, Albuquerque Studios, and Hyatt Regency. Films made here have later been presented in other festivals around the world. Duke City Shootout went on hiatus in 2009 but plans to return in 2010 to celebrate its tenth anniversary festival.

EXPERIMENTS IN CINEMA
Various locations
(505) 842-9977
www.basementfilms.org/experiments.html

Presenting international indie and underground movies, organizer Basement Films aims to promote underrepresented film and video. The emphasis here is on the visionary, and there is an impressive showing of films from all corners of the planet. Usually held over four days in April, venues have included Guild Cinema, 516 Arts, and Southwest Film Center.

48 HOUR FILM PROJECT
Various locations
www.48hourfilm.com/albuquerque

The 48 Hour Film Project national tour comes to Albuquerque every summer for a mad-dash weekend, during which filmmakers have exactly 48 hours to make a seven-minute film. Teams write, shoot, edit, and add the music soundtrack in those 48 hours, and nobody can cheat in advance because teams are assigned a movie genre, character, prop, and line of dialogue that they have to use in the film. At the end of the weekend, the movies are premiered, usually at the KiMo Theatre, and a winner is picked to compete for the national contest.

ITALIAN FILM FESTIVAL

Various locations

www.italianfilmfest.org

The Italian Film Festival shows Italian movie classics and contemporary award winners, plus it holds a gala dinner and a few other social events. Marco Tullio Giordana's epic six-hour-long *La Meglio Gioventù* has been screened for the festival (over two sessions!). The event is a fund-raiser for the University of New Mexico Chidren's Hospital and usually runs over eight days in February at venues that include the Guild Cinema and the South Broadway Cultural Center.

LOCAL SHORTS FILM FESTIVAL

Various locations

www.localshorts.com

This accessible and friendly festival showcases local voices with an eclectic lineup of short movies up to 15 minutes long that all have a connection to Albuquerque or New Mexico. A real community gathering, it usually takes place in July or August at the Lobo Theater.

SIN FRONTERAS FILM FESTIVAL

Various locations

www.unm.edu/~lasunm/solas.html

Presenting Latino films and filmmakers, Sin Fronteras is organized by UNM's Student Organization for Latin American Studies (SOLAS). The program's range of films includes documentaries, animations, and shorts. Screenings are at the UNM Southwest Film Center, and the festival has previously run over a weekend in February.

i **A New Mexico movie news blog, chat forum, cast and crew calls, and other resources for industry insiders and those who want to be can be found at www.CrewNewMexico.com.**

SOUTHWEST GAY & LESBIAN FILM FESTIVAL

Various locations

(505) 243-1870

www.closetcinema.org

A weeklong festival screening more than 80 features, documentaries, and shorts that showcase the richness of the GLBT experience. Organized by Closet Cinema since 2003, attendance has previously surpassed 4,000, making this one of New Mexico's biggest film festivals. Programming includes international films, and there are audience awards for movies in various categories. The festival usually takes place in September/October, and screening venues have included the Guild Cinema and South Broadway Cultural Center.

i **Albuquerque has the honor of entering the biggest team ever to the national 48 Hour Film Project—a contest to shoot a seven-minute film in 48 hours. Albuquerque's team boasted 116 people . . . and 30 horses!**

ALBUQUERQUE FILM CREDITS

A selected list of movies and TV shows filmed partly or in whole in Albuquerque. Films are listed chronologically by date of shooting in Albuquerque, with the most recent first. A full list is available at the Albuquerque Film Office; www.cabq.gov/film.

Paul
Crash: Seasons 1–2, TV
The Resident
The Dry Land
The Book of Eli
Friendship!
In Plain Sight
The Men Who Stare at Goats
The Spy Next Door
Breaking Bad: Seasons 1–3, TV
My One & Only
Saint John of Las Vegas
Crazy Heart
Easy Money
Night and Day
Year One
Love Ranch
Game
Not Forgotten
Terminator Salvation
Observe & Report
Easier with Practice
Sex & Lies in Sin City
Legion
Dark Country
The Spirit
Hamlet 2
To Live and Die
In Plain Sight
$5 a Day
The War Boys
Love N' Dancing
Swing Vote
Linewatch
Afterwards
Husband for Hire
Love Lies Bleeding
The Eye
Sunshine Cleaning
Wildfire: Seasons 1–4, TV
Tennessee
Sarah Connor Chronicles
In the Valley of Elah
Urban Justice
Beerfest
Fanboys
Employee of the Month
The Lost Room
Save Me
Carriers
Transformers
The Hitcher
No Country for Old Men
Wild Hogs
Dreamland
Trade
The Flock
Astronaut Farmer
Three Wise Guys, TV
Bordertown
Rent
First Snow
Cruel World
Rx
Around the Bend
Elvis Has Left the Building
Formosa
North Country
Nothing But Life
In from the Night, TV
Cruel World
Believe in Me
Coyote Waits
A Thief of Time
Off the Map
Clockers
Buffalo Girls, TV miniseries
Speechless
Natural Born Killers
The Fire Next Time, TV miniseries
Project Eliminator (aka Gambit)
Animal Behavior
Outrageous Fortune
Silkwood
Hide in Plain Sight
Butch and Sundance: The Early Days
The Muppet Movie
Every Which Way but Loose
Sidewinder 1
Bobbie Joe and the Outlaw
The Man Who Fell to Earth
Lonely Are the Brave
Ace in the Hole

KIDSTUFF

Albuquerque is first and foremost a city for families, and many of the attractions, entertainment, and recreation options featured in this book are as relevant to kids as they are to adults. The majority of annual events and festivals cater to youngsters, too, with dedicated activities and craft areas. In this chapter we highlight some especially fun stuff for kids. Within each themed section there are suggestions to please all age groups. The Crafty Stuff section has ideas on creative expression from candlemaking to making magic. Critters Galore gives venues in which to see or interact with animals, from cuddly alpacas to slithery snakes, plus exotic species at the zoo and aquarium, and even a Wild West rodeo. Fun & Games showcases amusements, play, and activity centers. Outdoor Stuff suggests ways to get a breath of fresh air while enjoying Albuquerque's natural environment, right in the center of town. Smart Play highlights the elements of interest to kids in city museums and cultural centers, and Treats & Eats speaks for itself! Restaurants in Duke City are generally child-friendly, especially the mom-and-pop-style eateries serving New Mexican cuisine, and of course there are plenty of chain restaurants that you'll be familiar with. But if you're looking for ice cream, a cool Route 66 diner complete with old-fashioned soda fountain, or other family-oriented dining spots, check out our suggestions.

In Albuquerque's desert environment it's especially important to keep kids well hydrated, and to shield them from the piercing high-altitude sunlight with sunhats, sunglasses with UV protection for their eyes, and frequent applications of high-SPF sunscreen. On the hottest summer days, if you don't feel like an indoor attraction, then either pass your time at shady outdoor destinations like the Rio Grande Nature Center or head for higher elevations. The Sandia Peak Tramway and Tinkertown Museum in the mountains are good choices for everyone to keep cool.

Pick up a copy of the free *New Mexico Kids* magazine for a calendar of events, activities, summer camps, and entertainment shows for youngsters. You'll find it at libraries, cafés, and stores around town and at the visitor center booth at Albuquerque International Sunport on Level One.

Price Code

Price codes are based on admission or activity fees for one adult, unless otherwise indicated. Rates for children are usually lower. In the Fun & Games section, amusement pricings are complex for the various packages available and frequently vary according to age. Although you can often gain admission for the cost of one activity or amusement, realistically, you're likely to go for more than the minimum, especially once the kids see what's on offer! Therefore, we've indicated a more likely scenario of how much it will cost you, although you can usually do a bare-bones trip costing less than our price code. We've noted where there are free admission days and if there's no charge for children under a certain age.

$ . . . . Less than $5
$$ $5–10
$$$ $11–20
$$$$ . . . . More than $20

i Travelin' Tots Rentals supplies cribs, strollers, car seats, and other essentials to parents visiting Albuquerque. Rent items by the day, week, or month, from infant swings and baths to high chairs, nursery monitors, and baskets of toys for different age groups. They also rent family fun stuff like picnic blankets, coolers, and walkie-talkie sets. Items are sterilized between rentals. Travelin' Tots has been in business since 2004, and they deliver the items to you and set them up if relevant. You can even arrange for a crib and bedding to be installed and made up in your hotel room before you arrive. A price example is $25 a week for a car seat. Delivery is free in Albuquerque; there's a small delivery fee to surrounding areas; (505) 237-1066; www.travelintotsrentals.com.

CRAFTY STUFF

ART! ATTACK **$$$**
3137 San Mateo Boulevard NE
(505) 298-3275
www.artattacknm.com

This paint-your-own-pottery studio has great ceramic pieces for kids to stencil, stamp, and paint, including figurines of dogs, cats, lizards, fairies, ninja turtles, and dragons. There are also boxes, dishes, and other objects to use as canvases for creativity. The studio fee includes painting, glazing, and firing, and you choose your own item to decorate in a range of sizes and prices. Note that it takes three to five days for a piece to be fired and ready to collect, so if you're on a short visit, it's best to come here early in your trip. The price code shown is for up to two hours of painting time, plus at least one figurine, depending on the size you pick.

CAKE FETISH **$**
2665 Louisiana Boulevard NE
(505)883-0670
www.cakefetish.com

Kids can decorate their own cupcake at Cake Fetish bakery in a party package—although you only need two people to count as a party! The price code shown is for a basic package including one unfrosted cupcake per person, vanilla and chocolate frostings, sprinkles galore, and a beverage. A deluxe party is also available with two cakes and more frostings. Both packages are for 2 to 10 people. Cake Fetish needs a week's notice on reservations, then they'll set up and reserve a table for you for an hour, and clean up afterwards. Available Monday through Saturday at both the Louisiana Boulevard store and the Westside location (Montano Plaza, 6200 Coors Road, Suite A9, 505-899-2425).

THE MAGIC AND JUGGLING SHOP
3205 Central Avenue NE
(505) 255-2303
www.magicandjuggling.com

Budding wizards will be enchanted by this Nob Hill store that supplies professional magicians but has plenty for the novice, too. There are tricks with coins and cards, magic sets, books, DVDs, and kits to learn how to juggle. A free Magician's Apprentice workshop offers an introduction to the craft each month, for participants 7 years and older. As we go to press, the workshop is at 1 p.m. on the third Saturday of the month, but that may change, so check with the shop before setting off. Closed Sunday and Monday.

NEW MEXICO CANDLE COMPANY **$$$**
523 Wyoming Boulevard NE
(505) 891-2366
www.nmcandleco.com

Kids (and parents!) create their own candles at this friendly family-run candle store and studio. Sand-cast candles are poured for you, and then you carve and paint! The sand- and wax-bonded candles are easy to sculpt, and they take paint beautifully for your own bright and unique design. If kids are too young to carve, the owner will carve for them—a pony, perhaps—and then the youngster can paint and decorate it. An extra candle is poured, so if you make a mistake, it's no big deal—grab the spare and start on that.

There's also a family room with air hockey, TV, beanbags, and Ping-Pong. Candlemaking workshops run several times a week, but if you call in advance, they'll set up for an individual or family anytime. If you just drop in, they might have candles you can carve, as long as you're willing to go with whatever shape is on hand. The price code shown is for the under-18s rate, including refreshments. Closed Sunday.

i **Children's Radio Hour on KUNM 89.9 FM on Saturday from 9 a.m. to 10 a.m. features stories, music, and news about kids' events. You can stream it online too: kunm.org.**

CRITTERS GALORE

ALBUQUERQUE ALPACAS
9721 Guadalupe Trail NW
(505) 269-6733
www.albuquerquealpacas.com

Visitors are welcome at this friendly alpaca ranch, where kids can pet, feed, and walk the alpacas around. There are often ultracute baby alpacas to play with, and you can find out about the whole process of rearing the animals; shearing their fleece; and spinning, weaving, and knitting the fibers, perhaps including a demonstration. The ranch has about 18 alpacas and is set around an adobe hacienda. There's no fee to take a tour, but you can pop into the ranch store to buy a souvenir of soft alpaca socks, gloves, mittens, scarves, sweaters, or rugs. The store only accepts cash or checks, and there also toys for sale and books on alpacas. It's best to call in advance and schedule a tour, as this is a one-woman working farm, but you can drop in if the gate is open. Open daily, but sometimes the owner is away with the animals at fairs and festivals, so call beforehand to check.

ALBUQUERQUE AQUARIUM AND RIO GRANDE BOTANIC GARDEN **$$**
2601 Central Avenue NW
(505) 768-2000
www.cabq.gov/biopark

This is a great combination destination for kids of all ages. The botanic garden includes a children's Fantasy Garden, guarded by a 14-foot-high dragon. Inside the warren-like garden, adults and kids alike are dwarfed by sculptures of giant ants, bees, flowers, and vegetables, and you can walk through a two-story-high pumpkin. Nearby in the botanic garden there's a lake and a model railway village in the Railroad Garden running around two 400-foot loops. Inside the seasonal PNM Butterfly Pavilion, brightly colored butterflies flutter around your head or—if you stand still long enough—might come to rest on your arm. See cows, goats, sheep, pigs, and horses at the Heritage Farm and creepy-crawlies at the new Insectarium. The Insectarium is opening in stages from fall 2009 to the main launch in 2010, with 8-inch emperor scorpions and foot-long millipedes from Africa; walking sticks up to 20 inches long from Asia; and tropical beetles, mantids, and tarantulas. From the end of November through December, the botanic garden hosts a River of Lights holiday light show with light sculptures and fiber-optic lit snowmen, and skaters can take to an outdoor ice rink on selected evenings.

At the Albuquerque Aquarium, a 285,000-gallon ocean tank is home to brown, sand tiger, blacktip, and nurse sharks, and you can watch twice-daily shark feedings and see divers descend into the tank daily through the 38-foot-wide floor-to-ceiling viewing window. Kids also love walking through the eel tunnel and spotting seahorses and jellyfish. There are also seasonal touch pools.

One entry fee covers admission to both the aquarium and the botanic garden. These two attractions, along with the neighboring Rio Grande Zoo, are part of the Albuquerque Biological Park. See the Attractions chapter for detailed information on all BioPark facilities, including the narrow-gauge Rio Line train that runs between them, and discount rate combo tickets. Free admission for under-3s. Open seven days.

If you're visiting the Albuquerque Aquarium and Rio Grande Botanic Garden in summer, it's a good idea to start at the gardens in the morning before the full heat of the day, then head into the cooler aquarium.

AMERICAN INTERNATIONAL RATTLESNAKE MUSEUM **$$**
202 San Felipe NW
(505) 242-6569
www.rattlesnakes.com

You get a certificate of bravery after moseying among 34 varieties of live rattlesnakes, as well as pythons, vipers, scorpions, poisonous lizards, and tropical spiders at this Old Town museum. They're all behind glass, but often there's the chance to touch a nonpoisonous snake, too! Open seven days.

Snooze beside the sharks in a "Sleep with the Fishes" sleepover at the Albuquerque Aquarium. These regular nights include activities such as games, crafts, a touch-pool visit, and a film. Adults must accompany under-18s, and the fee is $25 per person, registered in advance; (505) 848-7180; www.cabq.gov/biopark.

RIO GRANDE NATURE CENTER STATE PARK
2901 Candelaria Road NW
(505) 344-7240
www.nmparks.com

Walking into the nature center feels like you're entering a hobbit house. A tunnel entryway leads into a circular hall that's a cross between a secret laboratory and a Tolkien-esque chamber, with water pillars reaching to the ceiling. Because the building is sunk into the ground, you're on a level with the three-acre pond outside, which comes right up to the big curved windows in the cozy lounge. Here kids can watch pond wildlife up close, and depending on the time of year, you might see a family of Western painted turtles with their babies sunning themselves on the logs, geese waterskiing in to land, hummingbirds, dragonflies, and ducks. The outdoor birdsong and other natural sounds are piped into the lounge so it's the next best thing to actually being in the pond yourself! There are binoculars, identification guides, and children's books in the lounge and hands-on exhibits for children in the Discovery Room. Two easy nature trails take you into the shady cottonwood and willow bosque and down to the river. You can walk just a little way or follow the complete round-trip loops, which are each a mile or just under. The 270-acre park also includes the Candelaria Wetland and outdoor blinds to remain concealed while observing wildlife. There's a small shop but no café. A calendar of activities for kids and adults, including talks and demonstrations, guided nature walks, and evening moon walks, is available from the park or from the Friends of the Rio Grande Nature Center, www.rgnc.org. They're usually free, but some require advance registration. In just a few minutes' drive from the city center, you can drop into this serenely beautiful spot. Park admission is free for pedestrians and bikes. Motor vehicles pay $3. The park is open from 8 a.m. to 5 p.m. The nature center is open 10 a.m. to 5 p.m.

RIO GRANDE ZOO **$$**
903 Tenth Street SW
(505) 764-6200
www.cabq.gov/biopark

Watch the year-round daily feedings of the seals, sea lions, and everyone's favorite, the polar bears. In spring and summer kids can hand-feed lorikeets and giraffes, with their 18-inch tongues, and watch the Animal Encounters show and Porcupine Stroll. There are also bumpy, humpy camel rides available seasonally. You'll find a Gator Swamp, 15-foot-long crocodiles, gorillas, elephants, cheetahs, and cute koalas in the 64-acre zoo, which is inhabited by over 250 species of exotic and native critters. The zoo, along with the adjacent Albuquerque Aquarium and Rio Grande Botanic Garden, is part of the Albuquerque Biological Park. See the Attractions chapter for detailed information on all BioPark facilities, including the narrow-gauge Rio Line train that runs between them, and discount-rate combo tickets. Tots under 3 are free. Open seven days.

On Mondays from after Memorial Day through Labor Day, a paying adult can bring up to four kids free of charge to the Rio Grande Zoo or to the Albuquerque Aquarium and Rio Grande Botanic Garden.

RODEO AT THE STABLES AT TAMAYA $$$$
Hyatt Regency Tamaya Resort & Spa
1300 Tuyuna Trail
Santa Ana Pueblo
(505) 771-6037
www.tamaya.hyatt.com

Summer rodeos are open to visitors not resident at the resort, and children under 14 enjoy free admission to watch team roping, barrel racing, and other events. Rodeos include fun activities for kids to participate in, like stick-horse racing and pretend "branding." Rodeos have previously taken place on Thursday evenings from late May; check with the venue for current schedules. The price code is for nonresident adult entry. Take exit 242 from I-25 north of Albuquerque and west onto Highway 550 toward Bernalillo. The resort is signed after about 2.4 miles on your right.

FUN & GAMES

ABQ JUMP $$
2731 Broadway Boulevard NE, Suite E
(505) 344-5437
www.abqjump.com

This indoor inflatable play center has slides; basketball and other ball games; and plenty of fun bouncy shapes and structures to climb in, on, under, and around! It's open on weekdays and occasionally on weekends, although weekends are mainly reserved for kids' parties. Kids must wear socks to play here. The price code shown is per child over 2 years; admission for parents is free. With parental discretion some slightly younger jumpers may join in, for a reduced rate or free with a full-price admission. Find ABQ Jump on Broadway two blocks west of the Menaul exit from I-25, between Candelaria and Menaul.

CLIFF'S AMUSEMENT PARK $$$
4800 Osuna Road NE
(505) 881-9373
www.cliffsamusementpark.com

The newest thrill at this summer-only park is the Fire Ball, a 60-foot-high looping ride that turns you upside down 13 times a minute in the turquoise New Mexico sky. Screamers also get to test their lungs on the gravity drop from the top of the Cliff Hanger and as they spin 80 feet high in the air on the SideWinder. At the very least, you'll get great views of Albuquerque! Other highlights include the 3,000-foot-long New Mexico Rattler wooden roller coaster ride, 100 feet of which is in an underground tunnel; a Sea Dragon swinging boat; and Demolition Disco bumper cars. Watery adventures include a Rocky Mountain Rapids river ride, with a long splashing drop from the "peak," or hang on to your raft on the Big Flush water coaster. There is also a water play area with a wading pool. In the Kiddieland area younger kids can perch on a giant pup on the Doggie-Go-Round ride, do the bouncy Frog Hopper, or drive a buggy. Snacks available are mainly classic funground fare: burgers, hot dogs, pizza, popcorn, and cotton candy. The price code shown is for an all-day unlimited-ride pass for a kid under 48 inches tall. Or you can pay as you go. General admission is $2.50 at time of writing, and individual rides are in the $2 to $6 range, with no minimum purchase. Check out the Web site for discounts on ride passes bought online in advance. Open April to September; days vary by month.

HINKLE FAMILY FUN CENTER $$$
12931 Indian School Road NE
(505) 299-3100
www.hinklefamilyfuncenter.com

The great variety of things to do here includes the popular go-karts on an eighth-of-a-mile-long outdoor track, an arcade with over 100 games, and Lazer Tag in a 4,500-square-foot arena. There's also paintball, bumper cars, a pool with bumper boats, and two 18-hole miniature golf courses complete with waterfalls, flower beds, tree houses, ponds, and streams with bridges; trailing up and down between the multiple levels will use up plenty of energy! Climbers can don a harness to tackle a 32-foot-high climbing wall shaped like a boulder—make sure to wear closed-toe shoes if you want to climb. The Eats & Treats snack bar serves pizzas, hot dogs, and other munchies. You can pay as you go for individual attractions, buy a pass for two to five attractions, or choose a five-hour or full-day pass for unlimited play. The price code shown is for a package of three attractions and 90 arcade credits. If you just want to bring your little one for a round of mini golf, for example, entry will be lower. Open seven days year-round.

i **It's worth checking out the Hinkle Family Fun Center Web site before setting off, to find current coupons and special deals. Their discount coupons and two-rides-for-the-price-of-one deals can add up to big savings, especially if you're taking several kids.**

IT'Z FAMILY FOOD & FUN **$$$**
4595 San Mateo Boulevard NE
(505) 883-3677
www.itzusa.com

At iT'Z you'll find over 130 video and ticket games, 10-pin bowling, bumper cars, the Miner Mike indoor roller coaster, and a Spinoli ride. There's also a bounce house and toddler area. The all-you-can-eat buffet gives a choice of themed dining rooms, including a cartoon room, a drive-in-style room with movie screen, and the Gametime room with sports on TV. The buffet offers pizza, pasta, salads, and desserts, including some sugar-free desserts. You can come just for the buffet, which also gives access to a bounce house, but to really take advantage of the facilities here, buy a Game Card or a play package, either with or without the buffet. Children 3 and under eat free. Open seven days.

STONE AGE CLIMBING GYM **$$$**
4201 Yale Boulevard NE, Suite I
(505) 341-2016
www.stoneageclimbinggym.com

The indoor rock-climbing gym at Stone Age has 12,000 square feet of climbing terrain, including walls suitable for beginner climbers. There are 40 top-rope stations, 4 bouldering areas, and 2 lead climbing areas, with walls nearly 30 feet high. Challenges include a 20-foot overhanging-lead cave, and a 1,000-square-foot bouldering cave featuring an entrance arch. Stone Age has climbing shoes and equipment available for rent and offers climbing classes and private lessons. The price code shown is for a day pass, plus the package rental of climbing shoes and a harness and belay device. Minors need their liability waiver form signed by a parent or guardian, and belayers (the person holding the rope) must be 14 or over. Open seven days.

OUTDOOR STUFF

DOWNTOWN GROWERS' MARKET
Robinson Park at Central Avenue and 8th Avenue SW
www.downtownabq.com/growersmarket

Local children enjoy this outdoor community market on Saturday mornings from June through October; there's music and different entertainment and activities every week, such as face painting and fun jump bounce structures. There are always free samples of local fruits, jams, cheeses, and other produce to try, plus vendors of pastries and cookies, breakfast burritos, and fry bread. The grassy, tree-lined area is great for picnics and play. Hours vary by month, so check at the Web site.

SANDIA PEAK TRAMWAY **$$$**
East end of Tramway Road, NE
(505) 856-7325
www.sandiapeak.com

From a distance the cable cars on the world's longest aerial tramway look like shiny UFOs as they glide up to Sandia Peak. Inside, it feels like you're flying, too, on the 15-minute ride up to the 10,378-foot summit, with spectacular views over 11,000 square miles. Children can look out for wildlife in the canyons below and at the top explore the trails in the Cibola National Forest. Take your own picnic, buy snacks to take up from Sandiago's Deli by the ticket office at the base station, or eat at the High Finance restaurant on the peak. Full details on this feat of engineering are in the Attractions chapter, but suffice it to say that kids will be thrilled. Be sure to take a sweater or jacket no matter how warm it is in the city when you set off, as temperatures are substantially cooler at this altitude.

Children under 5 years ride free accompanied by an adult. In addition to tram tickets, a fee of $1 is charged to cars at the entrance to the tramway base terminal between 8:30 a.m. and 5 p.m. The tramway is open seven days year-round, except for two 10-day maintenance periods in April and November. There are also very occasional stoppages for bad weather or high winds. The Sandia Peak Tramway is at the east end of Tramway Road, where it dead-ends in the parking lot. Tramway Road intersects at the north end of Tramway Boulevard, and the turnoff from Tramway Boulevard is clearly signed. By interstate it's approximately 9 miles north from I-40 exit 167, or follow Tramway Road east from exit 234 on I-25.

TINGLEY BEACH
1800 Tingley Drive SW
(505) 768-2000
www.cabq.gov/biopark

Feed the ducks or have a picnic on the tables beside three fishing lakes on this "beach" conveniently central to town. You can also sail a model yacht (buy tokens inside Tingley Beach Station) or bring your own boat for the model boat pond, and in summer rent pedal boats. Children must be 3 or over to ride in the pedal boats. Bicycles can also be rented for a trip onto the Paseo del Bosque, a 16-mile paved bike trail that runs through here. Children 12 and under have their own fishing pond, and older kids can fish in the other two ponds. Anglers 12 and up need a fishing license, available for a day, five days, or annually from the Tingley Beach Outfitters; call to check their opening hours in advance, as they vary (505-248-8522). Drinks and snacks are sold at the Tingley Café, and outside you can shake hands with the jovial Clyde Tingley statue; he was a former governor of New Mexico. Swimming isn't allowed at Tingley Beach, which is part of the Albuquerque Bio Park, which also includes the nearby Rio Grande Zoo, Albuquerque Aquarium, and Rio Grande Botanic Garden. A narrow-gauge Rio Line train runs a loop between the BioPark facilities with a stop at the Tingley Beach Station. This train is included in the price of the Combo Ticket admission fee for visitors to the zoo, aquarium, and gardens. You can also buy individual journey tickets with some limitations—see the Attractions chapter for info—if your little ones are eager to ride the open-air train on its loop, which shows you a little of the botanic garden and the Heritage Farm and also runs past the elephants at the zoo. If you're just visiting Tingley Beach, it is free and open seven days, from sunrise to sunset.

i Children under 10 ride free on ABQ Ride buses, when traveling with a paying adult. Adult fare is $1.

SMART PLAY

ANDERSON-ABRUZZO ALBUQUERQUE INTERNATIONAL BALLOON MUSEUM $
9201 Balloon Museum Drive NE
(505) 768-6020
www.cabq.gov/balloon

This colorful museum dedicated to all things ballooning has interactive exhibits about the science and skills of ballooning that kids will enjoy. Probably the most fun (for kids of all ages) is the flight simulator. Standing safely on the ground inside a balloon gondola, with a big screen showing the target destination, the flyer steers using pulleys to ascend and descend, finding the winds that lead to the target—without landing in the river or getting caught in the trees! You can also practice ballooning knots, "release" a mini hot-air balloon, or weave a balloon basket and see displays of balloons and airships, plus gondolas from record-setting flights. Take the Alameda Boulevard exit 233 from I-25, go about 1 mile west on Alameda to Balloon Museum Drive (on the north side of Alameda). Closed Monday. Admission is free on Sunday from 9 a.m. to 1 p.m. and free all day on the first Friday of the month. Always free for toddlers 3 and under.

i **The free Stories in the Sky storytelling program at the Balloon Museum is for kids from 6 months to 6 years, on Wednesday morning from 9:30 a.m. to 10:15 a.m, with songs, games, and crafts. Accompanying adults get free admission, too.**

EXPLORA **$$**
1701 Mountain Road NW
(505) 224-8300
www.explora.us

Kids get hands-on at Explora, a children's museum and learning-and-play center for science, technology, and art. As they try out 250 tabletop activities, designed to be easy for child-sized hands, each child has a unique experience, whether creating their own music in the Shapes of Sounds area to learn about wavelength or placing their hand on the heat camera to see the hot and cold areas. Build a motor or gear shift, and join with others to make a moving contraption in the My Chain Reaction exhibit, perhaps starting with a feather or nail, or dropping a marble in to kick the movement off. Budding inventors love Explora, but children don't need a special knack for science to have plenty of "Aha!" moments when experimenting in the Water Lab or with light and optics in the Strange Light area. There are also plenty of fun tests with moving air, weaving, density of liquids, colors, construction, and geometry. See how fast cheese molds in the environmental chamber, or touch tarantulas and snakes in the nature area. Short theater performances once a week give life to characters like Marco Polo and Marie Curie. The Knee Hi Sci section is geared to the younger set, and Explora opens an hour early, at 9 a.m., on Monday for toddler time, aimed at under-4s who are accompanied by an adult and including stories and music. Free to tots under 1 year. Open seven days.

INDIAN PUEBLO CULTURAL CENTER **$$**
2401 12th Street NW
(505) 843-7270, (866) 855-7902
www.indianpueblo.org

The IPCC's adobe Pueblo House, looking like an authentic pueblo home, is an activity center for children to learn about daily pueblo life. Listen to traditional storytellers; make a drum; or try weaving, pottery, stone carving, and baking in the horno. It's best to plan ahead to visit Pueblo House—there are two sessions a day (morning and afternoon) from Tuesday to Thursday during the school year and two a day on weekends, but spaces are limited, and they get very booked. Call ahead for current times and to reserve your place, although if you turn up when a session is due, they'll let you in if there's room. A visit to Pueblo House is included with Indian Pueblo Cultural Center admission. You can also watch Native American dances every weekend in the IPCC's courtyard, and between June and September there is a daily dance on Thursday and Friday, too. Times vary seasonally, so contact the center for the current schedule. Other special events might include magic shows or art demonstrations, and the center's museum has artifacts and exhibits suited to older children interested in Indian history. Take a break at the Pueblo Harvest Cafe for authentic fry bread and homemade pueblo fruit pies. Admission is free for children under 5. Open daily.

NATIONAL MUSEUM OF NUCLEAR SCIENCE & HISTORY **$$**
601 Eubank Boulevard SE
(505) 245-2137
www.nuclearmuseum.org
Historic planes, rockets, and missiles are displayed in the 9-acre Heritage Park outside the museum, and inside there are hands-on activities for junior boffins, including Little Albert's Lab, where an Albert Einstein puppet helps kids understand scientific principles through interactive exhibits. In the Energy Encounter section, you produce a chemical reaction by cranking a handle, in order to thrust a Ping-Pong ball into the air. Admission is free for children 5 and under. Open seven days a week.

NEW MEXICO MUSEUM OF NATURAL HISTORY AND SCIENCE **$$**
1801 Mountain Road NW
(505) 841-2800
www.nmnaturalhistory.org
Outer space and dinosaurs—it's hard to find a better combo for kids. Here they can face off with a 40-foot-long T. rex; find out about dinosaurs unique to New Mexico, including the five-horned Pentaceratops; walk through a rumbling volcano; and ride in the Evolator time machine. Move the camera on a model of the Mars Rover in the "Making Tracks on Mars" area; and explore space exploration in New Mexico in the Space Frontiers exhibit, due to run at least through 2011. The planetarium presents child-friendly shows several times daily, perhaps showing presentations on space exploration or a journey through the solar system. The awesome five-story screen at the Lockheed Martin DynaTheater makes you feel like you're right inside films on dinosaurs, the natural world, and wild adventures. (Both venues charge separate entrance fees.)

Hands-on exhibits in the StartUp gallery on Albuquerque's place in computer history include a design-your-own-icon exhibit and a clever game to design a computer program—you have to order and pick up a pizza on a mini city map. Kids can also touch fossils; stroke a snake; and see turtles, lungfish, and other critters in the Naturalist Center. There are plenty of science and dinosaur treats in the museum store, and the M Cafe has a children's menu, plus exhibits inside the fun glass-top tables. Museum entry is free on the second Tuesday in January, second Tuesday in February, September 11, November 11, and Christmas Eve day. Residents of some New Mexico counties enter free in specified months—details at the Web site. There is always free admission for kids under 3. Open seven days but closed on all Mondays in September and January.

TINKERTOWN MUSEUM **$**
121 Sandia Crest Road / Highway 536
Sandia Park
(505) 281-5233
www.tinkertown.com
Kids are captivated by the imaginary world created in Ross J. Ward's carved miniature Western town and circus. Press the buttons on the intricately detailed scenes with doll's-house-size shops and hotels to make the characters and animals move. Or let 'em loose with a handful of quarters to animate some of the musical and antique arcade machines including a fortuneteller. Punch a lucky penny, find out your personality by the strength of your handshake, and see numerous curiosities in this mazelike 22-room folk art museum with walls constructed from over 50,000 glass bottles. There's a special children's visitors' book with crayons for drawing their favorite exhibit. To reach Tinkertown Museum take I-40 east to exit 175, then head north on Highway 14 for 6 miles through Cedar Crest, and turn left on Highway 536/Sandia Crest Road, the road that leads to the Sandia Peak ski area. Tinkertown is 1.5 miles on the left. Free admission for children under 4. Open seven days a week from April 1 through November 1.

TREATS & EATS

ELEPHANT BAR RESTAURANT **$$$**
2240 Louisiana Boulevard NE
(505) 884-2355
www.elephantbar.com

This kid-friendly chain restaurant is exotically themed with jungle animals and prints, and a children's menu for under-10s includes an entrée, beverage, and ice cream at less than $5. Aside from the spot-the-safari-animal fun, it's grown-up enough to keep parents happy, too, with Asian dishes and steak, fish, burgers, and salads on the broad menu. It can get quite busy and noisy at peak times. The price code is for the more expensive adult entrées; you can get away for less. Open seven days.

FLYING STAR CAFE **$$**
3416 Central Avenue SE
(505) 255-6633
www.flyingstarcafe.com

The locally owned chain of relaxed, spacious, and family-friendly Flying Star Cafes has a kid's menu that includes a petite burger, mac and cheese, a natural beef hot dog, and a pasta dish. At this original Nob Hill Flying Star and in the seven other locations around town listed below, the cool decor is modern and bright, and although each café is slightly different in style, you can count on fresh, healthy food for breakfast, lunch, and dinner, including organics, fair trade, and local produce, with no trans fats. You can also just pop in for a drink and a snack or one of their brilliant desserts. If you ask for a Kid's Club pass, you only need to rack up five stamps—one for each kid's menu item—to get a free dessert. The price code is for an average adult dish, although you can pay slightly more for some of the dinner entrées. Open seven days. Other locations are:

8000 Paseo del Norte NE; (505) 923-4211
8001 Menaul Boulevard NE; (505) 293-6911
4501 Juan Tabo NE; (505) 275-8311
4026 Rio Grande Boulevard NW; (505) 344-6714
723 Silver Avenue SW, (505) 244-8099
10700 Corrales Road, Corrales; (505) 938-4717
200 South Camino del Pueblo, Bernalillo; (505) 404-2100

I SCREAM ICE CREAM **$**
2000 Carlisle Boulevard NE
(505) 268-0139

Kid heaven with ice cream, this fun and colorful café is wildly decorated and packed with games, puzzles, and toys, plus plenty of nostalgic memorabilia for parents, too—Rubik's Cube, anyone? You can pretty much have a play date on your own. In addition to ice creams with tons of toppings, you can enjoy coffees, shakes, splits, and malts. Open seven days.

66 DINER **$$**
1405 Central Avenue NE
(505) 247-1421
www.66diner.com

This neon 1950s-style diner on Route 66 has an old-fashioned soda fountain where kids can order thick malts, shakes, floats, and ice cream sodas. If you need to get something sensible into them, too, there's a full breakfast, lunch, and dinner menu, including superburgers and blue plate specials such as spaghetti and meatballs. There's also a children's menu, with generous portions, at an average of $3.99 a meal. The best fun is to sit on a stool at the counter to enjoy the nostalgic decor evocative of *Happy Days,* listen to the jukebox, and watch the busy waitresses dressed in '50s bobby-soxer style. The price code is for an adult full-sized entrée. Open seven days.

TOMATO CAFE **$$**
5920 Holly Avenue NE
(505) 821-9300
www.tomatocafe.com

This smart Italian café serves an all-you-can-eat buffet that kids love, as they can help themselves to around six types of pizza, multiple pastas and pasta sauces, a choice of soups and side dishes, and a salad bar. Ice creams and toppings are also included. The food is fresh and high quality, and the restaurant also serves wine for parents. The price code is for an adult lunch buffet; it's slightly more at dinner. Kids' meals vary by age. As a guide, lunch and dinner buffets for 5- to 10-year-olds are $4.99 as we write. Tots 2 and under eat free. Tomato Cafe has recently relocated and is just east of I-25, Paseo del Norte exit, across from Target and Lowe's. Lunch and dinner is served every day.

Recipe for a Piñata

In Old Town buy a piñata in shapes that include cartoon characters and traditional star designs from La Piñata shop. (You'll also see gorgeous porcelain dolls here, in authentic Native American attire, although prices are beyond pocket-money reach.) Then cross the Old Town Plaza diagonally, turning right just past San Felipe de Neri church onto Romero Street to buy sweet treats at Rocky Mountain Chocolate Factory. Or head farther up Romero to the wonderful Candy Lady store, with old-fashioned fudge, licorice, caramels, rock candy, and chocolates. Once you've bought your candy, fill the piñata. Now all the kids need is a tree to hang it from and a big stick to thwack it with!

The Candy Lady: 524 Romero Street NW; (505) 243-6239; www.thecandylady.com

La Piñata: 2 Patio Market, NW; (505) 242-2400; www.rhondacacy.com

Rocky Mountain Chocolate Factory: Plaza Don Luis, 303 Romero Street NW; (505) 842-8883; www.rmcf.com

ANNUAL FESTIVALS AND EVENTS

Albuquerque is a year-round destination, and it has a healthy calendar of year-round events to please art lovers, foodies, music fans, and culture buffs. With the city's lively mix of cultures, there is always a party going on somewhere. Your problem won't be finding an event to go to; it will be choosing which of the many on offer to plump for. Many people plan their visits around special events such as the Albuquerque International Balloon Fiesta—one of the most photographed events in the world, with around 700 balloons and some 800,000 balloonatic spectators. The Native American Gathering of Nations is another big draw, as representatives from 500 tribes across the continent meet for their annual reunion and powwow, and many of the nearby pueblo resorts and casinos also host special events at this time. The New Mexico State Fair is the hub of the state for 17 days in September, and visitors might reasonably wonder if there is anybody left in any other part of New Mexico. If you plan to travel to Albuquerque during any of these three events, it's wise to book accommodations well in advance.

We're highlighting some of the top annual events, festivals, and celebrations that give the city so much of its vibrancy. It's worth noting that in laid-back Albuquerque, the complete festival or event program is sometimes not finalized till close to the date. If an event is listed here, though, you can be sure that it has earned a good reputation over time, and you're unlikely to be disappointed. Dates, venues, and prices given are accurate at the time of writing, but of course, changes may occur, so check with the organizers.

JANUARY

REVOLUTIONS INTERNATIONAL THEATRE FESTIVAL

Various locations
(505) 254-8393
www.tricklock.com/revolutions

Tricklock Company brings groundbreaking theater from around the world to this annual festival, established in 2001. Thirty-five events are presented from mid- to late January, and the festival emphasis is on imaginative and inventive theater and performance art. Theater companies are invited from as far afield as Israel, Germany, Spain, England, Scotland, Ireland, Norway, Poland, Serbia, Russia, and Australia, as well as closer-to-home artists from Mexico and across the United States. Albuquerque venues include the KiMo Theatre, the Journal Theatre at the National Hispanic Cultural Center, the N4th Theatre, the Filling Station, and UNM's Rodey Theatre and Theatre X. Some festival performances are also held at the Lensic in Santa Fe. Ticket prices vary according to show and venue, but some start at under $10; the main events are $18, and others go up to around $25. Buying a passport online for multiple shows offers a saving on individual ticket prices. For example, a passport for four shows costs around $65. Students can buy rush tickets for some events at $5, which are on sale 10 minutes before curtain-up.

MARCH

FIERY FOODS AND BARBECUE SHOW

Sandia Resort and Casino
I-25 and Tramway NE
(505) 873-8680
www.fiery-foods.com

Make sure you turn up hungry to the largest show in the world dedicated to spicy foods and barbecue. You'll sample your fill of the thousands

EXPO New Mexico

If you ask an old-timer for directions to EXPO New Mexico, you might draw a blank. Many people still refer to the venue as the State Fairgrounds, despite the fact that Governor Bill Richardson changed the name in 2003 to EXPO New Mexico, to reflect the diversity of the hundreds of other events that take place there each year. In addition to the New Mexico State Fair, EXPO New Mexico is currently home to the Downs Racetrack and Casino, the weekly Flea Market, the Albuquerque Thunderbirds basketball games and other sports, and more than 200 annual events and festivals, including arts and crafts shows; home and garden shows; car shows and monster truck rallies; and rodeo, horse, and livestock events. It is also used as a location by film companies.

The 236-acre grounds are bordered on the south by Central Avenue SE, on the west by San Pedro Drive NE, on the north by Lomas Boulevard NE, and on the east by Louisiana Boulevard NE. The fairgrounds have been in this spot for over 70 years. If you attend an event at EXPO New Mexico, check the specific details for which entry gate to use, but the main entrance is at 300 San Pedro NE.

The state fair has its roots in the territorial fairs that were held in Albuquerque from 1881. They ran for over 30 years, until one year the fair was badly rained out. The fairs died off until the 1930s, when Governor Clyde Tingley and some developers got the money together to buy a small parcel of land, and in 1938 the first New Mexico State Fair was held at the current location. Tingley's good relationship with President Franklin D. Roosevelt helped secure substantial "New Deal" funds for the new fairground buildings, as well as many other Albuquerque projects. According to the New Mexico Office of the State Historian, $500,000 in Works Progress Administration (WPA) funding was allocated to help revive the New Mexico State Fair. Many of the buildings still standing on EXPO grounds were WPA projects. The 60-stall Palomino Barn, used to stable horses during the rodeo and other equine events, were the first WPA buildings completed, constructed in true New Mexico style with adobe walls and viga ceilings. The quality of workmanship was so fine that they stood for 70 years without any renovation. In 2008 the barns were finally updated to bring them up to code. The original adobe bricks were removed one by one, new electric and water lines were installed, and then everything was put back together, so it looks exactly as it always did and uses most of the original materials. The mature elm trees that line the fairgrounds' Main Street, and which provide much charm and plenty of shade for summer events, are also part of the original WPA project, planted around three-quarters of a century ago.

The first state fair manager was Leon Harms, and the way he came to the job is typical of many "strange but true" stories Albuquerque residents tell of how they ended up living in this city.

of products available, from fiery fudge to spicy sausages, salsas, and hot sauces and even pasta, pasta sauce, and gourmet chocolate truffles.

The three-day show is held on the first weekend in March. Depending on how the calendar falls, that might include the last days of February. Around 15,000 people attend each year, and unlike many food shows, Fiery Foods and Barbecue Show is open to the public as well as trade visitors. This is just as well, or hotheaded chile lovers might bust down the doors to get to the source of their passion. Serious collectors buy products in threes—one for collection, one that they actually eat, and one that they trade. A bottle of hot sauce can sell for a few dollars up to thousands of dollars for signed and collectible jars. Foodies whose objective is to explore new ingredients rather than breathe flames will also find plenty of

Leon Harms was a former state legislator in Kansas, where he'd started a successful county fair. He had an asthmatic son, and in 1937 he and his family moved west, as many did in that era, in search of healthier climes and drier air. The family was heading for Arizona, but the story goes that as they drove over Raton Pass into New Mexico, the boy announced, "I can breathe." Leon Harms continued to Albuquerque, and when they stopped, Harms knew that this was the place to make their home instead. The timing was perfect because the city was still looking for a manager for the new State Fairgrounds, and Harms became the brains behind the enterprise, from organizing the layout of the building and grounds to running the show for the next 20 years. The Leon Harms Youth Hall is named for him.

One of the most eye-catching buildings on the grounds is the Tingley Coliseum, named in honor of Clyde Tingley. Despite its ultramodern-looking façade, Tingley Coliseum opened in 1957, and King of the Cowboys Roy Rogers was one of the first to grace the stage, headlining with his wife, Dale Evans, Queen of the West; his horse Trigger; and the Sons of the Pioneers. It was built as a multipurpose arena for rodeo and concert events, and such stars as Clint Eastwood, James Dean, and Elvis Presley helped promote the rodeo. The State Fair Rodeo is still held there today. Seating 9,286, the Tingley Coliseum is also the home venue for the Albuquerque Thunderbirds pro basketball team and has hosted ice hockey, car shows, and other events.

Other buildings of note include the Fine Arts Gallery, the Hispanic Arts Center, the Manuel Lujan Jr. Exhibit Complex, and the Alice K. Hoppes African American Pavilion Art Center. The Albuquerque and Santa Fe Indian schools have exhibited crafts and sold jewelry and pottery on the steps of the Native American Indian Art Gallery, built in 1938. All of these venues host arts and craft shows and other exhibits and events during the year, as well as during the New Mexico State Fair.

Recently there has been talk about moving the state fair to another location, although Governor Bill Richardson has been cited as saying that the fair will not move on his watch. Perhaps Richardson has a soft spot for this venerable institution; during the 2002 governor's race, he shook hands 13,392 times in an eight-hour visit to the New Mexico State Fair, thus making the *Guinness Book of World Records* for the feat of shaking the most hands in a single day.

Discussions are underway, however, about developments at the site, especially if the Downs Racetrack and Casino moves to Moriarty as originally planned. Much is in the air at the time of writing, but for now, as has been true for well over a century, a vital center for Albuquerque community is entrenched in these historic fairgrounds, whatever name you choose to call them. Information on EXPO New Mexico is available at www.exponm.com or call (505) 222-9700.

inspiration; for example, habanero key lime dessert sauce—served over cheesecake or ice cream, it's piquant but not too hot. In addition to local Albuquerque and New Mexican products, you'll find fiery foods from across the United States, and international exhibitors have come from South America, South Africa, China, and Australia. Exhibitors include both big household-name companies and small gastroentrepreneurs.

Personalities are as important as products at the show, and chileheads tend to have big personalities! Some come in costumes, perhaps as pirates, or with tropical themes or wearing giant chile peppers. One year a group flew in from Stuttgart, dressed as the German Hot Sauce Police. There are chef demonstrations, sometimes book signings, and other events. The 2009 Great Grill-Off, featuring celebrity chefs and experts on grilling and barbecue, was filmed by PBS for its *Barbecue America* series. The public is allowed in to the show from 4 p.m. on the opening Friday and after 11 a.m. on Saturday and Sunday. Buy tickets in advance; adult entry is $10. Tickets at the door are $15. Entry for under-18s is $5.

RIO GRANDE ARTS & CRAFTS FESTIVALS

EXPO New Mexico,
Home of the New Mexico State Fair
300 San Pedro NE
(505) 292-7457
www.riograndefestivals.com

Since its debut in 1989, the Rio Grande Arts & Crafts Festivals have become highly regarded juried shows, selecting exhibitors from hundreds of national applicants. A family-friendly event, with prices to suit every pocket, there are three editions a year, in March, October, and November. Depending on the season, there are between 200 and nearly 300 artists selling paintings, pottery, jewelry, furniture, decorative objects for the home, apparel, accessories, and all manner of arts and handcrafted items. Artist demonstrations give a peek into the creative process and might include a potter at her wheel or a display of glass blowing. There's often the option of buying a piece that you've watched being created. You can sample food at the gourmet cuisine booths, and live entertainment includes music and magic shows. At the Kid's Creation Station, children learn about art and create their own little masterpieces. The March festival is held over a three-day weekend, and adult admission is $6 a day, or $8 for a three-day pass. Free for children under 12.

APRIL

AMERICAN INDIAN WEEK & SPRING INDIAN MARKET

Indian Pueblo Cultural Center
2401 12th Street NW
(866) 855-7902
www.indianpueblo.org

Starting on the third weekend of April, this nine-day celebration of Native American culture and arts features daily tribal dances in the semicircular courtyard. Dancers come from New Mexico's pueblos and tribes, including Navajo and White Mountain Apache, and sometimes from as far afield as Canada and Alaska. There are artist demonstrations in which they show and discuss their skills with pottery, leather, beadwork, jewelry, metalwork, and fetish carving. A film series is always on the calendar and sometimes variety shows featuring contemporary dance, comedy shows, and plays. American Indian Week coincides with the Gathering of Nations, and the Indian Pueblo Cultural Center becomes the place that many Native Americans come to hang out when they're not at the Powwow, especially on the final Sunday of the week when the Gathering of Nations is over. The atmosphere is relaxed and familial, and on this final Sunday the newly crowned Miss Indian World traditionally drops in, too. Albuquerque public radio station KUNM usually broadcasts from the Sunday event for their popular Native American show "Singing Wire," and this radio remote gives Miss Indian World one of her first opportunities to talk to her constituency.

Over the course of this week, 3,000 to 5,000 Native American visitors come to the center, far more than during the rest of the year. During this last weekend of American Indian Week (and sometimes on the first weekend, too, although the schedule varies) the Spring Indian Market takes place. Artisans line the courtyard around the dancers, selling their beautiful jewelry, pottery, and other handcrafted works direct to the public. American Indian Week events and Spring Indian Market are included in the price of entry to the Indian Pueblo Cultural Center. Adults pay $6, with discounts for seniors, New Mexico residents, and students. Entry for children is $3, and under-5s are free.

FOUNDERS DAY FIESTA

Old Town
(505) 768-2000
www.cabq.gov/crs/specialevents.html

Many still refer to this Duke City birthday party by its former name: Fiestas de Alburquerque (note the extra "r," in honor of the city's original name). A celebration of the founding of Albuquerque on April 23, 1706, the festivities naturally center around Old Town. The schedule of events varies each year, and the fiesta date in mid-April varies, too, but there is always a Founders Day Parade and a colorful array of entertainment. The narrow streets around Old Town Plaza are filled with music, from mariachi ensembles to country music, bluegrass, and brass bands. You might watch flamenco dancers, Native American dancers, street performers from magicians to jugglers, or a Western show by the New Mexico Gunfighters Association. (Don't worry; they fire blanks.) There's an outdoor market, the San Felipe de Neri Church serves chili cheeseburgers, and the local retailers and restaurants have their own special events, too, and sometimes free treats. Old Town is packed, so arrive early for limited parking spaces, or better yet, take public transport. Details of each year's fiesta are posted in advance at the City of Albuquerque Web site on the Cultural Services Department Special Events page. Or call the general City of Albuquerque information line above.

GATHERING OF NATIONS
UNM Arena (the Pit)
Avenida Cesar Chavez Boulevard SE
www.gatheringofnations.com

Indian Country comes together in North America's biggest powwow of over 3,000 dancers and singers from more than 500 tribes. The Gathering of Nations has taken place annually in Albuquerque since 1983, as a social meeting place for Native Americans, as well as a competitive event between dancers and singers trying for over $175,000 in prizes. It's a truly unique experience as the enormous Pit resounds with chanting and the beating of hundreds of drums, and thousands of dancers make their grand entrance in brightly colored traditional outfits and headdresses, intricately decorated with feathers and beads. Everyone stands and removes their hat when the eagle staff comes in during the grand entry, and if an eagle feather falls during the dances, everyone stops until it is back in place.

As part of the Gathering of Nations Powwow, the Indian Traders Market gives the opportunity to shop for arts and crafts from 800 traders, and food vendors keep the crowd satisfied with treats that include Indian Tacos made with fry bread. Entertainment is provided by Native American performers on Stage 49, presenting an eclectic program. Of course, you'll hear singers and bands presenting contemporary Native music but also blues, rock, reggae, and hip-hop and interesting fusions between genres. On the Thursday evening, the Miss Indian World pageant is held at the Albuquerque Convention Center. Rather than a beauty contest, this competition between young women from many tribes is judged according to personality, knowledge of tribal tradition, and dancing skills. The new Miss Indian World is crowned on the Saturday night during the Gathering of Nations Powwow.

There are dozens of dancing, drumming, and singing contest categories in the powwow, for elders, men, and women and in different styles. You'll even see tiny tots decked out in full regalia, although all the small children who are dancing are rewarded with a prize.

Everyone is welcome to the Gathering of Nations, and when invited by the master of ceremonies to join the intertribal dances, you have a chance to participate. However, it's important to remember that the dances are not just entertainment but a form of worship. Each dance has a meaning or story attached and is part of a spiritual, cultural, and social tradition. It's fine to take photos (not videos), but don't use flash photography during contests, as it distracts the dancers, and ask individuals for permission before taking their photo outside the dances. The intricately decorated outfits are often handmade or family heirlooms, worth thousands of dollars. Don't call them costumes, and tempting as it is, don't touch the clothes or their ornamentation. They can be fragile and often have religious significance or symbolize an important event, honor, or legend.

The Gathering of Nations takes place on the last full weekend of April. The UNM Arena is on the southwest corner of Avenida Cesar Chavez and University Boulevard. Buy tickets in advance by credit card from the Web site or for cash only at the door. Tickets are approximately $15 to $19 per day for the Friday and Saturday, giving access to all events in the arena. There is no assigned seating, and single-day tickets do not have in-and-out privileges. A limited number of two-day passes are available, at double the one-day price but with the advantage of in-and-out privileges. Infants under 1 year are admitted free. Tickets for Miss Indian World on the Thursday evening are about $12 to $14.

MAY

ALBUQUERQUE WINE FESTIVAL

Balloon Fiesta Park
From south access via Alameda Boulevard NE / Balloon Museum Drive
From north access via I-25 Frontage Road / Balloon Fiesta Parkway
www.abqwinefestival.com

A great way to step into summer is to taste the fruits of previous harvests, and 15,000 people come to the Albuquerque Wine Festival to do just that over three days every Memorial Day Weekend. Around 21 wineries from Albuquerque and throughout New Mexico present their often award-winning tipples, and the entry fee includes a souvenir glass so you can taste your favorite varieties from the outdoor tented booths. The crowd is a good mix of wine buffs looking to restock their cellars, and families enjoying a spring day out, relaxing on a blanket on the grass, and maybe taking home a bottle or two. Live entertainment has included blues, funk, Cuban and African drum rhythms, and flamenco dancing. Entry is approximately $15 including the souvenir glass, and under-21s have typically been admitted free when accompanied by a parent or guardian. The festival usually runs from noon till 6 p.m. each day. Remember to bring ID with proof of age if you want to taste wines, as they do check.

EL CINCO DE MAYO

El Cinco de Mayo, which means "the fifth of May" in Spanish, is often mistakenly associated with Mexican Independence Day (actually September 16). In fact, Cinco de Mayo commemorates an often-overlooked event, the defeat of Napoleon III's army on May 5, 1862, after French forces unsuccessfully attempted to invade Mexico more than 50 years after it had declared independence from Spain. A national holiday south of the border, it commemorates the victory of the relatively small and poorly armed Mexican forces, who turned back an overwhelmingly superior army of would-be conquerors some 100 miles from Mexico City in the Battle of Puebla.

It's not clear why Cinco de Mayo has caught on as the major Mexican-American day of celebration in the United States. Some speculate that it may be because the defeat at the Battle of Puebla also disrupted the flow of French weapons to Confederate forces, whom Napoleon III was supporting in the Civil War. This disruption contributed to an eventual Union victory.

Whatever the reasons, Cinco de Mayo means fiesta time all across the Southwest, including Albuquerque, where the event is celebrated throughout the city at restaurants, bars, and cultural centers. Past festivities have included song, dance, and folklore events at Old Town Plaza, Civic Plaza, the National Hispanic Cultural Center, and the historic Barelas district. There may be neighborhood parades, fireworks, art shows, and musical and theater performances. And of course there's lots of traditional food and good cheer. Check local papers and events listings for the current year's events.

JUNE

ALBUQUERQUE FOLK FESTIVAL

EXPO New Mexico,
Home of the New Mexico State Fair
300 San Pedro NE
(505) 710-9641
www.abqfolkfest.org

Listen to and participate in music, dance, and more at this friendly folk festival, held on the third weekend in June. The festival expanded from one to two days in 2009, adding a new talent contest and a barn dance. The program includes performances by national and local musicians, dance from flamenco to African dance, and workshops for vocalists and instrumentalists in styles from bluegrass to Celtic. Bring your own instrument; there's a space to check it in if you don't want to carry it around all day. Beginners are equally welcome, and if you don't have an instrument, others in the workshop might loan you one. Dance workshops get you tangoing or two-stepping, or they teach more exotic forms like Hawaiian hula or Yiddish dance. Songwriters talk about their creative process, storytellers capture the imagination, and as you wander round the tents you'll find musicians who've only just met jamming together.

Everyone at the festival can enter the Band Scramble, in which musicians, singers, and dancers randomly assigned to groups have just 50 minutes to practice and give themselves a name (the kookier the better) before taking to the main stage to give a 6-minute performance. There's a Kid's Fiddle Contest for youngsters under 18, and sometimes an instrument "petting zoo" so children (and their parents) can touch and try out unusual instruments like bazoukis or didgeridoos. This celebration of creativity includes craft exhibits, workshops, and demonstrations, and vendors sell handicrafts, foods, and gifts. Adult tickets are between $10 and $20, depending on how much of the program you attend over the two days. Buy tickets in advance for a 20 percent discount. Seniors over 60 and children 11 to 17 are $5 a day or $8 for two days. Free entry for children under 11.

ALBUQUERQUE PRIDEFEST
EXPO New Mexico,
Home of the New Mexico State Fair
300 San Pedro NE
(505) 873-8084
www.abqpride.com

This celebration of Albuquerque's Gay, Lesbian, Bisexual and Transgender (GLBT) community paints the Expo New Mexico state fairgrounds with a fluttering array of rainbow flags on the second weekend in June. The city's first gay rights march in 1976 was a small affair of 25 to 30 people walking along Central Avenue. Over the years the rallies grew bigger, with a 2-mile parade that still starts at Central Avenue, a host of entertainment, and everyone in the community joining in. It's now reckoned to be New Mexico's largest GLBT event and one of the biggest parades in the state. Around 20,000 joined the parade in 2009. Entertainment ranges from belly dancers and improv theater to chart toppers like Taylor Dayne. The Pride Art Show features artists discussing their work, and many pieces are available for sale. Prizes are awarded to the best parade entries, and other contests include Pride Idol and a Queer Bake-Off and Recipe Auction, with awards for best pie, cake, and cookies. Previous fairs featured a car show, line dancing and hip-hop lessons, and a pet parade. A Children's Corner has activities and entertainment to keep the kids occupied. Admission is $13 a day, and children under 12 are admitted free.

i Look out for special displays in storefronts along Central Avenue during the Albuquerque Pridefest weekend. They're participating in Pridefest's annual window display contest, and the public can vote on their favorite at Albuquerque Pride's Web site.

NEW MEXICO ARTS & CRAFTS FAIR
EXPO New Mexico,
Home of the New Mexico State Fair
300 San Pedro NE
(505) 884-9043
www.nmartsandcraftsfair.org

The state's longest continuously running arts festival is held over three days on the last weekend in June. It presents work by more than 220 of New Mexico's most outstanding established and emerging artists and craftspeople. If you've come in previous years when it was held partly out of doors in the tree-lined fairgrounds, note that in 2009 the fair moved all booths indoors, to avoid wind damage to the art at night. Competition is tough to get into the juried show, and a total prize-money purse of $4,500 is awarded to winning artists in various disciplines. Artists sell directly to the public, and you'll see paintings; drawings; digital art; sculptures; photography; ceramics; jewelry; mixed media; fiber arts; and works in glass, wood, and metal. Maria Martinez, the acclaimed San Ildefonso Pueblo potter, cut the ribbon on the first fair in 1962 with then governor Edwin L. Mechem. They gave it a good kickoff, as the fair quickly outgrew its original location in Old Town Plaza and moved to the state fairground in 1969. Around 15,000 art lovers have turned up to browse and buy and to enjoy live music, including jazz and dance bands. There are also craft activities and entertainers like storytellers and clowns. A youth exhibit of work by students through grade twelve is designed to encourage and showcase budding New Mexican artists. A three-day pass for adults and seniors is $10. Daily admission $5, $4 for seniors over 65. Children 12 and under are free.

JULY

MARIACHI SPECTACULAR DE ALBUQUERQUE

Various locations
(505) 255-1501
www.mariachispectacular.com

Hear some of the world's most accomplished mariachi musicians at this renowned event that runs over five days, usually starting on the Wednesday after the Fourth of July. Spectacular is definitely the word, as the ensembles perform in their traditional suits, handsomely decorated with ornate embroidery and studded with rows of silver *botonadura,* or buttons. The sight is impressive and complements the stirringly passionate music. There are two mariachi performances. On the Friday evening a free public Showcase Concert and Competition is held at the Downtown Civic Plaza, where up to 20 different ensembles compete for prizes. (Budding mariachi aficionados might note that they don't like to be called bands, preferring the terms "ensemble" or "group.") On Saturday night the Showcase Grand Prize winners open the bill for the Spectacular Concert at the Sandia Resort and Casino. Here around 4,000 people gather in the resort's stunning open-air Amphitheater, for a sunset-to-starlight concert featuring leading professional mariachi groups. Tickets start at around $45, and it's worth buying them early, as they may sell out. Prior to the performances, a three-day conference and workshop with mariachi maestros runs at the University of New Mexico, where around 700 students learn about mariachi culture and music. This is open to any singers or musicians wishing to explore how to play in mariachi style, using guitar, violin, trumpet, *vihuela* (a small guitar), *guitarrón* (a bass guitar), and harp. There are also voice classes and sometimes classes for Ballet Folklorico. The conference costs around $80, and there is the opportunity to buy discounted tickets for the Spectacular Concert. The whole Mariachi Spectacular de Albuquerque concludes with an outdoor Mass on Sunday morning at the New Mexico Veteran's Memorial Park, where the large congregation has previously been presided over by the Archbishop of Santa Fe.

NEW MEXICO JAZZ FESTIVAL

Various locations
www.newmexicojazzfestival.org

This festival during the last two weeks of July brings jazz fans to their feet at venues in Albuquerque and Santa Fe. A combination of star international performers and the best New Mexico talent gives the festival its own special flavor. Past lineups have included Sonny Rollins, McCoy Tyner, Branford Marsalis, Cassandra Wilson, Pharoah Sanders, Kenny Garrett, Dianne Reeves, Cathryn McGill, the Albuquerque African Ensemble, and the always popular Preservation Hall Jazz Band. The festival started in 2006 and is a collaboration between the Santa Fe Jazz Foundation and the two hosting venues, Albuquerque's Outpost Performance Space and Santa Fe's Lensic Performing Arts Center. Ticket prices vary by artist and venue but average between $20 and $50.

There's a 10 percent discount if you buy tickets for three or more concerts, and students also receive small price breaks. A few free festival events are usually staged in Santa Fe in the plaza, and in Albuquerque at the Downtown Harry E. Kinney Civic Plaza, and in Old Town Plaza.

AUGUST

THE GREAT SOUTHWESTERN ANTIQUE SHOW

EXPO New Mexico,
Home of the New Mexico State Fair
300 San Pedro NE
(505) 255-4054
www.greatsouthwesternantiqueshow.com

Running for over a decade, this weekend show in early August is one of the largest antiques events in the Southwest and is organized by Nob Hill's Cowboys & Indians Antiques gallery. Over 200 dealers sell furnishings, American Indian and Western art, folk art, tribal and ethnographic antiques, vintage and estate jewelry, rare books, photography, and other collectibles. The art and antiques range broadly in price and style, including museum quality pieces. Many of the 3,000 visitors are not antiques experts but come to admire the art and maybe pick up a decorative piece for their home. Serious collectors, or those looking for a more exclusive experience, might pony up $75 for the Sneak Preview as the dealers set up on Friday afternoon. This gives you first chance to buy and chat with the dealers without the crowds. The admission for the Sneak Preview is tax deductible as a charitable donation, and proceeds go to arts and education causes in Albuquerque. Entry to Sneak Preview also includes entry to the show throughout the weekend. Otherwise, general admission on Saturday and Sunday is $8 a day or $12 for a two-day pass. A May edition of this show launched in 2009 and is about half the size of the August event.

SEPTEMBER

¡GLOBALQUERQUE! WORLD MUSIC FESTIVAL

National Hispanic Cultural Center
1701 4th Street SW
(505) 724-4771
www.globalquerque.com

This festival has grown fast since its debut in 2005, putting down roots in Albuquerque as a leading celebration of world music and culture in the Southwest region. ¡Globalquerque! prides itself on bringing artists to town that you might not expect to see on the festival circuit, representing all corners of the world, from Peru to Sweden and Ghana to Tibet. Grammy winners and nominees have graced the indoor and outdoor stages at the National Hispanic Cultural Center, with past performers that include Koko Taylor; the Global Drum Project, featuring the Grateful Dead's Mickey Hart; Lila Downs; Rahim AlHah; Indian Ocean; Kusun Ensemble; Native American "First Lady of the Flute" Mary Youngblood; and Taos Pueblo star Robert Mirabal. Events take place in the Albuquerque Journal Theatre with its terrific acoustics, the Fountain Courtyard stage, and the large outdoor Plaza Mayor, which has plenty of space for dancing against a backdrop of the impressive Mayan temple–style architecture. International cuisine and crafts shopping can be found in the Global Village booths. Free activities might include dance workshops, instrument making, African drumming, and crafts, open to both kids and adults. Scheduling may vary, but ¡Globalquerque! has usually run over the last weekend of September, coinciding with GO! Downtown Albuquerque Arts Festival, with a free shuttle between the two events. Ticket prices are tiered into three rates, depending on when you buy; the further in advance the cheaper the deal. A guideline for an adult one-day pass is $25 to $35; a two-day pass is $40 to $60. Children 12 and under are around half the adult rate. No charge for kids under 3.

GO! DOWNTOWN ALBUQUERQUE ARTS FESTIVAL
Gold Avenue between 2nd and 5th Streets, SW
(505) 243-2230
www.downtownabq.com/go

This free street party for the arts along hip and happening Gold Avenue runs for three days over the last weekend in September. The festival essentially turns the area into an outdoor gallery, and the aesthetic from mainly younger artists in this revitalized Downtown district is urban and edgy, rather than crafty or traditionally southwestern. Well over a hundred artists present contemporary fine arts, jewelry, furniture, ceramics, glass, wood, fiber arts, sculpture, photography, print, and lots of mixed media. An estimated 15,000 people join the party over three days. Street entertainers such as drummers, jugglers, mariachis, and clowns add to the carnival atmosphere, and bands also perform on the 4th Street festival stage. The beer garden opposite the stage is a good place to try some local brews, and a food court feeds the crowds with goodies from roasted corn to ice cream. Sometimes there are impromptu live-art demonstrations. The safely enclosed "GO! Wild" kids' zone has arts and other activities for children. The festival started in 2001 and in 2008 expanded from featuring just New Mexico talent, with cutting-edge artists coming from Texas and Colorado and as far afield as Wyoming and Florida. To date the festival weekend has coincided with the ¡Globalquerque! World Music Festival at the National Hispanic Cultural Center, with a free shuttle between the two events. Gold Avenue runs parallel to Central Avenue, one block south. Festivities start pretty much as you step out of the Alvarado Transportation Center, from the New Mexico Rail Runner Express station and other transport at the ATC.

i **The first winery in Bernalillo opened in 1883. Called La France Winery, it was operated by the La Salle Christian Brothers religious order to help fund their boys' school. A French winemaker was first hired to produce the wine, resulting in over 10,000 gallons of wine a year. An Italian immigrant from Tuscany took over the task and continued making wine even through the Prohibition era. The Archbishop of Santa Fe allowed the winery to stay open during Prohibition, as it supplied all of New Mexico's Catholic churches with sacramental wine.**

NEW MEXICO STATE FAIR
EXPO New Mexico,
Home of the New Mexico State Fair
300 San Pedro NE
(505) 222-9700
www.exponm.com

A 17-day extravaganza that starts the first weekend after Labor Day at the 236-acre state fairgrounds, this (along with the Albuquerque International Balloon Fiesta) is one of the big daddies of all Albuquerque's annual events, indeed of all New Mexico events. The fair parade alone usually takes over two hours to complete its 2.2-mile route. Unlike many state fairs that have moved on from their agricultural origins, New Mexico's fair retains a heavy focus on agriculture and livestock, as these are so important to the state economy. The annual eight-night rodeo is a standout event. Concerts in the Tingley Coliseum feature such rock and country stars as Huey Lewis & The News and Montgomery Gentry, and all around the grounds there are daily performances by Indian dancers, mariachi ensembles, and every variety of entertainment from New Mexico's homegrown talent. The Indian Village is the hub for native culture and activities, with tribal music and dance, arts, crafts, cookery demonstrations, and fresh-cooked Indian foods in the cafés. Authentic pottery, jewelry, rugs, and paintings are shown in the Native American Indian Arts Gallery. Artisans in the Villa Hispana sell santos, *retablos,* tinwork, and other traditional crafts, and Hispanic cultural events and performances are presented on the gazebo stage. In the Alice K. Hoppes African American Pavilion, you can hear rhythm and blues and gospel, eat soul food, and learn more about New Mexico's African-American heritage. A juried art show takes place at the African American Arts Gallery.

Around 500 booths sell arts, crafts, produce, and other merchandise, and there are cooking contests, livestock competitions, around 20 horse shows, pony rides, petting zoos, acrobats, science exhibits, and watermelon carving. Just about anything New Mexicans can do, they do here at the state fair, and approximately 700,000 people come each year to watch and participate. Old-timers have recalled that in the early years a man was shot from a cannon over a ferris wheel. Events are slightly tamer now, but you can still expect some high jinks. In 2008 fairgoers attempted to set a new record for the world's longest chile *ristra*. Unfortunately, *Guinness World Record* officials said the resulting ristra didn't make the grade, but at 157 feet and 7 inches, it was still a spectacular effort and kept the crowds happy for the seven hours it took to assemble it. Admission fees vary.

NEW MEXICO WINE FESTIVAL

Loretto Park, Camino del Pueblo
Bernalillo
(505) 867-3311
www.newmexicowinefestival.com

Launched in 1988, this is the state's oldest wine fair, and it gives you the opportunity to sample dozens of New Mexico wines over Labor Day weekend in Bernalillo's Loretto Park. About 19 wineries from throughout the state come to share their bounty, and the grassy, tree-lined park is filled over the three-day weekend with around 15,000 visitors. A tasting glass is provided with your admission fee; then you can browse the tents, try the wines, and buy a glass or a bottle of your favorite (although you cannot open purchased bottles on the festival grounds). The food is all locally made, including barbecue, Mediterranean plates, hamburgers, and turkey legs, plus the ever-popular *queso pan y uvas*—cheese spread on bread with grapes. Live entertainment focuses on jazz, with a dance floor in the music tent. Browse the good-quality juried arts and crafts show, plus the agricultural products for sale and produce such as nuts and lavender. The show is organized by the town of Bernalillo, in cooperation with the New Mexico Wine Growers Association. Note that you can't bring your own picnic in to the festival, and only service animals are allowed, no pets. Adult admission is around $12 a day. Under-21s must be accompanied by an adult. Remember to bring a proof-of-age ID if you want to taste wines; they do check.

OCTOBER

ALBUQUERQUE INTERNATIONAL BALLOON FIESTA

Balloon Fiesta Park, north of Alameda Boulevard, 1 mile west of I-25
(505) 821-1000, (888) 422-7277
www.balloonfiesta.com

The Albuquerque International Balloon Fiesta started as a modest balloon rally in 1972, with 13 balloons launching from the Coronado Shopping Mall parking lot. Now it's grown into the world's largest hot-air balloon festival, starting on the first Saturday of October for nine days of high-flying fun. There are jaw-droppingly gorgeous mass ascensions of around 700 balloons, contests of speed and navigation skill, Balloon Glow events at dusk with balloons lit up from within, and special-shape balloons to amuse young and old, plus plenty of on-the-ground activities. See the Close-up for a detailed look into this annual spectacular that is unique to Albuquerque.

The Balloon Fiesta has 14 sessions, 9 in the morning and 5 in the evening. The adult ticket price for any one session is $6. Children 12 and under are admitted free. Parking is $10 per car. You can buy tickets in advance or at the door on the day. In the event of bad weather or other cancellation, rain checks are issued so you can use your ticket for another session. Buy online in advance, and get tickets for 5 sessions for $25 plus a $1 handling charge. Entry routes into Balloon Fiesta Park vary; see the instructions for your event. If you are driving to the fiesta, you are encouraged to use the Park and Ride system, which effectively gives you

Albuquerque International Balloon Fiesta

When the world's largest hot-air balloon festival lifts off, the spectacle is awe-inspiring. Over 700 balloons participate in the fiesta, in every color and shape imaginable. As these bright, beautiful giants drift silently across the Rio Grande Valley against the Sandia Mountains and crisp turquoise skies, it's easy to see why the fiesta is reckoned to be one of the most photographed events on the planet. Around 800,000 spectators attend over nine days in October, but despite the fiesta's scale, it still manages to feel like a happy family reunion. Balloonatics young and old wander the launch field, talking to the pilots, and possibly even helping to prepare balloons for takeoff. The roar of hundreds of burners kicking hot air into the balloon envelopes prickles the back of your neck, and the excitement of being part of the on-the-ground action is hard to beat. Or maybe you'll take a champagne balloon ride yourself, for a bird's-eye view of the party.

FIESTA FAVORITES

The schedule varies each year, but here are some regular favorites, starting with Dawn Patrol Shows, when a dozen balloons take off in a choreographed launch set to music. Mass Ascensions commence around 7:15 a.m., as all 700 balloons launch in two waves, led by a balloon flying the American flag to the tune of the "Star Spangled Banner." In under two hours all the balloons are up, up, and away. In addition to balloonists from most U.S. states, a couple of dozen countries are represented, including Canada, many European nations, and some as far afield as Japan, New Zealand, and South Africa. The Wednesday morning Flight of the Nations Mass Ascension reflects the event's global spirit, with pilots sporting their national flag.

In balloon competitions pilots test their precision flying, steering toward a target on the ground to drop a weighted marker. The one closest to the center wins. Or they play aerial poker, where each pilot has to draw two cards for a winning hand, selecting their cards by placing markers on them while flying overhead. Similarly, in the Black Jack race, pilots try to score 21 from the giant cards spread on the ground. The Key Grab is one of the most adrenaline-packed contests, testing both speed and accuracy. Flyers launch from a mile away and dash to the field, trying to jostle ahead of hundreds of other balloons while avoiding collisions, to grab the prize key by hand from the top of a tall pole. Evening Balloon Glows, which are now a popular feature of balloon fests all over the world, began in Albuquerque on Christmas Eve 1979. Duke City pilots inflated their tethered balloons as a mark of gratitude to local residents, and the balloons, illuminated from within like giant lightbulbs, twinkled in such a festive fashion that they've become a year-round celebration. At dusk over 300 balloons at the Albuquerque fiesta fire up to magical effect, followed by fireworks.

The Special Shape Rodeo showcases balloons fashioned as bumblebees, eagles, dragons, dinosaurs, cacti, wagons, shoes, and soda cans. If you think you just saw a flying cow, a floating house, or a ship sailing overhead, it's not a figment of your imagination. Kids love the mass ascensions of the special shapes, and the Glowdeo brings the animals and other artistic creations to life in a shapes-only evening glow.

AMERICA'S CHALLENGE GAS BALLOON RACE

The most extreme fiesta competition is the America's Challenge Gas Balloon Race to fly the farthest distance from Albuquerque. Gas balloons fly higher and farther than hot-air balloons, and competitors often stay in the air for three nights or more, testing their stamina, courage, and skills. The race motto is "Go the Distance," and they do. Winners might fly 1,000 miles from Balloon Fiesta Park, finally touching down on the East Coast or Canada. You can track the gas balloons' progress and see video feeds on the Albuquerque International Balloon Fiesta Web site (www.balloonfiesta.com). Balloonist Mark Sullivan, an Albuquerque native and recipient of the Montgolfier Diplome, the sport's highest honor, from the Fédération Aéronautique Internationale, founded this race in 1995.

ON THE GROUND

The launch area at Balloon Fiesta Park is the size of 56 football fields, covering around 72 grassy acres. A virtual city springs up here for nine days, with entertainment, vendors, and other services. Launch officials are easy to spot: Wearing black-and-white-striped shirts, they're fondly known as Zebras, and they keep everything running safely and on time.

You can bring a lawn chair or blanket to sit on the soft grass, and bring a picnic if you want. Or check out over a third of a mile of vendors providing a variety of dishes from New Orleans filet gumbo to Wisconsin fried cheese curds. Hot breakfast burritos wrapped in foil serve as instant hand-warmers on cool mornings, or for sweet tooths there are warm mini cinnamon rolls drizzled with icing served in a paper-cone cup.

Previous fiestas have featured bands like the Coasters; Aztec dancers; barbershop quartets; air force bands; and jazz, blues, and Native American singers. Performances are on the Main Street stage, and there are also roving entertainers. The Chainsaw Wood Carving Contest buzzes away in hour-long Quick Carves or Master Carves over three days, transforming huge logs into works of art interpreting the annual fiesta theme. Some sculptures are raffled and auctioned off. The Fiesta of Wheels Car Show is also a popular event. Kids have an arts and crafts space or amuse themselves flying kites once the balloons have taken off. Each year 30,000 visitors of all ages drop into the free Balloon Discovery Center to learn about ballooning history and science. There is a simulated balloon flight, a theater with guest speakers, videos, puppet shows, and classes to build your own tissue-paper balloon. Merchandise for sale ranges from balloon-inspired wind chimes to pajamas.

AN ELEVATED EXPERIENCE

Even rookies can see fiesta action from the air during events, including the Mass Ascensions, the contests and Key Grab, and the Special Shapes Rodeo. Book with the fiesta's official balloon-ride operator Rainbow Ryders (800-725-2477, www.rainbowryders.com). Another way to ensure an extra-special experience of the balloon fiesta is to join the 1,500 volunteers who keep the show running. Anyone can volunteer for the chase crews, which help set up and launch balloons, follow them to landing, and assist in recovery and packing up. Register online, or show up on the day. Chase-crew volunteers must wear sturdy, covered shoes and also bring gloves.

Finally, the Gondola Club package provides a VIP experience in a reserved area with private indoor and outdoor seating. A full breakfast or dinner buffet is included, plus special parking, a shuttle to pop you down to the Fiesta Main Street with all its activities, and a souvenir gift. The Gondola Club is staffed by balloonists and New Mexico experts, so it's like having your own concierge—they have the inside scoop on anything you'll want to know. You can book the Gondola Club package for one session or more; be sure to book early for weekend sessions. The Gondola Club package including fiesta admission is $100 for the first session, $50 for additional sessions ($50/$25, respectively, for children 12 and under).

THE ALBUQUERQUE BOX

The famous Albuquerque Box wind pattern means that the wind blows reliably north at one elevation, then turns south at another. Pilots can use this predictable pattern to launch and fly at one altitude, then when they want to return to their start point, they change altitude and are blown back to base. These upper- and lower-level winds are created by the geography of the Rio Grande Valley and the Sandia Mountains, but the Albuquerque Box effect usually dissipates by noon, when the ground is heated by the sun, disturbing the thermal patterns.

Albuquerque International Balloon Fiesta, continued

The box pattern occurs frequently on early October mornings, aided by the clear skies and low humidity. It helps the balloon fiesta's hundreds of balloons remain close to the field during Mass Ascensions, resulting in the amazing display that makes the fiesta unique. Sometimes, a pilot does a quick "splash and dash," dipping his gondola into the Rio Grande.

Fortunately, the early-morning hours that work so well for balloonists are also some of the best times to take photographs! The light is soft, with gentle shadows as the low sun creates more texture and depth than when directly overhead. Photographers' favorite "magic hours" of dawn and sunset lend a beautiful warm glow to photography, which is also perfect for evening events at Balloon Fiesta Park. As they say in the balloonists' prayer at the Albuquerque International Balloon Fiesta: *"May the winds welcome you with softness. May the sun bless you with its warm hands."*

free admission. You'll also have a faster journey, as Park and Ride shuttles have special lanes to zip into the grounds. Another option is the New Mexico Rail Runner Express to the Los Ranchos/Journal Center Station, where shuttles are provided to Balloon Fiesta Park. Be warned, though, that you must purchase a combined Rail Runner/Park & Ride/ Balloon Fiesta Admission pass in advance, as they are not available at the Rail Runner Station. Order the pass online at the Balloon Fiesta Web site. For dawn events it's wise to be on the launch field by 5 a.m., or you might become stuck in traffic getting there. For evening Balloon Glows, the gates open at 3 p.m., and the Glow starts right at dusk, so it's recommended to arrive by around 4:30 or 5, before rush-hour traffic starts.

Hotels and B&Bs in the Albuquerque area fill up over Balloon Fiesta week, even as far as Santa Fe. Many people book their rooms a year in advance, so make early reservations. RV facilities at the fiesta are excellent, and you can park in the RV grounds, with an easy walk or a quick shuttle to the launch field. Reserve well in advance for these popular RV spaces, as they also fill up fast. Book online at the Web site, or call 888-422-7277 and ask for an RV representative.

i In 2005 Governor Bill Richardson signed a bill that designated the hot-air balloon as New Mexico's official state aircraft.

Dress in layers to stay comfortable through the changing temperatures. October days in Albuquerque are still very warm, around 70°F, but mornings are much cooler, around 40°F. The temperature also drops substantially once the sun sets, so you want to be able to add and remove layers to suit. Also wear comfortable shoes, as there's plenty to stroll around and see on the grassy launch field. For early morning events remember to bring sunscreen and sunglasses for later in the day. Similarly, for evening events, although you'll arrive in daylight, it will be dark when you leave, so bring a flashlight, and make a note of where you've left your vehicle so you can find it. Smoking is strictly forbidden anywhere near balloons. Also note that animals are easily spooked by balloon noise and movement, and no pets are allowed except service animals.

FALL INDIAN MARKET
Indian Pueblo Cultural Center
2401 12th Street NW
(866) 855-7902
www.indianpueblo.org

Coinciding with the International Balloon Fiesta, the Fall Indian Market provides the opportunity to buy authentic Native American jewelry, pottery, and other traditional arts, crafts, and artifacts directly from the artisan. There are also artist demonstrations, tribal dances, and film screenings. Entry to the Indian Pueblo Cultural Center is $6 for adults, with discounts for seniors, New Mexico residents, and students. Entry for children is $3, and under-5s are free.

RIO GRANDE ARTS & CRAFTS FESTIVALS
Big Top Tent at I-25 and Paseo del Norte
(505) 292-7457
www.riograndefestivals.com
Held on the first and second weekends of the Albuquerque International Balloon Fiesta, this popular juried festival features work from national artists and craftspeople. There are three editions of the Rio Grande Arts & Crafts Festivals each year, in March, October, and November. See the March entry for full details of what you can find at this family-friendly event. The October festival is held in a three-story-high, 400-foot-long Big Top tent, on the southwest corner of I-25 and Paseo del Norte, one exit south of the balloon fiesta site. Adult admission is $7 or $10 for a pass for all six days over the two weekends. Free for children under 12. Park at no charge off the southbound Frontage Road.

NOVEMBER

RIO GRANDE ARTS & CRAFTS FESTIVALS
EXPO New Mexico,
Home of the New Mexico State Fair
300 San Pedro NE
(505) 292-7457
www.riograndefestivals.com
The holiday edition of this popular juried festival is at the perfect time to shop for your gift list from a huge array of arts and crafts from all over the country. There are three Rio Grande Arts & Crafts Festivals each year, in March, October, and November. See the March entry for full details of what you can find at this family-friendly event. The November festival is usually held for three days over Thanksgiving weekend and has the added attraction of the annual Cookie Walk. In this charitable benefit you buy an empty box ($15) and then fill it with your choice of holiday cookies. Adult admission is $6 a day or $8 for a three-day pass. Free for children under 12.

i The Twinkle Light Parade is the first major event for the festive holiday season. Floats, custom cars, marching bands, dancers, and merrymakers follow the parade route from Central Avenue to the Rio Grande Botanic Gardens. Here Santa awaits and the River of Lights opens for the holidays. The date of the Twinkle Light Parade varies, but it usually falls at the end of November; www.cabq.gov/crs/twinklelight.html.

WEEMS INTERNATIONAL ARTFEST
EXPO New Mexico,
Home of the New Mexico State Fair
300 San Pedro NE
(505) 293-6133
www.weemsinternationalartfest.org
Usually held on the first or second weekend of November, this three-day arts and crafts fest has flourished over more than a quarter of a century. From its origins as a small local fair, it's grown into a big and lively event featuring celebrity artists. VIPs appearing at the show in previous years have included Jane Seymour, Anthony Quinn, Sophia Loren, and Bo Derek. Around 270 artists and craftspeople sell their work, including paintings in all styles from southwestern to abstract, pottery and ceramics, sculpture, jewelry, textiles and apparel, works in glass and metal, and an eclectic array of decorative objects for the home. The show is organized by the dynamic Mary Ann Weems of Weems Art Gallery. As a former art teacher, Weems is a big believer in introducing children to art, and the Children's ArtSMart is a unique part of the festival. Only kids 12 and under can go into this section—adults are forbidden—and here they can buy artworks for $10 and under. Any artist participating in the festival can present their pieces here, as long as it fits the maximum $10 price tag. This helps to get youngsters into the habit of buying art and builds their confidence about their personal tastes. To date, at least 40,000 children have bought work at ArtSMart. Previous years' shows have also

Day of the Dead

If you spend much time in Albuquerque, you'll start to notice imagery involving skeletons, skulls, and even death carts in art galleries, museums, and gift shops. The influence of old Mexico crosses the border when it comes to the Day of the Dead—or *el Día de los Muertos*—a traditional celebration of those who have passed on but have not been forgotten. El Día de los Muertos is commemorated on November 1 and into November 2, coinciding with the Catholic calendar's All Saints Day and All Souls Day, respectively.

An occasion for parties, parades, and dressing up in costume, the Day of the Dead goes back to Aztec rituals that originally occurred in late summer. Early Spanish explorers often found these celebrations unsettling because they appeared to mock the fact of death, but like many indigenous traditions it proved impossible to eradicate and so was eventually moved to a date that corresponded with the Catholic calendar and incorporated into the church.

An oddly uplifting celebration of mortality, el Día de los Muertos is a lot of fun once you get used to it—picture Halloween with a twist of tequila, and you're in the right zone. Of course, there is also a somber side, and people may visit ancestors' graves to pay their respects or make altars, called *ofrendas,* brightly adorned with decorations and mementos. A feast of food and alcohol is often left for the departed one. The skeleton icons associated with this day of remembrance may be sad and weeping or joyfully dancing, symbolizing both the sorrow of loss and a celebration of the loved one, joining with them beyond the grave in the eternal dance of life and death. Since "All Hallow's Eve" falls immediately before, on October 31, in multicultural Albuquerque you can wear that skeleton costume at least twice in the same week!

Albuquerque's Day of the Dead is celebrated each year with a public festival at the South Broadway Cultural Center (505-848-1320, www.cabq.gov/sbcc) and the annual South Valley Dia de los Muertos Marigold parade. At the Open Space Visitor Center (505-897-8831, www.cabq.gov/openspace/visitorcenter.html), Day of the Dead activities have included making an altar and cutting out festive *papel picado* paper banners. More recently, a fun run/bike/walk charity event known as "Day of the Tread" (www.dayofthetread.com) has been added to the customary celebrations—and yes, it happens in costume. Other festivities occur throughout the city, including music and arts and crafts, and bars and restaurants often host their own events. Because details change each year, it's best to check local newspapers.

included a silent auction and a charity benefit preview on the Thursday evening before Artfest opens, hosted by the celebrity artist, with admission of around $85 per person.

Weems International Artfest is a nonprofit organization, and proceeds from the show have benefited many regional causes. Adult admission is $5 or $4 for seniors over 65. Free for children 12 and under.

DECEMBER

One of the delights of December is the beauty of the city lit up by luminarias, or *farolitos,* as they're sometimes called by towns farther north. Luminarias are small brown paper bags with a votive candle inside, set into sand to hold the candle and weigh the bag down. When hundreds are lit in rows along the side of the street, atop adobe walls and around roofs, the sight is magical. The golden glow reflects against old adobe, and the twinkling candles immediately inspire a sense of festivity. They are traditionally lit on Christmas Eve, to light the path and help guide Mary and Joseph on their way and also to guide the faithful to midnight Mass. But whatever your religion, the aesthetics of this New Mexican tradition are bound to please, and these simple lanterns are a comfort on the longest nights around the winter solstice. Of course, in the early days of the luminaria tradition, they were not made from brown paper bags but were small bonfires of interwoven piñon branches. In some parts of New Mexico, you'll still see the piñon fires as well as the candles. Luminarias continue to evolve in the 21st century: Sometimes strings of shop-bought plastic ones are used to circle rooftops or other places where paper and fire would not be a match made in heaven, but they look just as pretty from a distance. Mostly though, you'll see people hand-lighting rows of luminarias through December for evenings of caroling and celebration.

Here are some favorite December festivities that usually take place each year. Contact individual venues for information, as details and dates change. The City of Albuquerque Web page www.cabq.gov/fun/winter is a good source for major holiday event listings.

The annual River of Lights sparkles from the end of November through the month of December at the Rio Grande Botanic Garden. This splendid evening display of holiday lights and light sculptures creates dinosaurs, flying birds, giant sparkling sunflowers, and all kinds of fantasy still and moving images, and a collection of miniature glass snowmen is staged as a winter wonderland scene, lit by fiber optics. An outdoor skating rink in the botanic garden plaza is open on some evenings; check for dates, and bring your own skates (505-768-2000; www.cabq.gov/biopark/garden).

The Old Town Holiday Stroll features dancers, singers, and other performers; the lighting of the giant Christmas tree; and the Santa Claus parade around the plaza. The Old Town Plaza and the streets all around are beautifully lit up by thousands of luminarias, and shops stay open late, many serving holiday treats such as biscochitos, hot chocolate, and cider. The Holiday Stroll usually takes place in early December. Arrive in good time to park, as the surrounding parking lots and streets get packed. Throughout the holiday season Old Town is a special place to be. Look out for a holiday concert on Christmas Eve (505-319-4087; www.albuquerqueoldtown.com).

The Hanging of the Greens is a long-standing tradition at the University of New Mexico, usually held on an evening in early December. It's drawn from the old English custom of decking the halls with boughs of holly (and other evergreens) for Advent. Lena C. Clauve, a UNM student and later dean of women, started the ritual at UNM in the 1930s. Students used to drive into the Sandia Mountains and gather greenery to decorate the Student Union Building. Now the Hanging of the Greens involves a procession through the campus adorned with luminarias, to present a wreath to the university president, before enjoying caroling, hot chocolate, and *biscochitos* (505-277-0111).

Other events include the annual Nob Hill Holiday Shop & Stroll (rt66central.com) with music, food, and holiday sales and a Holiday Open House at Casa San Ysidro in Corrales, where the historic home is decorated with holiday greens and luminarias, with activities like ornament making and carol singing (505-898-3915; www.cabq.gov/museum/history/casatour.html). A Santa's Workshop (complete with elves) is part of the fun in Christmas at Kuaua at the Coronado State Monument in Bernalillo, plus Native American dancing and storytelling around the bonfire (505-867-5351; www.nmmonuments.org). A Christmas Eve Luminaria Tour on ABQ Ride buses takes you round the light displays in Old Town, the National Hispanic Cultural Center, and other neighborhoods (505-243-7433; www.cabq.gov/transit).

Las Posadas is a Christmas tradition throughout New Mexico—a procession that reenacts Joseph and Mary's search for lodging (las posadas means "the inns"). In Albuquerque Las Posadas de Barelas has continued this holy ritual for more than 60 years. The date varies, but it starts from the Barelas Community Center, and anyone can join the procession. Singers and Matachines dancers follow Joseph, Mary, and the donkey as they go house to house seeking refuge, following a route lit by luminarias. They are turned away at every stop, until they reach Sacred Heart Church, where they are welcomed in. Afterwards, cookies and cocoa are served back at the Barelas Community Center, and there's a visit from Saint Nicholas. The Barelas Community Center, completed in 1942, is one of the oldest community centers in Albuquerque, built in Pueblo Revival style (801 Barelas Road SW; 505-848-1343; www.cabq.gov/communitycenters/barelas.html).

Many arts venues present seasonal entertainment like mariachi or Celtic Christmas music, plays such as *A Christmas Carol,* and the favorite Christmas ballet, *The Nutcracker.* Also check out holiday programs at the National Hispanic Cultural Center (505-246-2261; www.nhccnm.org) and the Indian Pueblo Cultural Center (505-843-7270, www.indianpueblo.org). Some Indian pueblos have special holiday dances and processions, and the Santa Ana Pueblo maintains a good calendar of annual events for all the 19 New Mexico pueblos. For latest information see www.santaana.org/calendar.htm.

PARKS AND RECREATION

Studies by the Trust for Public Land have ranked Albuquerque high for its land area dedicated to parks and preserves. Albuquerque's Open Space program protects and manages over 28,000 acres of lands in and around the city, and many of these areas of natural and cultural significance are open to the public. Open Space areas include the Rio Grande Valley State Park, the Sandia Foothills Open Space, Elena Gallegos Picnic Area and Albert G. Simms Park, Petroglyph National Monument, West Mesa Open Space, East Mountain Open Space, and Open Space Farmlands. Highlights for visitors in the Open Space areas are detailed in this chapter, and the Open Space Visitor Center is well worth a stop, as it tells you more about the areas included in the program and is a lovely destination in itself, with trails, wildlife watching, and gardens. There are plenty of recreation opportunities on the Open Space areas, which cover a diversity of environments, from the volcanic escarpment to the cottonwood bosque to the lower elevations of the Sandia Mountains. Trails within the lands vary from the easiest stroll to the highly challenging trek. One easy (if long!) trail in the heart of the city is the 16-mile Paseo del Bosque trail, which you can join at several places or just access by a short stroll from the Rio Grande Nature Center. Hiking, bicycling, mountain biking, horse riding, and in-line skating are permitted in most Open Space areas but not all, so look out for signs. High-impact recreation, such as playing Frisbee or softball, are not allowed on Open Space lands. Open Space area information and trail maps are available by calling the City of Albuquerque Open Space Division at (505) 452-5200 or from the Web site www.cabq.gov/openspace, or you can call the Open Space Visitor Center for information at (505) 897-8831.

Other recreation opportunities in Albuquerque range from its world-famous ballooning to Ice skating and skiing. The temperate climate and stunning geography ensure the city's popularity for all kinds of outdoor adventures, but there is also a good range of indoor leisure activities, including bowling and karting. Even if you're not an angler, it's worth checking out the fishing section, as these attractive waterside areas offer a cool escape from summer in the city, either for family picnics or for artists seeking to paint en plein air!

PARKS AND OPEN SPACE

ALBUQUERQUE BIOLOGICAL PARK
(505) 768-2000
www.cabq.gov/biopark

Albuquerque BioPark is an environmental park that includes the 36-acre Rio Grande Botanic Garden, the Albuquerque Aquarium, the Rio Grande Zoo, and Tingley Beach. The park areas stretch along the east side of the Rio Grande, and a narrow-gauge train runs a 1.5-mile journey to connect each facility. The Rio Grande Botanic Garden and Albuquerque Aquarium are on the same property (2601 Central Avenue NW). The botanic garden features a lake and lawns, a series of regionally themed gardens, a 10,000-square-foot conservatory, and a 10-acre Heritage Farm with vineyards and orchards. There is a children's Fantasy Garden, a Japanese garden with koi pond, and in summer the PNM Butterfly Pavilion. The aquarium contains about 3,000 salt- and freshwater aquatic animals and provides up-close encounters with moray eels in the eel tunnel and sharks through a 38-foot-wide viewing window into the 285,000-gallon ocean tank. The 64-acre Rio Grande Zoo (903 Tenth Street SW) is home—

in naturalistic habitats—to over 250 species of animals from New Mexico and around the world. Tingley Beach (1800 Tingley Drive SW) is a landscaped space to walk and feed the ducks or bring a picnic (no alcohol permitted). There are three fishing ponds, including a children's pond for those 12 and under (you need a license to fish if 12 or over, and day licenses are available). Despite the name, no swimming or floating devices are allowed here, but you can rent a pedal boat in summer and also bicycles. Tingley Beach is free and open daily from sunrise to sunset. We've given detailed information on the Albuquerque Biological Park facilities in the Attractions chapter.

ELENA GALLEGOS PICNIC AREA AND ALBERT G. SIMMS PARK

East end of Simms Park Road NE
(505) 897-8831
www.cabq.gov/openspace/lands.html

Part of the Sandia Foothills Open Space lands, this 640-acre park sits at about 6,500 feet elevation, with seven covered picnic areas and trails for hikers, bikers, and horse riders. Restrooms are available at the picnic area. The park is covered with piñon trees, chamisa, cholla cactus, yucca, and native grasses, and there are views west to Mount Taylor, north to the Jemez Mountains, and south over Tijeras Arroyo. The Elena Gallegos Information Center at the entrance to the park provides background information on the area. Visit the pond and wildlife blind via the easy half-mile round-trip Cottonwood Springs Trail, with shaded stops en route featuring artwork by Margie O'Brien related to the environment around you. (The Cottonwood Springs Trail is fully accessible.) The park is a popular spot for evening family picnics to watch the sunset as the skies change color behind Mount Taylor. The park's summer hours from April 1 to the end of September are 7 a.m. to 9 p.m. From October 1 to March 31, the winter hours are 7 a.m. to 7 p.m. Park admission is $1 per vehicle during the week, $2 on weekends. Simms Park Road is off Tramway Boulevard, north of the Academy Road junction. Turn east on Simms Park Road to the Information Center.

i **An old tale about the Dolores Treasure says that gold coins are buried beneath a grinding wheel somewhere in the Sandia foothills around the Elena Gallegos area. So keep your eyes open!**

OPEN SPACE VISITOR CENTER

6500 Coors Boulevard NW
(505) 897-8831
www.cabq.gov/openspace

As a central hub for the Open Space program, the visitor center has exhibits and information about all Open Space lands, including the habitats, ecosystems, and wildlife and the cultural and historical significance of these areas. The building is a renovated residence from the 1970s (the center's main room used to be the garage!), and the streamlined modern architecture sits pleasingly in this serene green spot just west of the Rio Grande. The center is popular with bird and wildlife photographers and with families. There are excellent views of the Sandias, the bosque, and also of the visitor center's 24 acres of agricultural fields, where sorghum, corn, millet, and alfalfa are grown. These fields draw diverse wildlife, and you can borrow a pair of binoculars to watch from the observation deck. They also serve as wintering grounds for migratory birds including sandhill cranes. Mid-November is the peak time to watch the flocks of sandhill cranes on their dramatic fly-outs to the river in the evening. The center's Traditions Garden demonstrates a variety of agricultural techniques used through the area's history by Native American and Spanish farmers, including a terraced arroyo garden, native plants, and waffle-grid gardens. Access to bosque trails is right on the doorstep of the visitor center. You can take the 1-mile round-trip River Loop trail, or the 2-mile round-trip Canopy Loop. The center opened in 2006 and also houses an art gallery presenting work related to open space. Education and arts programs and entertainment take place here through the year. The entry to the Open Space Visitor Center is off Coors, at the end of Bosque Meadows Road, between Montaño and Paseo del Norte. There is no admission fee. Closed Monday.

Don't miss the "Arbol de la Vida" outside at the back of the Open Space Visitor Center. This chainsaw sculpture by Joseph Mark Chavez is a tree of life with 26 animals, including bears, bats, snakes, and owls, carved out of a cottonwood tree stump.

PETROGLYPH NATIONAL MONUMENT

Las Imágenes Visitor Center
Unser Boulevard NW at Western Trail
(505) 899-0205
www.nps.gov/petr

This monument covers 7,236 acres on the 17-mile-long West Mesa escarpment, and there are four day-use areas amid the petroglyphs and around the volcano area. The petroglyph images were pecked into the boulders by Native Americans some 300 to 700 years ago, and later Spanish settlers added their own etchings 200 to 300 years ago. For more information on the monument, see the Attractions chapter. It is part of the Open Space network of facilities, so there are various hiking trails and picnic areas, but as this is a protected historical and environmental site, please stay on established trails. Wildlife here includes lizards, rattlesnakes, 6-inch-long dark brown desert millipedes, and the more rare gray slate millipede, about 3 inches long. Plants you might see include prickly pear, purple aster, broom dalea or purple sage, the sculpturally handsome cane cholla, and poisonous jimsonweed. You can go directly to any of the day-use areas, but you are strongly encouraged to go first to the Las Imágenes Visitor Center for trail guides, orientation, and important safety information. The visitor center also has a bookstore and a picnic area. Boca Negra Canyon is the only fully developed area, with restrooms, shaded picnic tables, and drinking water. There are three self-guided hiking trails, which lead you past around 200 petroglyphs; allow about an hour to take all three, or you can take just one or two trails from the parking lot. No pets are allowed here. Boca Negra Canyon is about a 2-mile drive north of the visitor center. Open hours are 8 a.m. to 5 p.m. There is no admission fee, but there is a parking fee of $1 during the week and $2 on weekends. Rinconada Canyon, Piedras Marcadas Canyon, and the Volcanoes area are less developed, with no water available. Dogs are permitted on leashes in these areas, but be aware that there are rattlesnakes, predators, and plants that could harm a dog, so keep your pet close. Trail and orientation information for these areas is available at the visitor center. Las Imágenes Visitor Center is open year round from 8 a.m. to 5 p.m.

RIO GRANDE NATURE CENTER STATE PARK

2901 Candelaria Road NW
(505) 344-7240
www.nmparks.com

Managed by New Mexico State Parks, the park has three ponds, a five-acre wetland, nature trails, and great opportunities to view wildlife both out on the land and from the nature center (also called the Visitor Center) designed by Albuquerque architect Antoine Predock in 1982. The tunnel-like entrance to the nature center leads you into a circular hall with environmental exhibits. The observation lounge has a curved glass wall that looks directly out to the three-acre pond surrounding the center, for an up-close view of geese, ducks, turtles, hummingbirds, and other wildlife. Speakers on the pond pipe the bird sounds from outside into the room, so you feel you are actually out in the environment with the creatures, from the comfort of the lounge. There are identification guides available, plus binoculars, trail guides, and a nature library. Over 270 species of birds have been spotted in the park. There are two easy trail loops of a mile or just under, a river walk, and a bosque loop. The 16-mile-long Paseo del Bosque multiuse paved trail also passes through the park, just a few steps from the nature center. The park also includes the Candelaria Wetland, and outdoor blinds to hide in for wildlife watching. There is an active program of activities and events for adults and children, including guided bird walks, nature walks, and evening moon walks—the walks are free, but some require registration. Call the park

Paseo del Bosque Trail

Running approximately 16 miles from north to south, the Paseo del Bosque Trail stretches along the east side of the Rio Grande, passing through the Rio Grande Valley State Park. A favorite with locals and visitors alike, the fully paved trail, with a corresponding natural-surface trail in some areas under a canopy of cottonwoods, is perfect for cycling and mountain biking, hiking, horse riding, and in-line skating. It leads you through the cottonwood bosque, wetlands, and open space, and no roads interrupt the flat trail. Although this north/south vein is right in the heart of Albuquerque, you could be excused for believing the city is a long way away. Wildlife on view, depending on the season, might include geese, ducks, sandhill cranes, herons, and hawks, as well as coyotes on land, and you could easily find yourself running alongside a roadrunner! *Sunset* magazine included the trail in its "Top 10 city bike rides." There are plenty of shorter sections to tackle if you don't feel up to doing the whole length. From the Rio Grande Nature Center to Campbell Road is just about three-quarters of a mile, or there's a 1-mile section between Alameda Boulevard and Paseo del Norte. Various access points with parking include the Rio Grande Nature Center; Alameda Boulevard at the southeast side of the Alameda Boulevard bridge; Pueblo Montano Picnic Area and Trailhead; Central Avenue at the northeast corner of the Central Avenue bridge; Marquez Street; and Rio Bravo Boulevard (turn north on Poco Loco Street, west of 2nd Street and just before the bridge crossing the river). The trail also leads you past the Albuquerque Biological Park and the National Hispanic Cultural Center. A downloadable trail map is available at www.cabq.gov/openspace.

or check the calendar of activities at the Friends of the Rio Grande Nature Center Web site, www.rgnc.org. (The Rio Grande Nature Center is also part of the Rio Grande Valley State Park system.) Park admission is free for pedestrians and bikes. Motor vehicles pay a $3 fee. The park is open from 8 a.m. to 5 p.m., and the nature center is open between 10 a.m. and 5 p.m.

RIO GRANDE VALLEY STATE PARK
(505) 897-8831
www.cabq.gov/openspace/lands.html

Stretching over 4,300 acres from Sandia Pueblo to Isleta Pueblo, and part of the Open Space lands, this park contains several areas of interest along the Rio Grande and bosque. The bosque is a riverside forest of towering cottonwoods, and you'll also see coyote willow and New Mexico olive. Wildlife in park areas includes many species of birds and waterfowl, turtles, beaver, coyote, raccoons, lizards, and snakes. The park's daily operating hours are April to October from 7 a.m. to 9 p.m; November to March from 7 a.m. to 7 p.m.

ALAMEDA / RIO GRANDE OPEN SPACE

The constructed Alameda Wetland reproduces natural wetlands that once occurred on the Rio Grande's floodplains. The Paseo del Bosque trail passes through here, and the area features cottonwoods and wildlife, including ducks and geese. Two picnic areas under the trees are on the northeast corner of the Alameda Boulevard bridge. Parking and access are on the southeast side of the Alameda bridge.

PUEBLO MONTANO PICNIC AREA AND TRAILHEAD

The picnic area is ADA-accessible in this Open Space recreational area. Note the wood carvings by artist and firefighter Joseph Mark Chavez. After bosque forest fires in 2003 caused severe damage, Chavez carved animals, birds, and figures of people into the remaining cottonwood tree stumps. You can also access the Paseo del Bosque trail here. Parking and access to Pueblo Montano Picnic Area and Trailhead is south of Montano Road, between Coors Boulevard and the Rio Grande.

RIO BRAVO RIVERSIDE

Here there is a quarter-mile nature trail loop through the shady cottonwoods beside the river, plus three picnic areas and a fishing pier. The Paseo del Bosque trail also leads from the parking lot. On Rio Bravo Boulevard turn north on Poco Loco Street, west of 2nd Street, before the bridge over the river.

RIO DEL NORTE PICNIC AREA

The trail loop here has super views of the river and wildlife such as ducks and geese as you amble beneath the cottonwoods. There are plenty of shady picnic tables en route, and the trail loop is fully accessible. This area is on the east side of the river and can be reached from the Paseo del Bosque Trail. There is limited parking near the Albuquerque Biological Park, north of Central Avenue and west of Tingley Drive.

City Parks

Albuquerque's Park Management administers more than 286 park sites around the city, and in every neighborhood it's hard to turn a corner without discovering another green space tucked away for local leisure and relaxation. Here are three of the most popular in Old Town, Downtown, and on the Westside of Albuquerque. For a full list and details on amenities, see the city Web site: www.cabq.gov/parks.

Skate Parks

Five city skate parks are available for in-line skaters, BMX bikers, and skateboarders. Los Altos Skate Park is said to be the largest in the Southwest, with a street course and two bowls included in its 35,000 square feet. This park is at 10140 Lomas NE, west of Eubank and east of Easterday. The $650,000 Tower Skate Park is located at Tower Road and 86th Street SW. The others are Alamosa Skate Park (6900 Gonzales Road SW); Coronado Skate Park (4th Street and McKnight NW); and the Northwest Modular Skate Park opposite the Cottonwood Mall, at Coors Boulevard Bypass and Seven Bar Loop. Under-18s must wear helmets at city skate parks, and other protective gear is heavily encouraged. Parks are open between May and August from 7 a.m. to 11 p.m., and for the rest of the year from 9 a.m. to 10 p.m. No dogs or alcohol allowed—just skating!

MARIPOSA BASIN PARK
6701 Taylor Ranch Road NW

Mariposa is a 47-acre park west of the Rio Grande, with a pond, playgrounds, picnic tables, soccer fields, courts for basketball and volleyball, and 12 horseshoe pits. This is a good spot for bird-watching. There are three trail loops of between half a mile and a mile, and on-site parking. The park is bordered by Taylor Ranch Road and Kachina Street NW.

ROOSEVELT PARK
Coal Avenue SE

A pretty and popular park in the Downtown area, famous for its gently rolling hills and old trees. The 11 acres offer plenty of space for letting off steam, walking in the shady grass, playing Frisbee golf, or just pausing for a picnic at one of the tables. A perimeter trail is .65 of a mile long, a mix of concrete and packed gravel. The trail is flat at the northern end, but steeper and not fully accessible at the southern. Dogs are allowed off leash here. The park is three blocks east of I-25 on Coal Avenue, between Spruce and Sycamore. Parking is near Hazeldine and Sycamore SE.

TRICENTENNIAL TIGUEX PARK
1800 Mountain Road NW

This Old Town park (pronounced TIG-oo-ay) is right beside the Albuquerque Museum of Art and History, the New Mexico Museum of Natural History & Science, and Explora museum. There are two easy loop paths, which also intersect. Both are flat, paved, and wheelchair accessible. The outer loop is half a mile, the inner loop just under a third of a mile. You'll find exercise stations along the paths, a children's playground area, basketball courts, grassy areas, and picnic tables. Also note the striking Patrick Alo sculpture celebrating Albuquerque's tricentennial. Parking is on the street or in the Old Town parking lot by the Albuquerque Museum.

i **If you want a faster flying thrill than a balloon ride, take a helicopter tour over the majestic landscapes of Albuquerque and farther afield in New Mexico with Enchantment Helicopters. The helicopter can also pick you up or deliver you to approved locations, such as resorts and casinos. The company provides helicopters to movie producers for aerial filming, so regular tourists are probably well advised to bring their cameras to capture some breathtaking shots! Enchantment Helicopters can be reached at (505) 831-4354, www.enchantmenthelicopters.com.**

RECREATION

Ballooning

See Albuquerque from the sky in a balloon ride! The city has an international reputation as the hot-air ballooning capital of the world, with its famous Albuquerque Box wind pattern and the annual nine-day Albuquerque International Balloon Fiesta in early October, which draws around 800,000 spectators to watch more than 700 colorful balloons take to the air. However, balloon companies fly year-round, and anyone can take a trip. Most balloon rides launch from the west side of the Rio Grande, where conditions tend to be most favorable. The early morning is the best time for launchings, as that is when the air is most stable, so you'll probably meet with your pilot and crew around sunrise. A ride typically lasts an hour in the air, but allow three to four hours for the whole experience, which includes prep time and inflation of the envelope—the formal name for the actual fabric part of the balloon. You can help the crew with inflation or just take pictures. Afterward, there will be time for packing up the balloon and usually a champagne toast, a light continental breakfast, and some kind of souvenir gift. You are of course returned to your starting point, as the balloon is followed by a chase crew, which will drive you back to the launch site.

So where will you fly? Experts from both the companies recommended below emphasize that every flight is different. Depending on wind speed and direction, you may cross the Rio Grande to the east side, fly west over the Petroglyph National Monument, drift upriver over the bosque, or follow the river south and land in the desert. Some flights land 8 miles from their starting point; others travel around so that you touch down just a half mile from where you took off! Part of the fun is the adventure of discovering where the morning will take you, but in any event you'll enjoy the peaceful sensation of floating in the sky with splendid bird's-eye views of the city and surrounding scenery.

Make sure you wrap up warmly for the early takeoff, but wear layers, as temperatures may change as the morning progresses. Women should leave the high heels at home for this trip—wear pants and sensible flat shoes for climbing into the gondola (the wicker basket that you ride in). Note that women who are pregnant or who may be pregnant cannot fly. Other health or minimum height/age restrictions may apply, so check with the balloon company. Adults can expect to pay upwards of $150 for a balloon ride and substantially more during the October peak weeks of the Albuquerque International Balloon Fiesta. It also costs more to guarantee a private ride, where the basket is reserved exclusively for you and your sweetheart, family, or friends. There are many excellent balloon companies in Albu-

Ballooning Briefs

The hot-air balloon was designated New Mexico's official state aircraft in 2005.

In 1783 the first-ever balloon passengers were a rooster, a duck, and a sheep, on a Montgolfier brothers' balloon that launched from Versailles, France, watched by Louis XVI and Marie Antoinette.

The first manned balloon flight in Paris, also in 1783, was witnessed by Benjamin Franklin.

The traditional champagne toast after a balloon ride dates back to the early history of ballooning in France. Pilots took along a bottle of bubbly so that wherever they landed they could appease mistrustful locals, who were understandably alarmed at the sight of these newfangled flying contraptions.

Balloon pilots can't steer their craft in the way that a plane or car is steered. Instead, they navigate by skillfully changing altitude up or down to catch the wind currents moving in the direction they want to go.

The Albuquerque Box is a wind pattern created by the Sandia Mountains and Rio Grande Valley. The wind blows north at one elevation, then turns south at another. Pilots use this reliable pattern to launch and fly at one altitude, then change altitude to return to base.

Three Albuquerque citizens made the first successful balloon flight across the Atlantic in 1978. Ben Abruzzo, Maxie Anderson, and Larry Newman made the crossing in the Double Eagle II helium balloon.

Duke City's Double Eagle II Airport was named for the balloon flown on that first historic flight across the Atlantic.

Abruzzo, Anderson, fellow Albuquerquean Ron Clark, and Rocky Aoki of Tokyo made history again in the first crossing of the Pacific Ocean by helium balloon with a 5,768-mile voyage in the Double Eagle V.

Albuquerque's Troy Bradley earned 24 ballooning world records for duration, distance, and altitude, including the longest manned balloon flight of 144 hours and 23 minutes.

querque offering flights with FAA-certified pilots, but the two below are recommended for their strong reputations, experience, and customer service. In the unfortunate event that the balloon company has to cancel your ride due to adverse winds or weather—there is no flight in any kind of precipitation—they will reschedule you for another day. (Reputable companies, including our recommendations below, do not charge you if they cancel your trip due to weather and you can't reschedule. Always check cancellation policies at time of booking.) So it's advisable if you're only in town for a few days to book your ride early in your stay. Chances are, you won't need to change, but if you do, you're covered. In any case, it's hard to think of a more spectacular and exhilarating introduction to Albuquerque than by floating overhead in its huge turquoise skies.

Rainbow Ryders: Locally owned and operated by the same owner for over 26 years, Rainbow Ryders is the official balloon-ride operator of the Albuquerque International Balloon Fiesta.

Balloon rides are in baskets carrying from 2 to 12 passengers. Fliers receive a commemorative flight certificate and balloon flight pin. Contact them at (505) 823-1111 or 800-725-2477; www.rainbowryders.com.

World Balloon: Originally founded by Albuquerque native and ballooning Hall-of-Fame's champion flyer Sid Cutter, World Balloon has been in business for over 37 years. Balloon rides are in baskets carrying from two to eight passengers. Fliers receive a commemorative flight certificate, lapel pin, and baseball cap. Contact them at (505) 250-2300 or (800) 351-9588; www.worldballoon.com.

Bowling

LEISURE BOWL
7400 Lomas Boulevard NE
(505) 268-4371

You'll find good old-school bowling here in a fun atmosphere on 32 lanes with automatic scoring. This is not the place to find laser shows, but there's nightly karaoke in the lounge and a deli and pizzeria for when you get hungry. Open seven days.

LUCKY 66 BOWL
6132 4th Street NW
(505) 345-2506

The Lucky 66 Bowl has bowling, billiards, video games, and a pro shop, and on several evenings a week you'll hear (and perhaps join in with) karaoke and live bands in Dewar's Pub. The Ezra's Place restaurant, tucked around the side of the bowling alley, overlooks the action. Open seven days.

SKIDMORE'S HOLIDAY BOWL
7515 Lomas Boulevard NE
(505) 268-3308
www.holidaybowlabq.com

This lively venue has 30 lanes and automatic scoring, and later on some nights there is "After Dark Bowling," with glow-in-the-dark pins, atmospheric music, and special-effects lighting and fog. Facilities include the 300 Club Bar & Grill, a pro shop, and an arcade. Open seven days.

Cycling

The Paseo del Bosque trail is the city's pride for cyclists, with nearly 16 miles of paved trail uninterrupted by roads, extending north to south to the east of the Rio Grande, through the shade of the bosque. It was cited by *Sunset* magazine as one of its "Top 10 city bike rides." See our Close-up for more details. A downloadable trail map and access information is available at www.cabq.gov/openspace. The Tramway Recreational Trail runs parallel to Tramway Boulevard beneath the Sandia foothills, for a well-landscaped 10-mile ride with super views that also connects to the foothills trail system. This trail is also used by runners and walkers. Tougher trails for mountain biking can be found in the Sandia Foothills Open Space area (505-897-8831; www.cabq.gov/openspace/sandiafoothills.html). There are also summer mountain bike trails around Sandia Peak, from novice to challenging. You can either drive around to the Sandia Peak Ski Area or take the Sandia Peak Tramway. No bikes are allowed on the tram, but bike rental packages are available (www.sandiapeak.com; tram information: 505-856-7325; Sandia Peak Ski Area: 505-242-9052.)

Fishing

ISLETA RESORT LAKES AND RECREATION AREA
4051 State Road 47 SE
(505) 244-8102
isleta-casino.com

This area is operated by Isleta Pueblo and is right by the Isleta Eagle Golf Course and just opposite the pueblo's casino. Two lakes are stocked with catfish in spring and summer and rainbow trout for the rest of the year. There is a fish-cleaning station, 44 shelters, picnic areas, and a volleyball court. A store sells tackle and bait, fishing accessories, fishing licenses and permits, and groceries and drinks. Restrooms can be found at both lakes. Daily limits are five fish for adults and three for children, and the recreation area is open from 6 a.m. to 8 p.m. in spring and summer, 7 a.m. to 5 p.m. in fall and winter. Rates vary for adults, seniors, and children.

Biking Resources

If you're a two-wheel wonder, here are some useful resources to help you get the most out of your biking time in Burque. New Mexico Cycling (www.nmcycling.org) has ride descriptions and maps, including a good number in Albuquerque, and a calendar of group rides. The New Mexico Touring Society (505-237-9700; www.nmts.org) is a club for recreational cyclists, with group rides, and it also has detailed descriptions of routes in Albuquerque. BikeABQ advocates for Duke City cyclists, whether for leisure or transportation (505-232-0120; www.bikeabq.org). The Bike Coop services bikes and sells cycling gear and accessories and new and used bikes. Find them at 3407 Central Avenue NE; (505) 265-5170; www.bikecoop.com. Two Wheel Drive also sells and services bikes, including recumbents, and has suggestions of popular bike rides on their Web site, or you can visit the store at 1706 Central Avenue SE; (505) 243-8443; www.twowheeldrive.com.

A map of Albuquerque's street-bike system and some of the many recreational trails can be downloaded from www.cabq.gov/bike, or call (505) 768-2526 to request a bike map. If you need to take public transportation, ABQ Ride buses and New Mexico Rail Runner Express trains all have bike racks.

RIO BRAVO FISHING AREA
(505) 897-8831
www.cabq.gov/openspace/lands.html

This area lies within the Rio Grande Valley State Park. There is a fully accessible fishing pier here, where you can fish for rainbow trout in the Rio Grande. There is also a quarter-mile trail loop beneath the cottonwoods and three picnic areas. Operating hours are 7 a.m. to 9 p.m. from April to October and 7 a.m. to 7 p.m. from November to March. Access the fishing area from Rio Bravo Boulevard, and turn north on Poco Loco Street, west of 2nd Street, just before the bridge over the river.

SANDIA LAKES RECREATION AREA
100 Highway 313
Sandia Pueblo
(505) 771-5190
www.sandiapueblo.nsn.us/lakes.html

Owned and operated by the Pueblo of Sandia, there are three lakes totaling 18 surface acres stocked with catfish in summer and rainbow trout through the rest of the year. Largemouth bass also reproduce naturally here. There are shade shelters here along the bosque with its mature cottonwoods and lots of wildlife and bird-watching including of wild geese and blue heron. Only shore fishing is permitted, and most fish are over 14 inches. Daily limits are five fish for adults and three fish for youths, and you don't need a state fishing license. Facilities include a bait-and-tackle shop, a playground and picnic areas, a softball field, and wheelchair-accessible trails. There's also a market selling drinks and snacks and restrooms. Fishing is year-round, from 6 a.m. to 8 p.m. April through September, and 7 a.m. to 5 p.m. in other months. Fees vary by age and whether you're fishing or just visiting. Sandia Lakes Recreation Area is on Highway 313, just north of the intersection of 2nd and 4th Streets. Or take exit 234 west from I-25 to Highway 313, then go north for a mile.

SHADY LAKES
11033 Highway 313 NW
(505) 898-2568
www.shadylakes.com

Fish for trout, bass, catfish, and bluegill in two trout ponds and five fishing lakes at the privately owned Shady Lakes in the bosque, which has been in business since 1962. It's also home to water lily gardens and is a wildlife refuge inhabited by beavers, raccoons, turtles, and birds, including owls and ducks. There is catch-and-release on bass and bluegill. Kids are very welcome, and one trout pond is an "easy catch" pond. Artists and picnickers come here, too, just to enjoy the cool shade and waterside scenery. You don't need a state fishing license. Rates vary by age and according to your use of the area. Open daily from March through October and weekends only in February; closed in winter. Exit I-25 at Tramway, go west for 1.5 miles, then right (north) on Highway 313 (Old Highway 85) for half a mile to the Shady Lakes sign on your left.

TINGLEY BEACH
1800 Tingley Drive SW
(505) 768-2000
www.cabq.gov/biopark

Tingley Beach is part of the Albuquerque Biological Park; there are two adult fishing ponds and a children's fishing pond for those 12 and under. The central pond and the children's pond are stocked with catfish in summer and rainbow trout in winter. Daily limits are four trout and two catfish, and you can use live and artificial bait in both ponds. The central pond is wheelchair accessible. The south pond is a catch-and-release stocked with rainbow trout all year, and no artificial or live bait is permitted, just flies and lures with single barbless hooks. Anglers 12 and up need a fishing license, which you can purchase for one day, five days, or annually. Licenses are for sale at the Tingley Beach Outfitters (505-248-8522), but their opening hours are limited, so check in advance so as not to turn up with your rod and be disappointed. You can also buy tackle and bait and other items here, and the Tingley Beach Café serves lunches and snacks. There are restrooms and picnic tables. Tingley Beach is free to visit; it also has a model boating pond and pedal boats to rent in the summer. It's open daily from sunrise to sunset.

Hiking

We've outlined some of the easier trails in our Parks section, but hikers seeking more of a challenge can find plenty of options both on the Westside and in the Sandia Mountains and Cibola Forest to the east of the city. At Petroglyph National Monument both Rinconada Canyon and Piedras Marcadas Canyon have unpaved trails of approximately 2.5 miles round trip, while the Volcanoes area has trails from 0.8 to 2 miles round trip. Although relatively short, these trails are of varying degrees of difficulty, in undeveloped areas with limited or no facilities and no water available, so stop in the Las Imágenes Visitor Center for trail guides and orientation (Unser Boulevard NW at Western Trail; 505-899-0205; www.nps.gov/petr). The Sandia Foothills Open Space area, which covers around 2,650 acres of steep, sloped hills, from 5,720 feet elevation to nearly 7,000 feet above sea level, includes various trails, including the challenging 11-mile Embudito Trail (505-897-8831; www.cabq.gov/openspace/sandiafoothills.html). There are also summer trails on Sandia Peak, accessible via the Sandia Peak Tramway (505-856-7325; www.sandiapeak.com). Don't forget the Paseo del Bosque Trail along the banks of the Rio Grande (see Close-up). Paseo del Bosque is not difficult to tackle, but at its full length it leads you through nearly 16 miles of terrific scenery, without leaving the city.

Horse Riding

THE STABLES AT TAMAYA
Hyatt Regency Tamaya Resort & Spa
1300 Tuyuna Trail
Santa Ana Pueblo
(505) 771-6037
www.tamaya.hyatt.com

Even if you're not staying at the resort, you can enjoy a trail ride from the stables in the Santa Ana Pueblo backcountry. Guides lead you through the pristine and peaceful cottonwood bosque beside the Rio Grande, with terrific views of the Sandia Mountains. Trips take about two hours, and times change seasonally. Customized rides

For Mountain Men (and Mamas)

With the Sandia, Manzano, and Jemez Mountains right outside Albuquerque's back door or a short drive away, peak experiences are not too hard to find with the guidance of these local experts. Suntoucher Mountain Guides offers mountaineering trips in the Sandia Mountain Wilderness and other ranges in New Mexico, plus experienced guide services and rock-climbing lessons. Routes vary from moderate to advanced. Contact Suntoucher at 751 Tramway Lane NE; (505) 400-5590; www.suntoucher.com. The guides at Stone Age Climbing Gym lead half-day or day-long climbs around Albuquerque, suited to different levels, and they also offer skills instruction. Find them at 4201 Yale Avenue NE, Suite I; (505) 341-2016; www.climbstoneage.com. The Albuquerque-based New Mexico Mountain Club (www.swcp.com/~nmmc) has regular activities, include hiking, technical rock climbing, backpacking, camping, snowshoeing, skiing, and cycling for all levels from easy to strenuous. The club has nearly 1,000 members and around 500 outings a year for members and guests. Active Knowledge (505-604-2177; www.activeknow.com) leads adventure trips and camps for adults and youth, from half a day to multiday, including rock climbing, rappelling, skiing, biking, geocaching, hiking, and white-water rafting. Gear and transportation are provided in all-inclusive adventures, and expert guides tailor the adventure to the fitness levels and expertise of the traveler.

are also available. Children must be at least 7 years old and 4 feet tall to join the ride. The resort is about 26 miles north of Albuquerque International Sunport. Take exit 242 from I-25, west onto Highway 550, to the west toward Bernalillo. Proceed 2.4 miles to the intersection of Tamaya Boulevard and Highway 550, just past the Santa Ana Star Casino. Turn right at Tamaya Boulevard, and proceed 1.2 miles to the three-way stop (Tuyuna Trail). Turn right, and proceed 1.3 miles to the resort. Proceed to the front-entrance courtyard. Approximate driving time: 30 minutes.

i **The friendly Albuquerque Road Runners hit the trails for regular weekly runs, jogs, and walks, suitable for all levels. Visitors are welcome: www.aroadrun.org. New Mexico Wilderness Alliance organizes hikes into the Sandia Wilderness and other areas. Upcoming hiking events are listed on their Web site: www.nmwild.org.**

Ice Skating

OUTPOST ICE ARENAS
9530 Tramway Boulevard NE
(505) 856-7595
www.outposticearena.com

There are daily public sessions in this expanded facility. Try to go for a "CooLLoop" session, when Outpost links twin NHL-size rinks with two smaller rinks, providing a skating loop of one-fifth of a mile. You can rent skates here, and take private lessons and group classes. Outpost Ice Arenas hosts a hockey program with clinics, classes, and league games. New Mexico Ice Hockey Foundation (505-797-PUCK; www.nmice.org) also holds programs and tournaments here. Open seven days.

Karting

ALBUQUERQUE INDOOR KARTING
5110 Copper Avenue NE
(505) 265-7223
www.abqkarting.com

Stay Safe, Have Fun

Although many of Albuquerque's outdoor recreations are just a short hop from the city center, don't let that lull you into a false sense of security. We're lucky to have the wilderness as our backyard to play in, but it's still a wilderness, and the deserts and mountains can be ruthless to those who are ill-prepared. A few precautions help keep you safe and let you make the most of your visit. Check the official info at each destination for specific advice, but at the very least:

Always take drinking water. In this high-desert climate, you need to guzzle more than you'd think to avoid dehydration. Knocking back the H_2O also helps prevent altitude sickness. It's easy not to notice how hot you're getting because in the low humidity here, any sweat just evaporates—so the upside is that you don't get clammy! The downside is that your body can overheat, especially if you are partaking in strenuous activity. Take plenty of water, and keep drinking it, and if you go for a drive away from civilization, make sure you have spare water bottles in the car.

Always wear a high-SPF sunscreen, good sunglasses to protect your eyes, and a sunhat. At high elevation the sun's UV rays are stronger—even on the rare cloudy days.

Don't push your body. The air is thinner at altitude, and it can take a few days to adjust, especially if you've arrived from sea level. You may notice you get a little more breathless on a walk than at home. That's normal; just take it easy, keep drinking the water, and pace yourself. If you feel you may be coming down with altitude sickness (symptoms include headaches, dizziness, fatigue, weakness, shortness of breath, loss of appetite, nausea, disturbed sleep, irritability, and a general feeling of malaise), consult a medical professional immediately.

Race to win or just have fun at this remodeled facility with the latest timed racing equipment that provides drivers with a printed record of lap times, finishing position, and ranking among previous drivers. There are two kinds of karts available: Fun kid karts are for drivers 7 or over, minimum 51 inches tall; the speedy GT3 Karts are for drivers 14 and over, minimum 55 inches tall. Spectators watch for free. There are also arcade games and pool, pinball, and gaming equipment. Open seven days.

Skiing

Duke City's home ski resort of Sandia Peak is terrific for beginner- and intermediate-level skiers and snowboarders, with long, wide mountain runs in a friendly and easily accessible environment. Skiers looking for further challenges might head north to Santa Fe (www.skisantafe.com) or Taos Ski Valley (www.skitaos.org), where there are more expert runs and where the higher elevations also tend to bring more snow.

SANDIA PEAK SKI AREA
Crest Scenic Byway 536
(505) 242-9052
www.sandiapeak.com

On the east side of the Sandia Mountain range, in the Cibola National Forest, the Sandia Peak Ski Area is great for family skiing and snowboarding, with 30 runs over 200 skiable acres. Ten

Wear suitable shoes and clothing. That means sturdy closed shoes for hikes (to protect against critters or even the odd cactus spine), and take layers, as the weather can change quickly. Once the sun goes down, the temperature drops substantially, or a sudden rain shower may cool the air.

Look out for snakes and other wildlife. Much of the beauty of the wilderness lies in the range of wildlife it contains, and although creatures rarely attack unless provoked, once we get out of the city, this is their territory, and staying aware of what's around us helps avoid any unfortunate encounters.

Always hike in pairs or stay in pairs or groups for backcountry expeditions, and let others know where you are going.

Even in city parks, observe the same security precautions that you would at home. It is generally unwise to wander around after dark in unpopulated areas.

Be aware of approaching storms and lightning, so you have time to take shelter if needed. In winter check the weather forecast before setting off for day trips—although Albuquerque itself doesn't tend to have severe snow, once you're out in more rural areas or take a trip into higher elevations, snow can come in quite fast and poses a threat to unprepared travelers. It's a good idea to have emergency supplies in the car, such as extra layers of clothing, blankets, a flashlight, water, and snacks. Heed any snowstorm advisories, as these are not picturesque sprinklings but can be sudden and severe. It's much better to stay put, stay safe, keep off the roads, and watch the wild and wonderful snow fall from indoors.

percent are expert runs, including the fiendish Diablo, and 55 percent are intermediate. Average annual snowfall here is 125 inches, and there is snowmaking on 15 percent of the trails. The base elevation is 8,678 feet, with the peak being 10,378 feet. The Scrapyard terrain park has small and medium jumps, rails, and boxes. Sandia Peak also provides access to a network of cross-country ski trails. Facilities include the Double Eagle Day Lodge and Cafe at the base of the ski area, the Wintermill Sports Shop, and a ski and snowboard rental shop. Half- and full-day lessons are available for skiers and snowboarders, and the Cubby Corner ski school is for 4- to 6-year-olds. On Sandia Peak the High Finance Restaurant serves lunch and dinner and has a full bar. You have two choices to access the ski area: Either drive around to the east side of the mountain (30 to 45 minutes) or hop on the Sandia Peak Tramway, which takes you to Sandia Peak in 15 minutes. If you take the tram, you must have your own equipment (or rent it in town), as there is no ski rental facility at the tram terminal.

To drive to Sandia Peak, take I-40 east to Cedar Crest, exit 175, then go north on Highway 14 to the Crest Scenic Byway 536 to your left; then it's 6 miles to the ski area. To reach the Sandia Peak Tramway, take exit 167 from I-40, and follow Tramway Boulevard north 9 miles. From I-25 take exit 234 to Tramway Road and continue east to the Sandia Peak Tramway.

Ski New Mexico provides snow reports, information on all the state's ski areas, and current ski deals at (505) 858-2422 or www.skinewmexico.com.

Swimming Pools

There are 12 municipal pools in the city. Five indoor pools are open year-round, while the 7 outdoor pools are open in summer only. Fees are very reasonable, maxing out at $3 for adults at the West Mesa Aquatic Center or $2.25 at other pools, and there are discounts for teens, kids, and seniors. Special deals on Friday night let you swim for pennies, and under-18s are free during Sunday Recreational Swim Hours. We've highlighted two of the biggest pools below, but you can find the pool nearest you on the map at www.cabq.gov/aquatics.

SUNPORT POOL
2033 Columbia Drive SE
(505) 848-1398
www.cabq.gov/aquatics

Albuquerque's second-largest municipal pool after the West Mesa Aquatic Center, this outdoor 40-meter by 22-yard pool bordered by trees is deliciously inviting on hot summer days, and youngsters will enjoy the wading pool. There are dedicated times for lap swims for adults. The pool is open seven days but only during summer months.

WEST MESA AQUATIC CENTER
6705 Fortuna Road NW
(505) 836-8718
www.cabq.gov/aquatics

Olympic-size swimming at this cool and modern aquatic center includes an indoor 50-meter pool with lap swimming, exercise classes, and diving boards of 1 meter and 3 meters in height. Indoor and outdoor recreational pools with great water slides keep the kids happy. The indoor recreational pool has a beachlike design that is fully accessible. Open seven days, although hours vary by season and day.

Tennis

JERRY CLINE TENNIS COMPLEX
7205 Constitution Avenue NE
(505) 256-2080
www.cabq.gov/recreation

This is the largest public tennis complex in town and the host for many USTA and regional tournaments. There are 18 courts, and 13 of these are lighted. Courts feature a Laykold surface and nylon nets, and ball machines are available to rent by the hour. Rates are very reasonable at $2 per person, with discounts for seniors and juniors. Make reservations for the courts up to two days in advance, although reservations for both Saturday and Sunday are taken on Thursday. You can book a court by phone or in person. Tennis lessons are available here, and there's an adult drop-in league throughout the year and an adult challenge ladder. Courts are available every day, from sunrise to sunset or from sunrise to 10 p.m. for lighted courts.

SIERRA VISTA WEST TENNIS COMPLEX
5001 Montaño NW
(505) 897-8815
www.cabq.gov/recreation

You'll find 10 courts at this public tennis facility, plus a swimming pool for an after-game dip. Reservations aren't required, but you can make a reservation two days in advance to be sure of nabbing a court. Rates here are also a reasonable $2 per person, with discounts for seniors and juniors, and ball machines can be rented by the hour. Tennis lessons are available. Courts are open seven days a week, from 8 a.m. till dark during the week and from 8 a.m. till 5 p.m.on weekends.

It is dangerous to swim in Albuquerque's Rio Grande, and government agencies strongly advise against it. There are strong undertows and other hazards that have resulted in loss of life. So no matter how tempting or calm it looks, it is not safe. Please go to a pool instead, where you can enjoy yourself safely.

SPECTATOR SPORTS

The name of the game in Albuquerque is college sports, with the UNM Lobos football and basketball teams at the top of the list, followed by baseball. However, Albuquerque also has professional NBA basketball in the Albuquerque Thunderbirds and pro baseball in the Albuquerque Isotopes. Ticket prices for these professional teams start at under 10 bucks and are exceptionally good value for the quality of play and the venues. Efforts to start an Albuquerque pro football team have not yet borne fruit, partly because of the lack of a suitable downtown arena, although an Albuquerque Arena Football franchise is rumored to be in the works, and conversations among investors continue.

Rodeo, marathons, and motor sports all add to the mix, and top women tennis players come to town every year to compete in the United States Tennis Association Pro Circuit ColemanVision Championships.

Much of the team game action centers around the University of New Mexico South Campus trio of Isotopes Park (baseball), University Stadium (football) and University Arena/The Pit (basketball). These are all near the intersection of Avenida Cesar Chavez SE and University Boulevard SE. From I-25 exit at Avenida Cesar Chavez and head east. The Pit will be on the right as you come to University Boulevard. Isotopes Park is on the left, northeast corner of University Boulevard. University Stadium will be to your right, after you cross University Boulevard.

AUTO RACING

SANDIA MOTOR SPEEDWAY

Sandia Motorsports Park
100 Speedway Park Boulevard
(505) 352-8888
www.sandiamotorsports.com

A multiuse auto racing and training facility located 14 miles west of Downtown Albuquerque, the Sandia Motorsports Park hosts weekly Saturday night racing events and other national and local events year-round. The 86-acre park includes two paved ovals of a half mile and a quarter mile and a 1.7-mile road course. Sandia Motorsports Park hosts the Rio Grande Region of the Sports Car Club of America (SCCA), the South West Motor Sports vintage racers, the Porsche Club, the Corvette Club, and Sandia Motorcycle Racing Inc. Saturday night oval racing includes late models, supertrucks, street stocks, hobby stocks, and VW Beetle "slug bugs." Over 40 road-course events a year feature all vehicle makes and models, as well as motorcycles. There is a motocross track, a paved quarter midget track, and a paved remote-control track. The $4 million Sandia Motorsports Park opened in 2000 and has TV-quality Musco lighting, family-friendly spectator facilities, and a playground for children. For Saturday night racing, adult entry is $10. Military, police, firefighters, teenagers to age 16, and seniors over 60 are admitted for half price; kids 12 and under watch the wheels for free.

BALLOONING

ALBUQUERQUE INTERNATIONAL BALLOON FIESTA

Balloon Fiesta Park, north of Alameda Boulevard, 1 mile west of I-25
(505) 821-1000, (888) 422-7277
www.balloonfiesta.com

The big ballooning event for spectators is the Albuquerque International Balloon Fiesta, for nine days each October, starting on the first Saturday of the month. If you have never considered the serene art of ballooning to be a competitive sport, try watching the Key Grab race, where pilots try to beat hundreds of other hot-air balloons flying from the start point a mile away, back to Balloon Fiesta Park to grab their prize by hand from the top of a tall pole. Aerial poker and Black Jack are just two of the fiesta competitions to test the pilots' precision flying skills, giving a whole other meaning to the phrase "aces high." The America's Challenge Gas Balloon Race is the equivalent of the marathon for the hardy pilots competing to fly the farthest distance from Balloon Fiesta Park. Be warned that you won't see the finish of this race; the winners typically fly for three nights or more, covering 1,000 miles before they land. See the listing and the Close-up in the Annual Festivals and Events chapter for full details on the balloon fiesta.

BASEBALL

ALBUQUERQUE ISOTOPES
Isotopes Park
1601 Avenida Cesar Chavez SE
(505) 924-BALL
www.albuquerquebaseball.com

A Triple-A affiliate team of the Los Angeles Dodgers, the Isotopes, affectionately called the 'Topes, play professional baseball from April through September. The team's home is Isotopes Park, a multimillion-dollar stadium with a capacity of 13,279, shared with the nationally ranked UNM Lobos baseball team. Isotopes Park is a stunning facility, with excellent amenities, opened in 2003 and built on the site of the historic Albuquerque Sports Stadium, which stood here from 1972 until 2002. In their opening 2003 season, the Isotopes sold more than half a million tickets and won the Central Division Title. They've enjoyed ongoing success, consistently ranking among the Pacific Coast League's leaders in attendance, and in 2007 received the Bob Freitas Award from Baseball America as the best overall organization in Triple-A Baseball. Isotopes Park is nicknamed the Lab—a nod to the team's scientific name. The Isotopes name is said to derive from an episode of *The Simpsons,* in which Homer manages to stop his favorite "Springfield Isotopes" baseball team from moving to Albuquerque. The name has other resonances with New Mexico, as the state is the birthplace of the first atomic bomb and the Albuquerque area is home to military and scientific laboratories for nuclear technology. An online survey of the community voted the name into place. The Isotopes' logo is an electron in orbit around the letter A. The team mascot is Orbit, a big fluffy electron. Isotopes Park is a very family-friendly venue. The Creamland Berm area beyond the right-field fence is a space with grass and ledges where families can relax and spread out on blankets. Behind the berm the Fun Zone for children has games and carnival rides, including a tower ride and a new carousel.

UNM LOBOS BASEBALL
Play at Isotopes Park
1601 Avenida Cesar Chavez SE
(505) 925-LOBO, (800) 955-HOWL
www.golobos.com

The University of New Mexico boasts a nationally ranked Lobos baseball team, from which an unprecedented six graduating players were drafted in 2009 into the Major Leagues. Sharing Isotopes Park with the pro 'Topes, the UNM Lobos help make Albuquerque a great city for baseball. The Lobos baseball season lasts from February to May, meaning that between the two teams there are only four months in which Duke City baseball junkies have to suffer withdrawals. The first Lobos baseball team took to the field in 1899.

BASKETBALL

ALBUQUERQUE THUNDERBIRDS
Tingley Coliseum
EXPO New Mexico,
Home of the New Mexico State Fair
300 San Pedro NE
(505) 265-DUNK / 3865
www.abqtbirds.com

The Albuquerque Thunderbirds D-League (NBA Development League) is an affiliate of the Miami

The Pit

The UNM Lobos Basketball's home venue is "The Pit," formally known as University Arena and noted for its cavernous interior, featuring tricky lighting for uninitiated competitors and also for its enormous and vigorous fan turnouts. Attendance is generally over 90 percent per season based on a capacity of over 18,000. The Pit is notorious for its thunderous outpourings of home-team support, guaranteed to intimidate, or at least distract, competing teams, who often develop supplementary hand signals in advance to be sure they can communicate on the court. Spectators might consider carrying their own earplugs, as noise levels at major games—the combined result of foot stomping, hand clapping, and general vocal vehemence—have been measured up to 125 decibels, right at the threshold of pain. The Pit's combined features give Lobos such a recognized advantage in home games that competitors have at times refused offers of Lobo games to avoid playing there.

The venue earned its nickname as a result of its unusual construction. Built in 1966 in an enormous hole dug out of Albuquerque's southeast mesa, 37 feet below ground level, it was apparently designed this way for reasons of economy. Fan enthusiasm necessitated an expansion in 1975, and a cantilevered upper deck was added with 2,300 seats, at a cost of $2.2 million, nearly twice the cost of the original building. This brings current capacity to 18,018; audience response remains avid enough that this figure includes reserved standing-room-only spaces. A current $60 million renovation project, expected to be completed for the 2010 season, will provide upgraded team and audience facilities, including views of the city and the Sandia Mountains from the upper reaches of its formerly subterranean interior. The home court itself will remain untouched. Renovations have been scheduled and designed so they don't disrupt the Lobos' season or the building's infamous aura of competitor intimidation. Games will continue, although portions of the arena may be temporarily closed to audience members. The Pit is host to other events, such as the annual Native American Gathering of Nations Powwow and the Ty Murray Invitational contest for Professional Bull Riders, Inc.

Heat and the Dallas Mavericks in 2009. The T-Birds play at the Tingley Coliseum from November to April, and this is the place to see future NBA stars. In 2006, their first year in Albuquerque, the team won the D-League Championship game over the Fort Worth Flyers. In the 2008–09 season, the Thunderbirds had the leading scorer in the league, Will Conroy, and the New York Knicks signed Thunderbirds player Mouhamed Sene. You could also see Dallas and Miami players here, sent from the affiliates. In the intimate space of Tingley Coliseum, spectators are close to the action, and the players make a good job of mingling with the crowd. Ticket prices start at around $5, which is a pretty good deal for professional NBA basketball. As Head Coach John Coffino says, "You can't get a movie ticket for that."

UNM LOBOS BASKETBALL
University Arena—The Pit
1111 University SE
(505) 925-LOBO, (800) 955-HOWL
www.golobos.com

Lobos basketball season runs from November to March, and both men's and women's basketball inspire fervent enthusiasm among fans. The Lady Lobos rank in the top 25 in the nation in home attendance, while the men's team ranks in the top 20. Usually, when men's basketball is playing away, women's basketball is at home and vice versa. One of the major claims to fame of Lobos basketball is their home venue, "'The Pit" (University Arena). This is one of the most instantly recognizable arenas in college basketball, infamous for striking fear in the hearts of visiting Lobos competitors (see The Pit Close-up).

FOOTBALL

UNM LOBOS
University Stadium
Avenida Cesar Chavez and University Boulevard
(505) 925-LOBO, (800) 955-HOWL
www.golobos.com

Dating from 1892, when they were simply known as "the University Boys," the UNM Lobos football team continues to fill University Stadium in record numbers. Nine of their top 10 crowds have occurred in the last decade, and season-ticket sales have more than tripled in recent years. The Lobos won the New Mexico Bowl in 2007, defeating the Nevada Wolfpack, in a streak of five bowl games played in seven seasons. Their highly anticipated 2009 season was the first under new head coach Mike Locksley. University Stadium opened its gates in 1960 and was expanded prior to the start of the 2001 season. Now standing at a capacity of more than 38,600, the stadium in recent years generally averages attendance of over 30,000 per game. It features its own state-of-the-art videoboard and scoreboard, LoboVision. The football season runs from September to November, although post-season bowl events occur through the first week of January. Lobo fans ensure that home games become all-day celebrations, with tailgating parties and festivities extending nearly till kickoff.

HORSE RACING

THE DOWNS AT ALBUQUERQUE RACETRACK & CASINO
201 California Street NE
(505) 266-5555
www.abqdowns.com

You can watch and wager on simulcast horse racing every day on over 500 TV monitors. There is live racing at the track from August to October. Stakes include the Albuquerque Derby, New Mexico Breeders' Quarter Horse Championship, and the New Mexico State Fair Thoroughbred Breeders' Derby. The casino has 330 slot machines and video poker gaming. The Downs Racetrack & Casino is on the grounds of EXPO New Mexico, Home of the New Mexico State Fair. For parking, enter at Gate 1 from Central Avenue, between Louisiana and San Pedro. In 2008 the New Mexico Racing Commission gave the Downs permission to move to Moriarty, 40 miles east of Albuquerque on I-40. At the time of writing, the move is on indefinite hold, but call before setting off.

MARATHONS

DUKE CITY MARATHON
(505) 880-1414
www.dukecitymarathon.com

With as many as 4,000 registrants and 10,000 in attendance, the Duke City Marathon is a top event for regional runners. It's been established for more than a quarter of a century. Events include the marathon, half marathon and 5k runs, plus half marathon and 5k walks, and a Miracle Mile event to benefit the New Mexico Cancer Center Foundation. The course is described as flat and fast. The marathon is held on a Sunday in October, with opening ceremonies at 6:30 a.m. The course starts and ends at the Downtown Civic Plaza and covers a good portion of the Paseo del Bosque trail. There is a postrace festival once the runners have departed at Civic Plaza, and events awards are announced there, too.

NEW MEXICO MARATHON
(505) 489-9484
www.thatsawrapevents.com

The New Mexico Marathon has been an institution for over a decade and is another premier regional runners' event. It is held on a Sunday in late August or early September, but the marathon starts at 5:30 a.m. to avoid the day's heat. Competitors at least get to run downhill for much of the

i **Buy an Olympic Sports Season Pass for admission to all Lobos baseball games for $50 (discounts for seniors and youths), and the pass takes you into all Lobos volleyball, men's soccer, women's soccer, and softball games, too; www.golobos.com/tickets/basebl.html.**

UNM Lobos

The Lobos name dates back to 1920, when George S. Bryan, a sophomore, editor of the *U.N.M. Weekly*, and student manager of the football team, suggested Lobo as a mascot name. Lobo means "wolf" in Spanish, and the creature's qualities of cunning, prowess, and leadership grabbed everyone's imagination. Shortly after adopting the name, the Lobos football team did in fact adopt a captured wolf cub. The cheerleaders were responsible for the animal, and it turned up harnessed at every game as their on-field mascot. Sadly, the wolf was put down after it bit a child in the audience who unwisely attempted to play with it. The Lobos' name lived on, however, though sometimes you'll hear "Slobos" instead when their performance is off. Around the UNM campus are some wonderful wolf sculptures.

Lobos team colors are cherry and silver. They are said to have replaced the black and gold combo of the 1890s after a faculty member suggested picking something a little more evocative of New Mexico. After some deliberations, the silver was chosen to symbolize the Rio Grande, as it appeared like a silver ribbon down in the valley to students picnicking high in the Sandias. The cherry tone represents sunset over the Sandias. Apart from a brief 1970s deviation adding turquoise into the school colors for the athletic teams, the school colors have been cherry and silver ever since.

As lobo means wolf, fans of Lobos teams are sometimes referred to as "howl raisers." With 21 sports offered through UNM Athletics, 10 for men and 11 for women, the Lobos are a major force in keeping the Albuquerque sports scene in the front of the pack. Over 450 UNM student athletes compete at the NCAA Division 1 level for national recognition. Sports include not only the big three most popular team sports—football, basketball (men's and women's), and baseball—but also women's and men's soccer. Nationally ranked and a winner of six conference titles, the men's soccer team has participed in six NCAA championships.

UNM Athletics also features indoor and outdoor track, cross-country, golf, skiing, swimming, volleyball, and many others. UNM is well known for its top-of-the-line athletic facilities and has hosted NCAA championships in men's basketball, as well as golf, women's tennis and volleyball, and men's gymnastics. Venues include University Stadium, Isotopes Park, and the Pit basketball arena, famous for its outlandish displays of Lobos loyalty. Local support for Lobos teams is fierce and faithful—you can always tell when it's a Lobos night in Albuquerque. The mood is up, people are on the streets, and the electricity is palpable.

The UNM Lobos ticket office is open weekdays 8:30 a.m. to 5:00 p.m. at 1155 University SE, first floor, on the northwest corner of University and Cesar Chavez. Or call (505) 925-LOBO or (800) 955-HOWL.

route, as it starts beneath the Sandia Mountains at 5,800 feet elevation, and finishes at Tigeux Park in Old Town at 4,800 feet. If the runners have any breath left to appreciate it, the marathon's scenic course from the Sandias leads down the length of Tramway and across the valley to the Rio Grande in a sweeping counterclockwise circle, with sunrise views over the mountains and balloons rising over the city. The final leg of the route is down Rio Grande Boulevard into Old Town. The spectators can certainly enjoy the vistas, and it's a spectator-friendly course, with only 4 miles (between mile 18 and 22) not accessible via car. There is also a half marathon and 5k run, which start a little later. The New Mexico Half Marathon route is the second part of the full marathon course, and this is a very fast race. The New Mexico 5k follows the final 3.1 miles of the same route. The race festival and awards ceremonies at the finish have included live music and mariachis, Spanish and Native

American dancers, and children's activities. On the Saturday before, there has previously been a New Mexico Marathon Health and Fitness Expo in Old Town's Hotel Albuquerque.

The same organizers host the annual World's Toughest 10k in Albuquerque in May, which starts at around 5,000 feet elevation and climbs to 6,500 feet at the base of the Sandia Tramway, with a challenging 12 percent grade in the last mile.

RODEO

PRCA RODEO
Tingley Coliseum
Expo New Mexico,
Home of the New Mexico State Fair
300 San Pedro NE
(505) 222-9700
www.exponm.com

The Professional Rodeo Cowboys Association shows the audience how the West was won in the eight-night rodeo at the New Mexico State Fair in September. The show stars world champions and the best cowboys in America, for events like saddle bronc riding, with its roots in the tradition of Old West ranch hands who used to compete to see who rode untrained horses with the best style. Competitors give the horse an advantage by beginning their ride with their feet over the horse's shoulders. Tie-down roping also goes back to the days when sick calves were roped down for medical treatment and requires teamwork between cowboy and horse. Barrel racing is a dash against the clock to ride a tight cloverleaf pattern around three barrels without overturning them. Winners and losers can be decided by a hundredth of a second, so the race is fierce and the tension high as barrels wobble, but will they fall? Other events might include steer wrestling, team roping, bull riding, and bareback bronc riding. The rodeos are followed by a concert.

TY MURRAY INVITATIONAL
At UNM University Arena / The Pit
1111 University SE
(877) 664-8661
www.pbrnow.com

Professional Bull Riders, Inc., comes to Albuquerque for three days of competition each spring for the Ty Murray Invitational. The 2009 event was at the end of March, and future dates should be similar. The Ty Murray Invitational pits tough men against tough animals in, appropriately enough, the Pit. The event has been held in Albuquerque since 1997 but moved from Tingley Coliseum to the University of New Mexico's Pit in 2009. The elite contest has four competition rounds, with the first three randomly matching the sport's top 40 bull riders against the toughest bulls. The leading 15 scorers move on to the finals on the third day to compete for the coveted title. The 2009 winner, Zack Brown, took home over $34,000 and was the only competitor to ride every one of his bulls over the three-day challenge. Tickets can be purchased from www.unmtickets.com or by calling (877) 664-8661.

TENNIS

COLEMANVISION TENNIS CHAMPIONSHIPS
Tanoan Country Club
10801 Academy Road NE
(888) COLEMAN
www.colemanvision.com/news/tennis.html

The annual $75,000 United States Tennis Association (USTA) Pro Circuit ColemanVision Championships for women has featured top-100 Grand Slam women's players since 1999. Traditionally scheduled for fall, three weeks after the U.S. Open, the tournament draws players from 30 countries. The USTA Pro Circuit event is held at the Tanoan Country Club, which has 14 courts. Tennis fans in Albuquerque appreciate the intimacy of the venue and the opportunity to see top-ranking players close to home. In 2008 29-year-old Julie Ditty made tennis history at the championships in Albuquerque. By winning both the singles and doubles events, she achieved her thirty-first and thirty-second USTA Pro Circuit titles. Ditty thus became the all-time record holder, inheriting that position from Paul Goldstein and Nana Smith, who each have 30 USTA Pro Circuit titles.

GOLF

Albuquerque's high-desert climate and sunny turquoise skies make golfing a year-round pleasure, and diverse course terrains here include desert, parkland, and mountain settings. Course designers take advantage of the natural beauty of New Mexico's rich landscapes, leading players through features (and obstacles!) that don't let you forget you're in the Land of Enchantment, whether you're navigating arroyos, forestry, mountain foothills, rugged rock mesas, rolling hills, the riverside cottonwood bosque, or crystal blue lakes. Spectacular big sky views of the Sandias and the Rio Grande valley are a given, as well as distractingly gorgeous sunsets. Those courses that wind their way across ancestral Native American Pueblo lands have a special touch of atmospheric magic. As icing on the cake, visitors are often surprised by the highly competitive greens fees compared to courses of equal quality in other parts of the country.

Albuquerque courses have garnered numerous accolades from golf and travel media, consistently appearing in "best of" national rankings and readers' choice selections. In *Golfweek*'s 2009 selection of Best Courses You Can Play in New Mexico, four of the top six public-access courses are in the Albuquerque area and are listed in this chapter: Paa-Ko Ridge, Twin Warriors, University of New Mexico Championship, and Sandia Golf Club. Among the many shiny virtual trophies on local courses' shelves, Paa-Ko Ridge crops up regularly in *Golfweek*'s Best Modern Courses selections, and Sandia Golf Club was listed in *Golfweek*'s 2009 Best Resort Courses. *Golf Digest* ranked Twin Warriors, Sandia Golf Club, and Santa Ana Golf Club in its 2007 Top 40 Casino Golf Courses. There are courses here suited to all skill levels and also plenty of choices for practice facilities.

The reliable and temperate weather is another ace in the hole for Albuquerque golfers. You can count on 310 days of sunshine a year, but even in high summer the elevation keeps temperatures pleasant, and low humidity also helps golfers stay comfortable. The higher the course elevation, the lower the temperature, and mornings are also substantially cooler. The long peak golf season is April to October, but play continues through all four seasons. Winter temperatures average a 50°F high, under dazzling blue skies.

Greens fees for the privately owned courses listed below, all of which are open to the public and require no membership, are very accessible. Fees for an 18-hole round start under $50 and max out at around $100, but rates fluctuate according to the time of year and day of the week. Fees sometimes include a golf cart or other benefits, so check what's included in your price comparisons to make sure you're not comparing apples with oranges! The City of Albuquerque's municipal courses are even more affordable, costing in the twenties per round. Discounts are available at many courses for seniors, juniors, afternoon or twilight rounds, and New Mexico residents. Most courses also offer annual passes. Naturally, greens fees are lower for a 9-hole game. If you're on a budget, then with some canny planning to pick your day and tee time, you can probably afford to take a swing at every one of the superb courses in the Albuquerque area. If you're flying through Duke City without your gear, golf clubs are available for rent at most venues. All the facilities listed here prohibit metal spiked shoes. Men's and women's dress codes vary, so check with the club, although in general cutoffs, tank tops, gym shorts, and any kind of tattered garments are not considered appropriate golf attire. Although most courses are open daily, year-round, there may be occasional closures due to bad weather or for tournaments.

PUBLIC-ACCESS COURSES

ISLETA EAGLE GOLF COURSE
4001 Highway 47 SE
(505) 848-1900, (866) ISLETA-2
www.isletaeagle.com

This 27-hole course is part of the Isleta Pueblo's Casino & Resort due to be renamed Hard Rock Hotel & Casino Albuquerque in Spring 2010, but is open to nonresidents. It comprises three 9-hole loops named for their key geographical features: the Mesa 9, Lakes 9, and Arroyo 9. You can play 18 holes in any permutation, and course length from four tee sets ranges from 5,231 to 7,572 yards. The nicely contoured par-72 course opened in 1996 and was designed by Bill Phillips. It is set in modified parkland and features dense roughs surrounding the manicured fairways and multitiered greens. Elevation changes are less extreme here, and it's more rolling than rocky. Seven of the 9 holes in the Lakes complex are designed around water, and the Lakes signature hole, the fourth, is a par 3, 193 yards from the back tee, with a challenging island green. Isleta Eagle offers splendid sweeping vistas over the Rio Grande and Mount Taylor to the west. Facilities include a practice range, a golf shop, and a clubhouse restaurant serving casual fare. Greens fees include golf carts, and reservations are taken seven days in advance, year-round. Metal spikes aren't allowed here. Isleta Eagle Golf Course is approximately 5 miles south of Albuquerque airport. Take I-25 south to exit 215; stay in the left lane onto Highway 47/ Broadway SE.

PAA-KO RIDGE GOLF CLUB
1 Clubhouse Drive
Sandia Park
(505) 281-6000, (866) 898-5987
www.paakoridge.com

Since opening in 2000, this highly acclaimed 27-hole course on the east side of the Sandia Mountains has received numerous laurels from golfing and travel press, both at the regional and the national level. It ranked third in the nation in *Golf World*'s Readers' Choice Awards for best public golf courses in October 2008. Paa-Ko Ridge was designed by Ken Dye, with five sets of tees playing from 5,702 to 7,562 yards. The course is par 72 for any 18-hole permutation of the three 9-hole tracts. The exciting mountain layout winding through ponderosa, piñon, and juniper trees requires strategic control to navigate landing areas and greens divided by challenging arroyos, native vegetation, and rock outcroppings and with dramatic changes in elevation. Elevations are from 6,500 to 7,000 feet, and it's worth noting on hot summer days that this high mountain area is 10 to 12°F cooler than in the city of Albuquerque. There are magnificent top-of-the-world views from all areas of the course. Hole names like Postage Stamp, Ambush, Narrow Passage, Gambler, and Dye-abolical give you an idea of what you're matching up against! The long par-5 dogleg Turquoise Trail (hole 15) drops 100 feet from tee to green over 640 yards from the back tee, and the par-3 Dye-abolical (hole 4) features a 100-yard-deep green, the largest in New Mexico, with a 13-foot drop from the lowest to the highest level on the green, demanding excellent control in placement. There are putting greens, chipping areas, a practice bunker, and a multitiered driving range, plus a golf shop. Carts with GPS are available, as are pro lessons. You can't rent a pull cart here, but you can use your own. Only approved soft-spiked shoes are permitted on the course. The Grille at Paa-Ko Ridge offers casual dining and a full bar with indoor seating in rustic wood decor, but most golfers will be tempted by the peaceful covered patio overlooking the lake and greens. Daily greens fees include a cart and warm-up range balls, and there are also lower rates for 9 holes. Bookings can be made a month in advance, or for longer advance bookings there is a small fee of $10 per person. Open March through November. Paa-Ko Ridge Golf Club is about 28 miles from Albuquerque airport, on the Turquoise Trail. Take exit 175 from I-40 east, and continue north on Highway 14. About 3.5 miles past the Sandia Crest turnoff to the ski area, you'll see Paa-Ko Ridge clearly signed on the left.

SANDIA GOLF CLUB
At the Sandia Resort and Casino
30 Rainbow Road NE
(505) 798-3990
www.sandiagolf.com
Developed by Sandia Pueblo and part of the Sandia Resort and Casino but open to nonresidents, too, this 18-hole par-72 championship golf course was designed by Scott Miller. The course unfurls expansively under Sandia Peak on sloping terrain across the changing elevations and natural folds of the landscape. Yardage is from 5,113 to a mighty 7,772 yards on the back tees. Twelve holes play toward the peak for excellent views, and there are also panoramic vistas across the valley. The course offers generous fairways and forgiving greens, although there are plenty of strategic challenges in holes guarded by water features, bunkers, and arroyos. However, obstacles are sometimes deceptively intimidating, testing you to keep your cool to ensure a safe landing. Hole 5 is the longest on the course, a challenging 662 yards over rugged terrain. There is a double-tier driving range, a 10,000-square-foot practice putting green, and a chipping green with bunker. On opening in 2005 the course was quickly recognized as a best new development by Golf Inc. and *Golf Magazine* and has continued to rank highly in golfing media. Golf carts are available (and recommended, although walking is permitted), and fees include range balls and GPS. Nonmetal spiked shoes must be worn on the course, and the dress code includes collared shirts. Golf instruction is available. The 16,000-square-foot circular Pueblo-style clubhouse includes a pro golf shop, which *Golf World* ranked in its 100 Best Golf Shops in 2009. The family-friendly clubhouse restaurant is a great place for cocktails and dinner, with a 3,000-square-foot covered patio that is refreshing in more ways than one, as it looks north over the Sandias and the stunning fountains and waterfalls of the 18th hole. Reservations for resort guests are taken up to 180 days in advance; otherwise, seven days in advance. Reservations are taken outside the above timings for a small ($10) nonrefundable booking fee. Longer advance bookings are available for group events of 17 players or more—contact the club. Open year-round. Take I-25 to the Tramway exit 234, and head east to the clearly signed resort.

i **Your golf ball flies farther at Albuquerque's average elevation of 5,500 feet, as the thin air at high altitude offers less resistance. Dana Lehner, the golfing expert for Albuquerque's Convention and Visitors Bureau, reckons you can anticipate an additional 25 yards on a drive. So enjoy the extra muscle in your game, not forgetting to hit maybe one less club than usual on long approaches to the green.**

SANTA ANA GOLF CLUB
288 Prairie Star Road
Santa Ana Pueblo
(505) 867-9464
www.santaanagolf.com
Santa Ana is said to have been the first true links-style golf course in New Mexico. It boasts eight sparkling lakes and 27 holes—the Tamaya 9, Cheena 9, and Star 9. You can play all 27, but most players choose a configuration of any two 9s for an 18-hole round of par 72. The course was designed by Ken Killian and opened in 1991; multiple tee boxes give a yardage range of between 4,924 and 7,239. As the sister course to Twin Warriors Golf Club just a 5-minute drive away, it shares similar scenic beauty on the Santa Ana Pueblo, with views of the Sandia and Sangre de Cristo Mountains. The natural terrain and native vegetation bordering each hole keeps players on their toes, and the greens are challenging here. However, the gently rolling hills to each side of the fairway feed errant shots back on track. The number 8 hole on Cheena tests all your skills on a 633-yard par 5, bordering the bosque along the Rio Grande. Carts equipped with GPS and pull carts are available. Soft spikes only are allowed on this course. There is a putting green, pitching green, and practice range, plus a pro shop, and lessons are available. The course has been highly

ranked by golf publications, and over 40 USGA qualifying events have been held here, as well as the 2009 PGA Professional National Championship. The Prairie Star restaurant in a picturesque adobe mansion by the clubhouse offers fine dining and cocktails and is known for its award-winning wine selections, including more than 50 wines by the glass. The club's Wind Dancer Bar and Grill serves golfers with more casual fare. The course is open year-round and reservations are taken up to a week in advance. Santa Ana Golf Club is about 24 miles north of the Albuquerque airport. Take I-25 north to exit 242, then head west on Highway 550 about 2.5 miles to Tamaya Boulevard on your right. Almost immediately, the turnoff for Prairie Star Road and the Santa Ana Golf Club are clearly signed.

TWIN WARRIORS GOLF CLUB
At the Hyatt Regency Tamaya Resort and Spa
1301 Tuyuna Trail
Santa Ana Pueblo
(505) 771-6155
www.twinwarriorsgolf.com

Designed by Gary Panks and opened in 2001, this 18-hole championship golf course is part of the Hyatt Regency Tamaya Resort and Spa but is also open to nonresidents. The 72-par course offers five tee positions, with yardage ranging from 5,843 to 7,736 yards. Land features in this spectacular high-desert environment with superb views of the Sandias include expansive grassy knolls, juniper- and piñon-studded ridges, arroyos, and the sacred butte called Tuyuna, or Snakehead. Holes 15 and 16 run alongside the butte.

The signature hole 4 is a par 3, with the green protected by a large lake and a series of ponds and waterfalls. This is the only water feature on the course, but it's an impressive one! Probably the most challenging hole is number 10, a par 4, where you're forced to hit over a large box canyon and then avoid a ruthlessly positioned deep bunker by the green.

The club is named for the twin warriors who guided the ancestral people of Santa Ana Pueblo, showing their path to the "Upper World" along the Rio Grande. As it is set on ancient Indian grounds, the course is routed around 20 cultural and archeological sites, including a cave dwelling and horse corral; the protected sites themselves are off-limits. The nationally acclaimed course, which has placed consistently in rankings by *Golf Digest* and *Golf Magazine*, hosted the 2003 and 2009 PGA Professional National Championship. Greens fees include a cart with GPS. You can walk the round (fees are discounted), but carts are encouraged, as the walk is quite demanding. Only soft spikes are permitted. There is a driving range, a large putting green, short game practice areas, and a private teaching area for lessons with the club professional. The Atush Bar & Grille with a shady porch serves a casual-fare menu, including popular breakfast burritos and hot dogs, and players can order ahead on their cart GPS, pick up their food, and keep playing. A beverage cart also runs round the course. Fine dining is just next door in the Corn Maiden restaurant at the Hyatt Regency Tamaya Resort and Spa, plus the Santa Ana Cafe and a lovely lounge bar and patio. There is also a large golf shop at Twin Warriors, including Native American art and craft works. Resort guests can book up to 150 days in advance, non-guests seven days in advance. Longer reservation periods are possible for groups of 16 golfers or more; contact the club. Twin Warriors is open year-round and is about 26 miles north of the Albuquerque airport. Take I-25 north to exit 242, then head west on Highway 550 about 2.5 miles to Tamaya Boulevard on your right. From here the turnoff to Tuyuna Trail and the Hyatt Regency Tamaya Resort and Spa are clearly sign-posted.

i **New Mexico Golf Destinations (www.newmexicogolfdestinations.com) provides information on New Mexico's golfing opportunities, including overviews and online video tours of Albuquerque golf courses and others in the region.**

UNM CHAMPIONSHIP GOLF COURSE
3601 University Boulevard SE
(505) 277-4546
www.unmgolf.com

The 18-hole University of New Mexico Championship course, also known as UNM South, is something of a granddaddy of local courses, designed by Robert (Red) Lawrence and established in 1967. It's a lush and hilly modified-parkland course with rolling fairways; there are five sets of tee positions offering from 5,381 to 7,248 yards. The par-72 course is full of surprises, with water hazards and traps in the form of sneaky bunkers, gullies, ridges, and inconvenient trees! Multitiered deep greens keep you alert once you get near the pin. Even the shorter par 3s challenge your accuracy, and the elevated green on the par-3 eighth hole demands a committed tee shot to get in position past the bunkers. Throughout the round there are great vistas over the Rio Grande valley and the towers of Downtown Albuquerque. The difficult but scenic par-4 signature hole 10 requires a drive to the top of a hill on a dogleg-right fairway. For the second shot to the hole, 200 yards away downhill, there are excellent views of the west mesa. The course has won its fair share of honors from golfing magazines and has long been a host for college tournaments, including the William H. Tucker Invitational and the women's Dick McGuire Intercollegiate, and for NCAA Golf Championships. Within the complex you'll find a large driving range, a putting green and two chipping greens, and a 3-hole beginners' course. There is a pro shop and instruction if required. The clubhouse includes a restaurant and bar. Carts are available and, while not necessary, are recommended on the hilly course. There are also pull-cart rentals. Soft spikes only are permitted at this course, and players must wear collared shirts. Open year-round. You can reserve a tee time up to 7 days in advance or 30 days with a credit card.

MUNICIPAL COURSES

Although Albuquerque's municipal courses designate their tees as men's or women's, golfing gals may play from any tees as long as play pace is maintained. Metal spiked shoes are prohibited on all city courses. At the time of writing, rates for 18 holes at the City of Albuquerque's golf courses are $22 during the week, $28.50 on weekends. There are discounts of 25 percent for seniors 55 and older and 50 percent for juniors 17 or under. There are also discounted greens fees for afternoon players, applicable from 4.5 hours before sundown. Rates vary for 9 holes, so check with the course. Carts cost extra, and golf clubs are available for rent at all facilities. Municipal courses are open dawn to dusk seven days a week.

i **Night drivers can enjoy evening practice at two municipal facilities with artificially lit driving ranges. The Puerto del Sol golf course 80-tee driving range is lit up late from Memorial Day to mid-September (1800 Girard SE; 505-265-5636). The Golf Training Center driving range (9401 Balloon Museum Drive NE; 505-857-8437) is open year-round, except for several weeks in October for the balloon fiesta, and in winter it closes earlier, at around 6 to 7 p.m. Summer hours are until 10 p.m. Information on both ranges can also be found at www.cabq.gov/golf.**

ARROYO DEL OSO
7001 Osuna Road NE
(505) 884-7505
www.cabq.gov/golf

Intermediate and advanced golfers enjoy the varied terrain and challenges of Arroyo del Oso's 27 holes, with expansive greens, gently rolling fairways with a hillier back nine, mature ponderosa pines, water hazards, hardpan, and sand traps. The 18-hole championship course designed by Arthur Jack Snyder opened in 1965. Oso means "bear," and this course is likely to bring out your inner bear, as well as every golf club in your bag! It plays 6,545 yards for men, or 6,936 yards from the longest tees, for par 72. The par-73 women's tees yardage is 6,015. There are two water hazards on the course. The signature hole is number 17, which is a long, uphill-haul par 4, stretching 405 yards from the back tee, with bunkers front, right, and left, and out of bounds on the right. Players are, however, rewarded with terrific views of the Sandias to the east. There are also a couple of long par 3s on the course, which push you over 190 yards from the back tees. Dam 9, an additional 9 holes added in 1987, is a 3,300-yard par-36 course, designed by Richard M Phelps. It zigzags across Bear Canyon Arroyo, with hilly fairways and rolling greens, and it also features two water hazards. Arroyo del Oso has a driving range, practice putting and chipping greens, a pro shop, cart rentals, and a café with indoor and covered outdoor seating. Golf lessons are available. The Dam 9 course doesn't take tee-time reservations. For the 18-hole course, options for tee-time bookings vary by day of the week and time of year. For weekdays bookings are accepted for play between noon and 3 p.m. only, between April and November. For all other weekday hours and for the rest of the year, it's a case of first come, first served. For weekends and holidays year-round, reservations for tee times may be made from 7 a.m. on Wednesday morning.

GOLF TRAINING CENTER
9401 Balloon Museum Drive NE
(505) 857-8437
www.cabq.gov/golf

Not a golf course but a practice facility next to the Anderson-Abruzzo Albuquerque International Balloon Museum, this center is (literally) a breath of fresh air under the Sandias for golfers seeking to polish their skills. It features an expansive driving range with night lighting and a five-hole pitch-and-putt, and you can also book lessons here. The center is open year-round but closes for several weeks in October for the Albuquerque International Balloon Fiesta. Hours vary, but as a guideline summer hours run to around 10 p.m., and in winter they put the buckets of balls away around 6 to 7 p.m.

LADERA
3401 Ladera Drive NW
(505) 836-4449
www.cabq.gov/golf

On the west side of the Rio Grande, with big-sky views back to the Sandia Mountains and to the nearby Volcanoes area, Ladera is the longest-yardage municipal course. The 18-hole championship golf course and the 9-hole executive course were both designed by Richard M. Phelps and opened in 1980 and 1981 respectively. There is plenty for players to get their teeth into on the main par-72 course, which stretches 7,060 yards for the championship tees, 6,618 for the regulation tees, and 5,966 yards for women's tees. You'll find four lakes here, plus broad fairways and roomy undulating greens. Hole 7 poses a gambling quandary, with its dogleg right turn, navigating trees to the right, and rough and bunkers to the left. To make your par 4, you can choose to take the straight, long course over the hole's 441 yards or try to carry the trees to make the hole shorter. The 9-hole executive course is moderate to advanced in challenge and is popular with beginners and seniors. Men's tees cover 2,053 yards; women's, 1,852 yards. The course mainly consists of par-3 holes, with a couple of par 4s and a single par 5. There is a spacious driving range and practice putting and chipping greens. Golf carts and pull carts are available to rent, and you can book a golf lesson here from the course pro. There is a pro golf shop and also a café. You can't book for the 9-hole executive course, but Ladera accepts tee-time reservations seven days in advance for the 18-hole course.

LOS ALTOS
9717 Copper NE
(505) 298-1897
www.cabq.gov/golf

Great for beginners and intermediate players, with plenty of challenges on the course, Los Altos features two lakes and mature trees on fairly flat ground. There is an 18-hole regulation course, plus a 9-hole executive par-3 course for time-

Golf on the Santa Fe Trail

Golf on the Santa Fe Trail features eight outstanding but diverse golf courses along the Rio Grande valley and was recommended as one of the country's top four trails by *Golf Magazine* in 2007. Six of the eight trail courses are in and around Albuquerque and are described in this chapter: Paa-Ko Ridge, Sandia Golf Club, Santa Ana Golf Club, Twin Warriors, Isleta Eagle, and UNM Championship. The other two are north of Santa Fe: Black Mesa Golf Club and Towa Golf Resort. All are open to the public.

Black Mesa is a highly praised Baxter Spann course on the Santa Clara Pueblo, playing 7,307 yards from the back tees through rugged landscapes and stunning sandstone formations. The "tough but fair" 18-hole course poses plenty of challenges for players of all levels and is about 90 minutes north of Albuquerque airport (115 State Road 399, La Mesilla; 505-747-8946; www.blackmesagolfclub.com). Towa Golf Resort on Pojoaque Pueblo, part of the Buffalo Thunder Resort complex, offers 27 scenic holes in a modified desert-links course with panoramic views of the Sangre de Cristo and Jemez Mountains. The course designers are Hale Irwin and William Phillips, and another 9 holes are due to be added. The current three 9s stretch between 3,380 and 3,640 yards each. Towa is about 75 minutes north of Albuquerque airport (47 Towa Golf Road, Santa Fe; 505-455-9000, 877-465-3489; www.towagolf.com). Obviously, you can play just one or several of the Santa Fe Trail courses or tee up for them all if you really want to take a Wild West challenge! Information on golf packages and free trip planning to customize golf tours for groups is available from Golf on the Santa Fe Trail at 110 Roehl Road NW; (505) 922-1323, (866) 465-3660; www.golfonthesantafetrail.com.

crunched golfers. Los Altos opened in 1960, making it the oldest of Albuquerque City's courses. Men's yardage is 6,180 for par 71, and women's yardage is 5,895 yards for par 74. Look out for the challenging hole 12, which, although a par 3, is a long 250 yards, and is well protected by surrounding bunkers. You'll find a driving range at Los Altos, plus practice putting and chipping greens. There are carts for rent, and golf lessons are available. There is also a pro shop and grill restaurant. During the week, play is purely first come, first served on the 18-hole course. For the weekend and holidays, reservations for tee times may be made from 7 a.m. on Wednesday morning. No reservations are needed for the 9-hole course.

PUERTO DEL SOL
1800 Girard SE
(505) 265-5636
www.cabq.gov/golf

A 9-hole course that's won accolades from the National Golf Federation, Puerto del Sol is a par-35 course tucked into a residential area near the airport, with a lovely grassy park feel and mature trees. There are three tee positions; the course measures 3,030 yards from the back tees and 2,525 yards from the forward tees. The easy-to-walk course is a winner with beginner players and seniors, who appreciate the generous greens, wide and fairly straight fairways bordered with trees, and the mainly flat terrain. Bunkers are the only hazards; you won't find any water features here. One of the trickiest holes is the par-4 hole 5. If you don't get your ducks in a row approaching the sharp dogleg with out of bounds on either side, you're in trouble! The longest hole, 8, is a par 5 at 478 yards. Of the two rolling fairways, the sloping hole 6 with bunkers poses a challenge. Due to the close proximity to the airport, players must allow landing aircraft to pass before teeing off at holes 1 and 9. This is the city's only golf course with a lighted driving range; the 80-tee range is open from Memorial Day to mid-September. There is also a putting green and chipping green, a pro shop, electric cart rentals, and a snack bar. Note the bronze statue by Reynaldo Rivera near the clubhouse. The statue portrays the late Jack Hardwick, a highly acclaimed teacher and head golf professional at the Puerto del Sol course from 1978 to 1994. There are no reservations for tee times at this course; play is purely on a first-come, first-served basis, but waits are typically brief.

SHOPPING

There are plenty of shopping temptations in Albuquerque, from the trendy to the traditional, and each of the main shopping areas has a slightly different feel. Nob Hill on Central Avenue, otherwise known as Route 66, shines a spotlight on hip boutiques with an eclectic range of fashion, arts and handcrafts, and super little lifestyle stores where you can browse for hours to find items for the home and design-savvy gifts. In Historic Old Town, specialty shops in quaint adobe buildings line the narrow streets around the plaza. Find Native American and Hispanic arts, pottery, and jewelry here, plus quirky Burque gifts that you won't find anywhere else. Don't forget to wander along the row of artists under the portal on the east side of the plaza. They sell jewelry and other handcrafted items directly to the public. Downtown offers a good mix of the traditional and the contemporary, with stores selling Native American and New Mexican artisan goods, and it's worth checking out the interesting young boutiques springing up along Gold Avenue. In all of these districts, it's best to park and walk. There's no better way to soak up the atmosphere and slow down enough to spot an interesting shopping opportunity or perhaps just an example of old city architecture. Also, the stores in these areas are close to each other, and there are plenty of restaurants and cafés, often with patios.

The Uptown area is home to the ABQ Uptown mall, plus many other contemporary retailers. If you're shopping for fine art or crafts, there is also a guide to some of the best Albuquerque art galleries in our Arts chapter.

Shopping Malls

ABQ Uptown: This stylish new open-air mall opened in 2006, with a definite urban edge, "bright lights, big city" feel, and distinctive architecture, plus blue, yellow, and red "Q" signage. It is home to upscale specialty stores; fashion, interior, and lifestyle retailers; and restaurants; Indian School NE and Louisiana Blvd; (505) 880-7030; www.abquptown.com.

Coronado Center: This is a long-established destination for Duke City shoppers—the balloon rally that was a precursor to the current Albuquerque International Balloon Fiesta launched from its parking lot in 1972. You'll find Macy's, JCPenney, and Sears here, plus over 150 specialty stores; 6600 Menaul Boulevard NE; (505) 881-4600; www.coronadocenter.com.

Cottonwood Mall: A large shopping complex on the west side of the Rio Grande River, Cottonwood Mall opened in 1996 and features Dillard's, Macy's, Sears, JCPenney, over 135 specialty stores, and the multiscreened United Artists Theaters; 10000 Coors Boulevard Bypass NW, at the intersection of Coors Boulevard and Coors Bypass; (505) 899-7467.

ANTIQUES

ANTIQUE SPECIALTY MALL
4516 Central Avenue SE
(505) 268-8080

Fifty traders in this 18,000-square-foot mall sell antiques and collectibles from no later than the 1950s, and you won't find any reproductions here. There's a little bit of everything in this treasure trove, from furniture to glass and even pre-Columbian Indian pieces. Open seven days.

ANTIQUES & THINGS
4710 Central Avenue SE
(505) 268-1313
www.antiquesandthingsabq.com

The 15,000-square-foot Antiques & Things used to be a McClellan's Five & Dime Store, and some of the original display cases are now used for antiques and mid-century vintage pieces, from toys and dolls to tools and pianos, plus cameras, books, furniture, clothing, and textiles. Home decorators looking for quirky vintage statement pieces might pick up a bargain here. There's also some contemporary jewelry. The price range from the 82 vendors is broad, with plenty of low-budget items. Closed Sunday and Monday.

COWBOYS & INDIANS ANTIQUES
4000 Central Avenue SE
(505) 255-4054
www.cowboysandindiansnm.com

Representing 15 national antiques dealers, Cowboys & Indians sells Western, Indian, and Hispanic art and antiques. The early southwestern pieces here primarily date back to the 1950s and earlier and include Native American pottery, baskets, rugs, jewelry, kachinas, and fetishes and Spanish religious art. There is also a diverse collection of Old West American memorabilia, cowboy gear, and art. The gallery also organizes the Great Southwestern Antique Show every August at EXPO New Mexico, Home of the New Mexico State Fair, and in 2009 also launched a smaller May edition of the show. Cowboys & Indians is open seven days.

Antique Mile

North 4th Street has been dubbed Albuquerque's Antique Mile, with a string of galleries selling antiques and vintage items from a variety of eras. The film industry picks up period props from this collection of stores, as they do from other Duke City purveyors of antiques. Antique Mile is located in the Village of Los Ranchos, bordered by Ortega Road on the north down to Osuna Road. All the stores are open from Tuesday through Saturday, and some have a welcome sign on the door on Sunday and Monday, too. Here are the participating stores, running north to south:

A Few Old Things: 8833 4th Street NW; (505) 922-1209

Legacy Antiques: 7809 4th Street NW; (505) 265-5827

Antique Co-Op: 7601 4th Street NW; (505) 898-7354

Antiques Consortium: 7216 4th Street NW; (505) 897-7115

Accents: 7209 4th Street NW; (505) 898-4488; www.AccentsInside.com

Vintage & More: 7005 4th Street NW; (505) 344-7300

Cabin & Cottage: 6855 4th Street NW (behind Calico Cafe); (505) 344-1168

A Few Old Things: 6711 4th Street NW; (505) 922-1209

GERTRUDE ZACHARY ANTIQUES
416 2nd Street SW
(505) 244-1320

Jewelry & Antiques
3300 Central Avenue SE
(505) 766-4700
www.gertrudezachary.com

Gertrude Zachary's antiques showroom on 2nd Street is only open on Friday and Saturday, but it has an impressive selection of American, European, and Asian antiques from the 18th and 19th centuries, including furniture, religious items, and architectural pieces such as doors and pillars. The showroom is also strong on vintage chandeliers.

The Central Avenue store at Nob Hill carries both antiques and contemporary and pawn southwestern jewelry and is open seven days.

MORNINGSIDE ANTIQUES
4001 Central Avenue NE
(505) 268-0188
www.morningsideantiques.net
Antiques aficionados will find a wealth of temptation in the fine-quality specimens in this Nob Hill store, ranging from the Colonial era to the mid-century modern era. The stock is pretty much evenly split between European and American pieces, including porcelain, silver, glass, furniture, jewelry, bronzes, and paintings. There are no reproduction items. Prices are from the low-mid range to high end. Open seven days.

VINTAGE & MORE
7005 4th Street NW
(505) 344-7300
Nine dealers display in the rooms of this old adobe house on Albuquerque's Antique Mile (see sidebar). Shop for mainly American antique furniture, decorative items, and a good selection of textiles, including quilts, linens, and vintage clothing, plus jewelry and accessories. Some contemporary pieces are sold here, too. Prices range from about $10 to four figures. Closed Sunday and Monday.

BOOKSTORES

There are several superb independent bookstores in Albuquerque, plus the national book chains. As most people are familiar with the wide array of products and services offered by Barnes & Noble, Borders, and Hastings, we've just picked out some of the local highlights for those stores.

BARNES & NOBLE
Cottonwood Corners Shopping Center
3701-A Ellison Drive NW
(505) 792-4234

Coronado Mall
6600 Menaul Boulevard NE
(505) 883-8200
www.barnesandnoble.com
Both of these stores hold regular story times and book clubs for teens. The stylish Coronado Mall Barnes & Noble, with its distinctive round tower over the entrance, also presents author events. Open every day.

BOOKWORKS
4022 Rio Grande Boulevard NW
(505) 344-8139
www.bkwrks.com
A popular North Valley independent bookstore for over 25 years and a great supporter of the literary arts, Bookworks hosts frequent readings by regional and nationally acclaimed authors. It also keeps a supply of autographed books from visiting writers, including the celebrated New Mexico author Rudolfo Anaya. There's a great collection of titles across all subjects and genres in this comfortably inviting store, and it's worth browsing the artsy and book-related selection of gifts. Bookworks is right next door to the Flying Star Cafe, so you can drop in to buy a book, then head next door to eat. Open seven days.

BORDERS
5901 Wyoming Boulevard NE
(505) 797-5681

2240 Q Street NE
(505) 884-7711

10420 Coors Bypass NW
(505) 792-3180
www.borders.com
The friendly staff at the Borders stores are good at recommending books of local interest and suggesting regional authors. There are weekly coffee specials in the in-store coffee house. Open seven days.

HASTINGS
Fair Plaza Shopping Center
6001-R Lomas Boulevard NE
(505) 266-1363

6051 Winter Haven Road NW
(505) 898-9227

Manzano Center
800 A Juan Tabo
(505) 296-6107

12501 Candelaria Road NE
(505) 332-8855

La Mirada Shopping Center
4315 Wyoming NE
(505) 299-7750
www.gohastings.com

Hastings stores host author readings and signings, craft events for kids, and other arts events, including live music.

PAGE ONE
11018 Montgomery NE
(505) 294-2026
www.page1book.com

The biggest independent bookstore in New Mexico, the recently remodeled Page One is nearly 30 years old and has friendly and knowledgeable staff. In addition to a big stock of recent releases, there's a large selection of rare and collectible books, autographed books, and a spotlight on local authors. There is also an excellent children's books section, complete with a fantastic hand-painted mural, and children's story time and puppet shows. Page One also sells magazines, software, cards, and gifts and has a store café. Open seven days.

TREASURE HOUSE BOOKS & GIFTS
2012 South Plaza Street NW
(505) 242-7204
www.myspace.com/oldtownbookseller

This characterful Old Town bookstore only stocks titles related to New Mexico and the Southwest, including fiction and mystery novels and books on the Old West, Indian, and Hispanic cultures. There are regular signings by regional authors, and you can also find cards here. Open seven days.

UNIVERSITY OF NEW MEXICO BOOKSTORE
2301 Central Avenue NE
(800) 981-2665 or (505) 277-5451
bookstore.unm.edu

Owned and operated by the university, this store does, of course, sell textbooks for students but also books on various subjects published by UNM Press, including poetry, fiction and nonfiction, and Southwest and regional titles. It also hosts book signings and sells gifts. Closed Sunday.

CLOTHING STORES

Children's Clothing

ADDISON MARIE
North Towne Plaza Shopping Center
5901 Wyoming Boulevard NE, Suite V
(505) 242-6027
www.addisonmariebaby.com

A baby boutique for newborns to age 4, Addison Marie retails fun and fashionable little dresses, onesies, rompers, and coordinated sets from American, Canadian, and European designers. Started by a mom and her own mom, the store focuses on finding clothing that's a little out of the ordinary, such as cute Juicy Couture velour all-in-ones that make a tiny tot even more squeezable. There's a good selection of organic lines, plus trendy diaper bags, and American and European toys. Open seven days.

AQUI
101 Bryn Mawr Drive SE
(505) 255-2926
www.aqui-nobhill.com

The stock here is divided roughly 60/40 between women's fashion and kids' clothing, so moms have a good excuse to bring their offspring here and make it a family shopping expedition! You'll find stylish casual separates for girls and boys, including pants, jackets, hoodies, tees, and girls' colorful skirts and dresses with a decent sprinkling of sweet prints. Babies are kitted out with separates and onesies. There are also children's shoes, including the favorite Tiny Toms, which serve a good cause, too, as the Toms Shoes brand matches each purchase by giving a pair of shoes to a child in need. Open seven days.

BABY BEAR
4801 Lomas NE
(505) 265-2922
www.babybearstore.com
Carrying clothes, accessories, and toys for babies and toddlers from infants through to age 3, Baby Bear features organic and natural fabrics and brands such as Sage Creek, Kate Quinn, and Under the Nile. The boutique's cloth diapers are a top seller, as well as their charming wooden toys. There are also baby shoes in soft leather, slings and wraps, and other accessories for the busy mom and her brood. Closed Sunday and Monday.

ZAP . . . OH!
103 Amherst Drive SE
(505) 268-2050, (866) 473-9350
www.zapoh.net
This family-owned store sells casual and special-occasion clothes for boys and girls up to age 8. Brands include the cute and colorful Zutano, classic pieces by Tea Collection, and infant wear Baby No Tags. You'll find separates from tees to capris, in Nob Hill's Zap . . . Oh!, plus onesies, shoes, accessories, and blankets. Open seven days.

Maternity Clothing

GLOWING MATERNITY & BABY BOUTIQUE
600 Central Avenue SE
(505) 243-4569
www.glowingmama.com
Mothers-to-be will love this EDo district boutique's high-fashion maternity wear, from casual-chic daywear and denim brands like 7 For All Mankind to designer dresses for special occasions. Labels include Juicy Couture, Serfontaine, Maternal America, Michael Stars, Momzee, and Olian. You can find intimate apparel here, too. The boutique also sells clothes for the stylish baby around town, from infant to 24 months, plus a few T-shirts for older children, up to about 6 years. There are also baby toys, blankets, and furniture, Uppababy and Bagaboo strollers, and trendy diaper bags. Open seven days.

Men's Clothing

BERT & JESS CLOTHIERS
2671 Louisiana Boulevard NE
(505) 345-9329
bertandjessclothiers.com
Dapper gents do well to head uptown to Bert & Jess Clothiers, which sells stylish formal tailoring and casual wear, plus shoes and accessories, including hard-to-find items like ascot cravats. There is a well-selected collection of suits with a classic contemporary vibe, and the store also offers custom-tailored suits. Labels here include Hickey Freeman, Jack Victor, and Luigi Bianchi Mantova. The owners are strong on customer service and go the extra mile to search for unusual items requested by customers. The store is closed on Sunday, although Sunday appointments can be arranged.

LOBO MENS SHOP

As of 2007 the bolo tie is the official state tie of New Mexico.

2120 Central Avenue SE
(505) 243-6954
www.lobomensshop.com
The shop has no connection with the University of New Mexico Lobos nor does it sell Lobos athletics gear, as the name might suggest. Instead, it's a venerable retailer providing fine menswear since 1963, including suits, dress and casual shirts, some other casual wear, ties, belts, wallets, hats, and shoes. Labels include Calvin Klein, Montefino, Dockers, Giorgio Brutini, and Frye Boots. Many customers also come here to buy Levi's jeans. There's a traditional menswear-store feel in the garment displays on dark wood shelves and cabinets. Open every day.

THE MAN'S HAT SHOP
511 Central Avenue NW
(505) 247-9605, (877) 239-9871
www.manshatshop.com
A handy (or heady?) Downtown store with a huge range of hats and caps, including stylish panamas, spiffy boaters, casual safari hats, and debonair fedoras. Of course, there are cowboy hats, although you can always go continental and try a beret instead. From a Cossack hat to a leather kepi, basically, if you can put it on your head, the Man's Hat Shop sells it. They've been in business for over 60 years, and if you can't find what you want, they'll design and make a hat for you. Closed Sunday.

ROBERT R. BAILEY CLOTHIER
6640 Indian School Road NE
(505) 881-2750
robertrbailey.com
Selling upscale contemporary tailored and casual wear, mainly from European brands, the store has the aura of a classic men's clothier, with a couple of big-screen TVs and a billiards table. Labels include Canali of Italy, Iton of Sweden, Jhane Barnes, and Robert Graham, and you can also opt for custom-made suits. There's a nifty range of haberdashery, too. The store claims something of a cult following for its sportswear, and the Tommy Bahama collection is a big magnet for customers. Closed Sunday.

TOAD ROAD
Suite C, 3503 Central Avenue NE
(505) 255-4212
This cool Nob Hill store opened at the end of 2006 and quickly established itself as a go-to for guys looking for casual wear and classy jeans and Ts, featuring brands like Diesel, Modern Amusement, and Alternative Apparel. They also carry local designers and accessory ranges. The friendly store owners are musicians, so don't be surprised if you find an impromptu jam session taking place. Toad Road sells women's wear, too, so it's a great place for couples to shop together. Open seven days.

i **DiPietro's Custom Clothing sells custom-made men's suits and shirts by Valentino, Hugo Boss, Dormeuil, Holland and Sherry, Ermenegildo Zegna, and shoes from Allen Edmonds. There is no storefront; service for a made-to-measure suit is by appointment only on a flexible schedule to suit the client, including weekends. Contact DiPietro's Custom Clothing at (505) 298-2699; www.dipietros.net.**

Vintage Clothing

OFF BROADWAY
3110 Central Avenue SE
(505) 268-1489
www.offbroadwaycostumes.com
There's a big stock of women's vintage clothing here, plus a smaller selection for men. You can pick up pieces from the Victorian era through to the big-shouldered glamour of the 1980s, including lots of chic 1940s and '50s looks. Off Broadway is especially popular for high-end vintage garments and is a go-to shop for special occasion evening, cocktail, and party gowns. If you fancy yourself as a 1920s flapper, you'll probably find your match here. There are also reproduction period outfits. The store also rents vintage ensembles and character costumes for parties, theatrical productions, and seasonal events. Get there early to pick your Halloween costume, as that's when there's the biggest rush on rentals. Open every day.

Women's Clothing

AQUI
101 Bryn Mawr Drive SE
(505) 255-2926
www.aqui-nobhill.com
The mother-and-daughter team running this Nob Hill boutique has a great eye for easy-to-wear pieces with an original fashion edge. Find dresses and separates here featuring fresh contemporary prints, plus casual jackets, jeans, tops and sweaters, and accessories. Jeans include Union Jeans and Earnest Sewn. The broad range

of labels range from the eco-friendly Edun to the always eyecatching Aoyama Itchome. There is also a good selection of handbags, jewelry, and shoes, including the popular Toms Shoes. Aqui stocks clothes for children and babies, too. Open seven days.

ELSA ROSS
3511 Central Avenue NE
(505) 265-2070
www.elsaross.com

Originally opened as a shoe shop in 1989, this Nob Hill store run by Elsa Ross and daughter Emma soon stepped out into a full fashion boutique and now has the Albuquerque exclusive on about 95% of the lines it carries. The collection includes Diane Von Furstenberg, Haute Hippie, 3.1 Phillip Lim, and the trendy denim label Current/Elliott. Designer accessories also factor strongly, including shoes, bags, and sunglasses, from names like Roberto Cavalli and L.A.M.B. Open seven days.

GEE LORETTA!
10655 Montgomery Boulevard NE
(505) 292-6652
geeloretta.com

A good destination to find ultrafeminine fashion, including cocktail and evening wear and special-occasion dresses, flirty skirts, and casual wear with a kick. They also stock handbags, accessories, and jewelry, and the girl's best-friend Spanx brand. There are three stores under one roof here, with ¡Zapatos! shoe shop and Arteriors lifestyle and interior design. Closed Sunday.

MAGNOLIA LE BOUTIQUE
4605-B Menaul Boulevard NE
(505) 881-0561
www.magnolialeboutique.com

Owners Irene Jack and Erin Ingersoll offer a carefully selected range of women's fashion and accessories, with an emphasis on classic styles with a fashion edge for smart investment dressing. This is the place to pick up a great little jacket with trendy touches that won't look dated after one season. Labels include the popular LAmade, and designer denim includes Citizens of Humanity and AG Adriano Goldschmied. Closed Sunday.

SEVENTH GODDESS
3503 Central Avenue NE, Suite A
(505) 243-8025
www.seventhgoddess.com

A heavenly lingerie boutique for goddesses and ordinary mortals, Seventh Goddess has collections of European and American intimate apparel, including customer-favorite labels Cosabella, Claire Pettibone, and Mary Green. The frillies here range from the playful to the outright seductive, and plus sizes are available. The store specializes in ready-made and custom-designed corsets, and other treats in the store include hosiery, scented lotions and potions, candles, and accessories from the vampy to the romantic. Complimentary coffee, tea, and truffles are served to customers. Open seven days.

TRES BOUTIQUE
3021 Central Avenue NE
(505) 255-8737
www.tresboutique.com

A relatively new addition to the Nob Hill fashion scene at the end of 2008, Tres Boutique has already made its mark with Duke City women, from teens looking for something hot for a night out to mothers and daughters shopping together. They stock just about everything except jeans—from cocktail dresses to casual wear and business attire. New designers are in the spotlight, and there are also jewelry, bags, shoes, and belts. Closed Sunday.

VINTAGE COWGIRL
Patio Market
206½ San Felipe Street NW
(505) 247-2466

Despite the name, this Old Town boutique sells all new contemporary clothing and accessories, but the fashion style is definitely feminine, flirty, vintage cowgirl!

Kick up your heels in their dynamite colorful cowgirl boots, or check out the vintage-look shirts. They also stock hats. The store sponsors the fashion show for the New Mexico State Fair Queen contest, so they're popular with younger women, but women of all ages who like the romantic retro Western aesthetic with a trendy edge will find something here. Open seven days.

i **Although the majority of the stock in Larry's Hats on Central is for men, the store also carries women's hats, including Wallaroo Hat Company and Parkers labels. It's worth dropping in to check out their vintage costume jewelry, bags, scarves, and gloves. Larry's Hats is open seven days at 3102 Central Avenue SE; (505) 266-2095.**

Women's Consignment

2 TIME COUTURE
600 Central Avenue SE, Suite C
(505) 242-3600
www.2timecouture.com

On first entry into this smart boutique, you wouldn't guess it was a consignment store, until you realize that each item is a one-off. The store is beautifully designed to present its upscale selection of new and gently used women's fashion, shoes, and accessories, and it only accepts certain contemporary designers and brands in excellent condition. If you have a taste for labels like Chanel, Dior, Gucci, Marc Jacobs, Juicy Couture, BCBG Max Azria, Nicole Miller, Vera Wang, Kate Spade, and Lulu Guiness, then this is the place to browse. It's worth checking out the designer bags, especially as one size fits all! 2 Time Couture is next door to the Grove Cafe and Market and is open seven days.

Women's Shoes

DEBENEDETTOS
6855 4th Street NW
(505) 345-9948
debenedettos.com

DeBenedettos is a good stop for gals with a passion for shoes, as they specialize in stylish women's footwear from Europe and Brazil, ranging from casual summer sandals to elegant business heels. They are the exclusive Albuquerque suppliers of Manas, A. Marinelli, Berando, and Zita Maria. Most popular for their A. Marinelli line, they also feature Matisse and Tsubo, plus Latico purses and Icon purses and accessories. The boutique caters largely to locals, but as the Los Ranchos area becomes more popular among tourists, out-of-towners are discovering it, too. You'll spot customers in there from 20-somethings to retirees, but as the owner says: "We'll put nice shoes on 80-year-olds!" Closed Sunday and Monday.

i **Don't forget to check out the boutiques and fine-clothing stores in our men's and women's clothing sections, as several of those also sell a great selection of shoes. Dan's Boots and Saddles (listed under Western Wear) stocks a huge collection of cowboy boots for all.**

TERRA FIRMA
113 Carlisle Boulevard SE
(505) 260-0507

Women come here for comfortable fashion footwear, including shoes, boots, clogs, and sandals that look good without killing your feet. Leading brands at Terra Firma include Dansko, Keen, Naot, Wolky, and Frye Boots. As well as the Nob Hill store, there is one at North Town Shopping Center, 5901 Wyoming Boulevard NE; (505) 856-7200. Open seven days.

COMICS & COLLECTIBLES

ASTRO-ZOMBIES
3100 Central Avenue SE
(505) 232-7800

Voted best comic-book store by the weekly *Alibi* newspaper for eight years solid, Astro-Zombies sells new- and back-issue comics from DC, Marvel, Dark Horse, Image, and independent publishers, plus graphic novels and comic- and movie-related toys, action figures, T-shirts, and collectibles. The store also stocks new and used vinyl records. Open seven days.

COMIC WAREHOUSE
9617 Menaul Boulevard NE
(505) 293-3065
www.c-warehouse.com

Warehouse is the word! There is a huge selection of new comic books and over 200,000 old comic books at this 30-plus-year-old business. You'll also find Anime and Manga, trading cards, and related comic items, including T-shirts, posters, and toys, plus collector supplies such as bags and storage sleeves. Open seven days.

LOUIE'S ROCK-N-REELS
105 Harvard Drive SE
(505) 232-7510

Movie and music fan Louie Torres has created a treasure trove for customers who share his passions, and as Louie says, "The only person who'll ever answer my phone is me or my dog!" His store stocks 20,000 movie and music posters, plus movies on DVD and VHS video, film books, and related movie paraphernalia. You can pass a nostalgic few hours here browsing movie postcards, lobby cards, and press photos. Music posters include commercial American, imported British, and promotional posters that record companies sent out to promote new releases. Closed Sunday.

FARMERS' MARKETS

Here are our top picks of the farmers' markets in and around Albuquerque. Market seasons and times for these lovely community gatherings can be as organic as the produce they sell and may well change each year. We've indicated the most recent times as a guideline, but please check with the market Web site for the latest news. If no Web site is provided, you can find information on these and other Albuquerque and New Mexico farmers' markets at the New Mexico Farmers' Marketing Association Web site: farmersmarketsnm.org.

CORRALES GROWERS' MARKET

You can count on this charming old agricultural community just north of Albuquerque to put on a good spread of fruits from local orchards, plus vegetables and herbs, honeys, jams, chiles, salsas, baked treats, and plants and flowers for the home. There is also music, and other entertainment and events.

Where: Recreation Center, 500 Jones Road and Corrales Road, Corrales (south of the post office)

When: Summer market (April to October) is on Sunday mornings (previously 9 a.m. to noon) and in high summer from July on Wednesday afternoon (previously 3 p.m. to 6 p.m.). Winter market (November to April) is on the first Sunday morning of the month (previously 10 a.m. to 1 p.m.).

DOWNTOWN GROWERS' MARKET
www.downtownabq.com/growersmarket

All produce on sale here was grown less than 60 miles away, and vendors also offer artisan breads and pastries, goat cheese, pasta, honey, plants and flowers, soaps, and even dog biscuits! This community market includes arts and crafts, live music, and activities such as face painting and chef demonstrations. Grab a breakfast burrito, muffin, or fry bread and a cup of Joe and make a picnic under the park's shady cottonwoods.

Where: Robinson Park at Central Avenue and 8th Avenue SW

When: On Saturday morning from June through October. Hours vary by month, so check at the Web site.

LOS RANCHOS GROWERS' MARKET
www.villr.com/market.htm

There is plenty of fruit from local orchards, plus veggies, eggs, honey, grass-fed beef, pasta, bread, pies, jams, and jellies at this Village of Los Ranchos market, which is also strong on arts and crafts. Vendors sell original and handmade items, including jewelry, soaps, candles, tinwork, pottery, cards, and clothing and scarves. You can also find houseplants and flowers here. Snacks might include burritos and posole, to keep you fueled while shopping. The market features a lively cal-

endar of entertainment, from music to pottery or origami demonstrations.
Where: 6718 Rio Grande Boulevard NW
When: The summer market, from May to November, is on Saturday morning (previously has been 7 to 11 a.m.). The winter market, from December to April, is on the morning of the second Saturday of the month (previously has been 10 a.m. to noon).

NOB HILL GROWERS' MARKET

Browse New Mexico produce and grass-fed beef, eggs, honey, breads, pies, goat cheese, and jellies. There are also vendors of flowers and herbal skincare at this expanding market, with live music and a cool Nob Hill vibe. Kids are entertained with craft activities and a playground.
Where: Morningside Park at Lead Avenue and Morningside Drive SE
When: Thursday afternoons (previously has been 3 to 6:30 p.m.), May to November

i If you miss the farmers' markets, you can still find good fresh and organic produce at these stores—Sunflowers Farmers Market: 5112 Lomas NE, (505) 268-5127, or 10701 Corrales NW, (505) 890-7900, www.sfmarkets.com; La Montañita Co-op: 3500 Central SE, (505) 265-4631, or 2400 Rio Grande NW, (505) 242-8800, www.lamontanita.coop.

FLEA MARKET

EXPO NEW MEXICO FLEA MARKET

Expo New Mexico, Home of the New Mexico State Fair Gate 9, Louisiana Boulevard and Central Avenue NE
(505) 222-9766
www.exponm.com

Roll up, roll up, for New Mexico's oldest and biggest flea market at the state fairgrounds, with over 1,300 vendors selling furniture, clothing, music, jewelry, and even fresh produce. As anyone can come and sell here for the day by registering for a vendor space, you never know exactly what riches you might find, from crafts to collectibles to businesses selling off overstocks. Or it may turn out that the clutter from someone else's garage might be exactly the treasure you've been looking for. Food concessions help stave off hunger pangs while you're browsing. The flea market runs in all kinds of weather, every Saturday and Sunday from 7 a.m. to around 6 p.m., except during the annual state fair in September or if Christmas coincides with a weekend. Enter the state fairgrounds by Gate 9 at Louisiana and Central. Admission to the market is free, but there is a fee for parking.

GARDEN CENTERS AND NURSERIES

JERICHO NURSERY

101 Alameda Boulevard NW
(505) 899-7555
www.jerichonursery.com

At this colorful 2.25-acre full-service garden center, you can find a wide array of trees, shrubs, and plants, from cacti to kale, with plenty of unusual varieties for gardeners seeking something a little different. Jericho also sells pottery, yard art, pond plants, bird feeders, tools, and other garden accessories. Although it's a relatively young garden center, opened in 2005, the owner and most of the expert staff here are from the now-closed Rowland Nursery, which had a long and popular reputation. Owner Rick Hobson appears on TV and radio gardening shows, and the nursery hosts gardening seminars. There is also a branch at the Village Mercantile in Corrales (3675 Corrales Road, 505-897-9328). Both stores are open seven days, year-round.

OSUNA NURSERY

501 Osuna Road NE
(505) 345-6644
www.osunanursery.com

This large nursery covers 10 acres and is a family business run by owner Chang An since 1980. It offers a wide selection of bedding plants, trees, shrubs, native varieties, and tropical houseplants. The store offers a good selection of garden tools and indoor and outdoor garden accessories, ornaments, and gifts, including pottery, fountains, and birdbaths. Locals enjoy the good service from "Team Osuna" staff, who will also diagnose plant problems if you bring a photo or sample. There is also a "plant interiorscape" service for businesses and homes. Open seven days, year-round.

PLANTS OF THE SOUTHWEST
6680 4th Street NW
(505) 344-8830
www.plantsofthesouthwest.com
Specializing in native southwestern plants and trees, Plants of the Southwest has its own farm in Galisteo, and harvests its own non-GMO (genetically modified organism) seeds, which are also for sale. Seed selections include wildflowers, grasses, chiles, herbs, and vegetables. The business started from its Santa Fe location in 1976. Although not the largest nursery, this is a popular spot among North Valley gardeners, not least for its knowledgeable employees who are always helpful in making recommendations. Open seven days in summer, closed Sunday in winter.

GOURMET FOOD

THE GROVE CAFE AND MARKET
600 Central Avenue SE, Suite A
(505) 248-9800
www.thegrovecafemarket.com
The shelves of this popular café are a cloud nine for foodies, with a modest but perfectly selected range of local and international food products, including artisan breads, cheeses, and chocolates and premium olive oils, vinegars, condiments, olives, jams, coffees, teas, and other culinary items. There are plenty of nicely packaged and unusual products here that would serve as gifts. Closed Monday.

JEWELRY

GERTRUDE ZACHARY JEWELRY
1501 Lomas Boulevard NW
(505) 247-4442, (800) 682-5768
Jewelry & Antiques
3300 Central Avenue SE
(505) 766-4700
www.gertrudezachary.com
Designer Gertrude Zachary works with Native American silversmiths and artists to produce a wide selection of handcrafted jewelry in both traditional and contemporary designs. The store is popular with locals for its bold silver and turquoise pieces, but there are plenty of other high-quality gemstones, too, and you can also find concha belts and old pawn jewelry. The Nob Hill store on Central Avenue has 18th- and 19th-century antiques as well as jewelry. Both stores are open seven days.

i **Pawn jewelry has been used as collateral for a loan from a pawn shop. If the jewelry owner doesn't reclaim his or her property by repaying the loan and interest in a certain period, the shop owner keeps the item and sells it. In New Mexico, you'll frequently see old Indian jewelry that originally came onto the market in this way, and it continues to be called pawn jewelry, even if the dealer now selling the jewelry isn't a pawn shop.**

OOH! AAH! JEWELRY
110 Amherst Drive SE
(505) 265-7170
oohaahjewelry.com
Expect to see a nicely edited selection of jewelry here from about 100 local, national, and international artists. This Nob Hill boutique sells both contemporary and traditional designs, and refreshingly unusual fashion pieces start under $25. Metals include silver, gold, platinum, and titanium, and there are plenty of pieces set with gemstones, in addition to gold vermeil, bridal collections, wedding bands, and watches for men and women. A range of handbags features labels like Tutela, Hobo, Latico, and Nino Bossi. Ask for a frequent-shopper punch card to receive $15 store credit for every $150 spent. Open seven days.

i **See the Native American section for stores selling beautiful hand-worked Indian jewelry.**

LIFESTYLE

HEY JHONNY
3418 Central Avenue SE
(505) 256- 9244
www.heyjhonny.com

It's always a pleasure to putter around Hey Jhonny—and yes, that is how they spell the name! You're guaranteed to find unusual decorative items for the home in this chic boutique, including contemporary pottery and ceramics, glasswear, vases, candles, bowls, and goblets, as well as jewelry, gifts, scarves, and an always-hot selection of Hobo International purses. Many pieces are one of a kind, and the owners bring pieces back from their travels to keep their Nob Hill clientele coming in to see what's new. Open seven days.

HISPANIAE
410 Romero Street NW
(505) 244-1533
www.hispaniae.com

This Old Town store is packed with traditional south-of-the-border arts and crafts, especially from Mexico, Peru, and Guatemala, plus retablos by New Mexican artisans. Hispaniae specializes in Day of the Dead iconography, often with a dash of mordant humor or a splash of Frida Kahlo. Also look out for beautiful black La Chamba cookware from Colombia and tinwork from Mexico. Open seven days.

JACKALOPE
6400 San Mateo Boulevard NE
(505) 349-0970, (866) 867-9813
www.jackalope.com

A riotous bazaar of eclectic home accessories, pottery, rugs, furniture, folk art, and gifts, Jackalope started as an importer of Mexican pottery in Santa Fe (where there is still a store). It has expanded over more than three decades to stock colorful merchandise from around the world, including China, India, and Africa, and it's always an adventure to see what you might find. There is also a store in Bernalillo, just north of the city (834 W Highway 550, #44, Bernalillo; 505-867-9813). Open seven days.

LA CASITA DE KALEIDOSCOPES
Poco-a-Poco Patio
326-D San Felipe NW
(505) 247-4242
www.casitascopes.com

Allow plenty of time for a foray into this Old Town store that captivates adults and kids alike with its wide range of kaleidoscopes from exquisite artist-designed pieces with prices into the hundreds (or thousands), down to simpler examples at around ten bucks or less. Many of the kaleidoscopes are not only delightful to use but make beautiful decorative items for the home. It's easy to spend an hour oohing and aahing your way around the shop as you try out all the kaleidoscopes, and it's a good spot to pick up an unusual gift. Open daily, although Sunday hours are usually limited to the afternoon, and it may be closed Sunday in January. Check in advance.

LA PIÑATA SHOP
2 Patio Market Street NW
(505) 242-2400
www.rhondacacy.com

Choose from a selection of different styles of piñatas—including bowls, burros, and cartoon characters—to fill with your own goodies. Traditional star-design piñatas are always a good pick in this Old Town specialty store. You can also buy leather hats, pillows, vests, and jackets, plus handmade porcelain dolls with clothes made by the store owner and Native American jewelry, paper flowers, and artwork. Open seven days.

NEW MEXICO CANDLE COMPANY
523 Wyoming Boulevard NE
(505) 891-2366

Watch the candlemakers at work, and find unusual candles here, including candles that are sand-cast using sand from a New Mexico mesa and hand-carved into distinctly local shapes. Favorites are the adobe casas that are miniature versions of the real thing, complete with chile *ristras* hanging round the door and candlelight shining through the windows. Other candles are carved into mission churches and pueblos or feature cut-out chile pepper, cowboy boot, or alien motifs. The store's exclusive Corndles, candles realistically shaped like a corn husk in various colors, are sold all over the world. Fragranced candles include a popular pear scent, local desert sage and piñon scents, and quirkier fragrances like clean sheets! You can also mix your own blend from about 60 scents. The store also stocks pottery candles and wind chimes, or you can order a custom-shaped and -decorated candle. There are regular candle-carving workshops for adults and children. See the entry in the Kidstuff chapter for more details on the workshops. Closed Sunday.

PATRICIAN DESIGN
216 Gold Avenue SW
(505) 242-7646
www.patriciandesign.com

This stylish Downtown boutique is a good source for unique art, gifts, and decorative home accessories. Patrician Design began as a spinoff of owner Patty Harrell Hoech's interior design business, in which she made a point of featuring local artists. Responding to the needs of the nearby loft community, as well as stop-ins from out of town, the shop expanded to offer its varied and colorful range of art, cards, and bath and body lotions and soaps, as well as mirrors, colorful tableware, handmade jewelry, and scarves and other accessories by local artisans. Particularly sought after are lotions and potions by Archipelago and Thymes, Votivo long-burning fragrant candles, high-quality "functional art" tableware by Penne Roberts and Maggie Beyler, and award-winning pieces by such local artists as Michelle Chrisman, Susan Weeks, and Meg Leonard, the creator of Albuquerque's 2009 Balloon Fiesta poster. The owner tries not to duplicate the styles of each artist, so all the work here is diverse. Textile artist Renee Gentz is popular for her wall hangings, as well as one-of-a-kind "wearable art" pieces, including caftans, jackets, and scarves. Patrician Design is also the exclusive source for the work of the late New Mexico expressionist artist Peggy Zuris. Open seven days.

QUE CHULA
3410 Central Avenue SE
(505) 255-0515
www.quechulastyle.com

Que Chula means "How cute!" and that's a good description for this retailer of Mexican imports, textiles from Guatemala, and locally made jewelry. You can pick up Mexican folk art and hand-blown Mexican glasswear, traditional equipale furniture with a colorful twist, tooled leather purses, punched-tin decorations, framed mirrors, linens, pottery, and adorable hand-painted children's furniture. There are lots of Virgin of Guadalupe–themed items, from mouse pads to shopping bags. Open seven days.

i **Find interesting gift items at Little Shops on Rio Grande, a collection of specialty shops all under one roof. It's an eclectic array of art; furniture; southwestern clothing; home and office accessories; jewelry; religious items, including baptismal gowns; candles; dolls; chile products; piñatas; crystals; dragon- and fairie-theme items; and more. Open seven days. Little Shops on Rio Grande is located at 1507 Rio Grande Boulevard NW; (505) 765-5489.**

MUSIC STORES

CHARLEY'S RECORDS & TAPES
7602 Menaul Boulevard NE
(505) 296-3685

Serving music fans since 1988, Charley's sells new CDs and has a big stock of used CDs and up to 4,000 tapes for sale, too. Vinyl LPs and singles ranging from classics to imports and indie labels are a big draw for local customers. You can find all kinds of collectibles in this vintage-music store, as well as rock T-shirts and a huge poster collection. There is also used equipment for sale, from turntables and cassette players (to play your vintage technology music on!) to DVD players. Open every day.

NATURAL SOUND
3422 Central Avenue SE
(505) 255-8295
This is a Duke City favorite for its wide range of new and used CDs, with a good selection of indie labels. Natural Sound also sells used tapes, LP records, and DVDs. Although the music assortment is diverse, there's a strong collection of electronic and house music, in keeping with the staff's personal tastes. The flyer table here is a popular community resource to find out what's going on. This 37-year-old business is due to move to another location within Nob Hill in early 2010 but hopes to keep the phone number, so call for the new address. Open every day.

NATIVE AMERICAN

BIEN MUR INDIAN MARKET CENTER
100 Bien Mur Drive NE
(505) 821-5400, (800) 365-5400
www.bienmur.com
Owned by Sandia Pueblo, this kiva-shaped center sells Native American arts and crafts, including jewelry, pottery, fetishes, baskets, and rugs. There is a large stock of over 19,000 handmade pieces from artists in various tribes and pueblos, and shoppers on all budgets should find something to suit. The showroom has been here since 1975, and the center's name means Big Mountain. You'll often find special-event sales taking place and changing showcases highlighting selected artists. There's a tobacco store here, too. Open seven days.

i **A fetish is a carved or otherwise crafted image of an animal that offers religious meaning or spiritual protection. It is traditionally blessed by a shaman or priest. Zuni Pueblo Indians are legendary for their fetish carvings.**

SKIP MAISEL'S
510 Central Avenue SW
(505) 242-6526
www.skip-maisels.com
You'll find shelf upon shelf of Indian jewelry, pottery, and other crafts in this Downtown landmark store. Although Skip Maisel's bills itself as a wholesaler, it sells direct to the public but at wholesale prices. There are thousands of pieces of pottery from different pueblos and tribes, including Santa Clara Pueblo's famous black pottery, and just browsing the different styles and motifs is an education in itself. There is also a wide range of Navajo, Hopi, and Zuni jewelry; Navajo rugs; and handmade kachinas. There are usually Indian artisans in the store, so you can watch them at work. Closed Sunday.

i **Architect John Gaw Meem designed Skip Maisel's 1930s building. Look for the murals on the façade portraying Native ceremonial life. When artist Olive Rush was commissioned to create the murals, she involved other—then unknown—artists to paint the long panels, including Pablita Velarde, Harrison Begay, Ben Quintana, and Pop Chalee.**

SOUTHWESTERN FLAVORS

THE CHILE CASA
Plaza Hacienda
1919 Old Town Road NW
(505) 242-2111
www.thechilecasa.com
Find popular hot sauces and award-winning salsas in this Old Town store. Traditional New Mexican food items include Carne Adovada Mix and mole sauce; piñon coffee; margarita mix; and, of course, a variety of crushed and powdered chiles and other regional seasonings, spices, and rubs.

Jams and honeys include Green Chile Blueberry Preserve, and there are bread and cake mixes to make your own sopaipillas, jalapeño cornbread, and adobe mud cake. You can also find chile ristras here or even buy a "just add water" green chile stew to satisfy your chile cravings once you get home from New Mexico. Most products are made in New Mexico. The store is in an old adobe that used to be the stable area of the main house, which is now La Hacienda restaurant. Find Plaza Hacienda behind the restaurant, near the east gate entrance to the plaza. Open seven days.

i **Pick up salsas at local restaurants that also retail the fiery stuff they serve, including Sadie's, El Pinto, and the Garduño's chain. Paisano's Italian restaurant sells its own marinara sauce.**

SPORT

SPORT SYSTEMS
6915 Montgomery NE
(505) 837-9400
www.nmsportsystems.com

This locally owned retailer has equipment, clothing, and specialty shoes and boots for sports people and lovers of the great outdoors. Runners, hikers, cyclists, swimmers, yoga practitioners, and winter sports fans will find a good selection of brand-name gear here, such as Nike, Adidas, Salomon, Teva, Speedo, the North Face, and Patagonia. Additional services include rental of ski and snowboarding equipment and gear, and Sport Systems also organizes group cycle rides and clinics. There's also an in-store coffee shop. Open seven days.

i **Chile ristras are traditionally a popular buy for visitors. These long ropes of dried red chile peppers make a festive decoration in a kitchen or hanging on a door or in a porchway.**

SWEET TREATS

AMOUR CHOCOLATES
2412 San Mateo Place NE
(505) 881-2803, (888) 422-6687
www.amourchocolates.com

Handmade fine chocolates full of southwestern heart include chocolate seasoned with a dash of spicy red chile. Espresso-roasted Costa Rican coffee beans covered in bittersweet chocolate also give quite a kick, while nut nuts will enjoy the pecans and almonds coated in chile and chocolate. Look for the chocolate bars with a Duke City twist; they're very reasonably priced, in cute packaging, and they make great stocking-filler gifts. Choose from flavors that include the dark Cowboy Coffee Crunch, the Cowgirl Coffee Crunch Bar with white chocolate, and Lil' Wrangler Mocha Crunch. Or opt for the more romantic Dark Cherry Pecan Bar. Amour also cooks up a handful of sugar-free chocolate treats. Find Amour Chocolates at stores around town, or drop by their San Mateo showroom, where you can buy retail and even enjoy tastings.

CAKE FETISH
2665 Louisiana NE
(505) 883-0670

Montano Plaza
6200 Coors Road, Suite A9
(505) 899-2425
www.cakefetish.com

Decadent cupcakes in dozens of flavors fill the shelves of the two Cake Fetish stores. Piled high with hand-frosted decoration, cupcakes include Sleepless in Albuquerque (chocolate cake, with mocha buttercream, chocolate ganache, and an espresso bean); Velvet Elvis—a red velvet cake with cream cheese buttercream and a sparkle of red sugar sprinkles; and the delectable Piña Colada coconut cupcake with pineapple and coconut buttercream. Their Fluffer Nutter flavor made MSN.com's 2008 list of The Country's Best Cupcakes, and Cake Fetish also appeared in *Forbes Traveler*'s 2009 round-up of America's Best Cupcakes. If you can't make up your mind which one to try, buy a variety tray of mini cupcakes. There are daily specials, and even doggie-treat cupcakes. Closed Sunday.

THE CANDY LADY
524 Romero Street NW
(505) 243-6239, (800) 214-7731
www.thecandylady.com

Candy lady Debbie Ball tempts Old Town visitors with a wonderland of treats, from good old-fashioned licorice, caramels, and rock candy to hand-molded chocolate tool sets. The fudge here (in 20 flavors!) is especially worth checking out, and chocolate-covered strawberries are a favorite with customers. More adventurous sweet tooths will enjoy trying the red or green chile peanut brittle or piñon brittle. There are also sugar-free candies here. There is an adults-only selection of naughty novelty candies in a separate room.

THEOBROMA CHOCOLATIER
12611 Montgomery Boulevard NE
(505) 293-6545, (877) 293-6565
www.theobromachocolatier.com

The Theobroma name derives from two Greek words translating to "food of the gods," and this small family firm does its best to live up to the name, with hand-dipped chocolate assortments; truffles; after-dinner mints; chocolate-covered cherries, blueberries, and almonds; glace apricots; and nut bark. Popcorn fans will enjoy the milk chocolate–covered old-fashioned or caramel popcorn. Theobrama Chocolatier also sells Taos Cow ice cream and fresh fruits, including strawberries and pineapple, dunked in white, dark, and milk chocolate. Kids will love the UFO—a disk of chocolate studded with caramel and pecans and topped with white chocolate. Closed Sunday.

i Look for AlbuqCookie's locally made cookies, including biscotti in flavors such as chocolate piñon, pistachio chocolate chip cranberry, and lavender lemon. Shortbreads include tasty chocolate pepper chile flavor and green chile pecan Sandia cookies. Find them in gourmet and food stores, including La Montañita Co-op, or order a bag from the AlbuqCookie online store: www.albuqcookie.com.

THRIFT STORES AND RESALE

BUFFALO EXCHANGE
3005 Central Avenue NE
(505) 262-0098
www.buffaloexchange.com

Trade and buy new and recycled women's and men's fashion at the bright and breezy Albuquerque branch of this national chain. There are some clothes for juniors, too, but not for small kids. This is also a good place to find retro clothing, shoes, hats, accessories, and ties for theme parties, especially from the 1970's, '80s, and '90s, but there is also lots of funky and fun contemporary gear, and customers come back often to see what's new. Open seven days.

SUPER THRIFT STORE
615 Virginia Street SE
(505) 255-5523

This is Animal Humane's thrift store, and as animal lovers are generous with their donations, it's a good place to sniff out antiques, furniture, household items, clothes, collectibles, and low-cost books. Bargain hunters love their prices, but note that the store closes for lunch. There is a second store at 7901 North 4th Street NW; (505) 217-3476. Both are open every day.

THRIFT TOWN
3900 Menaul NE
(505) 872-0647
www.thrifttown.com

You can't miss the large storefront of this emporium that's earned its place as a long-time favorite of Duke City's pennywise shoppers. Part of a chain of 15 thrift stores across western states, Thrift Town sells everything from TVs to sports gear, but it's the enormous range of bargain clothing that proves most popular, from casual kit to formal wear. Open seven days.

WESTERN WEAR

DAN'S BOOTS AND SADDLES
6903 4th Street NW
(505) 345-2220
www.dansboots.com

This is the place to buy cowboy boots! The store carries 4,000 pairs in a gamut of styles for men, women, and children. It is also a genuine supplier to Western equestrians, selling saddles and tack, with a feed store, too. The authentic atmosphere at Dan's gets you in the mood to find the boot to fit, from classic rugged looks to fancy tooled-leather designs. There are also cowboy hats and Wrangler jeans for adults and kids. Closed Sunday.

DAY TRIPS AND WEEKEND GETAWAYS

Centrally located Albuquerque is in a good position to take advantage of New Mexico attractions at all points of the compass via I-25 and I-40, and the added benefit of a road trip in the Land of Enchantment is that the journey is just as beautiful as your ultimate destination. This chapter highlights some of the most popular and interesting destinations within easy reach of Albuquerque. These include the day trips of the Turquoise Trail, Acoma Pueblo, and, of course, Santa Fe, just an hour's drive away, for a complete change of pace from Duke City. Santa Fe's museums, galleries, entertainment, shopping, and restaurants are so easily reached that many people pop up just for an evening at the opera or a Friday afternoon stroll down Canyon Road to drop in at the gallery openings, followed by a spot of dinner. Slightly farther afield, the Georgia O'Keeffe country of Abiquiu and Ghost Ranch make a scenic day trip, with options for O'Keeffe tours, hiking, and a soak in the nearby Ojo Caliente mineral springs, but if you want to stretch it into an overnighter or a long weekend, some accommodations are suggested. Taos, at around two-and-a-half hours' drive from Albuquerque or more if traffic is against you or you decide to stop off en route in Santa Fe, can be done in an early-start day trip. The more relaxing choice, however, is to stay over and drop into the much slower pace of this small town that can almost feel like another world once you emerge from the deep rift of the Rio Grande Gorge. And talking of other worlds—alien hunters and art lovers alike will enjoy Roswell, a three-hour drive southeast of Albuquerque, with its landscape that is quite different from the more rugged northern destinations featured here but equally beautiful in its sense of immaculate open space. These are numerous other places to discover, but these will kick off your New Mexico explorations and provide a taste of the diversity of land, culture, and activities available on Albuquerque's back doorstep. In the destinations spotlighted there are, of course, many other attractions and further side trips, too. The selections point out some of the best of these destinations, knowing that you'll find the rest of the best as you travel around and enjoy the discovery even more. And of course, then you can return and dig deeper into the places you love most.

While main highways are well maintained and fairly fast, be aware that once you get out into smaller villages or into the mountains, you may encounter dirt roads that are sometimes rutted to washboards or with potholes, slower speed limits, and lots of winding lanes. Take it easy, and enjoy the adventure, but allow plenty of time for journeys off the beaten track.

If you're making a special trip to see a museum or other attraction, call ahead to be sure it's open that day. Hours may change seasonally, and opening days in New Mexico can change rather spontaneously!

ACOMA PUEBLO: THE SKY CITY

Rivaled in antiquity only by Taos Pueblo, the pueblo of Acoma is not only one of the oldest continuously occupied settlements in North America, it is arguably the most dramatic in its setting. Built atop a 367-foot-high sandstone mesa whose sheer cliffs fall steeply away to the desert below, the location was chosen for defensive purposes, and it is partly for this reason that it was among the most difficult of the pueblos for the Spanish conquerors to subdue and control. Located an hour's scenic drive west of Albuquerque, it's still an adventure not to be missed for anyone who wants a glimpse back into time. Sky City's San Esteban del Rey Mission Church dates back to as early as 1640, and the surrounding original adobe village on the 70-acre mesa top is as much as 500 years older than that. At 6,460 feet above sea level, its views of sky, mountains, and desert are magnificent. Acoma is famed for its fine traditional pottery, as well as jewelry and other craft items, which can be viewed at the Haak'u Museum and purchased at locations throughout the pueblo or at the Sky City Cultural Center. Tours and guided hikes by pueblo residents are available, and traditional festivals open to the public are held several times a year. While the mesa-top pueblo remains in its original condition as a designated National Historic Landmark, the nearby Sky City Casino Hotel provides accommodations for overnight visitors, gaming, and entertainment. There's also an RV park. Call ahead before visiting, as the pueblo may be closed to visitors some days for ceremonial events.

Acoma Pueblo is 65 miles west of Albuquerque. Take I-40 west to exit 102, and follow the signs 16 miles to the Sky City Cultural Center (800-747-0181; www.acomaskycity.org).

THE TURQUOISE TRAIL

On the east side of the Sandia Mountains—also known as "the greener side of the mountain"—the 62-mile Turquoise Trail National Scenic Byway runs from Albuquerque to Santa Fe along Highway 14, passing through old mining towns and offering splendid vistas of Cibola National Forest and the San Pedro, Ortiz, Jemez, and Sangre de Cristo Mountains. Take I-40 east to exit 175, for Highway 14 North. At this turnoff by Tijeras, you are at an elevation of 6,300 feet.

The first highlight along the trail is actually a digression to the Tinkertown Museum on NM 536/Sandia Crest Road—a left turn at Sandia Park. Open from April 1 through November 1, Tinkertown Museum houses an incredible collection of folk art and eclectic Americana, centered around animated hand-carved figures and miniature Western and circus scenes, all created by Ross J. Ward (505-281-5233, www.tinkertown.com; see the Attractions chapter for a full description). If you continue past Tinkertown Museum on NM 536, you'll rise on the winding road through the Cibola National Forest to the Sandia Peak ski area and then to the 10,678-foot Sandia Crest with panoramic views and hiking trails. If you're getting peckish by now, Sandia Crest House Gift Shop and Restaurant (505-243-0605) is handily located right at the crest, open year-round and serving snacks such as quesadillas and sandwiches. From the Highway 14 junction with NM 536, it's 1.5 miles to Tinkertown Museum, 6 miles to the ski area, and 14 miles to Sandia Crest, with picnic areas along the way. The mountain road to the crest is all paved and well maintained, but to drive it safely can be slower than you'd expect; allow an hour for the round trip, plus however long you want to stop at the top. You pass through five different ecological zones on the way, home to mule deer, bighorn sheep, black bear, and golden eagles. In winter be alert for snowstorms.

When you return to Highway 14, you'll want to check out the village of Golden, which earned its name from the site in the Ortiz Mountains that in 1825 created the first gold rush west of the Mississippi—even before the more famous California and Colorado gold rushes.

The buzziest town along the trail is Madrid (pronounced with the emphasis on the first syllable, MAH-drid, which makes it easier to distinguish from the Spanish city of the same name). Once a booming coal-mining town that fed the Santa Fe Railroad from the late 1800s, Madrid's fortunes changed when the demand for coal declined. The coal mines closed in 1954, and Madrid became a ghost town. It was revived in the 1970s when artists moved into the old cabins and claimed it as an arts colony. Now the main street along Highway 14 is lined with brightly painted storefronts housing funky and fun shops, restaurants, and around 30 art galleries (www.visitmadridnm.com). Madrid puts on a good show with its Fourth of July parade and its festive Christmas celebrations, decorations, and lights.

Take a peek into Madrid's history at the Old Coal Mine Museum, with its mining relics, a 1901 Richmond Steam Engine, and antique cars. Entry is via Old West Bar and Antiques, summer only between April and October, from Friday through Monday (2846 Hwy 14; 505-438-3780).

The Mine Shaft Tavern—a rugged former miners' haunt—boasts a 40-foot lodge-pole pine bar and mural paintings by Tinkertown Museum's Ross J. Ward. The green chile cheeseburger is a popular menu item at this roadhouse, built in 1944, serving breakfast, lunch, and dinner and hosting live music on the weekend. Restrooms, however, can appear rather neglected (2846 Highway 14; 505-473-0743; www.themineshaft tavern.com). A little farther along on the right, you'll find beautiful glasswork, fine art, jewelry, furniture, and lighting at the Jezebel Gallery and Glass Studio (2860 Highway 14; 505-471-3795/866-539-3235; www.jezebelgallery.com). This is a good stop to find out-of-the-ordinary home decor and desirable trinkets to suit all pockets, and at the rear of the gallery a soda fountain dispenses good old-fashioned floats, malts, ice cream, snacks, and more modern Starbucks coffee. Perch at one of a few small boardwalk tables outside to watch Madrid's comings and goings.

i Much of the movie *Wild Hogs,* starring John Travolta, Tim Allen, Martin Lawrence, and William H. Macy, was shot in Madrid.

A little farther along Highway 14, take a left turn for Cerrillos, which is set back slightly from the main highway, amid beautiful old trees—you could easily drive past the town if you didn't know it was there. Cerrillos was a mining area for turquoise and lead since at least the 1300s. Later turquoise mined here was used in Spanish crown jewels, and later still Cerrillos supplied turquoise to Tiffany & Co. In the town's 1880s peak, miners also extracted gold, silver, and zinc, and there were 21 saloons and four hotels in this busy frontier town, which was visited by Theodore Roosevelt and Thomas Edison. Today Cerrillos is a small, sleepy village, with a ghost-town feel and not remotely trendified in the Madrid style.

Still, it's worth a drive around the few blocks that form the center, where the quiet dirt streets and original structures make it easy to imagine you're back in the old Wild West.

Also note the Iglesia San José (Saint Joseph's Church), with its white bell tower and the saint's figure carved from a tree trunk out front. The church was built in 1922, and Sunday Mass is still celebrated here. The Casa Grande Trading Post, Cerrillos Turquoise Mining Museum, and a petting zoo with llamas and goats are all on the same property; the 28-room adobe hacienda has its front windows lined with hundreds of old glass bottles. Follow the signs to the scenic overview; the road dead-ends by the Casa Grande Trading Post, 17 Waldo Street; (505) 438-3008.

Upon arrival at the end of the Turquoise Trail just south of Santa Fe, you can go on into the City Different or join I-25 to zip back to Albuquerque. Information on all the Turquoise Trail towns and attractions is available at www.turquoisetrail.org.

SANTA FE

Santa Fe was formally settled for Spain by Governor Don Pedro de Peralta in 1609–10 as La Villa Real de la Santa Fe de San Francisco de Asis—the Royal City of the Holy Faith of Saint Francis of Assisi. Now more catchily known as "The City Different," Santa Fe, an hour's drive north of Albuquerque, is set at 7,000 feet above sea level and is America's oldest and highest capital city. Although there's tons here for culture vultures, foodies, and shoppers to enjoy, it's the picture-perfect charm of Santa Fe that first captures the affection of visitors. Old adobe buildings glow golden in the high-desert sun, fronted by patios colorful with hollyhocks and chile ristras, along pretty winding streets that were once wagon trails, all posed against the stunning backdrop of the Sangre de Cristo Mountains. Thanks to strict building codes, the city has maintained its old-time feel—there are no high-rise tower blocks to mar the views, and even modern constructions in historic districts must blend in with the existing Spanish Pueblo and Territorial styles. Santa Fe celebrates its 400th anniversary in 2010, and information on special anniversary events can be found at www.santafe400th.com.

Santa Fe is the fourth largest city in New Mexico, after Albuquerque, Las Cruces, and Rio Rancho, but with a population hovering around 70,000, it still has a fairly intimate atmosphere and is easy to navigate. On arrival head first to Santa Fe Plaza, the historical and social center of town. This is a good spot to get oriented from, with many sites of interest within easy walking distance, and the plaza also provides an immediate sense of the city. Laid out by Don Pedro de Peralta in front of the Palace of the Governors, the shady plaza is a pleasant place to sit and watch the passersby, and it hosts the annual Indian and Spanish market and other community events. The Palace of the Governors was built in 1610, as Santa Fe became the administrative center for the Spanish Empire north of Mexico. The Palace of the Governors, with its 4-foot-thick adobe walls and inner courtyard, is the oldest continually occupied public building in the country. Today Native American artisans display their handmade jewelry, arts, and crafts along the palace's long portal facing the plaza. You can tour the Palace of the Governors, which contains period rooms and historical exhibits, including the Tesoros de Devoción—or Treasures of Devotion—collection of *bultos, retablos,* and *crucifijos* dating from the late 1700s to 1900 and the Palace Press exhibit of 19th- and 20th-century printing techniques and equipment. Call ahead for the current schedule of free daily docent tours (105 West Palace Avenue; 505-476-5100; www.palaceofthegovernors.org).

Behind the Palace of the Governors, with admission to both included on the same entry ticket, is the New Mexico History Museum, opened in May 2009. This lively 96,000-square-foot museum is home to interactive and multimedia exhibits on the state's history, from its early indigenous peoples through Spanish colonization, the Mexican Period, and the U.S. territorial days of the Santa Fe Trail, up to the atomic age and flourishing arts life of modern New Mexico (113 Lincoln Avenue; 505-476-5200; www.nmhistory museum.org).

Long established as an arts colony, Santa Fe is reckoned to be America's third-largest art market by sales. However, you don't have to an art lover to enjoy a stroll along Canyon Road, an eight-block stretch of old adobe houses, many of which are now home to around 100 art galleries, plus a sprinkling of cafés and restaurants. Canyon Road leads off Paseo de Peralta, south of East Alameda Street, and there are often gallery openings and artist events on Friday evenings, when the neighborhood has a festive open-house feel (www.canyonroadarts.com). The city also breaks out an arts party on the plaza for Spanish Market in July, with traditional Spanish colonial crafts that include santos, tinwork, handcrafted furniture, and weavings, and for Indian Market, usually held on the third weekend in August, when over a thousand Native American artisans representing around 100 tribes sell their handcrafted wares. On the second full weekend in July, the Santa Fe International Folk Art Market, considered the world's largest international folk art market, is held at Museum Hill with artists from around 40 countries and live entertainment.

i **Make hotel reservations well in advance if you're visiting Santa Fe during the July and August Indian, Spanish, and International Folk Art Markets, as city accommodations quickly fill.**

Museum Hill is a plaza of four excellent museums and the Museum Hill Café (open for lunch) on Camino Lejo, a little over 2 miles from the Santa Fe Plaza. The Museum of Spanish Colonial Art, in a converted home designed by John Gaw Meem, presents over 3,000 objects from throughout the Spanish colonial world, covering five centuries and four continents (750 Camino Lejo; 505-982-2226; www.spanishcolonial

.org). The Museum of Indian Arts and Culture leads you through the lives of southwestern native cultures, with artifacts that include pottery, basketwork, jewelry, and weavings and audio exhibits of Native Americans sharing their stories and songs (710 Camino Lejo; 505-476-1250; www.miaclab.org). The eight-sided building housing the Wheelwright Museum of the American Indian is inspired by a traditional Navajo *hooghan*. New Mexico's oldest private nonprofit museum, it showcases changing exhibits of Native American art (704 Camino Lejo; 505-982-4636; www.wheelwright.org). You'll find the world's largest collection of folk art from around the world at the Museum of International Folk Art. There are over 135,000 objects here, including textiles, religious art, and toys (706 Camino Lejo; 505-476-1200; www.moifa.org). The "M" line bus connects Santa Fe Plaza to Museum Hill, in a 15-minute ride that runs hourly, seven days a week, from the Santa Fe Trails downtown transit center on Sheridan Avenue, just off the plaza, one block west of the New Mexico Museum of Art.

i **Some Santa Fe Museums are closed on Monday or only open seasonally on Monday, so check before heading off.**

Other major arts attractions around Santa Fe Plaza include the New Mexico Museum of Art, in a 1917 Pueblo Revival–style building by architects I. H. Rapp and William M. Rapp. The museum holds over 20,000 art pieces in its collections, including works by New Mexico and international artists, including Peter Hurd, Ansel Adams, Georgia O'Keeffe, Agnes Martin, Elliot Porter, Gustave Baumann, Maria Martinez, and Bruce Naumann (107 West Palace Avenue; 505-476-5072; www.nmartmuseum.org; this museum changed its name from the Museum of Fine Arts in 2007). The Georgia O'Keeffe Museum (217 Johnson Street; 505-946-1000; www.okeeffemuseum.org) is a beautiful modern gallery that perfectly complements the world's largest permanent collection of O'Keeffe's paintings, drawings, and sculptures. It opened in 1997, 11 years after O'Keeffe's death. It's worth renting the audio tour guide here, with interesting narration and background on the art.

Art by and about native peoples is found in the National Collection of Contemporary Native American Art, the largest collection of its kind in the world, at the Institute of American Indian Arts Museum. More than 120 Native American nations are represented in over 7,000 works, in addition to touring exhibitions (108 Cathedral Place; 505-983-1777; www.iaia.edu).

In July and August the Santa Fe Opera performs at its splendid open-air amphitheatre, dramatically set on a hilltop 7 miles north of Santa Fe Plaza. The curving roof of the opera house protects against the elements, while the sides are open to views of the rolling desert landscape and night skies. Performances begin at sundown but arrive earlier—the outdoor bars and terraces offer great sunset views. The parking lot opens three hours before curtain time, and some patrons bring picnics for tailgating parties. Once you are in your seat, you can read a translation of the libretto on a display on the chair back in front of you (exit 168 on US 84/285; 505-986-5900; www.santafeopera.org).

The Lensic Performing Arts Center is a 1931 vaudeville and movie palace whose stage has been graced by such stars as Rita Hayworth, Judy Garland, and Yehudi Menuhin. After an $8.2 million renovation, the Lensic reopened in 2001 as an 800-seat arts center and is home to theater; music concerts, including the Santa Fe Symphony Orchestra; classic and contemporary dance, including Aspen Santa Fe Ballet; and a host of international and regional performers from comedians to acrobats. Santa Fe's Lannan Foundation also hosts author and speaker events here—previous literary highlights have included Pulitzer Prize–winning novelist Annie Proulx (211 West San Francisco Street; 505-988-7050; www.lensic.com).

The Cathedral Basilica of St. Francis of Assisi was built from 1869 and dedicated in 1887 under the direction of Santa Fe's first bishop—and later first archbishop—John Baptiste Lamy of France. Lamy brought French architects and Italian stonemasons to New Mexico to work on the Romanesque-style cathedral, and stained glass windows from France can be seen in the lower bay. The cathedral stands on the site of an older church that was destroyed during the 1680 Pueblo Revolt. In 2005 Pope Benedict XVI elevated the cathedral to a basilica, indicating its special importance in Catholic history. Many locals still refer to it by its familiar former name of St. Francis Cathedral, and its landmark twin bell towers dominate the southeastern view from the plaza. Archbishop Lamy and six other archbishops are buried here, and a statue brought from Spain in 1625 is considered the oldest Madonna in North America. Mass is held every day, including Spanish Mass on Sunday morning. There is a gift store by the front entrance (213 Cathedral Place; 505-982-5619; www.cbsfa.org).

The Gothic Revival Loretto Chapel was designed by the same French architects that designed the Cathedral Basilica of St. Francis of Assisi. Built between 1873 and 1878 and styled after King Louis IX's 13th-century Sainte Chapelle in Paris, this Santa Fe treasure is popular for weddings. Just like the cathedral basilica, it features stained glass from France that somehow survived the journey across the ocean and then a wagon ride along Old Santa Fe Trail. However, the Loretto Chapel's most famous mystery is the Miraculous Staircase. Upon completion of the Loretto Chapel, the space constraints were such that it was impossible to access the choir loft, except via a ladder—or so insisted the local carpenters. The legend continues that, after the Sisters of Loretto (meaning light) prayed to St. Joseph, patron saint of carpenters, a mysterious man rode up on a donkey seeking work. He set to building a spiral staircase with two 360-degree turns and no apparent means of support, then promptly disappeared without pay. The Miraculous Staircase, built some time between 1877 and 1881, was an innovative feat at the time, and some aspects of the construction are still under debate. Of course, some people reckon it was St. Joseph himself who arrived to help the sisters out of the dilemma. The Loretto Chapel was deconsecrated as a Catholic chapel in 1971 and is now a private museum (207 Old Santa Fe Trail; 505-982-0092; www.lorettochapel.com).

i Santa Fe's newly revitalized Railyard District is home to the New Mexico Rail Runner Express Santa Fe Depot, plus a small but growing number of shops, galleries, and restaurants; the farmers' market; and a 10-acre park at the south end. The area is bordered by Guadalupe Street and Cerrillos Road, and the Rail Runner station is about a half mile south or a 15-minute walk from the downtown plaza. Buses to downtown also serve the station; www.railyardsantafe.com.

Santa Fe's ski area lies 16 miles northeast of the city in the Sangre de Cristo Mountains. Base elevation is 10,350 feet, with chairlifts to 12,075 feet, and 72 trails run across 660 acres of the gorgeous Santa Fe National Forest. Twenty percent of the trails are designated "easier," with the remainder split between intermediate and difficult/expert runs. The longest trail is 3 miles. Average snowfall is 225 inches, and the season usually runs from Thanksgiving to around Easter. The Ski Santa Fe area welcomes skiers and snowboarders, and the "Bone Yard" Freestyle Terrain Park has features suitable for beginners to intermediates. Kids have their own ski and play areas. The ski area is at the end of New Mexico State Highway 475. Turn off Paseo de Peralta on the north side of town by the pink Scottish Rite Temple, onto Bishop's Lodge Road (Washington Avenue). Take a right onto Artist Road, which becomes Hyde Park Road, and follow the road up the mountain to the ski basin (505-982-4429; www.skisantafe.com).

Ten Thousand Waves is one of Santa Fe's oldest day spas and a perennial favorite with locals and visitors alike. The Japanese-style spa is a beautifully landscaped, serene haven about 20 minutes' drive from the plaza, in the piñon-studded foothills leading up to the ski area. You have a choice of soaking in the communal hot tubs or in private tubs. No reservations are required for the communal tubs—one mixed, one women only, and both featuring a sundeck, wet/dry sauna, plunge pool, and shower. The women-only tub is clothing optional at all times. The mixed tub is clothing optional until 8:15 p.m., when bathing suits are required (suits are available for rent). If nudity bothers you, be aware that most people do strip off, but nobody looks askance if you choose to keep your swimsuit on. You can also reserve a variety of private tubs for 55-minute periods, set in the natural environment, and some have features such as waterfalls. It's wise to make advance bookings for private tubs, although some might be available to walk-ins. The spa menu includes a broad range of massages, body treatments, and facials, including the Nightingale cleansing masque, made from (sanitized) droppings of Japanese nightingales. If you want to stay overnight, lodging is in a number of stylish and peaceful Japanese-style "Houses of the Moon." Note that there's no restaurant on site—day guests buy healthy and tasty snacks from the spa store in the reception area—but accommodations have microwaves and fridges; a couple offer full kitchens; and all rooms are supplied with granola, fruit, coffee, and tea. The admission fee to the spa and hot tubs includes a kimono, sandals, towels, lockers, tea, and well-equipped changing and shower rooms with toiletries. To reach Ten Thousand Waves, follow the same directions as for the ski area above. The spa is 3.4 miles on the left from the turn onto Artist Road, which becomes Hyde Park Road (3451 Hyde Park Road; 505-992-5025; www.tenthousandwaves.com).

You're spoiled for choice in this gastronomic city, with options ranging from homely local cantinas, to innovative chefs putting a fresh twist on classic southwestern cuisine, plus contemporary American, European, and Asian restaurants. Favorite Santa Fe–style restaurants around the plaza include Cafe Pasqual's, run by Chef Katharine Kagel and named after San Pasqual, the folk saint of kitchens and cooks. The intimate and festive dining room is decorated with colorful banners, Mexican tile, and murals by Mexican artist Leovigildo Martinez, and the largely organic menu offers new spins on New Mexican, Old Mexican, and Asian cuisine. Cafe Pasqual's serves breakfast, lunch, and dinner, and breakfast options range from huevos rancheros to *tamal dulce*—a tamal of sweet corn and raisin wrapped in banana leaves and served with black beans, mango, and Mexican hot chocolate. At lunch and dinner try the chicken and vegetarian mole enchiladas or the hearts of romaine salad with Maytag blue cheese, roast beets, and Asian pear with a spicy kick of Chile Pecans. Cafe Pasqual serves beer and wine (121 Don Gaspar Avenue; 505-983-9340; www.pasquals.com).

The Shed is tucked away in a 1692 adobe hacienda, with a series of nine cozy rooms leading off each other and patio dining out front on the spacious brick courtyard. Lunch and dinner is served at this family-owned restaurant, with a menu combining Pueblo, Spanish, and Mexican

i **Around 1.2 to 1.4 million people visit the City Different every year. Most travelers come between April and October, with July, August, and October being peak months.**

i **The Bell Tower Bar at the La Fonda on the Plaza hotel is a top spot for watching the sunset—literally. The fifth-floor open-air bar offers great views over the city and serves a mean margarita. The bar is open April to October, weather permitting. Fonda means "inn," and there's been a fonda on this site since Santa Fe's earliest days, including a former Harvey House. While staying here in 1925, author Willa Cather got the idea to write *Death Comes for the Archbishop,* her excellent and evocative historical novel based on the life of Archbishop Lamy (100 E. San Francisco Street; 800-523-5002; www.lafondasantafe.com).**

flavors. The notable house chile is grown in Hatch, New Mexico, exclusively for the restaurant and prepared fresh each day. Signature dishes include red chile enchilada with a fried egg on top and *carne adovada* for those who like it spicy. They also serve super soups here, good green chile stew with potato and pork, blue-corn tortillas with all traditional dishes, and some decadent desserts, including knockout zabaglione, and rich mocha cake. A full bar is available. The Shed is located at 113½ East Palace Avenue; (505) 982-9030; www.sfshed.com.

Santa Fe is approximately 63 miles north of Downtown Albuquerque, an hour's drive via I-25. You can also take the Turquoise Trail route to Santa Fe described elsewhere in this chapter. The Sandia Shuttle Express offers at least 13 daily bus shuttles each way between Albuquerque airport and Santa Fe (888-775-5696; www.sandiashuttle.com), or catch the New Mexico Rail Runner Express from Albuquerque, which takes about 90 minutes to get to the Santa Fe Depot, depending on the train you choose (www.nmrailrunner.com).

i **The Santa Fe Convention and Visitors Bureau is located at 201 W. Marcy Street and is open Monday through Saturday for visitor information. You also can call (505) 955-6200 / (800) 777-2489 or visit the Web site, www.santafe.org. At the Web site or by phone, you can request a free visitor's guide to be sent by mail.**

GEORGIA O'KEEFFE COUNTRY—GHOST RANCH AND ABIQUIU

If you're familiar with the New Mexico landscapes of artist Georgia O'Keeffe, you're bound to spot some familiar scenes in the red-rock country about 130 miles north of Albuquerque. O'Keeffe fell in love with this area—so much so that she moved here from New York and spent five decades capturing its austere beauty on canvas. She bought two properties here, one at Ghost Ranch and the other in Abiquiu, and divided her time between them. Both are now owned by the Georgia O'Keeffe Museum in Santa Fe.

Ghost Ranch

Owned since 1955 by the Presbyterian Church, Ghost Ranch is a 21,000-acre educational and retreat center. Ghost Ranch is traditionally known as El Rancho de los Brujos—Ranch of the Witches. O'Keeffe didn't own or live in the entire ranch but purchased a seven-acre property, called Rancho de los Burros, here in 1940, which became her summer home and the base for her art inspired by her beloved Ghost Ranch landscapes. O'Keeffe's personal property is not open to the public, but from mid-March to mid-November, you can take a one-hour guided tour of the Ghost Ranch lands to see the sites so precious to O'Keeffe; 90-minute horseback tours are also offered. There are only a handful of tours each week, and reservations are required; call (505) 685-4333. Ghost Ranch hosts numerous residential retreats and workshops throughout the year, including workshops for artists, photographers, and writers, as well as hiking and outdoor adventures. Day visitors are welcome, although, if you're traveling a long way, it's worth calling ahead to check that facilities are open, in case of special circumstances. On arrival register at the front desk.

There are several hiking trails from the central building; ask for trail maps and safety information. Note that you're quickly into remote country here, so be sure to take water, wear sensible hiking shoes and sun protection, and take the usual precautions when heading out. The Chimney Rock trail, about a 3-mile round trip of 90 minutes' to 2 hours' duration, takes you up to a spectacular 7,100-foot overview of the Chimney Rock spire and the entire Piedra Lumbre basin below, including Abiquiu Lake and the unmistakable profile of Cerro Pedernal to the south. The Pedernal, a 9,862-foot mountain with a broad, flat top, was immortalized by O'Keeffe, who considered it her own private mountain. She insisted that God had told her if she painted it enough times, he would give it to her. The

Chimney Rock trail is best taken early in the day or in late afternoon, when it's cooler. Other trails take you into a shady box canyon, to Kitchen Mesa, and along the Piedra Lumbre hike. Round trips vary from 3 to 5 miles, and the hikes are of varying difficulty from level to steep. The base elevation at Ghost Ranch is 6,500 feet. There's a Trading Post store in the main center.

Paleontologists struck dinosaur gold in this area, with findings of articulated fossils of the Coelophysis (New Mexico's state fossil), and Ghost Ranch's Ruth Hall Museum of Paleontology exhibits include a complete Coelophysis cast skeleton. The Florence Hawley Ellis Museum of Anthropology contains pottery and other artifacts excavated on digs in the Gallina, Chama, and Rio Grande region, plus contemporary arts and crafts from Native, Hispanic, and Anglo artisans. Both museums are closed on Monday.

Just north of the main Ghost Ranch entrance, the Piedra Lumbre Education and Visitor Center is located between mile markers 225 and 226. There are displays here on regional geology, paleontology, archaeology, and northern New Mexican culture and history, including touring exhibits from the New Mexico Museum of Natural History and Science. The visitor center hosts art shows, and there's a gift shop and outdoor picnic areas. The Piedra Lumbre Education and Visitor Center is closed on Monday and shuts down over the winter from October 31 to April 1.

Simple accommodations are available at Ghost Ranch, if it's not filled up with a retreat. These are mostly dormitory style, with a few private rooms, and there are also camping grounds. Dorms and private rooms are basic—they don't have TV, phones, or locks on the doors—but you can't beat the location.

Ghost Ranch is located on US 84, approximately 130 miles from Albuquerque. Take I-25 North to the 599 bypass around Santa Fe, then take US 84/285 north to Española. Follow signs in Española for US 84 to your left, toward Chama. Remain on US 84 North, passing though Abiquiu. Ghost Ranch is signed on your right between mile markers 224 and 225, about 13 miles north of Bode's Store in Abiquiu (505-685-4333 or 877-804-4678; www.ghostranch.org).

Abiquiu

In 1945 Georgia O'Keeffe bought a house in Abiquiu (pronounced ABeecue), in addition to her existing property at Ghost Ranch about 13 miles away. At first she split her time between New Mexico and New York, but after her photographer husband, Alfred Stieglitz, died, she moved permanently to New Mexico in 1949. Between March and November you can take a tour of O'Keeffe's Abiquiu home and studio, a 5,000-square-foot 18th-century Spanish colonial compound that was in ruins when O'Keeffe bought it. She directed its restoration with the aid of her friend Maria Chabot. The guided tour lasts about an hour and leads you through the house that is left much as it was when O'Keeffe, due to ill health, moved to Santa Fe in 1984, two years before she died. The fascinating tour of the reclusive artist's private home and studio, led by well-informed and lively guides, is packed with details describing O'Keeffe's life here and pointing out views that she painted from her studio. The March to November tours are operated by the Santa Fe Georgia O'Keeffe Museum, at set times and by appointment only. Numbers are limited to twelve visitors per tour, and you can't bring cameras or large bags or make notes or sketches. Due to the limited availability, tours often get booked three or four months in advance, so make reservations early.

The tour leaves from a tour office by the Abiquiu Inn, to avoid too much traffic into the small and private village of Abiquiu itself, set above Highway 84. You must arrive in good time so you don't miss the minibus that takes you on the couple of minutes' drive to O'Keeffe's house. Aim to get there even a bit earlier and grab a drink or a bite to eat first at the Abiquiu Inn's restaurant. Also use the restrooms here or in the tour office—there are none at the house. Make tour reservations with the Georgia O'Keeffe Museum by calling (505) 685-4539 or find information at the Web site: www.okeeffemuseum.org.

About a mile north of Abiquiu Inn on Highway 84, Bode's Store is a gas station and all-purpose store selling outdoor gear, gifts, general supplies, groceries, beer, wine, and spirits, and the place is pretty spirited, serving as a local trading post for this quiet corner of the Rio Chama Valley. Bode's Cafe and deli is a bargain stop for travelers hungry for a burrito, burger, Frito pie, and home-baked pastries (505-685-4422; www.bodes.com).

If you want to stop overnight, the Abiquiu Inn offers a choice of 19 casitas and suites comfortably decorated in southwestern style. Some feature viga ceilings, kiva fireplaces, full kitchens, and verandahs or patios, with a number of casitas arranged around a pretty courtyard and fountain. The green and wooded grounds around the inn are pleasantly landscaped and peaceful. The inn's friendly restaurant—Café Abiquiu—serves breakfast, lunch, and dinner. The cooking here is good and tasty, offering a broad menu of southwestern dishes, including vegetarian options. The restaurant is not licensed for any kind of alcohol, although it's fine for residents to bring their own if they want to take out their restaurant order and dine "at home" in their casita. The Abiquiu Inn gift shop is crammed with O'Keeffe memorabilia and books, plus a large selection of New Mexican and Native American arts, crafts, textiles, and regional souvenirs.

To drive to the Abiquiu Inn (21120 Highway 84), about 115 miles from Albuquerque, take I-25 North to the 599 bypass around Santa Fe, then take US 84/285 north to Española. Follow signs in Española for US 84 to your left, toward Chama. Remain on US 84 North to Abiquiu. The Abiquiu Inn is on your right, 3 miles past the SR 554 turnoff (505-685-4378 or 888-735-2902; www.abiquiuinn.com).

OJO CALIENTE MINERAL SPRINGS

Ojo Caliente Mineral Springs Resort and Spa opened as a health spa in 1868, although recent renovations have spruced up this popular destination for stressed-out New Mexicans seeking to soak their cares away. As a side trip from Abiquiu, it takes about 30 minutes to drive to Ojo Caliente. From Albuquerque it's approximately 112 miles. Ojo Caliente's sulphur-free, geothermal waters originate from an underground volcanic aquifer, and the 10 pools set under the rock cliffs, including 3 private pools, are fed by waters from an iron spring, a soda spring, and an arsenic spring. A pump dispenses water to drink from the lithia spring, reputed to aid depression and digestion. Water temperatures range from 80° to 109°F. Don't miss the mud pool (open seasonally, May to October). After covering yourself with warm clay, you let it bake dry in the sun, then jump into the pool to wash it off. Facilities include poolside lounging decks and a sauna and steam room. Bathing suits are required in the public pools. No reservations are needed for day guests to the public springs; admission includes one towel. A locker for stashing your gear is free, but if you want to actually lock it, bring your own padlock or purchase a padlock at the front desk. You can also rent a robe. Booking is recommended for the private pools, which feature kiva fireplaces and are available to rent in periods from 50 minutes upward. The spa menu offers facials, massages, and body and nail treatments. If you want to sleep over after a relaxing day at the springs, a wide range of accommodation options includes Cliffside suites with their own private outdoor tubs, cottages with a patio and kitchenette, and rooms in the main hotel building. There is also an RV park and tent camping along the Rio Ojo Caliente. Breakfast, lunch, and dinner are served in the Artesian Restaurant, a casual and friendly spot for good New Mexican and international dishes. Next to the restaurant, a new wine bar and lounge offers a bar menu. From Albuquerque the drive is around 112 miles. Take I-25 North to the 599 bypass around Santa Fe, then take US 84/285 north to Española. Follow signs in Española for US 84/285 to your left, toward Chama. Once on 84/285, turn right just past the Chevron station on the right to US 285 north. Follow 285 for 16.7 miles to Ojo Caliente, and look for the sign to the Ojo Caliente Mineral Springs left turnoff, just after mile marker 353 (50 Los Baños Drive, Ojo Caliente; 505-583-2233, 800-222-9162; ojocalientesprings.com).

i When setting off into more remote areas of New Mexico, make sure you have a full tank of gas. There are sometimes long intervals between gas stations.

TAOS

Famed for its natural beauty and classic northern New Mexico ambience, its vivid arts scene, and its tricultural heritage, Taos (approximately 135 miles north of Albuquerque) is considered by many to embody the essence of the "Land of Enchantment." Tucked at 7,000 feet beneath the Sangre de Cristo Mountains, between the heights of Taos Mountain and the depths of the Rio Grande Gorge, Taos is popular with motorcyclists, art enthusiasts, hikers, skiers, history buffs, and anyone who enjoys a strikingly beautiful outdoor setting without sacrificing the comforts of fine dining, charming lodging, and an open, anything-goes atmosphere in which everyone seems to be an artist, a writer, a musician, or a mystic. Taos has been known as a countercultural haven since the early part of the 20th century. Curious visitors continue to arrive looking for the original settings of the movie *Easy Rider* or the perfect spot to build an off-the-grid Earthship out of recycled materials or perhaps, if they are fortunate, hear the elusive "Taos hum." Depending on whom you talk to, this mysterious low-frequency phenomenon could be a spiritually generated vibe, the product of government or extraterrestrial interventions, or entirely nonexistent.

Driving up from Albuquerque on Highway 68, you'll enter the Rio Grande Gorge the last 30 minutes before hitting Taos. Traveling along the winding gorge road by the river, you might spot rafters running the white water, and you'll pass through villages with orchards and small organic farms nourished by the fertile river valley bed. In summer look for roadside fruit stands—Sopyns at Rinconada is one of the largest, decorated with dozens of chile ristras for sale. As you emerge from the gorge and crest the approach to Taos, a spectacular vista reveals itself at the Horseshoe Curve, with a pullout and an overlook at the top. From here you can see the Rio Grande Gorge crack the earth apart across the mesa to the west, with Taos Mountain ahead dominating the north end of the Taos valley.

When you enter Taos environs, the first community you pass through is Ranchos de Taos. Turn right into St. Francis Plaza to see the San Francisco de Asis church (505-758-2754). The curving organic lines and massive buttresses of this adobe Spanish Mission church have been immortalized by numerous painters, most famously Georgia O'Keeffe, and photographers including Ansel Adams and Paul Strand. Building began on this Spanish Mission church in the late 1700s and was completed in 1815. The thick fortresslike walls were a defense against raiding Apache, Comanche, and Ute tribes. To maintain the adobe walls, the local community remuds the walls every spring, with young and old pitching in. There is also a parish office and shop in the plaza, a café, and a few galleries and gift stores. San Francisco de Asis church is often referred to locally as the Ranchos church. It's oriented with the rear facing the main road. The right turn into the plaza is immediately before the Ranchos Post Office and traffic lights—the first traffic lights you'll encounter when entering Taos from the south.

The center of Taos is easily walkable, if you focus on the few blocks around the Taos plaza. The plaza—formally the Don Fernando de Taos Plaza, although nobody ever calls it that—has been a center of trading from the early Spanish colonial years. While the plaza itself used to be a main hub

i Pick up a copy of the weekly *Taos News,* published on Thursday. The Tempo arts and leisure supplement tells you everything going on during the week ahead, from festivals to art openings and live music; www.taosnews.com.

Taos has been dubbed the Solar Capital of the World; even the local radio station is powered by the sun. Tune into KTAO solar radio at 101.9 FM. Or stream it on the Web to warm up to the Taos vibe before you arrive: www.ktao.com.

of the local community, today it's heavy on souvenir shops, and Taoseños tend to gather elsewhere in the surrounding downtown area. There are a few notable exceptions, however, and a first-time visitor should definitely start with a stroll around the plaza. In the summer a series of Taos Plaza Live (www.taosplazalive.com) free music concerts are held here on Thursday evenings, and these lively events presenting some of the best regional bands and singers draw a cheerful toe-tapping (or outright boogying) crowd. Over the Christmas holidays glowing *farolitos* (votive candles in brown paper bags) line the plaza around the gazebo and town Christmas tree.

The Pueblo Revival–style Hotel La Fonda de Taos (575-758-2211, 800-833-2211, www.lafonda taos.com) on the south side of the plaza opened in 1937, although there has been a fonda, or inn, on this site since around 1820. Hotel La Fonda is home to author D. H. Lawrence's "Forbidden Art" collection—paintings by Lawrence that were considered obscene and banned in England in 1929. The images wouldn't raise any eyebrows now, and you can view them for a small fee. Inside the hotel you'll also find Joseph's Table restaurant and Butterfly Bar. Joseph Wrede is Taos's star chef, named by *Food & Wine* magazine in 2000 as one of "America's Ten Best New Chefs." The restaurant and bar ambience is elegantly cozy, the service immaculate, and the food superb, with innovative flavor combinations (575-751-4512; www .josephstable.com).

On the north side of Taos Plaza, walk through the connecting alley to the John Dunn House shops and Bent Street, where there are restaurants and cafés and outdoor entertainers, and you can shop for fashion, gorgeous yarns and textiles, hand-tooled leather goods, and gifts. One of the town's two best bookstores is here: Moby Dickens has a broad range of titles, including a strong mystery section, on two floors (124A Bent Street, 6 Dunn House; 575-758-3050; www .mobydickens.com). Brodsky Bookshop is the oldest bookstore in Taos and carries both new and used titles (226A Paseo del Pueblo Norte; 575-758-9468; www.taosbooks.com). Both stores have a good selection of Southwest titles and books by local Taos authors, including signed copies, and both host author events. Around the plaza and downtown area, you'll also find numerous art galleries.

Ledoux Street, southwest of the plaza, is a narrow, winding street lined with art galleries and photography studios in old adobe buildings. It's anchored at the far end by the Harwood Museum—the second oldest museum in New Mexico, founded in 1923 and owned by the University of New Mexico since 1936. It is Taos's flagship museum, and its permanent collection is an excellent introduction to the artistic heritage of the Taos region, with over 1,700 art works and a 17,000-strong photographic archive, from the 19th century to the current day. It also hosts temporary art exhibits. Highlights include paintings from the Taos Society of Artists, including Ernest Leonard Blumenschein, Oscar Edmund Berninghaus, and Victor Higgins, and works from American Modernists Marsden Hartley and John Marin. Upstairs you'll find a superb collection of 19th-century retablos and bultos and traditional New Mexican tinwork and hand-carved furniture. The octagonal Agnes Martin Gallery—a striking and meditative space—was built specifically to display seven oil paintings by Martin, who was a resident of Taos until her death in 2004. The museum is housed in a mid-19th-century adobe compound, remodeled by artist Burt Harwood between 1916 and 1918 into a handsome example of Pueblo Revival–style architecture and later expanded by John Gaw Meem. The gift store sells art books and jewelry, textiles, and decorative arts by local artisans (238 Ledoux Street; 575-758-9826; harwoodmuseum.org.) Also on Ledoux Street, the Blumenschein Home & Museum is kept much as it was when this cofounder of the Taos Society of Artists lived here. The oldest part of the house was built in 1797, and the home includes the personal belongings, paintings, and antiques of E. L. Blumenschein and his wife, Mary Greene Blumenschein, also an acclaimed artist (222 Ledoux Street; 575-758-0505; taosmuseums.org).

The Taos Art Museum has a fine collection of over 300 paintings by more than fifty Taos artists, including the masters of the Taos Society of Artists and Taos Moderns. The collection is housed in the studio and home of Russian artist Nicolai Fechin, built between 1927 and 1933, which blends Russian, Native American, and Spanish styles (227 Paseo del Pueblo Norte; 575-758-2690; www.taosartmuseum.org).

The Millicent Rogers Museum displays over 1,200 pieces of southwestern jewelry from the glamorous Standard Oil heiress Mary Millicent Rogers's own collection. Gathered during her years in New Mexico, when Rogers lobbied for the recognition of Native American arts, the jewelry represents traditional regional styles of Indian and Hispanic silversmiths and artisans. The museum also holds Rogers's collection of textiles and Navajo weavings, plus pottery, basketwork, Hopi and Zuni kachina dolls, and Hispanic religious and colonial arts, including santos, tinwork, and hand-carved furniture. A substantial collection of Maria Martinez pottery, donated by Martinez's family to the museum, includes not only the famous glossy black Martinez pottery but also photos, documents, and memorabilia. The Millicent Rogers Museum is located at 1504 Millicent Rogers Road, 4 miles north of Taos Plaza (575-758-2462; millicentrogers.org).

i The Taos Visitor Center is open seven days at 1139 Paseo del Pueblo Sur. You pass it as you drive into Taos from Highway 68, on the right corner at the traffic light intersection with Paseo del Cañon. Visitor information is also available from (575) 758-3873 or (800) 348-0696; taos vacationguide.com.

Taos Pueblo, a National Historic Landmark and UNESCO World Heritage Site, has stood at the base of sacred Taos Mountain for nearly 1,000 years, its multistoried adobe structure providing shelter to generation upon generation of Native Americans. Open to the public for a reasonable entrance fee (extra charge if you want to take photos or use your video camera), the site appears today much as it did when first seen by Spanish explorers in the 1500s. The two main structures are called Hlauuma (north house) and Hlaukwima (south house) and are regarded as the oldest continually inhabited communities in the United States. Approximately 150 Taos Indians live within the pueblo full time, where they keep to the old ways and have no electricity or running water. However, over 1,900 people live on Taos Pueblo lands in all, mostly in contemporary homes, with the old pueblo remaining the center of ceremony and tribal government. (Taos Pueblo is a sovereign nation, with independent authority to govern within its own territories, an area of 99,000 acres, most of it undeveloped.)

i A $25 combination ticket from the Museum Association of Taos gives access to five museums: Harwood Museum of Art, Millicent Rogers Museum, Taos Art Museum at Fechin House, E. L. Blumenschein Home & Museum, and La Hacienda de los Martinez. The combo ticket saves money on the regular admission rates and is valid for a year. Buy it from any of the member museums: taosmuseums.org.

Upon arrival at the pueblo, find out when the next guided tour is leaving. These informative and engaging tours by pueblo residents are highly recommended to get acquainted with the history, architecture, culture, and character of this beautiful old pueblo and its people. The patron saint of Taos Pueblo is St. Jerome, and the San Geronimo or St. Jerome chapel, built in 1850, is popular with photographers, with its squared bell towers and high white cross against the crisp turquoise sky. No photography is allowed inside

Close-up

Taos Art Colony

Taos's reputation as an arts colony dates back to the "broken wheel" incident of September 3, 1898, when two artists, Bert G. Phillips and Ernest L. Blumenschein, were traveling from Denver to Mexico and their wagon wheel broke 20 miles north of Taos, near the village of Questa. They tossed a three-dollar gold piece to see who'd carry the wheel to the nearest blacksmith for repair. Blumenschein lost, and off he rode to Taos. Fascinated by Taos and the pueblo, the artists stayed on to paint the land and people even after the wheel was fixed. Blumenschein returned to New York City after two months, leaving Phillips to make his home in Taos, and they corresponded with each other about the idea of starting an art colony. They encouraged other artists to visit, who also took a shine to Taos. In 1915 Blumenschein, Phillips, Oscar E. Berninghaus, E. Irving Couse, W. Herbert "Buck" Dunton, and Joseph Sharp formed the Taos Society of Artists. The society promoted members' work through traveling exhibitions to other cities, which drew further attention to Taos and attracted more artists to Taos. There were ultimately 19 members in the Taos Society of Artists, with Walter Ufer, Victor Higgins, Catherine Critcher, E. Martin Hennings, and Kenneth Adams, plus associate members Robert Henri, John Sloan, Julius Rolshoven, Albert Groll, Randall Davey, BJO Nordfelt, Birger Sandzen, and Gustave Baumann. The group disbanded in 1927. By this point Taos was already making its name as a significant art colony. This was championed further by New York heiress and patron of the arts Mabel Dodge Luhan, who moved to Taos, established a series of arts salons, and invited all number of creative stars to visit, including Georgia O'Keeffe, Willa Cather, Ansel Adams, D. H. Lawrence, and Martha Graham.

the church, however. You can still see the remains of the original mission church on the west side of the village, largely destroyed by the U.S. army in 1847 during the war with Mexico. Special events open to the public include San Geronimo Feast Day on September 29, as well as the Procession of the Blessed Mother on Christmas Eve, followed by the dramatic lighting of enormous bonfires throughout the pueblo. Public ceremonial dances occur on Christmas and New Year's Day (cameras and cell phones are not allowed for ceremonial and feast days). Taos Pueblo also hosts its Annual Taos Pueblo Pow Wow in July. Some 40 shops and galleries provide a large sampling of traditional pueblo arts and crafts, including mica pottery, silver jewelry, animal-skin moccasins and drums, and visual arts. Some pueblo artists also work in more contemporary forms—such as the outstanding photography of Bruce Gomez and the rock-meets-traditional-Native-flute music of two-time Grammy winner Robert Mirabal. The pueblo is closed to the public for private ceremonial purposes during part of the winter and early spring. Call or visit the Web site for closure days. There are two entrances to Taos Pueblo: Proceeding north from the plaza on Paseo del Pueblo Norte/Highway 64, take the right fork at Allsup's gas station. Or continue on Paseo del Pueblo Norte to the next signed entrance, about a mile along on the right. From either, it's a mile to the pueblo parking area, and both entrance roads lead you past Taos Mountain Casino (575-737-0777, 888-946-8267), a smallish smoke-free casino with slots and some table games. Taos Pueblo visitor information is available at 575-758-1028, www.taospueblo.com.

The Rio Grande Gorge Bridge spans the craggy chasm of the gorge at a height of 650

i Hernando Alvarado arrived in Taos Valley in 1540, as part of the Coronado expedition. Taos was established as a Spanish village by 1615, complete with an appointed *alcalde,* or mayor. The Town of Taos was incorporated in 1934.

feet above the river. You can park at the side of the bridge and walk to the middle for the full view up and down river. The cantilever truss-style bridge is the second highest of its type in the country. On the west side of the bridge, there's a rest area and parking lot, and from here a trail leads along the west rim. Stay well away from the edge—the cliff faces do crumble even if the rocks look stable, and don't set off along the exposed mesa trail—or indeed loiter on the bridge—if there's any sign of thunderstorms or lightning. The best time to visit the gorge bridge is in the morning or late afternoon, when the sun doesn't beat down as hard and the shifting shadows are especially photogenic in the gorge and on the backdrop Taos Mountain. From the center of Taos, head north on Paseo del Pueblo Norte/Highway 64 through El Prado, to the traffic light at the four-way intersection about 4 miles north of the plaza (a right turn here takes you to the ski valley). Turn left, following Highway 64 west for 8 miles.

Travel about 1.5 miles beyond the Rio Grande Gorge Bridge to reach the Earthship community of buildings that seem almost to grow out of the mesa. These self-sustaining, off-the-grid homes built from natural and recycled materials have been pioneered by Taos architect Michael Reynolds for nearly 40 years. Earthships are now built all over the world, and Reynolds is the subject of the movie *Garbage Warrior,* directed by Oliver Hodge and released on DVD in 2008. You can explore a fully functioning Earthship at the visitor center at the "Earthship World Headquarters," which also runs seminars on how to build Earthships (800-841-9249). For a more immersive experience, rent an Earthship by the night for up to six people, fully furnished and with all modern amenities (575-751-0462; www.earthship.net).

Skiers have always enjoyed Taos Ski Valley, with its European alpine feel, challenging runs, and a good dose of trails for beginners, too. The only hiccup in this otherwise family-friendly resort was that snowboarders were excluded. This changed for the 2008 season, and now snowboarders are also welcome on the slopes. The resort also features an "Out-to-Launch" terrain park. Taos Ski Valley is about 17 miles northeast of the town of Taos, in a snow basin north of Wheeler Peak (the highest mountain in New Mexico at 13,161 feet). Taos Ski Valley receives an average of 305 inches of snow a year and has 110 runs over 1,294 acres. Of these 24 percent are classified as beginner trails, 25 percent intermediate, and 51 percent expert. The base elevation is 9,207 feet, and the highest of the 13 lifts goes to 11,819 feet. For kids there's a children's center and ski school programs. Nightlife in the ski valley is pretty lively, and there are plenty of dining options right by the slopes. Taos Ski Valley was founded in 1955 by Ernie and Rhoda Blake, and the resort is still owned and operated by their family. The season runs from around Thanksgiving to early April. In the summer you can ride the chairlift in the ski valley and either take a picnic to the top or just go for a hike and the views. Head north on Paseo del Pueblo Norte/US 64 to the traffic light junction with NM 150 and NM 522. Turn right onto NM 150/Ski Valley Road, and continue 15 miles, through the town of Arroyo Seco, to the Taos Ski Valley (866-968-7386; www.skitaos.org).

Arroyo Seco (www.visitseco.com), en route to the Taos Ski Valley and about 8 miles from downtown Taos, is a small but charming village with gift shops, art galleries, and pottery and jewelry studios. Top off a visit at the Taos Cow Cafe, serving all-natural Taos Cow ice cream, which you can eat outside under the trees by the creek (505-776-5640; taoscow.com).

For a small town (Town of Taos population is around 5,000), there are a remarkable number of excellent dining choices. For the best sunset views in town and warm Italian hospitality, the Stakeout Grill & Bar, high on Outlaw Hill 9 miles south of central Taos, serves great steaks and Italian dishes, including vegetarian options (for dinner only). There's a large patio, and you can also stop in for cocktails. You pass the Stakeout on the right as you drive in from Santa Fe (575-758-2042, www.stakeoutrestaurant.com). At El Meze, Chef Frederick Muller, formerly of the favorite local haunt Fred's Place, serves a dinner menu influenced by Moorish Spain and a tender and juicy New Mexican Buffalo Short Ribs Adovada. The restaurant is located in an 1847 hacienda with a torreon, or watchtower, and a courtyard patio beneath Taos Mountain (El Torreon Hacienda, 1017 Paseo del Pueblo Norte; 575-751-3337; www.elmeze.com). Also check out Joseph's Table in the Hotel La Fonda on the Plaza, as described above in this section.

The Trading Post Café serves satisfying Italian and international dishes for lunch and dinner, in a historic trading post, with an open-style kitchen and changing art exhibits. Find it at the Ranchos de Taos intersection of Highways 68 and 518, 4 miles south of the plaza (575-758-5089). At a slightly lower price point, the Dragonfly Café & Bakery occupies a cozy 1920s adobe with a pretty front patio and pond and dishes up lunch, dinner, and Sunday brunch with market-fresh produce and an eclectic world menu from Bibimbop to Middle Eastern Lamb Plate to true-blue American bison burger (402 Paseo del Pueblo Norte; 575-737-5859; www.dragonflytaos.com). Gutiz is recommended for its innovative Latin/French fusion food, beautifully cooked by Chef Eduardo, including all-day breakfast, lunch, and dinner. This simple but colorful restaurant also serves tapas-style dishes. The stuffed Parisian crepe with yellow chili sauce is a knockout, especially teamed with homemade mint lemonade (812B Paseo del Pueblo Norte; 575-758-1226; www.gutiztaos.com). Locals head to Guadalajara Grill for Mexican comfort food at value prices, including great green chile–smothered enchiladas—in two bustling cantina locations on the north and south ends of town: 1384 Paseo del Pueblo Sur, (575) 751-0063; and 822 Paseo del Pueblo Norte, (575) 737-0816.

i **Live bands play at the Sagebrush Inn on the weekend for Taos two-steppers to pack the dance floor of this 1930 Pueblo Mission–style inn. Note the enormous wooden vigas and original paintings on the walls, including art by R. C. Gorman (1508 Paseo del Pueblo Sur; 575-758-2254, 800-428-3626; www.taoshotels.com).**

The Taos Inn is referred to as the living room of Taos for good reason: Everybody passes through here at some point, as they have done since 1936, when it opened as the Hotel Martin. Some of the inn's buildings date back to the 1800s; others are more recently added, and the inn is on both the National and State Registers of Historic Places. The large lobby with its double-high ceiling is a comfy place to have a coffee or a drink, and there's live music here most nights. In summer visitors and locals mingle to sip margaritas on the front patio with its iconic neon thunderbird sign, watching Taos cruise by on the main road. Doc Martin's restaurant is open for breakfast, lunch, and dinner, and a bar menu is also available in the Adobe Bar. There's a range of accommodations at varying price levels, either in the main building or in small blocks of casita-style rooms within the compound. Some have viga ceilings or kiva fireplaces, and all are very authentic Taos (125 Paseo del Pueblo Norte; 575-758-2233, 888-518-8267; www.taosinn.com).

Bed and breakfast at the Mabel Dodge Luhan House is another walk into history and the who's who of Taos society, as this is the place where Mabel Dodge Luhan held her arts salons that drew creatives and thinkers such as D. H. Lawrence, Carl Jung, Georgia O'Keeffe, and Ansel Adams. The rooms—many with kiva fireplaces and viga ceilings—are named after their former occupants, and one bathroom has windows colorfully painted by D. H. Lawrence to protect his modesty. Courtyards and a portal lead you into this warm adobe house that backs onto pueblo land. It is secluded but within 10 minutes' walk of the plaza, and the breakfasts here are a treat (240 Morada Lane; 575-751-9686, 800-846-2235; www.mabeldodgeluhan.com).

The upscale AAA Four Diamond El Monte Sagrado Living Resort and Spa has 84 plushly appointed guest rooms, suites, and casitas; the fine-dining De la Tierra restaurant; and the lively Anaconda Bar, all set in immaculately landscaped grounds. This is Taos luxe with an eco-edge (317 Kit Carson Road; 575-758-3502, 800-828-8267; www.elmontesagrado.com).

As a budget option just a couple of minutes' walk from the plaza, the Indian Hills Inn offers good standard accommodations, built around a large grassy courtyard with a swimming pool (233 Paseo del Pueblo Sur; 575-758-4293, 800-444-2346; www.taosnet.com/indianhillsinn). Tent and RV campers can find a place to rest at the 10-acre Taos Valley RV Park and Campground, 2.5 miles south of Taos Plaza. The spacious grounds with natural high-desert vegetation offer scenic views and amenities including a playground, store, and laundry (120 Este Es Road; 575-758-4469, 800-999-7571; taosrv.com).

Getting to Taos

From Albuquerque take I-25 North to the 599 bypass around Santa Fe, then take US 84/285 north to Española, then Highway 68 to Taos. The journey takes about 2.5 hours. In an ideal world you would make this drive in daylight: first, for the views and second, for safety on the winding two-lane road through the Rio Grande Gorge for the last part of your journey. There are no gas stations in the Rio Grande Gorge—fill your tank in Española, or there's one last gas station in Velarde, just at the mouth of the gorge. After that, it's a service station–free zone for around 30 miles till you reach Taos. Twin Hearts Express offers a bus shuttle between Albuquerque and Taos (via Santa Fe) with four daily departures; call (575) 751-1201 or (800) 654-9456.

Getting around Taos

There are no taxi services in Taos and only limited public bus transportation, on the Chile line (505-751-4459; www.taosgov.com/transportation/chile-line.php). You can do without a car if you stick close to the plaza and downtown, but generally, you need a vehicle to see the sites or even to have a full range of options for restaurants. Car rental is also limited; you're best off renting a car in either Albuquerque or Santa Fe.

i If you visit the pueblos of Acoma or Taos, or any other pueblo, check out the Close-up on Native American Pueblos in the Area Overview chapter, for advice on what to expect and a handy guide on etiquette.

ROSWELL

Although Roswell is best known for its alleged 1947 UFO crash, there's more to the town than just aliens, although Roswell certainly makes the most of its "Did they, or didn't they?" alien mythology, with flying saucers and benevolent big-eyed extraterrestrials a recurring motif around town. Even some of the streetlamps in downtown Roswell are shaped like alien heads.

The story that made Roswell famous started on July 8, 1947, with an official report that the wreckage of a "flying disk" had been found on a crash site in ranch lands northwest of Roswell. The next day the military corrected the earlier announcement, saying it was a weather balloon instead. This didn't stop stories from circulating of alien bodies found in the wreckage and arguments over whether the debris material found could really have come from a weather balloon. Was it a cover-up? Certainly, as you're driving to Roswell in Chaves County, 200 miles southeast of Albuquerque, the land drops from mountains to the wide plains of the Pecos Valley, where it's impossible to avoid watching the huge empty sky, just in case something might be out there.

And that speculation keeps people coming every year to the annual Roswell UFO Festival, when both believers and skeptics descend on the town for four days over the July 4th weekend. Festival events include lectures, shows, films, a parade, fireworks, alien disk golf, and a festival music concert (the 2009 big-name act was Jefferson Starship). The festival is also the only time of year when the public can tour Hangar 84, where the alien bodies were allegedly stored. Make hotel reservations well in advance if you're stopping over during the UFO Festival, as this small city, population around 50,000, gets packed (888-ROS-FEST, www.ufofestivalroswell.com).

The rest of the year you can find out about the controversial Roswell Incident at the International UFO Museum and Research Center. The museum doesn't have many bells and whistles to entertain younger kids, but it presents a documented history of the famous incident, including witness accounts and newspaper and radio reports from the day in question. The exhibits become increasingly compelling as you follow the unfolding story, weighing evidence from all parties to draw your own conclusions about what happened that summer night in 1947. The museum also contains photos of UFO sightings from around the globe. A new multimillion dollar UFO Museum and Research Center is due to open in early 2011 in a futuristic building with new displays, eight blocks north of the current museum. Until then find the UFO Museum and Research Center at 114 North Main Street; (575) 625-9495, (800) 822-3545; www.roswellufo museum.com).

The surprise for art lovers is that Roswell has a couple of excellent art museums and a number of galleries around town. The Roswell Museum and Art Center is a handsome 50,000-square-foot building, originally opened in 1937 as a WPA art center. It's now grown to 12 galleries with works by southwestern artists, including regionalists Peter Hurd and Henriette Wyeth, known for their studies of the southeastern New Mexico Hondo Valley; Taos artist Howard Cook; Marsden Hartley; and Georgia O'Keeffe, among many others. It also houses the Robert H. Goddard Collection of Liquid-Propellant Rocketry, with a reconstruction of Goddard's workshop and some fascinating videos of Goddard's early rocket-launching experiments—the ones that flopped and the ones that flew. The 120-seat Robert H. Goddard Planetarium is on the same site as the museum, with various programs throughout the year. The free Roswell Museum and Art Center is located at 100 West 11th Street; (575) 624-6744; www.roswellmuseum.org).

Although the Anderson Museum of Contemporary Art looks fairly low key from the outside, inside the free-to-enter gallery, you'll find seven galleries with an eclectic and colorful-in-every-sense display of over 300 art works, including shark sculptures made from golf bags hanging from the ceiling and an enormous rearing fiberglass bull with flashing red eyes by Luis Jiménez, one of several public art sculptures from Jiménez. The museum showcases works from the Roswell Artist in Residence program, and the broad array of media and styles here is well worth a visit (409 East College Boulevard; 575-623-5600; www.roswellamoca.org).

i The Tree of Knowledge sculpture outside the Roswell Public Library was erected to celebrate the library's centennial in 2006. The sculpture was designed by artist Susan Wink, but others in the community contributed to making the clay tiles that form the tree trunk—all inscribed with author names, poems, or literary quotes. It took 26 workshops over two years for contributing artists to complete the tree, with its 2,800-plus word tiles. Dedicated in 2008, the Tree of Knowledge stands over 17 feet tall, and the "leaves" are wrought from steel, spelling inspirational words such as "Create," "Laugh," and "Imagine." See it at 301 North Pennsylvania Avenue.

At the New Mexico Military Institute—dubbed the West Point of the West—the General Douglas L. McBride Museum presents a collection of exhibits on the history of NMMI, its Hall of Fame alumni, and military memorabilia. The free museum is located in a 1918 building that housed the first indoor swimming pool west of the Mississippi. Check the opening hours in advance—it's usually closed on weekends and may be closed for special events. Find it in the Enrollment and Development Center, New Mexico Military Institute, 101 West College Boulevard; (575) 622-6250, (800) 421-5376; www.nmmi.edu/museum. The public may also play at the NMMI 18-hole golf course at 201 19th Street; (575) 624-8240.

A stroll through Roswell's free Spring River Zoo in the 34-acre Spring River Park (1306 East College Boulevard; 575-624-6760), leads you through native and exotic species, including coyotes, lemurs, llamas, pronghorn antelope, bobcats, bison, black bear, and raccoons, and there's nothing like turning the corner of a city park and finding yourself face to face with a pair of mountain lions. The park also has an antique wooden horse carousel and a miniature train for rides around the park, as well as a small lake, playground, and picnic shelters.

A short drive east of Roswell, the Bottomless Lakes State Park is so named because the lakes, ranging from 17 to 90 feet in depth, are a deep blue-green that gives a never-ending illusion, and early attempts by cowboys to measure their depth by tying their saddle ropes together never touched bottom. The lakes are set amid red-rock bluffs, and you can swim from the sandy beach around Lea Lake or scuba dive, fish, rent a paddle boat, and also camp here on tent and RV sites. This was New Mexico's first state park, designated in 1933. Take US Highway 380 east for 12 miles; turn south on NM Highway 380 for 7 miles (575-624-6058 or 888-NMPARKS; www.emnrd.state.nm.us/prd/bottomless.htm).

Roswell is about three hours' drive from Albuquerque, and for overnight stays accommodation choices focus on chain hotels. The 70-room Hampton Inn and Suites is comfortable and spaciously designed, with a "still new" feeling—it opened about five years ago. There's a complimentary breakfast bar and an indoor swimming pool (3607 North Main Street; 575-623-5151; www.hamptoninn.com). For eats the smart Cattle Baron is part of a small chain founded in Portales, New Mexico, and specializes in steak and seafood (1113 North Main Street; 575-622-2465). Italian food lovers should head to Pasta Cafe Italian Bistro (1208 N. Main Street; 575-624-1111), which is romantically atmospheric in true Southern Italian style, offering a menu of mostly Sicilian dishes. The cheery, family-owned Peppers Grill and Bar (600 North Main Street; 575-623-1700) serves casual New Mexican fare, pastas, burgers, and steaks, with complimentary happy hour hors d'oeuvres in the bar.

i Fittingly, part of the 1976 David Bowie movie *The Man Who Fell to Earth* was shot in Roswell.

i Visitor information is available from the Roswell Convention & Visitors Bureau, 912 North Main Street. Or you can phone 888-ROSWELL or visit their Web site: www.roswellmysteries.com.

RELOCATION

Albuquerque is both the economic and geographic center of New Mexico, and the affordability of real estate and the reasonable cost of living have contributed to Albuquerque's hitting the nation's radar as a relocation destination. It doesn't hurt either that the city enjoys a gorgeous environment, unique culture, mild high-desert climate, and easy access to other places of interest in New Mexico and around the Southwest. The incoming population is a lively mix of students arriving to study at the University of New Mexico, young and more-established families relocating for work and quality of life, and retirees looking for a place in the sun with a good dose of culture and activities. Although Albuquerque has the amenities of a big city, it still retains a smaller-city feel at times, with a "mañana" atmosphere that sometimes requires adjustment for professionals coming from a faster-paced environment. On the other hand, the rather less-stressful quality of life and great outdoor recreation opportunities compensate enormously. And although locals still complain about the traffic, you can't beat that quick commute time—a drive of 20 to 30 minutes maximum is normal, or it could be even less, depending on where you live, which makes our friends from other, bumper-to-bumper metro areas sigh with envy.

In 2009 Albuquerque was placed sixth in the Best Cities in America list by *Outside* magazine, was put on the 10 Best Cities to Live by both *U.S. News & World Report* and *Relocate-America,* and notched up to second place in *Kiplinger's Personal Finance*'s 10 Best Cities of 2009. The growth of the metro area definitely raises some challenges regarding urban planning and future provision of water, but at the time of writing, the city is maintaining a fairly even economic keel despite the problems on a national level. Some slowdown is in effect but generally not at the same level as other states and cities, thanks to the diversity of industry. There is a lot of activity in the technology and renewable-energy sectors, and the health-care industry continues to grow. House prices also remain relatively stable.

REAL ESTATE

Almost 70 percent of Albuquerque metropolitan area homes are owner occupied, according to 2009 estimates. Housing choices include rural old adobes, grand haciendas, funky fixer-uppers, ranch-style houses and new starter homes in suburban developments, and upwardly mobile urban apartments and loft conversions. Roughly half the city's homes were built post-1970. The median sales price for an existing single-family home in the metro area was $182,600 in the first quarter of 2009, compared to the Western median of $237,600. New residents to the Albuquerque area tend to come from the East and West coasts and the neighboring state of Texas, and these competitive real estate prices compared to the newcomers' places of origin are especially favorable for single professionals, young families, and retirees. Homes in the $200,000 to $250,000 price range constitute the most dynamic and desirable market as of summer 2009. Rentals are also a good value, and there are around 79,000 apartment units in the city. The average monthly rent is 80 cents per square foot, utilities included, according to the Apartment Association of New Mexico. As the City of Albuquerque can't expand north or south because of the boundaries of the Sandia and Isleta Pueblos nor stretch any farther east because of the mountains, much of the population growth and new construction are on the Westside, where there is still vacant land, and up into the city of Rio Rancho.

The ACCRA Cost of Living Index produced by the Council for Community and Economic Research showed the Albuquerque metropolitan area had a cost of living index of 96.8 between the first quarters of 2008 and 2009 (100 indicates the national average; the index compares price levels for consumer goods and services for a midmanagement standard of living).

Real estate professionals broadly divide Albuquerque into four quadrants. Some areas within those quadrants will be inside city limits, others just a few blocks over will be outside city limits—falling under the jurisdiction of Bernalillo County or in the Village of Los Ranchos, for example. This section gives an overview of the neighborhoods within the four quadrants and nearby communities in the metro area.

The New Mexico Mortgage Finance Authority provides low-interest financing to low- to moderate-income New Mexicans, assisting first-time home buyers and teachers, health-care workers, police officers, firefighters, safety workers, or active members of the armed forces, even if they are not first-time homeowners (505-843-6880; www.housingnm.org).

METRO AREA NEIGHBORHOODS

Downtown

Downtown has benefited from a 10-year, $350 million revitalization program—it used to be rather dead at night after office workers went home, frequented more by panhandlers than city sophisticates out for a night on the town, but it's now a lively destination for restaurants, arts, and entertainment. As a center for business, it's home to the Albuquerque Convention Center, City Hall, courthouses, the Alvarado Transportation Center, and high-rise office buildings around the Harry E. Kinney Civic Plaza. Residential developments spotlight trendy urban apartments and loft conversions, including the 100 Gold lofts on Gold Avenue.

Call 311 for the City of Albuquerque's 24-hour Citizen Contact Center hotline. Operators are quick on the draw to provide answers on city amenities and events and to respond to requests for general services. (This number is for nonemergency requests only—call 911 for emergencies.) Outside city limits you can reach the Citizen Contact Center by phoning (505) 768-2000, or pop them a question via Twitter on their ID @cabq.

East Downtown (EDo)

Albuquerque's first planned suburb, in 1880, was the entrepreneurial Franz Huning's Huning Highlands Addition, east of the railroad tracks between Copper Avenue NE and Iron Avenue SE. This area now falls into the neighborhood lately tagged as EDo (East Downtown), riding the coattails of similar nicknames for hip city areas like Denver's LoDo and TriBeCa in New York. Cool new restaurants and shops have boosted EDo's image, and the Huning Highland Historic District is again a fashionable residential area, with its Queen Anne–style houses and conversions such as the Lofts at the old Albuquerque High School.

The New Mexico Historic Preservation Division, part of the Department of Cultural Affairs, gives state income tax credits to homeowners of listed historic structures or in registered historic districts for rehabilitation of the property. Credit is up to 50 percent of rehabilitation costs, to a limit of $25,000. Various work is eligible for the tax credit program, including roofing and window repairs. Information is available at www.nmhistoricpreservation.org or call (505) 827-6320.

Albuquerque Northeast

From the University of New Mexico to the base of the Sandia Mountains, this broad and well-developed area includes mature suburban neighborhoods with homes in many price ranges, from starter homes and fixer-uppers to seven-figure price tags. Generally, values grow steeper as you climb into the foothills. Properties in this quadrant are always in demand, with their speedy access to city amenities and major employment, and some of the most exclusive residential neighborhoods are found here. Custom homes in Sandia Heights perch in the foothills, looking as if they could be straight off the front cover of a chic shelter magazine with their stunning contemporary architecture, the mountains behind them, and extensive views over the city. The higher elevation comes with a correspondingly higher asking price, of course. North Albuquerque Acres offers luxury custom homes on lot sizes of an average of one acre or more, in a country setting, with horse facilities on larger lots. Wells and septic systems are the norm here for water supply and sewage treatment. Gated communities include Tanoan—a golf course community—and Towne Park. Other popular subdivisions include High Desert and Glenwood Hills. The Near Northeast Heights and Northeast Heights—covering the University area above Central Avenue, Uptown, and the area east to the Sandia foothills—offer a host of shopping, schools, and parks. Properties range from smaller vintage treasures to elegant older homes, often with larger lots, in mature landscaping. These areas offer more entry-level homes, including ranch-style properties. Popular Northeast Heights residential neighborhoods near the university include Altura Park, Netherwood Park, La Hacienda Addition, and Haines Park.

Albuquerque Southeast

In the Southeast Heights, affordable neighborhoods around the EXPO New Mexico Fairgrounds and directly north of Kirtland Air Force Base are interspersed with small enclaves of elegant upscale properties. First-time buyers wanting easy access to the university, the air force base, or Sandia National Laboratories will likely find something to suit their budgets and family needs. The Four Hills neighborhood, tucked just south of I-40 under the mountains, is just a few minutes' drive from the bordering Kirtland Air Force Base and Sandia labs and carries a higher price tag. The neighborhood is built around the Four Hills Country Club, and some properties back on to the golf course. Executive homes date from the 1960s through to recent constructions, and they often occupy larger lots. The Southeast Heights University area is always desirable, especially Nob Hill, which retains a friendly neighborhood feel despite its ultrahip vibe and tourist traffic. Luxury condos have been developed, while eclectic older homes, often renovated, have smaller yards and are inhabited by both university professors who've lived there for decades and smart young professionals. Other areas are the well-established and elegant Ridgecrest, including the Lofts at Ridgecrest, Parkland Hills, and Siesta Hills.

Albuquerque Southwest

The Albuquerque Country Club area—near Tingley Beach and the Rio Grande Zoo—is one of the most sought-after residential spots in the city. A wealthy old neighborhood with palatial vintage villas and haciendas, plus some more modern architecture, this beautifully landscaped area features wide residential streets with double rows of mature cottonwoods down the center of the divided road. Gardens are lush, and the area is remarkably peaceful considering it's just a few blocks from the heart of Downtown. You'll pay a pretty penny to live here. Farther out, the South Valley is largely agricultural, with southwestern-style homes often featuring barns and acreage for livestock. Recent subdivisions on the Southwest Mesa offer affordable housing to first-time buyers, and the area is expanding, as land is available for development. Prices here are far more competitive than in similar properties elsewhere in the city.

Albuquerque Northwest

North Valley

The North Valley, above I-40 and nestled between I-25 and the Rio Grande, is home to some of the earliest agricultural settlements in the Albuquerque metropolitan area, and the pastoral nature has been sustained even as the city has spread its tentacles out around the valley. It includes the Village of Los Ranchos, stretched along the river, with beautiful secluded estates on large acreage, including many horse properties. Homes are built in traditional Southwest style, and the highly desirable irrigated land is expensive. The lushness of massive cottonwoods and green pastures extends up into Corrales village, with its charming old adobe homes and artsy character. More recently established communities on custom-home subdivisions include Tinnin Farms, Los Poblanos Orchards, and Dietz Farms. These peaceful and affluent North Valley neighborhoods offer a rural lifestyle with all the facilities of the big city on the doorstep. Although prices reflect the high demand, there are also more modestly priced older homes in the North Valley, including properties in need of a little TLC.

Westside

As west is the only direction that Albuquerque can expand, given its bordering pueblo lands and mountain geography, new construction abounds west of the Rio Grande, offering more house for your money. Developers are creating housing in all styles and price ranges to meet the needs of the growing city, including custom and semi-custom homes. It can be windier and dustier in some areas of the west mesa. Leisure and shopping amenities are good, including the large Cottonwood Mall, although dining leans toward chain restaurants on the Westside. Petroglyph National Monument is convenient for hiking, and the Open Space Visitors Center offers easy access to river trails.

Paradise Hills, close to the Cottonwood Mall, has a mix of older (up to 30 years) homes and brand-new planned communities. The Ventana Ranch subdivision in west Paradise Hills is active, with new builds from affordable apartments to luxury family homes, and has parks, trails, and panoramic views. The Northwest Heights is also a popular area, including Taylor Ranch. These suburban neighborhoods include homes in southwestern or classic brick styles.

RIO RANCHO

Albuquerque's ambitious young neighbor, incorporated as a city in 1981, is a fast-growing master-planned community, anchored by the Intel Corporation campus. Population was estimated at 80,000 in 2008. The "City of Vision" is about 25 minutes' drive northwest of Downtown Albuquerque, and although the new town doesn't have the same old adobe charm as some other areas in the region, the good employment options and healthy economy create a vigorously optimistic atmosphere. A new Hewlett-Packard Company site is anticipated to add 1,350 to 1,800 jobs. Rio Rancho also serves as a bedroom community for Albuquerque city workers. It has the second lowest crime rate in New Mexico, after Los Alamos to the north, and there are ample shopping and leisure opportunities within Rio Rancho and nearby. Rio Rancho covers 65,290 acres, and real estate offers a wide range of new constructions, from affordable family housing on subdivisions stretching along State Highway 528 toward Bernalillo and upscale neighborhoods and golf communities. There are also retirement communities here. From Rio Rancho's slightly higher-in-elevation northwestern perch, the views across the valley to the mountains are superb.

BERNALILLO

Bernalillo is the county seat of Sandoval County, and this historic town of 8,500 residents retains a small-community feel along its classic western main street, Camino del Pueblo, which used to be part of El Camino Real and later Route 66. It's a far cry from the busy traffic on the main US Highway 240, a thoroughfare through Bernalillo to I-25 used by nearly 30,000 vehicles every weekday.

Bernalillo is about 17 miles north of Downtown Albuquerque, a quick zip for I-25 commuters, and there is also a New Mexico Rail Runner Express station. Population has been steadily growing in recent years, and there are many affordable older homes and priced-for-value small homes here for entry-level buyers, as well as some high-dollar rural estates. Retirees with a nest egg are buying in the Alegria Active Adult Community, about five minutes from the town of Bernalillo en route to Rio Rancho.

VALENCIA COUNTY—BELEN AND LOS LUNAS

The rapidly growing Valencia County lies at the southern end of the metropolitan area. Traditionally agricultural in nature and surrounded by wide open spaces, Valencia County communities are conveniently located on the I-25 corridor and, in addition to their own local employment, serve as bedroom communities for Albuquerque. Los Lunas and Belen also have New Mexico Rail Runner Express stations for speedy commuting. The county seat Los Lunas is about 24 miles south of Downtown Albuquerque and is expanding with new subdivisions; a major Wal-Mart distribution center is located here. Belen (Spanish for Bethlehem) is approximately 35 miles from Downtown. Founded in 1740, it's now home to manufacturing companies in industrial parks and historical-interest sites, such as an original Harvey House railroad hotel. The Village of Bosque Farms (approximately 18 miles south of Albuquerque) has a commercial strip surrounded by residential neighborhoods. Housing options in Valencia County are a mix of affordable new builds and rural properties and farms, including horse properties. These are quiet communities, with a small-town family focus and the benefit of access to city amenities and employment.

i The Greater Albuquerque Association of Realtors (GAAR) provides a monthly market report on its Web site: www.gaar.com. The report highlights residential real estate prices and trends, including notes on any areas showing substantial changes. The Web site also features spotlights on Multiple Listing Service (MLS) areas.

i Albuquerque Economic Development (AED) is a one-stop shop providing information and assistance to businesses interested in relocating to Albuquerque. Individuals heading to Duke City can also find helpful information on the region on their Web site. Contact AED at Suite 203, 851 University Boulevard SE; (505) 246-6200 or (800) 451-2933; www.abq.org.

EAST MOUNTAINS

Driving east on I-40 through Tijeras Canyon takes you in about 15 minutes to the start of the East Mountains communities. These enclaves vary enormously, from mountain villages to eastern plains towns. Along the Turquoise Trail on Highway 14 north to Santa Fe, you pass behind the Sandias, beneath the Sandia Peak Ski Area. It is quickly evident why this is dubbed "the green side of the mountains," with alpine landscapes at higher elevations and the forests of Cibola National Park. The climate in the Sandia Mountains is cooler and wetter than in the city of Albuquerque, with average annual rainfall of 40 inches and 111 inches of snow. Old Turquoise Trail villages include Tijeras, Cedar Crest, Sandia Park, and Madrid. Affordable mountain refuges are on lot sizes from small to several acres, often against wooded tracts, and are suitable for horse owners. There are also fixer-uppers available and some mobile homes. There are several new upscale developments, including Paa-Ko, by the acclaimed Paa-Ko Ridge Golf Course. The plains towns of Edgewood and Moriarty are east on I-40, approximately 30 and 45 minutes' drive to Downtown Albuquerque, respectively. These communities offer a combination of new developments and rural properties, as well as affordably priced land for those who want to build their own dream home.

EDUCATION

Albuquerque Public Schools (APS) is the state's largest school district, serving nearly a third of New Mexico's students. In the 2008–09 school year, 94,836 students attended APS schools. The diversity of the district is reflected in the fact that more than a third of APS students are from homes where English is not the primary language. There are 87 elementary schools, 26 middle schools, and 13 high schools. *U.S. News and World Report*'s assessment of "Best High Schools 2009" awarded two bronze medals to Albuquerque public schools—the Career Enrichment Center and Eldorado High—and a silver medal to La Cueva High. A number of magnet schools in the city—with a specific curriculum focus aimed at students with special interests—offer disciplines that include technology, science and scientific research, math, contemporary arts, and leadership and international studies.

Average class sizes are 20 students for kindergarten; 22 for grades 1 to 3; 24 for grades 4 to 5; 27 for grades 6 to 8; and a 30-student average in grades 9 to 12. APS students are assigned to a school according to their address, although it's possible to apply for a transfer to a school outside the immediate neighborhood. School transportation is available for elementary school kids living over a mile from school, for middle schoolers more than 1.5 miles away, and for high school students who have to travel over 2 miles.

Albuquerque has 36 charter schools, leading by a long measure New Mexico's flourishing charter school movement. The state's Public Education Commission gave the go-ahead for four new charter schools in September 2009.

Rio Rancho has its own public school district, created in 1994 and now enrolling over 15,000 students. It's the third-largest school district in New Mexico, and scores are above the average for the state in most areas of the New Mexico Standards Based Assessment.

i High school students in New Mexico with a minimum 2.5 grade point average (out of 4.0) are eligible for a New Mexico Lottery Scholarship, which pays for tuition at a state college. The scholarship covers tuition for eight semesters, starting with the student's second semester.

Private Schools

Around 13 percent of Albuquerque's children are educated at private or parochial religious schools, with over 40 to choose from in the area. The Albuquerque Academy is generally reckoned to be one of the top nondenominational private schools.

All the elementary schools listed here also teach preschoolers, and St. Mary's Catholic School offers both elementary and middle school. Hope Christian School, listed under High Schools, teaches pupils from prekindergarten through elementary school and up to grade 12.

Elementary Schools

ESCUELA DEL SOL MONTESSORI
1114 7th Street NW
(505) 242-3033
escueladelsol.org

While Escuela del Sol Elementary teaches kids from grades one through six, the school also has primary classrooms for ages 3 to 6, and a Toddler Community for tots from 18 months to age 3. Escuela del Sol is an independent nonprofit, founded in 1968. It uses the Montessori method to maximize children's potential and stimulate their inherent passion for learning, and the school asserts that its teaching method not only achieves academic excellence but fosters creative thinking and self-direction in the child. Students are educated in multiage classrooms, in a collaborative rather than competitive environment, with at least one trained and certified Montessori teacher in each class. Head of School Friedje vanGils will have been leading Escuela del Sol for 30 years in 2010, and the school is also an internship site for the American Montessori Society. The school's campus is on the site of the Harwood Art Center, which is owned and operated by Escuela del Sol. This registered historic red-brick neoclassical Revival-style building housed the Harwood Girls School—a Methodist boarding school—between 1925 and 1976. Now the Harwood Art Center is a community arts center and gallery, with programs that include visual arts, concerts, theater, and dance performances. Most of the main building is given over to the arts center, and the school occupies the north wing and other historic and recently constructed buildings on the site, including Hudd Hall, built in 1940. Students participate in a number of community outreach programs, and there is a natural relationship with the arts and the local neighborhood via the Harwood Art Center.

MANZANO DAY SCHOOL
1801 Central Avenue NW
(505) 243-6659
www.manzanodayschool.org

Manzano Day School, founded in 1938, teaches children from prekindergarten (four years old) to fifth grade. Children are educated on a six-acre campus near Old Town, with adobe buildings, gardens, and *placitas* (enclosed patios or courtyards), and an amphitheater. There is a maximum of 18 students to a class, and more than half the teachers have been with the school for over a decade. Traditional subjects are taught using new approaches, such as the F.A.S.T. Reading Program (Foundations of Analysis, Synthesis and Translation) and Mel Levine's Schools Attuned program. The core curriculum of reading, writing, math, social studies, and science is accompanied by cocurricular subjects, including visual arts, technology, Spanish, music and performing arts, physical education, environmental studies, and library studies. Students take several field trips a year, including one between one and three days annually at Manzano's Fenton Ranch in the Jemez Mountains, 80 miles northwest of Albuquerque. Homesteaded in the 1800s, the ranch, with residential dormitories, is part of Manzano's campus and is used for environmental education. This is the only elementary school in Albuquerque accredited by the Independent Schools Association of the Southwest (a voluntary membership organization), in addition to the New Mexico State Department of Education. The application process for all ages includes a school visit and testing or evaluations.

ST. MARY'S CATHOLIC SCHOOL
224 Seventh Street NW
(505) 242-6271
www.saintmaryscatholicschool.com

St. Mary's provides a Catholic education from kindergarten through eighth grade. There is also a preschool program for four-year-olds. The school was founded in 1863 by the Sisters of Charity from Cincinnati and the Jesuit Fathers of Immaculate Conception Parish. The school has a faculty of around 55 teachers and teacher assistants, who educate over 600 students. Preference for admissions is given first to siblings of current students, then to Catholic students registered at Immaculate Conception Parish, then to Catholic students registered at other parishes, and, finally, to non-Catholic students. St. Mary's Catholic School encourages involvement from parents in the child's academic and spiritual education and also requires parents to provide 20 hours of service to the school or 10 hours for single parents.

High Schools

ALBUQUERQUE ACADEMY
6400 Wyoming Boulevard NE
(505) 828-3200
www.aa.edu

Founded in 1955, this independent, college-preparatory day school educates nearly 1,095 students from sixth to twelfth grade. Originally a boys' school, Albuquerque Academy opened its doors to girls in 1973, and classes are now an even 50/50 for boys and girls. Albuquerque Academy focuses on academic excellence, inclusiveness, accessibility, and community outreach. The school enjoys high national rankings: There were 33 National Merit Semifinalists in the class of 2008 and 31 in the class of 2009; 162 students in the class of 2008 accepted $4.7 million in merit-based college scholarships, from over $17 million offered.

Albuquerque Academy's 312-acre campus includes the Simms Library, with a collection of over 100,000 volumes, a science center, a visual arts studio, two gymnasiums, a swimming pool, and the Simms Center for the Performing Arts, which presents events that include Chamber Music Albuquerque concerts. The average class size is 14.5, with a student-to-teacher ratio of nine to one. Students are required to study the core disciplines of English, history, math, modern languages, science, and performing and visual arts through grade nine. They also join experiential education programs, which are mostly taught in New Mexico's wilderness areas and around the Four Corners. All students participate in physical education or interscholastic athletics, and the school boasts 50 teams in around 20 sports, with 99 varsity athletics state championships under the school's belt in the last four decades. Domestic and international exchange programs are also available.

Youngsters enter Albuquerque Academy from over 100 schools in the Albuquerque area and beyond. Approximately 40 percent are students of color, with over 22 languages spoken in the homes of the class of 2015. There are 144 places available in grade six, with additional places added in older grades. The school has a $204 million endowment, and around a third of students receive financial aid totaling over $4 million a year.

BOSQUE SCHOOL
4000 Learning Road NW
(505) 898-6388
www.bosqueschool.org

This nonprofit, nonsectarian school was founded in 1994 and is set on a 45-acre site along the Rio Grande bosque. It has 545 students in grades 6 through 12, with an average class size of 16 and a 9:1 ratio of students to faculty. The school focuses on a traditional academic education and college preparation, while celebrating diversity and encouraging progressive approaches to learning. The arts curriculum includes visits to local community artists and galleries, and performing arts are core-curriculum activities rather than extracurricular, with all students participating. Students can also get involved in age-appropriate community service projects, including environmental and animal programs. Seventy-five percent of students participate in one or more of Bosque School's 35 interscholastic teams. A new 15,000-square-foot schoolhouse for the upper school is adding eight new classrooms, a technology center, and a college-guidance suite.

HOPE CHRISTIAN SCHOOL
8005 Louisiana Boulevard NE
(505) 822-8868
www.hopechristianschool.org

Hope Christian School educates youngsters from prekindergarten though grade 12. It was established in 1976, and its mission is "to pray for, equip and send Christ-centered, passionate leaders to change the world." Around 1,400 students attend, with approximately 600 in pre-K to fifth grade, and 400 students each in the middle school and high school. Average class size in the lower levels is 22, with a ratio of 16 students per teacher in the upper level. The school operates on a 20-acre campus, and students come from around 230 church congregations in the Albuquerque metropolitan area. Hope Christian School offers an academically challenging environment, an emphasis on teaching biblical principles, and an interscholastic athletics program—home of the Huskies! Over 95 percent of Hope graduates continue on to college. In addition to the usual testing, interviews, and teacher reference, the application process requires a character reference from the pupil's pastor.

MENAUL SCHOOL
301 Menaul Boulevard NE
(505) 345-7727
www.menaulschool.com

Menaul School was founded on its current site in 1896 by the Reverend James Menaul, a Presbyterian minister and founder of First Presbyterian Church of Albuquerque. It educates children from grades 6 to 12, and although it is a faith-based institution rooted in the Christian tradition, students do not have to be either Presbyterian or even Christian to attend. Menaul School offers an ecumenical learning environment and is open to students from all religious backgrounds. Between 225 and 250 students are taught on a peaceful 35-acre collegelike campus in the North Valley. Sports facilities include a soccer field, football fields, tennis courts, and a gymnasium. Class sizes are up to 16 in core courses, with between 6 and 9 students in elective courses. Menaul School prides itself on providing a high-quality college preparatory education to students of racial and economic diversity. Over 60 percent of students are from Hispanic, Native American, or other minority groups.

SANDIA PREP
532 Osuna Road NE
(505) 338-3000
www.sandiaprep.org

Sandia Prep's college preparatory education for grades 6 to 12 emphasizes a balance of "the Five A's: academics, arts, athletics, school activities and the atmosphere in which these events occur." Established in 1966 as a girls' school, Sandia Prep became coed in 1973. It offers strong college prep programs in English, creative writing, journalism, math, laboratory science, history, Spanish and French, and computer technology. A student population of 625 enjoys an average class size of 16 and a student-to-faculty ratio of 9 to 1. Many of the faculty have taught here for over 20 years, and each student is allocated a faculty member as a special advisor on academic or other issues. The school has a 30-acre campus, and in 2009 a new $5 million, 23,000-square-foot Performing Arts Center was completed, with new classrooms and a new admission center. Participation in sports is encouraged, and the school has a "no cut" approach to athletics: Any student wishing to play on a school team may do so. Twenty-three percent of students benefit from financial aid, with total aid of $1,169,900 awarded in the 2009–10 academic year. The school has an endowment of $3,550,000 and was profiled in *Newsweek*'s 2005 review of "America's Best High Schools."

ST. PIUS X HIGH SCHOOL
5301 Saint Josephs Drive NW
(505) 831-8400
www.saintpiusx.com

St. Pius X is a Catholic college preparatory high school for grades 9 to 12 under the archdiocese of Santa Fe. It educates around 950 students with a student/teacher ratio of 12 to 1. Approximately 98 percent of St. Pius X graduates continue to four-year colleges. St. Pius X High School opened in 1956 and moved to its current 40-acre campus on Albuquerque's Westside in 1988. The campus was formerly home to the Catholic University of Albuquerque. The school has a lively fine arts program, with performance and visual arts, and the music program includes band, orchestra, chorus, and jazz. In 2008 21 chorus and orchestra students from St. Pius X were recognized as New Mexico All-State Musicians. There are over 20 sports teams, with a substantial record of achievement in state championship titles for both boys' and girls' soccer and basketball teams, and students have received scholarships to Division 1 university athletic programs. At this faith-based school, student life includes daily prayer and monthly Masses and a required theology curriculum. In order to graduate, pupils must complete a given number of community service hours with a nonprofit organization.

Higher Education

Technical Schools and Community Colleges

ART CENTER DESIGN COLLEGE
5000 Marble Avenue NE
(505) 254-7575
www.theartcenter.edu

Albuquerque is a branch campus of the Art Center Design College. The main campus is in Tucson, Arizona. The college offers six bachelor of arts degrees, in illustration, advertising and marketing, interior design, animation, graphic design, and landscape architecture. The two bachelor of fine arts degree programs are in studio art and photography. In 2009 two Albuquerque students were awarded gold and silver ADDY Awards in the American Advertising Federation's annual ADDY Awards.

CENTRAL NEW MEXICO COMMUNITY COLLEGE
525 Buena Vista Drive SE
(505) 224-3000
www.cnm.edu

This community college offers 48 associate degree programs in the arts, sciences, and occupational disciplines and 52 certificate programs in business, health, technology, and vocational occupations. CNM has six schools of study: Adult and General Education; Applied Technologies; Business and Information Technology; Communication, Humanities, and Social Sciences; Health, Wellness, and Public Safety; and Mathematics, Sciences, and Engineering. Noncredit workshops and classes are also offered to the community in subjects from creative writing to conversational Spanish.

Other services offered by CNM include workforce training programs and distance learning courses. Tuition rates are low and vary by the student's area of residence; some courses are free of charge if you live within CNM's tax district. In addition to the main campus, the college has campuses in the Northeast Heights, the South Valley, and the Westside, and a new campus is under construction in Rio Rancho, due to open in 2010. CNM's Workforce Training Center, dedicated to job training and professional development, is located in the area of Balloon Fiesta Park.

i Learn how to tackle a chile head-on at the Jane Butel Cooking School's series of weekend and weeklong courses. Butel is an expert in southwestern cuisine, having taught cookery classes since 1983. The most recent of her 18 cookbooks is *Real Women Eat Chiles*. Classes are held in Jane's kitchen in Corrales. Online courses are also offered. Information is at (800) 473-8226; www.janebutelcooking.com.

Colleges and Universities

NATIONAL AMERICAN UNIVERSITY
4775 Indian School Road NE
(505) 348-3700
www.national.edu

National American University offers degree programs for working adults, with classes scheduled in the day, in the evening, and on the weekend to offer maximum flexibility for students juggling family, jobs, and studies. The university also offers courses that are taught 100 percent online, plus combinations of online and on-campus classes. Course options include associate's, bachelor's, and master's degrees, with a focus on business, information technology, medical administration, medical assisting, and health-care management. NAU has campuses in seven states, and the Albuquerque campus opened in 1975. Since 1997 there has also been a Rio Rancho branch of the university at 1601 Rio Rancho Drive SE; (505) 348-3750.

UNIVERSITY OF NEW MEXICO
(505) 277-0111
www.unm.edu

The University of New Mexico was founded in 1889 and has long been a key influence on city life, establishing Albuquerque as a center for academics, artists, and thinkers. The faculty includes a Nobel laureate, 2 MacArthur Fellows, and 35 Fulbright Scholars. The main 600-acre campus in Albuquerque enrolled over 25,000 students for the 2008–09 academic year. Statewide, over 32,000 students were enrolled, including those at the satellite campuses. Preliminary enrollment reports for fall 2009 suggest 2009–10 will be a record-breaking year. In 2008 *U.S. News & World Report* cited UNM's graduate programs in law, engineering, and medicine as among the best in the nation. The university also has major schools of education and business. *Forbes*'s 2009 America's Best Colleges report ranked the University of New Mexico at number 239 among the nation's top 600 colleges and number 38 among public colleges. Annual giving to the university in 2008 was over $85.5 million.

At UNM's main campus students may enroll in over 215 degree and certificate programs. These include 94 baccalaureate-, 72 master's-, and 38 doctoral-level degree programs. UNM is the state's major research university and enrolls 80 percent of the state's PhD candidates.

The UNM Health Sciences Center, established in 1994, is the largest integrated health-care research, education, and treatment organization in the state, with programs including the School of Medicine, College of Nursing, and College of Pharmacy. *U.S. News & World Report* ranked the School of Medicine in the top 25 medical schools in the nation.

Students at UNM enjoy a beautiful campus, with historic buildings set amid mature landscaping resplendent with over 300 tree species and a duck pond, right in the heart of the city. Those living in residence halls will benefit from a $4.8 million facelift in 2009 to renovate student housing. The campus is dotted with the university's art collection of over 200 sculptures, murals, and paintings. Famed architect John Gaw Meem designed 30 of the UNM buildings, and his oft-praised Spanish Pueblo Revival style indelibly stamped the campus with a character unique to UNM. Meem's Zimmerman Library was cited as the New Mexico building of the 20th century by the American Institute of Architects; Scholes Hall and the Alumni Memorial Chapel are also standout architectural examples.

Students have a pick of over 400 student organizations to join, from academic and cultural groups to fraternities and sororities. UNM Athletics offers 21 sports, and the university Lobos teams enjoy a loyal and passionate following of red-and-silver-hued fans from the greater community. Sports facilities include the renowned Pit arena, University Stadium, and Isotopes Park.

UNM's on-campus arts venues are some of the finest in the state and are central to the entire city of Albuquerque's arts life, as well as being popular attractions for tourists. In the Center for the Arts, the venerable 2,044-seat performance venue Popejoy Hall is home to the New Mexico Symphony Orchestra. The smaller Rodey Theatre, Keller Hall, and Theatre X present smaller music, drama, and dance productions. The UNM Art Museum houses New Mexico's largest fine art collection and also the Jonson Gallery. Other free museums are the Maxwell Museum of Anthropology, the UNM Meteorite Museum, the Geology Museum, and the Tamarind Institute's fine art lithography gallery.

WEBSTER UNIVERSITY
Suite 300, 4775 Indian School Road NE
(505) 292-6988
www.webster.edu

Webster University offers master's degrees through evening programs convenient for adults with day jobs. Each class is held one evening a week, typically between 6 and 10 p.m., over a nine-week block. There are two facilities in Albuquerque: The Kirtland Air Force Base campus was the first to arrive in 1977 (505-255-3645), and the midtown campus at Indian School Road, called the Metro Campus, followed in 1985. The school's MA programs include counseling, gerontology, information technology management, management and leadership, and human resources development, as well as a master's in business administration. There are also online master's degree programs in arts and sciences, communications, and business and technology. Webster University has its roots in Webster College, founded by the Sisters of Loretto in St. Louis, Missouri, in 1915.

MEDIA

Print Publications

Daily

ALBUQUERQUE JOURNAL
7777 Jefferson Street NE
(505) 823-3400, (800) 641-3451
www.abqjournal.com

The *Albuquerque Journal* is the state's newspaper of record, publishing seven days a week, with zoned editions for Rio Rancho, the West Side, and Santa Fe. In addition to covering the expected range of metro and state news, business, entertainment, politics, sports, and lifestyle subjects, the Journal carries a number of national magazine inserts such as *Parade, American Profile,* and *Relish*, and local-interest supplements. The *Journal* has a comprehensive online newspaper and archives, some of which can be read at no cost, but much of the content is available by subscription only. Subscribers who have the newspaper delivered automatically have free access to the Web site, or you can take an online subscription. (There are, however, individual-session trial passes to read with no charge after watching an advertisement.) The publishers also offer a rather smart eJournal format, which replicates the print-edition layout and lets Web readers leaf through the pages just as they would a hard-copy newspaper, with extra tools to navigate, enlarge articles and photos, or save them to a personal archive. *Albuquerque Journal* dates back to 1880 and is produced by the Albuquerque Publishing Company, which anchors the Journal Center Business Park just south of Balloon Fiesta Park.

NEW MEXICO DAILY LOBO
University of New Mexico
(505) 277-0111
www.dailylobo.com
The University of New Mexico's award-winning free newspaper is staffed by approximately 100 UNM students and covers not only campus activities and education subjects but also arts and culture around the city. It also has a strong sports section—and, of course, provides detailed reporting of the Lobos teams. It's published every weekday during the academic semester and distributed on campus and in nearby businesses.

Weekly

ALIBI
Suite 151, 2118 Central Avenue SE
(505) 346-0660
alibi.com
This free alternative weekly newspaper offers lively coverage of politics, news, local arts, music, film, and dining. It carries a comprehensive calendar of events and publishes special issues, including the popular annual Best of Burque readers' poll. Around 45,000 copies of the tabloid format *Alibi* are distributed each Thursday throughout the Albuquerque metro area and in Santa Fe.

MÁS NEW MEXICO
123 Palomas Drive NE
(505) 255-1928
www.masnewmexico.com
Más New Mexico launched in 2009 as a free weekly newspaper serving the Hispanic community. The bilingual publication reports in both Spanish and English on city, state, national, and international news. Published every Wednesday, 20,000 copies of *Más New Mexico* are distributed in Albuquerque and Santa Fe.

NEW MEXICO BUSINESS WEEKLY
Suite 202, 116 Central Avenue SW
(505) 768-7008
www.albuquerque.bizjournals.com
Part of the American City Business Journals network, *New Mexico Business Weekly* publishes every Friday, covering the state's business news and industry movers and shakers. Special reports and supplements examine various business sectors and cross-industry issues such as office design and green business. The Web site publishes some but not all of the print-edition content, but digital subscriptions are available, and you can also register for free business-news updates by e-mail.

Biweekly

LOCAL IQ
907 Third Street NW
(505) 247-1343
www.local-iQ.com
A free biweekly tabloid, *Local iQ* focuses on leisure and lifestyle and covers arts, music, film, food, and culture. It includes entertainment and event listings and annual roundups that scope out the scene on, for example, happy hours at bars, restaurants, and pubs across the city. *Local iQ* is distributed to 25,000 readers around the Albuquerque area.

Monthly

ALBUQUERQUE THE MAGAZINE
1550 Mercantile Avenue NE, Top Floor
(505) 842-1110
www.abqthemag.com

This glossy lifestyle magazine covers just about everything of interest to a Duke City dweller, including features on restaurants, arts, leisure, local businesses, and the personalities shaping city culture. Visitors just passing through will also find plenty of info on places to go and things to do. The chunky and beautifully produced *Albuquerque The Magazine* is available on newsstands or by subscription.

ALBUQUERQUEARTS
Suite 234, 600 Central Avenue SE
(505) 298-2155
www.abqarts.com

The free *albuquerqueARTS* tabloid is a source for comprehensive coverage of performance, visual, and literary arts. It includes information on upcoming arts events, plus interviews and behind-the-scenes insights, and it also publishes articles on food, travel, and leisure activities. It's distributed to 45,000 readers around Albuquerque, Santa Fe, and Taos.

LOCALFLAVOR
223 North Guadalupe #442
Santa Fe
(505) 988-7560
www.localflavormagazine.com

As the name suggests, localflavor is all about the food—and the wine and lifestyle that go with it. A free publication produced 10 times a year, localflavor offers in-depth features on restaurants in and around Albuquerque, Santa Fe, and Taos, including interviews with chefs and tidbits of the latest restaurant news, plus coverage of food-and-wine festivals and area farmers and food producers who are contributing to the New Mexican feast. Issues also spotlight interesting artists, designers, shops, and places to visit; 30,000 copies are distributed in the region.

Albuquerque Online

The New Mexico Independent (newmexicoindependent.com) covers news, politics, culture, and local issues. Thoughtful reporting and commentary is provided by editor Gwyneth Doland, formerly of the *Albuquerque Alibi* and *Santa Fe Reporter,* and a team of impressive staff reporters and columnists, including recruits from old-school newspaper journalism. The online newspaper is published by the nonpartisan, nonprofit Center for Independent Media.

The Duke City Fix blog (www.dukecityfix.com) is a community site featuring regular contributors and plenty of other opinionated locals weighing in on life in Duke City, from local politics and current events to arts, restaurants, and interesting places to visit. Newbies in town can ask questions in the discussion forums.

The Albuquerque on the Cheap blog (www.abqonthecheap.com) reports on the latest discounts and special offers in city restaurants, attractions, entertainment, shopping, hotels, and events, including some offers exclusive to the site. Bargains often include "kids eat free" deals and free family-friendly events. Yours truly is on the editorial team! The blog is part of the national Cities on the Cheap network and won the Best Blogger award in the 2009 Best of City reader poll by *Albuquerque The Magazine.*

NEW MEXICO MAGAZINE
495 Old Santa Fe Trail
Santa Fe
(505) 827-7447, (800) 898-6639
www.nmmagazine.com
The official state magazine, published in partnership with the New Mexico Tourism Department, was founded in 1923, making it the oldest state magazine in the country. However, readers turn to it not for its history but for insights into the culture, places, and people of the Land of Enchantment. The eternally popular humor column "One of Our 50 Is Missing" describes readers' encounters with officials, businesses, and even airline staff who are convinced New Mexico lies south of the border and thus refuse to ship items without overseas postage or to let travelers on a flight to Albuquerque without their passports.

Radio

ALTERNATIVE
KTEG 104.1 FM The Edge

CHILDREN'S
KALY 1240 AM Radio Disney

CLASSICAL
KHFM 95.5/102.9 FM

CLASSIC HITS
KABG 98.5 FM
KIOT 102.5 FM

CONTEMPORARY
KKOB 93.3 FM The Pop Music Channel
KSYU 95.1 FM Hot 95 Urban contemporary, R & B
KDLW 97.7 FM Contemporary rhythmic hits
KMGA 99.5 FM Adult contemporary, soft rock
KPEK 100.3 FM The Peak Modern Adult and Contemporary

COUNTRY
KRST 92.3 FM
KAGM 106.3
KBQI 107.9 FM

HIP-HOP
KDLW 97.7 FM

JAZZ
KAJZ 101.7 FM
KABQ 104.7 FM

NATIONAL PUBLIC RADIO
KANW 89.1 FM
KUNM 89.9 FM

OLDIES
KKJY 1550 AM
KANM 1600 AM

RELIGIOUS
KLYT 88.3 FM
KQRI 89.5 FM
KFLQ 91.5 FM
KEAR 91.9 FM
KSVA 920 AM
KKIM 1000 AM
KXKS 1190 AM

ROCK
KZRR 94.1 FM "94 Rock"
KBZU 96.3 FM Classic rock

SPANISH
KCZO 101.1 FM
KKRG/KJFA 101.3 FM
KDAZ 730 AM
KARS 860 AM
KRZY 1450 AM

TALK RADIO/NEWS
KBZU 96.3 FM
KLVO 106.7 FM Radio Lobo Mexican regional
KNML 610 AM The Sports Animal
KKOB 770 AM News, talk, Lobos sports
KTBL 1050 AM News, talk
KDEF 1150 AM News
KKNS 1310 AM News, talk
KABQ 1350 AM Progressive, talk

VARIETY

KBNM 98.1

KDRF 103.3 FM Adult hits: "We play stuff we like"

KAGM 106.3 FM The Range: The new, the known, the legends

Television

LOCAL STATIONS

KASA Channel 2 (Fox)

KOB Channel 4 (NBC)

KNME Channel 5 (PBS)

KOAT Channel 7 (ABC)

KCHF Channel 11 (Religious)

KRQE Channel 13 (CBS)

KFTQ Channel 14 (TeleFutura)

KWBQ Channel 19 (CW)

KNAT Channel 23 (TBN)

KQDF Channel 25 (Azteca America)

KAZQ Channel 32 (Religious)

KLUZ Channel 41 (Uni)

KASY Channel 50 (My50-TV)

WORSHIP

With over four centuries of Catholicism in the state of New Mexico, it's not surprising that Catholics still form the biggest single religious congregation in Albuquerque, with over a quarter of a million adherents in the metro area. Missionaries from other spiritual traditions mainly arrived with the railroad, which opened up the region to newcomers of other denominations and the ministers to tend the flocks. Hence, many of Albuquerque's oldest churches in faiths other than Catholicism were established from 1880 onward. Today Albuquerque citizens have their choice of a full roster of religious affiliations, from Adventists to Zen Buddhists. The Albuquerque Historical Society estimated in 2006 that the city had around 600 houses of worship. Baptists, Methodists, Lutherans, and followers of the Church of Jesus Christ of Latter-day Saints are all well represented in the city, and Albuquerque's rich ethnic mix also provides a Russian Orthodox, a Greek Orthodox, and an Armenian church, plus a number of Korean churches, an Islamic mosque, and a Thai Buddhist temple. Most of Albuquerque's larger churches have some kind of program for children during services, as well as a lively schedule of interest groups and religious and social activities for all congregants. Many are involved in outreach or social-action initiatives. Some of the churches below have a strong musical tradition, meshing music as praise with Albuquerque's enduring love of the arts. This section highlights some of the older, larger, or otherwise notable houses of worship in various spiritual traditions.

i **The new bell tower constructed in 2003 on Sacred Heart Catholic Church on Stover Avenue in Barelas incorporates two steel beams from the 78th floor of the collapsed World Trade Center.**

CATHEDRAL CHURCH OF ST. JOHN

318 Silver Avenue SW

(505) 247-1581

www.stjohnsabq.org

Originally an Episcopal parish church founded in 1882 at this location, St. John was designated the Cathedral Church of the Missionary District of New Mexico and Southwest Texas in the early 1920s. The current building was designed in 1951 by architect John Gaw Meem, who was a member of the church. The Cathedral Church of St. John serves in the Episcopal Diocese of the Rio Grande. Childcare is available for babies and young children during Sunday morning service, and there is also a Sunday school. Sunday Eucharist is followed by a coffee hour, and there are regular community events. The refurbished Reuter organ, built in 1952, has 3,800 pipes and is the largest organ in New Mexico; the cathedral is highly regarded for its organ and choral music of praise, including new works commissioned for the cathedral choir.

CHURCH OF JESUS CHRIST OF LATTER-DAY SAINTS NEW MEXICO TEMPLE
10301 San Francisco Drive NE
(505) 822-5110
www.ldschurchtemples.com/albuquerque

The Church of Jesus Christ of Latter-day Saints reports a New Mexico membership of 64,872 in 2009. This Albuquerque temple, set on over eight acres in the Northeast Heights, is the first Mormon church in the state and the 73rd operating temple. Its opening dedication was in spring 2000, and it serves a congregation from across New Mexico and southern Colorado. The church's missionary work among New Mexico's Native Americans began in the 1860s. There are Native American and Spanish sessions here, and clothing rental is available.

CONGREGATION ALBERT
3800 Louisiana Boulevard NE
(505) 883-1818
www.congregationalbert.org

The home of Albuquerque's Reform community, Congregation Albert was founded in 1897 and is Albuquerque's first synagogue and the oldest ongoing Jewish organization in the state. Congregation Albert moved to its current location in 1984 and is a member of the Union for Reform Judaism. A variety of formal and more informal worship services and gatherings is offered, as well as a busy schedule of events, classes, groups, and music activities. The Early Childhood Center offers prekindergarten and kindergarten education, plus daily programs for younger children and a Tot Shabbat Playgroup.

FIRST BAPTIST CHURCH
4101 Paseo del Norte NW
(505) 247-3611
fbcabq.com

Originally organized in 1853 and refounded in 1887, First Baptist Church is affiliated with the Southern Baptist Convention. Historically based in Downtown Albuquerque, in 2010 it is moving to the Westside from its home since 1937 on Broadway Boulevard. This follows a recent period of holding services in a Westside school as a temporary facility while maintaining the Downtown base—which in itself rather echoes the early years of the Broadway church, where building started in 1926 and the congregation held its services in the basement for a while as the church was constructed overhead. The atmosphere in First Baptist Church worship services is southwestern casual, with special services for children. Church membership is currently just over 1,200, although numbers may grow as it serves the expanding Westside population. The church also offers a "life group" system, teaming congregants into small groups according to age and other factors. The church has a blogging pastor, Michael Cook.

FIRST PRESBYTERIAN CHURCH
215 Locust Street NE
(505) 764-2900
www.firstpresabq.org

First Presbyterian Church had a congregation of over 1,000 in 2008. The church dates back to the mission of Dr. Sheldon Jackson in 1880, which led to the building of the original church on Fifth and Silver. That church went through several rounds of reconstruction to enlarge it for the growing congregation and to repair it after fire destruction in 1938. The church moved in 1954 to the current address. The church organ, with over 3,000 pipes, is one of the largest in the state. Two Sunday morning services are held here, plus Sunday school.

FIRST UNITED METHODIST CHURCH
314 Lead Avenue SW
(505) 243-5646
www.fumconline.org

The Reverend N. Hewitt Gale organized the First Methodist Episcopal Church in 1880, and by the following year a small adobe chapel had been constructed on the site of the current church (earlier Methodist services were conducted in an Old Town saloon). That building was replaced in 1905 by the current stone church, and subsequent additions have included the large cruciform sanctuary added in 1955. Church windows are said to have been designed by a student of Louis Tiffany. First United Methodist Church has grown with its congregation to now occupy much of a city block. The church holds two services on a Sunday morning—a contemporary service followed by a traditional one. The church's Wesley Kids preschool and childcare program operates five days a week, enrolling children from six weeks to age five.

HOFFMANTOWN CHURCH
8888 Harper Drive NE
(505) 828-2600
hoffmantownchurch.org

The Southern Baptist Convention forms the second-largest congregation in the Albuquerque metro area, after Catholics, according to the Association of Religious Data Archives, with 26,652 adherents in 2000 (the latest figures available). Hoffmantown Church is a large, modern SBC-affiliated church founded in 1954 with 5,800 members and an average attendance of 1,800. There are two Sunday morning services and a couple of children's programs to take care of infants through fifth graders. The pastor gives weekly radio and TV broadcasts, and the church has an active schedule of interest groups, miniseries, and events.

NAHALAT SHALOM
3606 Rio Grande Boulevard NW
(505) 343-8227
nahalatshalom.org

Nahalat Shalom Southwest Center for Jewish Renewal was started in 1982 by a group seeking a place to practice inclusive Judaism. The founding rabbi was Rabbi Lynn Gottlieb, one of the first women to be ordained. She was succeeded in 2006 by Rabbi Deborah J. Brin. The congregation did not have its own permanent space until 2000, when it bought an old Baptist church in the North Valley, and the former baptismal is now the spot where a 22-member klezmer band plays. Nahalat Shalom, meaning Inheritance of Peace, is a member of Aleph: The Alliance for Jewish Renewal.

SAN FELIPE DE NERI
2005 North Plaza NW
(505) 243-4628
www.sanfelipedeneri.org

Although a busy tourist destination in the Old Town Plaza, San Felipe de Neri, the third-oldest church in America, continues to serve the spiritual needs of its parish. The first church here was established under the direction of Franciscan priest Fray Manuel Moreno, to serve the small community of the newly minted Villa de Alburquerque in 1706. It was originally called San Francisco Xavier Church and changed to San Felipe de Neri in honor of King Philip of Spain. The first church construction was completed by 1718–19, on the west side of the plaza, but following its collapse in 1792, the church that stands today was built on the north side of the plaza in 1793. San Felipe de Neri is the oldest building in Albuquerque and is listed on the National Register of Historic Places. Mass is celebrated here daily, including a Sunday morning Mass in

i **In 1853 Bishop John Baptist Lamy of Santa Fe, who later became the first Archbishop of Santa Fe, appointed Father Joseph Machebeuf as pastor of Albuquerque. Willa Cather's beautiful novel *Death Comes for the Archbishop,* published in 1927 and drawing on historical accounts, tells the story of these two fellow Frenchmen and their pioneering work to organize a Catholic diocese during New Mexico's early years as a U.S. territory. Though the characters are disguised as Bishop Latour (Lamy) and Father Vaillant (Machebeuf), the book weaves a spellbinding story of the challenges of the territory at the time and depicts true events, such as Lamy's construction of the St. Francis Cathedral in Santa Fe (properly called the Cathedral Basilica of St. Francis of Assisi) and Father Machebeuf's later journeys into the mining towns of Colorado, where he went on to become the first Bishop of Denver.**

Spanish. The church has been actively involved in education since 1770, originally using the parish house for classrooms. Today's San Felipe de Neri School, on nearby Lomas Boulevard in Old Town, teaches children from prekindergarten through eighth grade. San Felipe de Neri is located in the Archdiocese of Santa Fe, which is responsible for 91 parish seats and 216 active missions across an area of over 61,000 square miles. Other Catholic churches in Albuquerque may be found on their Web site: www.archdiocesesantafe.org.

ST. PAUL LUTHERAN CHURCH
1100 Indian School Road NE
(505) 242-5942
www.stpaulabq.org

A member of the Evangelical Lutheran Church in America in the Rocky Mountain Synod, St. Paul Lutheran Church was founded in 1891 in Downtown Albuquerque and relocated to the current modern church in 1971, in Midtown near the Big-I interchange. The Rev. William Rosenstengel, a missionary from Nebraska, established the church, and early services were in German until 1910 when they switched to English. St. Paul's first female pastor arrived in 1987, and today there are two pastors, a man and a woman. The church reports a membership of over 1,200 and an average attendance of 159 congregants. There is a visitor center by the east doors to welcome new faces to Sunday morning services. Music is a big part of St. Paul's ministry, with choirs and a youth music program. St. Paul's Calico Butterfly Preschool opened in 1980 and has programs for infants through five-year-olds.

HEALTH CARE

Health seekers first headed for the clean air of Albuquerque's high-elevation dry climate to ease their respiratory ailments, especially the tuberculosis patients, known as "lungers," in the epidemic of the early 1900s. Interestingly, two of the people who later made a great impact on Albuquerque's medical landscape—Dr. William Randolph Lovelace and Carrie Tingley, wife of Governor Clyde Tingley—initially came to New Mexico seeking their own healing from tuberculosis.

In 1902 the Sisters of Charity opened St. Joseph Sanatorium to serve the lungers, and that first hospital is now part of the Lovelace Health System. The Southwestern Presbyterian Sanatorium, opened in 1908, grew into Presbyterian Hospital, and Presbyterian Healthcare Services now operates eight hospitals in New Mexico, with two in Albuquerque. From the seeds sown by those early religious hospitals, Albuquerque has grown into New Mexico's core provider of advanced medical treatment, and patients also come from bordering areas of Arizona, Colorado, and Texas. Because Albuquerque serves so many citizens from smaller communities across the state, the options available to city residents are more numerous and sophisticated than you might expect from other cities of a similar size. Hospital patients are reaping the benefits of recent major investments in medical technology, equipment, and hospital facilities, and cancer patients can expect state-of-the-art facilities and treatment at the University of New Mexico's new $90 million Cancer Center and at the M. D. Anderson Cancer Center at Presbyterian Kaseman Hospital. There are over 1,600 licensed beds in the metro area's largest general hospitals combined: UNM Hospital, Presbyterian and Presbyterian Kaseman, and Lovelace's Medical Center and Westside. Two new hospitals are due to open in Rio Rancho in 2011 to serve that community's fast-growing population.

This section provides an overview of Albuquerque's major hospitals. There are also many specialized treatment centers, outpatient clinics, alternative-medicine practitioners, and other health-care providers. Check the Yellow Pages, and also refer to the Lovelace, Presbyterian, and UNM networks on the Web or by phone, as they provide many varied programs to serve the health-care needs of the community.

HEART HOSPITAL OF NEW MEXICO
504 Elm Street NE
(505) 724-2000
www.hearthospitalnm.com

The state's first hospital dedicated to the prevention and treatment of heart disease, the Heart Hospital of New Mexico opened in 1999. It's owned by MedCath Corporation in partnership with the New Mexico Heart Institute, the largest cardiovascular medical group in the region. The hospital offers a full range of heart-care services and prides itself on its patient-centered approach. In 2008 it was the only New Mexico hospital to receive the Outstanding Patient Experience Award by Healthgrades, based on a survey of patients. The survey reported patients' experience of doctor and nurse communications, speed of responsiveness, medical information, the cleanliness and noise levels in hospitals, and instructions for postdischarge care. Heart Hospital of New Mexico came in within the top 5 percent for patient experiences out of 2,592 hospitals across the country. The two-story hospital is built on an eight-acre campus, with 55 patient rooms and sleeper beds available for family members wanting to stay close to the patient. There are three operating rooms, four cardiac catheterization laboratories, and seven emergency and trauma rooms. The hospital's performance is the fastest in New Mexico for the time from arrival at the 24-hour emergency room to the time of treatment. Programs to support patients at the Heart Hospital of New Mexico include a pet therapy program and a therapeutic music program. The hospital offers a reasonably priced full HeartScan screening package for early detection of heart disease.

i **An American Heart Association study ranked Albuquerque as the fifth most heart-friendly city for women among midsize metro cities. The study factored in risk indicators and statistics on heart disease.**

Lovelace Health System

Dr. William Randolph Lovelace started a medical practice in Albuquerque in 1913; as a TB sufferer he'd originally come to New Mexico for therapeutic reasons. In 1922 he founded the Lovelace Clinic with other physicians, modeled after the pioneering Mayo Clinic. Today Lovelace Health System operates a state-of-the-art Downtown medical center, a hospital on the Westside, and a women's hospital and provides health plans for individuals, families, and employers. In addition, Lovelace Rehabilitation Hospital has programs for patients suffering from brain injuries, spinal cord injuries, strokes, and other conditions. Lovelace also runs the outpatient Gibson Medical Center and services that include pharmacies. The Albuquerque and metro-area hospital network serves more than 250,000 people annually, and Lovelace Health Plan insures upwards of 190,000 people in the state of New Mexico. All three hospitals below have 24-hour emergency rooms.

i **Dr. Randy Lovelace, nephew of William R. Lovelace, was a groundbreaker in aviation medicine and contributed to the development of the BLB mask that provided oxygen to high-altitude aviators. Lovelace was himself a pilot and decorated World War II veteran. In 1946 he joined the Lovelace Clinic in Albuquerque, where potential astronauts were later put through their paces to check their health, resulting in the selection of the Mercury Seven. Lovelace was appointed NASA's director of space medicine in 1964.**

LOVELACE MEDICAL CENTER
601 Dr. Martin Luther King Jr. Avenue
(505) 727-8000
www.lovelace.com

The 11-floor Downtown medical center was on the receiving end of a $60 million renovation in 2007, and its high-tech care includes New Mexico's only Gamma Knife Center for noninvasive brain surgery and the only intravascular ultrasound. The new Cardiac Care Center offers wellness programs, diagnostics, and advanced cardiovascular surgery and rehabilitation. The top floor of the hospital is dedicated to the UNM Cancer Research & Treatment Center Medical Oncology unit. The hospital also offers general surgery and surgical services in gastroenterology, gynecology, neurology, orthopedics, podiatrics, urology, plastic surgery, and both thoracic and vascular surgery. Imaging technology includes a new million-dollar-plus 64-slice volume computed tomography scanner, which scans and produces high-resolution images faster than conventional CT scanners. It's used in emergency and trauma cases and for diagnostics that include cardiac, oncology, spinal injury, pediatric, and other exams. Lovelace Medical Center has 254 licensed beds.

LOVELACE WESTSIDE HOSPITAL
10501 Golf Course Road NW
(505) 727-2000
www.lovelace.com

Serving the Westside and Rio Rancho population, the hospital has 95 licensed beds and a full range of surgical services, including cardiology, neurosurgery, oncology, orthopedics, plastic surgery and reconstructive surgery, podiatry, thoracic surgery, urogynecology, urology, and vascular surgery. The hospital received 2,570 inpatients in 2008, more than 18,000 outpatient visits, and over 22,000 arrivals in the emergency room. Diagnostic facilities include MRI, a 64-slice CT scanner, and digital mammography. There is a full women's health service here, including gynecologists, obstetricians, and midwives.

LOVELACE WOMEN'S HOSPITAL
4701 Montgomery Boulevard NE
(505) 727-7800
www.lovelace.com

This is New Mexico's first and only hospital dedicated to women's health, with 98 licensed beds.

i **The Quit Now program for smokers offers a free personal quit plan, free nicotine patches or gum, referrals to community groups, and phone-coaching sessions. Call (800) QUIT NOW, (800) 784 8669; www.quitnownm.com.**

The hospital provides general surgical services and a family birthing center, which saw 3,600 births in 2008. The site has 16 labor and delivery rooms and a maternal-fetal medicine program to care for high-risk pregnancies. A recently expanded Level III Neonatal Intensive Care Unit has 53 beds. The Breast Care Center offers digital mammography to make examinations speedier and more comfortable.

Presbyterian Healthcare Services

Presbyterian is the only private, nonprofit healthcare system in the state. It's the largest healthcare provider, too, and 700,000 people—one out of every three New Mexicans—use Presbyterian's services. Founded in Albuquerque in 1908, Presbyterian has eight hospitals in New Mexico, plus primary, acute, and specialist care clinics, and offers a number of insurance plans for individuals, families, and employers. There are two hospitals in Albuquerque, and both have a 24-hour emergency room.

PRESBYTERIAN HOSPITAL
1100 Central Avenue SE
(505) 841-1234
www.phs.org

Presbyterian Hospital is New Mexico's largest acute-care hospital. This seven-floor facility provides full general and acute medical and surgical services and has 453 licensed beds. The Presbyterian Heart Center is located here, performing diagnostic catheterization, balloon angioplasty, and open-heart surgery. It's also home to the Women's Healthcare Center, which in addition to regular OB/GYN services was an initiator in offering New Mexico's first in-vitro fertilization program. Presbyterian Hospital brings more babies into the world than any other hospital in the state, and trained doulas are available to take care of moms-to-be. The Children's Center takes care of kids with 24/7 emergency and general care and offers 17 pediatric specialist medical services, including cardiology and neurology, with over 500 surgeries performed a year. The Children's Center's sixth-floor Rachel's Courtyard is a $1.5 million "playground in the sky" for young patients to play in and heal and share with their families.

The New Mexico Department of Health has information on health programs, including vaccination and prevention programs, plus information on hot health topics, support services, and services for those at risk; (505) 827-2613; www.health.state.nm.us.

PRESBYTERIAN KASEMAN HOSPITAL
8300 Constitution Avenue NE
(505) 291-2000
www.phs.org

Located in the Northeast Heights, this was the first satellite hospital to the original Presbyterian Hospital 6 miles away, and it provides general medical, surgical, and emergency services, with 170 licensed beds. In 2007 the top-notch M. D. Anderson Cancer Center at Presbyterian Kaseman Hospital opened, in partnership with the renowned M. D. Anderson Cancer Center at the University of Texas. The cancer center provides inpatient and outpatient care, using the latest oncology treatments. Other facilities at Kaseman include the Presbyterian Behavioral Health psychiatric unit, which also serves chemically dependent patients; the Sleep Disorders Center, accredited by the American Academy of Sleep Medicine; and a hospice unit.

The $165 million Presbyterian Rio Rancho Medical Center is under construction and is expected to open in 2011.

University of New Mexico Hospitals

With the University of New Mexico Hospital as the flagship medical facility, UNM's hospitals fall under the aegis of the University of New Mexico Health Sciences Center, which dominates UNM's campus north of Lomas. This is the largest academic health complex in the state, and in addition to the medical facilities listed below, UNM also operates the UNM Psychiatric Center, the UNM Children's Psychiatric Center, and 43 clinics throughout the state.

UNIVERSITY OF NEW MEXICO HOSPITAL
2211 Lomas Boulevard NE
(505) 272-2111
hospitals.unm.edu/hospitals

UNM Hospital operates the state's only Level I Trauma Center, caring for almost 90,000 emergency patients each year, and over 450,000 outpatients. The hospital is the primary teaching hospital for the university's school of medicine and has ranked in the 100 top-performing hospitals in the United States. The hospital handles general surgical procedures, chronic-disease management, and acute-care cases. In 2007 the impressive new Barbara and Bill Richardson Pavilion opened at the hospital, adding nearly 500,000 square feet of emergency and clinical space, and incorporating the latest surgical, imaging, and laboratory technology. As a research hospital UNM Hospital participates in numerous advanced clinical trials across many specialties. The American Hospital Association named UNM Hospital as one of the 100 Most-Wired Hospitals and Health Systems in the United States in 2009. Although this sounds like they perhaps have very good Wi-Fi access for patients, it actually refers to the use of IT tools to integrate and communicate medical information, thus improving the quality of health care and patient service and safety. The hospital was the only one in New Mexico to make the list in 2009, the sixth consecutive year that UNM was cited, out of seven years in all. Only eight other American organizations have matched that record.

The New Mexico Poison and Drug Information Center (800-222-1222) is part of UNM's College of Pharmacy. The 24-hour hotline handles calls about poisoning and exposure incidents regarding medications of all kinds, from prescription to illegal drugs, household products, work or environmental chemicals, carbon monoxide, food poisonings, plants and mushrooms, bites and stings, and even burns from handling chile peppers.

UNM CANCER CENTER
1201 Camino de Salud NE
(505) 272-4946
hospitals.unm.edu/hospitals

Since 2005, this facility has been a National Cancer Institute–designated cancer center, one of only 65 designated centers in the country and the only center in New Mexico. One criterion for NCI-designated centers is scientific excellence, and the UNM Cancer Center is the state's leading facility for advanced research and clinical trials, paired with innovative treatment. In August 2009 the center opened the first phase of its spectacular new $90 million cancer center, having outgrown its existing facilities. In 2008 the center served 7,600 patients in 90,000-plus patient visits—a figure that UNM says represents half the adults diagnosed with cancer in New Mexico and almost all the children. The new 206,000-square-foot construction could serve 200,000 patients a year and will be the core of a statewide network of cancer care. In addition to state-of-the-art diagnosis and imaging facilities, a Siemens-PET-NET cyclotron and radioisotope production facility, a diagnostic clinical laboratory, four vaults for radiation oncology and radiosurgery programs, the new center reflects a holistic approach to patient care, with healing gardens, a meditation chapel, and natural colors, materials, and designs informed by Native American philosophies and incorporating plenty of natural sunlight, mountain views, and rooftop garden. The full facility is expected to open in 2010.

UNM CARRIE TINGLEY HOSPITAL
2211 Lomas Boulevard NE
(505) 272-2800
http://hospitals.unm.edu/hospitals

Located in the Barbara and Bill Richardson Pavilion that was added to UNM Hospital in 2007, this is new Mexico's only pediatric rehabilitation hospital, with a 24-bed inpatient unit. Despite its spanking-new high-tech environment, Carrie Tingley Hospital has a 70-year history. Carrie Tingley was New Mexico's first lady, wife of Governor Clyde Tingley, and the couple originally moved from Ohio to New Mexico in the hope that the climate would alleviate Carrie's tuberculosis. The Tingleys were known for helping the sick and especially disabled children in need of medical care. The Carrie Tingley Hospital opened in 1937 in Hot Springs, later renamed Truth or Consequences, south of Albuquerque, and moved to the city in 1981. In 1989 it became part of UNM. Through inpatient care and 21 specialized clinics, the hospital treats children and adolescents with long-term physical disabilities, musculoskeletal and orthopedic conditions, developmental issues, brain and spinal cord injuries, and many other conditions.

UNM CHILDREN'S HOSPITAL
2211 Lomas Boulevard NE
(505) 272-5437
hospitals.unm.edu/hospitals

The only general hospital in New Mexico dedicated solely to children, UNM Children's Hospital serves nearly 60,000 children a year, more than half from outside the Albuquerque area. It occu-

i **Agora Crisis Center doesn't only take suicide and crisis calls—you can call them to talk about any emotional issue. The help line is open every day from 9 a.m. to midnight. You can also visit in person during clinic hours—call ahead to find out opening times. If needed, Agora's referral service will put you in touch with agencies or other resources to help. Some resources are on Agora's Web site. The service is free and confidential. Call (505) 277-3013; www.agoracares.org.**

Numbers for Health-Related Questions or Emergencies

Look to these phone numbers for help.

Emergency Police, Fire, Ambulance, or Rescue Units: 911

Agora Crisis Center: (505) 277-3013, 9 a.m. to midnight.

AIDS Statewide Hotline: (800) 545-2437

AIDS Testing and Counseling: (505) 938-7100, (888) 882-2437 (New Mexico AIDS Services)

Al-Anon: (505) 262-2177

Alcoholics Anonymous: (505) 266-1900

American Cancer Society: (505) 260-2105

American Diabetes Association: (505) 266-5716

American Heart Association: (505) 353-5800

American Lung Association: (505) 265-0732

American Red Cross: (505) 265-8514

Arthritis Foundation: (505) 867-7430

Gamblers Anonymous: (505) 260-7272

Information Center for New Mexicans with Disabilities: (800) 552-8195, (505) 272-8549

Narcotics Anonymous: (505) 260-9889

New Mexico Cancer Prevention and Control: (505) 222-8613

Poison Control Center: (505) 272-2222, (800) 222-1222

Suicide Hotline: (866) HELP-1-NM, (866) 435-7166

pies almost 500,000 square feet over three floors of the new Barbara and Bill Richardson Pavilion, opened in 2007 as a wing to UNM Hospital. The facilities include a maternity center, a pediatric emergency center, an intensive care unit for newborns, a pediatric oncology infusion center, and the Children's Hospital Heart Center.

i **A new University of New Mexico hospital is planned for Rio Rancho, with an opening date anticipated to be the end of 2011. The UNM Sandoval Regional Medical Center will initially have 75 beds, with health care that includes urgent care and general medical, surgical, and ob/gyn services.**

INDEX

A

S

ABOUT THE AUTHOR

Tania Casselle is a transplant to New Mexico from London, England, who fell hook, line, and sinker for the Land of Enchantment after first arriving in Albuquerque in 1998. She's worked as a magazine staff editor and freelance writer for 20 years and contributed stories on New Mexico to many publications, including *Indian Country Today, New Mexico Business Weekly, localflavor, Film Festival TV Channel,* and *Latitudes* in-flight magazine. She reports on travel, business, lifestyle, well-being, food, fashion, interior design, film, and performance and literary arts, and her work has appeared in magazines, newspapers, books, and online media in the United States, Europe, and Asia. As the host of Writers on Radio for five years, she's interviewed many fine New Mexican and national authors and poets for broadcast on stations that have included NPR-affiliate KRZA, KTAO, and KVOT. Writers on Radio is sponsored by the Society of the Muse of the Southwest and produced by Cultural Energy. Tania was awarded first place for both radio interviews and food writing in the 2009 New Mexico Press Women's Excellence in Communications Contest. She now lives in Taos, New Mexico, and gets desperate cravings for Albuquerque restaurants if she's away from them for too long. She's also been known to hole up in Duke City hotels for weeks at a time when focused on a writing project. Tania loves to hear what readers have to say and can be reached at Tania@WriteOnDeadline.com.